Landscapes of Preindustrial Urbanism

Landscapes of Preindustrial Urbanism

Georges Farhat

Editor

DUMBARTON OAKS RESEARCH LIBRARY AND COLLECTION   WASHINGTON, D.C.

LIBRARY OF CONGRESS CATALOGING-IN-PUBLICATION DATA

NAMES: Dumbarton Oaks Colloquium on the History of Landscape Architecture (41st : 2017 : Washington, D.C.) | Farhat, Georges, editor. | Dumbarton Oaks, host institution. | Dumbarton Oaks Colloquium on the History of Landscape Architecture.

TITLE: Landscapes of preindustrial urbanism / Georges Farhat, editor.

DESCRIPTION: Washington, D.C. : Dumbarton Oaks Research Library and Collection, [2020]. | "Dumbarton Oaks Colloquium on the History of Landscape Architecture XLI"—Page preceding title page. | Includes bibliographical references and index. | Summary: "The use of the word 'landscape' to describe the formation and infrastructure of cities seems to express contemporary preoccupations with the postindustrial urban condition. The Industrial Revolution is often seen as a turning point in the emergence of the urban landscape of the modern metropolis, and the large city as commonly experienced today in the world is certainly dependent on a range of recent (or quite recent) breakthroughs in construction technology, climate control, communication, and transportation. In this view, urban landscapes are a historically late development and are, therefore, seen to embody an essentially modern and Western concept. But features associated with contemporary urban Landscapes—most notably the forms of human adaptation to and reshaping of the sites where cities develop and expand—can also be found in preindustrial contexts in different time periods and geographical regions. Preindustrial urban settlements generally occupied land that had been used for other, mostly productive, purposes, and their development involved complex and dynamic relationships with the management of natural resources. Such cities are traditionally studied as the centers of commerce, trade, and artisan production as well as the seats of secular and religious authorities; the essays in this volume to examine how the original clusters of agrarian communities evolved into urban formations"—Provided by publisher.

IDENTIFIERS: LCCN 2019047893 | ISBN 9780884024712 (hardcover)

SUBJECTS: LCSH: Urbanization—History—Congresses. | Land use—History—Congresses. | Land use, Urban—History—Congresses. | Human ecology—History—Congresses. | Urban archaeology—Congresses. | Landscape archaeology—Congresses. | LCGFT: Conference papers and proceedings.

CLASSIFICATION: LCC HT361.D85 2020 | DDC 712.09—dc23

LC record available at https://lccn.loc.gov/2019047893

Volume based on papers presented at the symposium "Landscapes of Pre-Industrial Cities," held at the Dumbarton Oaks Research Library and Collection, Washington, D.C., on May 5–6, 2017.

GENERAL EDITORS: John Beardsley and Thaïsa Way
ART DIRECTOR: Kathleen Sparkes
DESIGN AND COMPOSITION: Melissa Tandysh
MANAGING EDITOR: Sara Taylor

COVER ILLUSTRATION: A prehistoric mounded site: Tell Surezha, Kurdistan region of Iraq. Drone photograph by Jason A. Ur, September 10, 2017.

FRONTISPIECE ILLUSTRATION: Lingas (phallic symbols of Hindu god Shiva) carved in the sandstone riverbed at Kbal Spean, ca. 1050 CE, Kulen Hills, upstream of Angkor, Siem Reap province, Cambodia. Photograph by Georges Farhat, July 2015.

www.doaks.org/publications

Programs in urban landscape studies at Dumbarton Oaks
are supported by a grant from the Andrew W. Mellon Foundation
through their initiative in Architecture, Urbanism, and the Humanities.

≈

CONTENTS

FOREWORD

In 2014, Dumbarton Oaks launched a new program in urban landscape studies funded by the Andrew W. Mellon Foundation through their initiative in Architecture, Urbanism, and the Humanities. Established by former Mellon executive vice president Mariët Westermann and the late Hilary Ballon, the initiative is intended to foster the joint contributions that the humanities and the design and planning disciplines make to understanding the processes and effects of burgeoning urbanization around the world. At Dumbarton Oaks, the program brings scholars and practitioners from multiple disciplines together to explore how urban environments as we know them today have emerged and how we might reimagine them for the future. The program involves three principal components: semester-long fellowships for both research and teaching projects, with additional opportunities for field research funding; a series of internal academic events that create a framework for interactions among the fellows as well as the humanities scholars at Dumbarton Oaks and neighboring academic institutions; and public programs, including lectures, colloquia, workshops, and publications, aimed at disseminating the initiative's work nationally and internationally.

This volume is the record of one of those public events, the proceedings of a symposium held May 5–6, 2017, under the title "Landscapes of Pre-Industrial Cities," co-organized by Georges Farhat and me. The event built on a series of previous symposia and subsequent books, including *Food and the City* (2012 symposium; 2015 publication) and *River Cities, City Rivers* (2015 symposium; 2018 publication). While both those initiatives featured a wide geographical and chronological range of subjects, they each focused on one particular landscape-related topic, chiefly but not entirely from the perspective of modern and contemporary urbanism. What was needed next, we thought, was a still deeper history of urban formation, in yet wider geographical and cultural contexts, one that might explore the origins of city building in preindustrial societies and begin to reveal whether the relationships of these early cities to their landscapes were similar to or different from more recent urbanism. That is to say, we sought a landscape-specific analysis, one that examined the role of such factors as climate, topography, and physical resources in urbanization, along with more familiar geographical and chronological distinctions.

What we sought above all was to challenge some of the binaries that continue to characterize both urban and landscape studies: the dualities of cities and their hinterlands;

the natural and the built (or, in other terms, naturally occurring and socially produced environments); and the human and nonhuman actors in urbanization. Many of the urban landscape formations presented in this volume—large-scale, low-density "megasites," "hydraulic cities," or agro-urban landscapes—seem like hybrids between these binaries. At the same time, we wanted to avoid imposing a new duality between industrial and preindustrial urbanization. Indeed, we hope that the theories, methods, and technologies devoted to studying recent urbanism might be useful in approaching the distant past, even as preindustrial cities might shed light on the problems and opportunities of contemporary and emergent cities. This poses challenges to be sure. In particular, while applying current, cutting-edge technologies to the study of past urban landscapes can bring about tremendous breakthroughs in knowledge and interpretation, we should be careful not to collapse the equally tremendous differences between current cultural circumstances and those which produced past urban landscapes, in order, for instance, to avoid pushing recent ecological thinking into the distant past.

Given my imminent retirement from Dumbarton Oaks, I asked Georges if he would undertake on his own the considerable effort of editing this volume and composing its introduction. He graciously agreed, and has done a superb job on both fronts. I am grateful to him for seeing the project to completion. His enlightening introductory essay builds on a study by a multidisciplinary team he supervised in 2015–2016. Funded by Agence française de développement (AFD), the study initially aimed to assist local authorities in defining the "cultural landscape" of the 400 km^2 UNESCO World Heritage site comprising Vat Phou and associated ancient settlements in Champasak Province, Laos. Additional grants from University of Toronto (SSHRC) and Laboratoire de l'école d'architecture de Versailles allowed him to further conduct fieldwork across Southeast Asia and in Mexico.

We have had support from many other quarters over the life of this project. Colin McEwan and Elena Boeck, former directors of Pre-Columbian and Byzantine Studies, respectively, at Dumbarton Oaks, deserve particular credit for sustained conversations about the state of urban studies in their disciplines and for pointing us to potential speakers in their fields. Their participation ensured a strong representation of the ancient Mediterranean and the Americas in both the symposium and this volume. No less constructive were discussions with all the speakers at the symposium, including Suzanne Blier, Alan Kolata, Timothy Murtha, and Christophe Pottier, who were prevented by scheduling conflicts from submitting papers for this volume. We are also thankful to a host of other scholars for offering help and suggestions at key moments: Damian Evans, École française d'Extrême-Orient; Roland Fletcher, University of Sydney; Steven Kosiba, University of Minnesota; María Olvido Moreno-Guzmán and Fernanda Salazar, Universidad Nacional Autónoma de México; Eduardo Neves and Jennifer Watling, Universidade de São Paulo; Alceu Ranzi, Universidade Federal do Acre; and Silvia Segarra, Universidad de Granada.

A special acknowledgement is directed to the five anonymous readers who thoroughly reviewed either the volume as a whole or topics related to their own areas of expertise: the Americas, Africa, the Mediterranean and Near East, and South and

Southeast Asia. Lastly, this book could not have materialized without the unique academic endorsement and logistical support provided at Dumbarton Oaks through director Jan Ziolkowski's inspiring leadership and, in Garden and Landscape Studies, the involvement of program director Thaïsa Way, coordinator Jane Padelford, former assistant director Anatole Tchikine, and the senior fellows. The final outcome owes much to the efforts and rigor of an exceptional publications team, including copyeditor Magda Nakassis, designer Melissa Tandysh, managing editor Sara Taylor, and director Kathleen Sparkes. We thank them all.

Under the new leadership of Thaïsa Way, the Dumbarton Oaks Mellon Initiative in Urban Landscape Studies is being renewed through a deeper inquiry into the legacies of race, identity, and difference as they shape the practice of democracy in the city, while acknowledging the crucial importance of sustainability, adaptability, and resilience in urban systems. I have every confidence that the studies of urbanism and landscape will continue to become more closely intertwined at Dumbarton Oaks, even as the institution continues to honor its long commitment to the histories of gardens and designed landscapes.

John Beardsley
Director, Garden and Landscape Studies, 2008–2019

Bridging Remote Sensing and Worldviews

Urban Landscapes from a Preindustrial Perspective

GEORGES FARHAT

EXCHANGES BETWEEN URBANISM AND LANDSCAPE HAVE REACHED
an unprecedented scale and critical significance over the past decades. As the
world's increasing population continues to urbanize, using fossil fuels technology
in growth economies, the extensive reshaping and ecological transformation of the
regions where cities develop have become mainstream concerns. Even the phrase
"urban landscape" has evolved from oxymoron to a commonsense category. It was
initially associated with modernity and industry; now, in the face of climate change,
it conveys hopes for green, responsive, and resilient urbanism. Yet, what exactly does
the notion of urban landscape cover? When did the phenomenon it denotes emerge?
How did the relationships between cities and landscapes evolve across time and space?
Could past dynamics of urban landscapes help reveal their present nature and antici-
pate future developments? These were some of the questions posed to participants of
the 2017 annual symposium in Garden and Landscape Studies at Dumbarton Oaks,
resulting in this volume on *Landscapes of Preindustrial Urbanism*.[1]

As reflected by a flourishing production in urban and landscape studies, answers
to such questions are far from evident. Moreover, research appears divided between
two distinct blocks of historical time. On one side, industrial pasts and postindustrial
transitions of cities and their landscapes are charted, theorized, and regulated following
a variety of complementary, sometimes conflicting, paths in different disciplines that
range from environmental humanities to ecology, planning, and design.[2] On the other,
preindustrial conditions of urban landscapes are being explored in a few rapidly expanding fields of archaeology,[3] historical geography, and heritage studies.[4] These areas have
benefited, over the past three decades, from tremendous advances and renewals in

technologies, methods, and conceptual frameworks. As a result, some well-studied sites have been thoroughly revisited while others are uncovered and new perceptions emerge. A wealth of knowledge has been unearthed and studies of preindustrial urbanism are being recentered on landscapes. Illuminated in unprecedented ways, landscapes turn out to be the very stuff of preindustrial urbanism. In fact, a paradigm shift is under way, according to which landscapes and urbanism are increasingly understood as formed in reciprocal relation during preindustrial times. This volume seeks to capture, frame, and introduce such a paradigm shift to landscape scholars and designers while offering alternative visions to urban historians and planners.

This introductory essay addresses the nexus between technologies and environments in urban landscapes. As a preamble, I will discuss critical notions and, in particular, the modern natural/built binary that still prevails within environmental studies. Then, I will survey the means, methods, and worldviews that we can entwine in various ways—as each essay herein illustrates—to reconsider preindustrial urbanism relative to landscapes.

Urban Landscapes and Techno-Environmental Frameworks

In this project, the phrase "urban landscape" necessarily reaches beyond "open spaces," "public places," "cityscape," and "urban forms" of the "built environment." Although commonly used, these categories are historically less universal than assumed. They stem from a specific, late modern episteme of landscape architecture and planning praxes.[5] Among these, urban morphology is the study of the long-term coevolution of cities' social structures and "urban tissue."[6] When considered synchronically, "urban forms" are associated with meanings or symbolism.[7] They have thus fed on visual-centric concepts like that of "cityscape."[8] However, since the 1970s, urban ecology and environmental history more completely apprehend the "built environment" as an ecosystem.[9] Yet, these methodologies operate within a modern environmental framework premised on the clear distinction between natural (objectified, physiographic) landscapes and their sociocultural (represented or built, anthropogenic) counterparts. This dualist conception—whose inherent contradictions have long been pointed out[10]—becomes ever less relevant. If it might have fit industrial cities, it was certainly foreign to earlier contexts.

In response to such limitations, *Landscapes of Preindustrial Urbanism* outlines a more inclusive and historical but less anthropocentric approach. It looks to expand humanistic definitions of landscape such as that of John Brinckerhoff Jackson: "a composition of man-made or man-modified spaces to serve as infrastructure or background for our collective existence."[11] Instead, in our project, (urban) landscapes are considered within their historically specific, technical, and environmental frameworks. In other words, landscapes here do not only encompass built and unbuilt areas from household to infrastructure but also integrate land tenure and use with material processes of mediation between human and nonhuman agents and phenomena—minerals, plants, animals, water, fires, weather, skies, forces, and other entities. This is precisely what a famous 1550s portrait-map captures of Paris, to which we'll return later (Figures 1.1 and 1.11).

Thus conceived, processes of mediation define techno-environmental frameworks of interweaving temporalities, techniques, and materialities. Prior to the First Industrial Revolution (1760–1840), varying calendars, astronomical mappings, and cosmologies informed regional ecologies as well as urbanism.[12] Similarly, preindustrial times require us to think of technologies as embodied skills (techniques) and embedded knowledge rather than as applied science.[13] In that sense, preindustrial technologies both shaped and were reshaped by a wide array of material practices or experiences that range from the production of artifacts to landscape engineering and urbanism.

Further to this, taken in relational webs of mediation, materials of urban landscapes become agents of historical change. Whether possessing intentionality or not, they exercise agency through performance, growth, weathering, and a myriad of other processes.[14] Anthropologist Tim Ingold's "ecology of materials" offers a phenomenological elaboration of such an agency. Matter, he argues, is to be "considered in respect of its occurrence in processes of flow and transformation"; it is not secondary to form (idea, knowledge), and, therefore, passive as in the "Western intellectual tradition."[15] Deceptively evident, this proposition further unfolds in archaeologist Chantal Conneller's words: "different understandings of materials are not simply 'concepts' set apart from 'real' properties; they are realized in terms of different practices that themselves have material effects."[16]

Accordingly, techno-environmental frameworks have their own history and historicity. Indeed, even within the West, polarities between culture or artifact (*techné*, *ars*) and nature (*physis*, *natura*) have been constantly reshaped.[17] Likewise, boundaries between natural elements, realms, and beings remained fluid in European thought, framed as they were by medicine, alchemy, and craftsmanship, until the mid-eighteenth century.[18] What then, of periods and places where, as in the Andes, animacy was an experiential constituent of (urban) landscapes?[19] Interplaying here are epistemic questions (knowledge systems) and ontological ones (the nature of essence and substance), which, however, are not to be conflated.[20] They urge us to refrain from projecting backward current binaries associated with notions of cultural landscape (tangible/intangible) or landscape ecology (abiotic/biotic). Shouldn't the same apply to "natural" and "built environments" to avoid colonizing the past in retrospect?

Natural and Built Environments in Modern Approaches to Preindustrial Urbanism

Over the past century, the natural/built binary, which reflects the modern epistemic natural/social sciences divide, has largely prevailed in landscape and urban studies. It still defines how geographers, historians, and archaeologists looking mainly at regional-scale patterns investigate the dynamics of past urbanization relative to landscapes. Scholars foreground interdependence between cities as social environments (centers of consumption and production) and their catchment areas or hinterland (depleted, transformed natural environment). They do so within a given technological system and resulting urban network.[21] Such constructs draw on two well-known and complementary modern precedents. The first one is economist Johann Heinrich von Thünen's

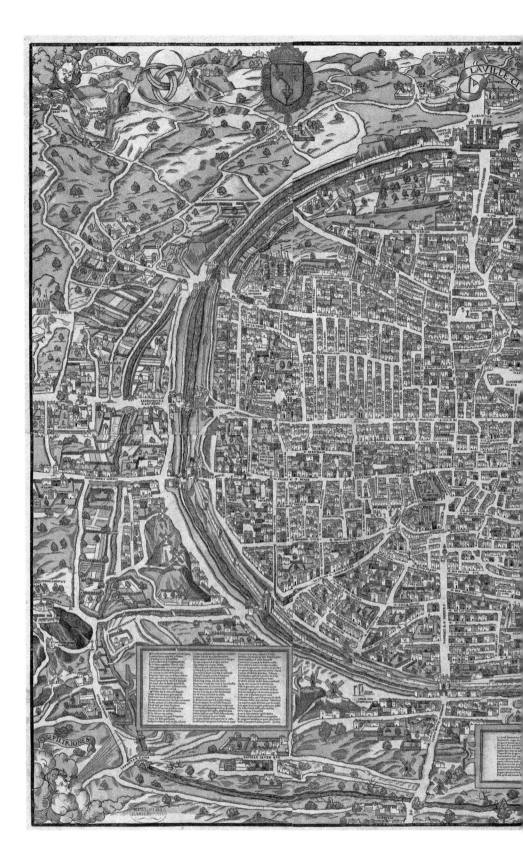

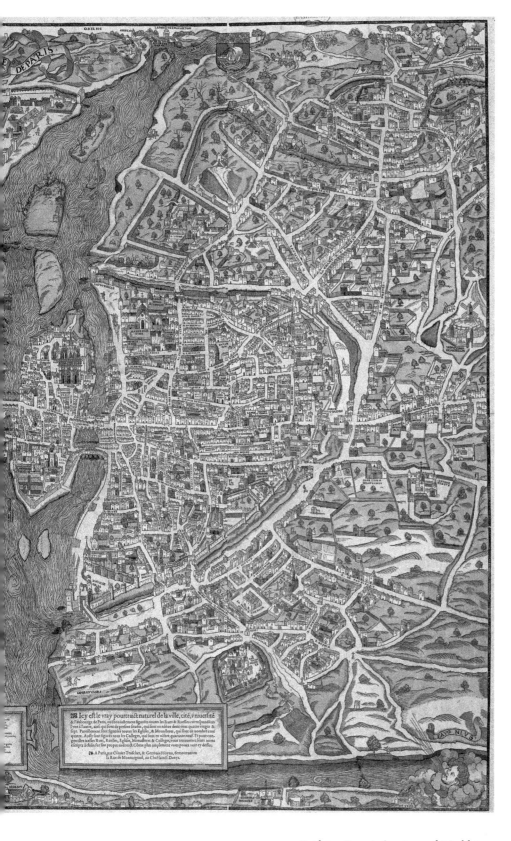

FIGURE 1.1

Olivier Truschet and
Germain Hoyau, *Ici est le vray
pourtraict naturel de la ville,
cité, université, & faubourgz
de Paris*, ca. 1550, woodcut,
eight plates assembled,
approx. 1:5,000, 96 × 133 cm.
North (*Septentriones*) is
in the bottom left corner.
Photograph courtesy of Basel
University Library.

(1783–1850) scheme of land "economic rent" (Figure 1.2).[22] It factors soil properties and distance along with time and cost of transport. The second precedent is geographer Walter Christaller's (1893–1969) "central place theory,"[23] which puts forth hierarchical systems of cities as long-distance interaction networks. Both concepts, though, it should be emphasized, stemmed from planning theory and were aimed at its practice. They were not devised by historians or archaeologists, whose disciplines they nevertheless much inspired.

The city/hinterland polarity is at the heart of other equally influential theoretical models, such as Max Weber's political economy of medieval Europe and Louis Wirth's social ecology of industrial North American cities.[24] It subsequently shaped archaeologist V. Gordon Childe's most famous and evolutionist paradigm, the "Urban Revolution," located in the Fertile Crescent and Indus Valley around 3000 BCE.[25] Childe's ideal type of "earliest cities" was precisely predicated upon "techniques" and the exploitation of "natural resources." This conjunction of technology and environment supposedly brought sedentary, agropastoral economies and settlements from "barbarism" into urban "civilization."[26] It guided Childe's list of "ten rather abstract criteria" of what originally constituted a city.[27] Along with centralized hydraulic systems (flood control, irrigation) and food surplus for larger, densely populated settlements, Childe's urban model involved other "inventions and discoveries."[28] These comprise occupational specialization and social hierarchy, long-distance trade, communication networks, taxation, and monumental buildings. In addition, the import of raw materials and the export of artifacts implied art, writing, and numerical records as well as practical, exact, and predictive sciences. Such were purportedly the preconditions of urbanism and state formation. They supposed top-down planning and the transformation of specific environments.

Childe's thesis inevitably raised questions that were then addressed by archaeologists and anthropologists. Among other noted issues is the status of technology. In Childe's rationale, it remains abstract as it reflects universal stages of evolution and is imposed from outside onto local practices and environments.[29] Further elaborations would, therefore, look more deeply into social complexity, regional-scale settlement patterns, and the latter's impact on specific hinterlands. In that regard, anthropologist Julian H. Steward's "cultural ecology," which postulates technology's role in social adaptation to given environments, would have an enduring appeal and influence.[30] It set the focus on "behavior" and collective responses to ecosystems. Conceptualized in relation to regional physiography and ecological processes, any "cultural evolution" was thereby to be reconstructed at all scales, from artifacts to settlement patterns.[31] Again, criticism would not be long to rise.[32] And for all the methodological refinements and accumulated data since Childe's "Urban Revolution," defining cities, urbanism, or urbanization in preindustrial times remains a central question that is worth reconsidering precisely relative to landscapes.

Recent Calls to Redefine Preindustrial Cities and Urbanism

As John N. Miksic points out, definitions of what constitute cities worldwide persistently depend upon idealized models of compact and dense settlements from ancient

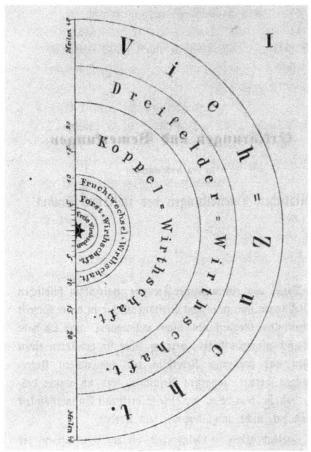

a

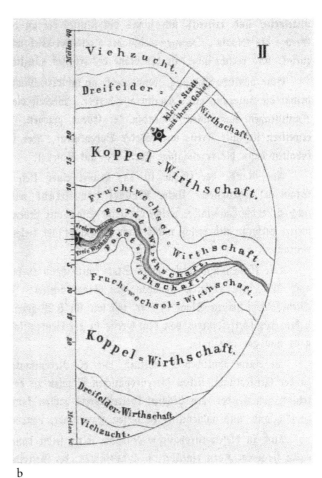

b

Mediterranean and southwest Asian sites.[33] Corresponding "monothetic, unilinear definitions of 'urbanization,'" Miksic observes, prove too rigid and unrealistic when considered outside their place of origin.[34] In fact, not only do non-Western types of polities, from Southeast Asia and Africa to the Americas, call for landscape-specific frameworks, but too often Western and Near Eastern urban models also turn out to be narrowly defined. For instance, within the confines of the former Roman empire, the characterization of urbanism during Late Antiquity or under Byzantium presents environmental challenges in a variety of cases. These range from newly founded settlements to uncertain, open-ended transitions of ancient ones, including their "ruralization" along with shrinkage or dispersal.[35] And, as research on nonelite urban households and hinterlands demonstrates, even Mesopotamia and the Levant feature regional variance in types and trajectories of urbanization with primary and secondary phases.[36] These preceded top-down planning and did not solely depend on agricultural surplus; they also fed on wetlands.[37]

Alternatives have been proposed by archaeologists to move beyond a priori definitions. Some, like George L. Cowgill, have opted for a loose, minimal definition of

FIGURE 1.2

Scheme of land "economic rent," showing optimal agricultural use of hinterland surrounding a city (central star) in two different cases: a) an abstract ideal space; and b) a river valley with secondary city (peripheral star). Reproduced from Johann Heinrich von Thünen, *Der isolierte Staat in Beziehung auf Landwirtschaft und Nationalökonomie* (1826; 3rd ed., Berlin: Wiegandt, 1875), 1:390–91.

"cities" (rather than "the city"), requiring, however, site permanence, a clear urban/rural distinction, and a shared urban identity.[38] Colin Renfrew, drawing on Childe's "checklist," suggested quite an opposite characterization that consists of "common aspects of urban structure" that would yet be "of very wide, if not quite universal, applicability."[39] Building on these and previous process-based approaches, Michael E. Smith has recently offered an elaborate multivariable matrix with twenty-one "urban attributes" to help "identify early cities."[40] Such a flexible urban typology is at once useful and revealing. It should help open the box. But, like its predecessors, it remains premised on the clear dissociation of a "built environment" from a "hinterland," the former bearing on the latter. It thus mirrors the very same epistemic "nexus" that undermines the field of urban environmental history, as Martin V. Melosi recently noted.[41] Furthermore, it is informed by the modern ecological paradigm—with attendant views of urban metabolism and materials flow—that still distinguishes socially produced from natural environments.[42]

Yet, lines between terms in such theoretical models are being blurred owing precisely to technologies, methods, and concepts developed over the past decades in at least three different areas: survey and mapping, environmental studies, and anthropology writ large. By changing our sense of spatiotemporal scales, approaches to ecology, and notions of materiality, these moves have allowed us to reconsider afresh and conjointly a number of urban landscape constituents such as settlement patterns, design processes, and worldviews.

Remote Sensing and Previously Unseen Settlement Patterns

Since the end of the twentieth century, remote-sensing technologies have presented renewed potential for the study of formerly abandoned urban settlements. Recently declassified aerial or satellite intelligence photographs from the Cold War period have provided invaluable information on site condition prior to later agricultural and urban developments.[43] From the 1990s onward, space and airborne synthetic-aperture radar (SAR), with their ground penetrating emissions, have enabled researchers to successfully detect subsurface features and small-scale terrain irregularities in arid areas or during dry seasons (Figure 1.3).[44] Conversely, airborne light detection and ranging (LiDAR) reveals a wide array of aboveground landforms in covered, forested areas under tropical climate conditions.[45] Meanwhile, digital image analysis, modeling, and integration of both historic maps and recently collected data into geographic information systems (GIS) reframe landscape-related spatiotemporal processes.[46] As a consequence, ways of perceiving and conceiving past landforms and earthworks, land use and cover, built structures and water features evolve. Settlements, agriculture, infrastructure, and engineered geosystems cohere as regional-scale webs. Unsurprisingly, recovered settlements do not match traditional models, hierarchies, or trajectories of dense cities. Nor, it should be stressed, do they fit the terms of the modern natural/built environment divide.

"Megasites" constitute one such newly defined and diverse type of large-scale and low-density preindustrial urbanism. This type comprises late fifth- to early fourth

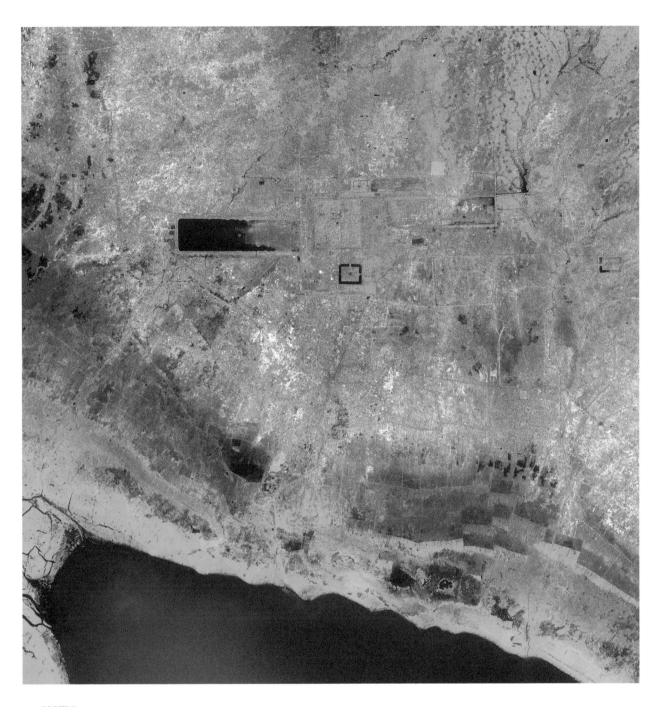

FIGURE 1.3

Urban landscape of Greater Angkor, Cambodia. Simulated natural color image acquired on February 17, 2004, by the Advanced Spaceborne Thermal Emission and Reflection Radiometer (ASTER) on NASA's Terra satellite. NASA image created by Jesse Allen, Earth Observatory, using data provided courtesy of NASA/GSFC/METI/ERSDAC/JAROS and the US/Japan ASTER Science Team. For further details, see Figures 1.4 and 1.5, as well as the discussion on page 11.

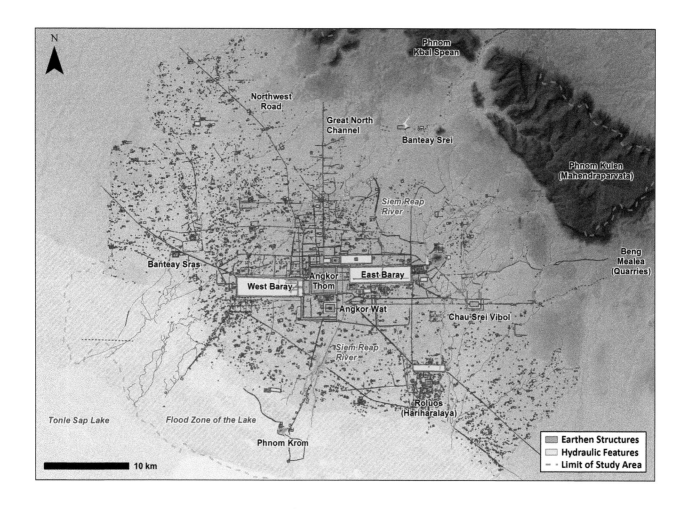

FIGURE 1.4

Map of the Greater
Angkor area. Map
by Christophe
Pottier and Damian
Evans of the Greater
Angkor Project. École
française d'Extrême-
Orient/APSARA/
University of Sydney.

millennium BCE, 300–350 ha settlement clusters in Mesopotamia (Jason A. Ur, this volume) and quasicontemporary, near-elliptical layouts at Maidanetske and Nebelivka in Eastern Europe (Romanian-Ukrainian Cucuteni-Trypillia civilization).[47] Late Iron Age oppida (fortified settlements) with denser walled urban cores and dispersed peripheries also fall into this category.[48] African examples that defy any simple conceptualization illustrate other instances of this type. Thirteenth- to sixteenth-century CE constellations of stone wall enclosures at Great Zimbabwe extended over 730 ha across rocky hills and valleys.[49] Ninth- to eleventh-century Esan-Edo agglomerations of concentric earthworks grew in Nigeria's rainforest belt to cover 6,500 km² comprising over five hundred agriculture-based settlements. It is at their core that, ca. 1200, the "urban kingdom" of Benin City emerged to control land, craft, and trade.[50]

Archaeologist Roland Fletcher uses the phrase "low-density, agrarian-based urbanism" to denote a type of extensive and dispersed settlement whose limits clearly rest in technology-environment interactions.[51] It defines the engineered plain where Greater Angkor (Cambodia) expanded from the ninth to fifteenth century, between Lake Tonlé

FIGURE 1.5

Rice fields cultivated within East Baray (tenth-century reservoir), Greater Angkor, Siem Reap, Cambodia. Note the scale of the afforested embankment in the background. Photograph by Georges Farhat, 2015.

Sap and the plateau of Phnom Kulen (Figure 1.4).[52] This reconceptualization of the Khmer empire's capital comes as the latest stride in a long history of modern survey. It originated in Bernard-Philippe Groslier's 1950s to 1970s "hydraulic city" construct, which drew on aerial archaeology to hypothesize an urban-rural continuum.[53] It continued with architect and archaeologist Christophe Pottier's systematic field survey and mapping during the 1990s. It eventually coalesced into the Greater Angkor Project as Damian Evans and teams integrated all existing cartography and aerial photography, radar imagery (2000s), and laser scanning (2010s) into GIS.[54] As a result, what is currently described as the "world's largest preindustrial settlement complex" appears to have formed a 1,000 km² mesh of infrastructure.[55] This urban landscape was composed of rectified rivers, embanked canals and reservoirs (baray), moats and causeways, dikes and earthen platforms. The resulting network was interspersed with innumerable local temples, house mounds, ponds, and, most of all, rice fields (Figure 1.5). Irrigated by gravity, the latter were worked by households with the help of water buffalo. Altogether, the urban landscape secured crops against erratic monsoon rain to feed an estimated resident population of seven hundred thousand inhabitants.[56]

Similarly, "agro-urban landscapes" have been recognized in tropical Mesoamerica as a common settlement type, materializing in manifold ways.[57] Seventh- to tenth-century Maya settlements at Tikal (Guatemala) and Caracol (Belize), extending respectively over 120 and 200 km², are well-studied cases that have been provocatively described as "green" and "garden" cities.[58] Yet it is an entirely other kind of dispersed forest urban settlement, dating from ca. 1250 CE, that Michael Heckenberger explores in the Amazon (this volume).

Pattern, size, and density in all such sites cannot but change our views of preindustrial urbanism. While this expectedly resonates with current urban sprawl and its theory, awareness of climate change or loss of soils and biodiversity inevitably inflect research on past urban landscapes.

Urban Landscape Materiality in Geoarchaeology and Historical Ecology

Environmental conditions, under which regional types of preindustrial urbanism formed, developed, and declined, have been lately reframed by geoarchaeology. The latter, which integrates a host of earth sciences, now benefits from larger, more reliable, or previously unavailable sets of data (from ice cores and speleothems to DNA and tree rings).[59] It enables researchers to more accurately reconstruct paleoenvironments as well as long-term climate dynamics; to correlate environments and societies; and to retrace land cover, land use, and associated foodways.[60]

Better understood, monsoon variability, droughts, floods, and warming cycles are now identified among factors that contributed to the collapse of urban systems under constant climatic stress.[61] Owing to urban population growth and agricultural needs, ensuing deforestation, soil exhaustion, and erosion would combine with siltation of hydraulic infrastructure while overflows interacted with earthworks (terraces, bunds, mounds, causeways).[62] In cases as diverse as Cahokia (United States), Caracol, Angkor, and Anuradhapura (Sri Lanka), climate variation and ecological instability conflicted with economic constraint and rigid management patterns. The result was failure of complex, large-scale infrastructure networks and urban collapse or, alternatively, peripheral dispersal and reconfiguration of settlements.[63]

Obviously, scholars' interests in such phenomena are driven by a quest for solutions to current environmental crises, for which they hope to learn from the past.[64] However, more significant for our present consideration is the fact that preindustrial urban settlements are now holistically studied as environments that can no longer be dissociated into built and unbuilt or core and hinterland areas. More important still is a rethink of human and nonhuman agencies based on archaeological finds. This has enabled historical ecology to frame a more integrative matrix accounting for the dynamics of long-term, human-environmental interactions—rather than a deterministic one-way adaptation as in cultural ecology.[65] One finds material practices of design and ecological processes entwined in such a matrix. Two opposite cases, one of sterile terrain formation and the other of organic soil creation (pedogenesis), should suffice to illustrate this interaction. Semiarid plains across the world are scattered with mounds and hills ("tells"), measuring up to 1 km across and 40 m in elevation, that once were urban settlement mounds in wetter climates. Now an integral part of their regional landscapes, these reliefs have emerged through subsequent phases of collapse, reconstruction, and abandonment. Returning to clay after melting, mud bricks formed

hills that, in turn, were subject to ecological cycles.[66] Under completely different conditions, across the Amazon, raised fields and anthropic "dark earths" accompany extensive precontact settlement earthworks and artificial islands (Figure 1.6). Vast swaths of the oft-fantasized pristine wilderness and biosphere turn out to have been human-managed forests.[67] Their fauna and flora were domesticated, selected, and reshaped for more than two millennia into what could ultimately be described as descendants of urban landscapes.[68]

FIGURE 1.6

Pre-Columbian earthworks and geometric geoglyphs, Bastião da Mata, Amazon, Acre, Brazil. Photograph by Diego Lourenço Gurgel, 2012.

Worldviews: From Historical to Ecological Anthropology

Perspectives on landscapes of preindustrial urbanism are undoubtedly changing through the lenses of remotely sensed imagery and historical ecology. The present volume seeks to bridge these methodologies with worldviews. However, along with the use of emic (insider) notions and views, as opposed to etic (outsider) ones, this involves more than beliefs, mentalities, and ideology. Indeed, the constituents of worldviews range widely from social institutions (such as kinship or land tenure structures) to cosmologies (conceptions of space and time), as studied by historical anthropology. They also include ever-mutating ontologies (with attendant techno-environmental frameworks) that ecological anthropology explores.[69] In this respect, urban landscapes constitute a major medium for worldviews.

FIGURE 1.7

Altepetl glyph of Cholula, Mexico, from the *Historia Tolteca-Chichimeca*, 1545–63, fol. 25. Département des Manuscrits, Mexicain 46–58, Bibliothèque nationale de France, Paris.

Recent studies have markedly focused on the ways in which preindustrial urbanism was shaped by institutional frameworks nested in the environment. Such is the case, for instance, in Mesopotamia, with the "patrimonial household" (Akkadian *bītum*), which—rather than abstract bureaucracy and centralized authority as in Childe's "Urban Revolution"—turns out to be the model for lineage, village, temple, city, and polity.[70] In the Andes, multivalent notions such as *ayllu* (social groupings and land tenure) and *wak'a*

14   GEORGES FARHAT

(collective, actual, or mythical stone ancestor) are tied to untouched or reshaped landscape features endowed with *camay* (vital force).[71] As Alan L. Kolata's work on ancient Peru demonstrates, around Chimú (1100–1470, desert North Coast) and Inca (1438–1533, highlands) urban settlements, crops, artifacts, kinship, and ritual intertwined dynamically in the ways communities built their environmental infrastructure.[72]

Such interrelatedness of urbanism and landscapes is precisely ingrained in the multilayered Mesoamerican territorial concept and glyph of *altepetl* (pl. *altepeme*), literally "water-mountain" in Nahuatl (Figure 1.7). Over the past decades, provocative studies have illuminated its many sociopolitical and spatial attributes: segmented territoriality, core and tributary communities or *calpulli* (later *tlaxilacalli*), dynastic lordship, pyramid, marketplace.[73] Within a worldview that paired rain and fertility with the human body's physiology and fluids, various relations existed between an *altepetl*'s tutelary deities and urban landscape constituents (Figure 1.8).[74] Built pyramids echoed surrounding mountains and volcanoes. Flows of sacrificial blood responded to life-giving spring waters. Political ceremonies magnified household rituals that involved edible effigies of the sacred geography.[75] Located northeast of the Basin of Mexico, the city-state of Teotihuacan (150 BCE–600 CE) epitomized many of these connections. They include the settlement grid's orientation (toward particular mountains) and topographic integration (earthworks), human-made hills (pyramids) and processional spaces, canalized bodies of water and irrigated *chinampas* (raised beds) (Figure 1.9).[76] Understandably, Teotihuacan's classic urban legacy (history, rituals, and layout principles) would later be emulated by the Triple Alliance (1428–1521 CE) or so-called Aztec empire.[77] It thus

FIGURE 1.8

Tlaloc Paradise mural, showing a mountain with water streams flowing into raised beds (*chinampas*) or fields with maize and other flowering plants. Tepantitla Patio 2 mural (detail), Teotihuacan, Mexico. Photograph by María de Jesús Chávez and Carlos M. de Rosas Landa, 2016; digital assembly by Carlos M. de Rosas Landa; courtesy of the Archivo fotográfico del proyecto "La pintura mural prehispánica en México," Instituto de Investigaciones Estéticas, Universidad Nacional Autónoma de México.

FIGURE 1.9

Plaza of the Moon and the Street of the Dead with the Pyramid of the Sun, built from 100 BCE to 250 CE, at the monumental core of Teotihuacan. Note the similarities between the pyramids and mountain range in the back. Photograph by Georges Farhat, 2016.

inspired the construction of the archipelago settlement of Tenochtitlan-Mexico in a vast system of shallow, cascading lakes and lagoons that once covered most of the Basin of Mexico. However, of equal importance for the region's urban evolution was its spatial conglomeration of *altepeme*. The institutional structure underlaid the distribution, construction, and operation of a centrally funded network of causeways, dikes, aqueducts, canals, and channels from 1325 to 1520 CE (Figure 1.10).[78] This infrastructure was necessary not only for defense and transportation but also for the supply, drainage, separation, and circulation of water (fresh, brackish, and saline). It controlled floods in resource-rich lakes whose flora and fauna were thereby recomposed. It also organized Tenochtitlan's expansion on reclaimed land whose street and canal gridiron layout interwove with central and peripheral *chinampas*.[79] The latter's labor-intensive maintenance depended upon the development of complex local ecological knowledge and management institutions within overlapping land tenure and economic structures: tenant farms, *calpulli* holdings, "noble" estates, and state taxation.[80] As a result, Tenochtitlan's outward-growing *chinampa* urbanism created a flat-bottom topography of soft substrate that would make later Hispanic extensions increasingly vulnerable to floods and earthquakes.

The complexity of territorial institutions that structured urban landscapes in the Americas was certainly not foreign to European counterparts. In France, for instance, two different land institutions that meshed and overlapped shaped all landscapes: the *seigneurie* (fiefdom), the basic political and economic unit (composed of demesne,

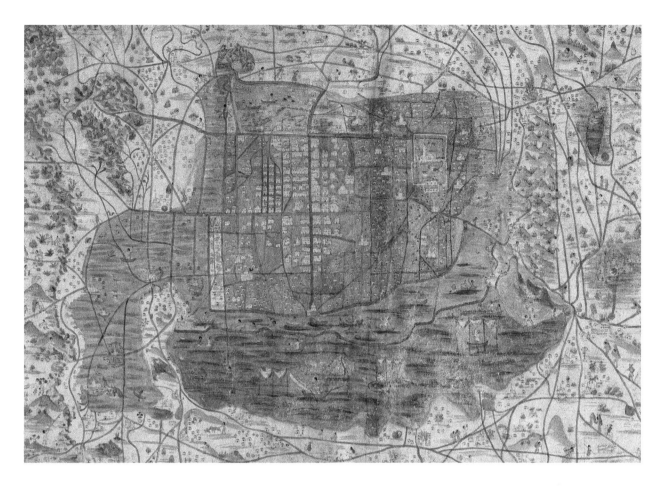

censive, commons, and wasteland); and the parish, at once a spiritual, social, and fiscal subdivision.[81] As they ruled land tenure, use, and taxation as well as justice and road construction in an order-based society, both institutions framed the interrelation of urbanism and landscape within and across any *ville* (town), *faubourg* (abbey-centered or craft-specialized suburb), and their surrounds.[82] They organized city and countryside alike, unhindered by fortification walls and administrative boundaries.[83] This held true for the entire *prévôté et vicomté de Paris*, forming a regional urban system with myriads of parishes and lay as well as ecclesiastical seigneuries.[84] Better than any other document, Truschet and Hoyau's *pourtraict naturel* shows how this materialized around 1550 when, within the capital's intramural area (approximately 480 ha), the population was about two hundred thousand (Figure 1.11).[85] Here, an urban landscape was seized in the making, with all constituents laid bare: from terrain and hydrology to parishes and *censives* (burgage), graveyards, fields, and gardens, through to building types, urban tissue, and technical devices.[86] The latter, in particular, conspicuously manifest material mediations between humans and nonhumans. Among others, they include earthworks and ramparts, furnaces and tileries, quays and inhabited bridges, moats and sewers, wells and fountains, windmills and watermills, spires and bell towers. In uniquely regional fashions, minerals, plants, and animals contributed to form, supply, and sustain this

FIGURE 1.10

Map of Tenochtitlan/Mexico City (detail), ca. 1550, painting on skin, 75 × 114 cm. Note the network of channels (blue), causeways (brown), and dikes across wetlands or fresh (bluer) and salty waters (greener) surrounding core island land (light brown) in archipelago settlement. Photograph courtesy of Uppsala University Library, Sweden.

FIGURE 1.11

Olivier Truschet and Germain Hoyau, *Ici est le vray pourtraict naturel de la ville, cité, université, & faubourgz de Paris* (detail), ca. 1550, woodcut. See Figure 1.1. Photograph courtesy of Basel University Library.

urban landscape. Masses of clay, stones, and gypsum were quarried from either the ground surface or a maze of subterranean galleries.[87] Vast forests were felled in surrounding provinces and turned into woodwork or fire and smoke. Thousands of horses roamed the streets while livestock was slaughtered in marketplaces.[88] Pillories and gallows exposed tortured bodies of criminals at major intersections.[89] As a result, tons of manure, saltpeter, carcasses, and wastewater were produced and recycled in agricultural practice and artillery or for bone artifacts and leatherwork.[90] But to fully grasp this material reality, one must recall other aspects of its techno-environmental framework. Back then and for another century, alchemy and craftsmanship collaboratively defined a conceptual horizon for material transformation and transmutation in the city's workshops and apothecaries.[91] Infrastructure and buildings were engineered in a world still organized by an elemental, qualitative physics of universal contrariety, whose mathematization was only beginning, while in colleges, geometry was taught as a means to access the mystery of the Holy Trinity.[92] No doubt, economic relationships between urban core and countryside, which would later inspire von Thünen's own scheme, shaped the entire region. But the divide between walled city and hinterland that this map exhibits was only apparent, transient, and therefore misleading. Both within and around city walls, landscape was at once the very material and outcome of urbanism. Here again, the natural/built binary proves to be an irrelevant lens.

Earthworks, Waterscapes, Forestry

To address the abovementioned theoretical and methodological challenges, this cross-cultural project brings together scholars from anthropological archaeology and historical geography as well as environmental and heritage studies. They engage with landscapes through survey, excavation, preservation, and commitment to local communities, which implies a good deal of ethnography. The resulting collection of essays is contingent upon the current state of research. It achieves diversity across time and place with no attempt yet at comprehensiveness or balance in sampling. Geographic areas of selected case studies include a variety of unexpected, unforeseen, or unlikely locales. These range widely from Southeast Asia (Cambodia) to the Amazon (Xingu River). However, although the volume opens with Mesopotamia in 4500–2500 BCE and closes in Africa on the eve of industrialization, it is organized thematically rather than historically or geographically. It is composed of three parts, each foregrounding a specific landscape theme: Earthworks, Waterscapes, and Forestry. Whether minor or major, these themes nevertheless appear in each of the parts, where they bring into play current landscape concepts with past contexts, sometimes by contrast or with irony.

Earthworks
Earthworks point to matters and structures that lay the ground for urban settlements or are the outcome of temporal processes. This actually includes substrates, outcrops, soils, earthmoving, leveling, terracing, and other topographic constructions such as embankments, causeways, platforms, mounds, and pyramids. In turn, these inflect and undergo

flows, erosion, collapse, and sedimentation. Earthworks are not only necessary to the foundation and spatial organization of urban landscapes; they constitute the matrix and agents of unanticipated long-term ecological developments. Oftentimes, they also are what becomes of urbanism.

To begin, Jason A. Ur's essay "Space and Structure in Early Mesopotamian Cities" challenges Childe's model of top-down, planned origins of urbanism. Using remotely sensed imagery and surface survey of artifacts, Ur investigates settlement mounds that exhibit alternatives to centralized, irrigation-based economies and urban/rural dichotomies. He reconceptualizes three different early urban structures, dating from ca. 4000–2500 BCE, in Syria and Iraq, respectively, as "megasite," low-density city, and city-state. Putting the focus on the agency of households and neighborhoods rather than that of kings and elites, Ur demonstrates that "even the most geometric of settlement forms" from these periods "can be explained through the concept of emergence." This precisely embodies landscape-specific processes of growth and organization. Enmeshed with land cultivation and the molding of clay, settlements evolved outward then inward and upward. Once abandoned, they turned into "tells" that reconfigured the plains' topography.

Next, from the perspective of historical geography, Hendrik W. Dey looks into the interrelation of "Landscape Change and Ceremonial Praxis in Medieval Rome: From the Via Triumphalis to the Via Papalis." He concentrates on the transition of the imperial city's decline to the Christian appropriation of its built structures as secondary substrate and ground as well as quarry. Dey unravels seemingly familiar but rarely scrutinized factors of historical soil formation in urban landscapes. He more specifically highlights a long-term interaction between two opposite phenomena: on the one hand, soil sedimentation and accretion of dirt, silt, building collapse, waste, and rubble; on the other, triumphal pomp, rituals, and processional routes. The conjunction of both processes ultimately fossilized into urban street layouts in the Tiber's floodplain. From this extremely detailed chronicle of many conspiring events, factors, and components, we learn how an urban landscape can mutate and evolve as a full-fledged historical agent.

Turning with Timothy R. Pauketat to the earth-mound-built and animal-populated urban complex of Greater Cahokia, which was planned ca. 1050 CE and stretched along the Mississippi River, we ask: "What Constituted Cahokian Urbanism?" Pauketat answers the question with a radical "approach to urbanism that is both less reductionist than older social-evolutionary models and less anthropocentric than historical or phenomenological" ones. Cahokia was composed of a collection of monumental core areas and precincts, with shrines and steam baths scattered across them. Open water, residential neighborhoods, and maize fields lay in between. In response to environmental conditions, Greater Cahokia remained under incessant construction and reconstruction until 1350 CE, when it was abandoned because of climate change. To characterize this "urbanism in the making," where sounds, lights, and textures are manifestations of its many inhabitants, Pauketat turns to weather and atmospheres, materials and substances, earth, water, heat, and pressure, as well as the agency of other-than-human beings. He comes to define the urban landscape of earthen mounds as a mediation between humans' affective experience, spiritual forces, and watery transubstantiations.

Waterscapes

Waterscapes focus on the ways in which urban landscapes are shaped by water as life-giving substance or source of energy, threat or resource, at once physical, political, ritual, and spiritual. From harvesting to distribution, their infrastructure and materiality are explored here in Mediterranean and monsoon climates. This section gets even closer to technical issues, involving environmental variability and management models along with their material implications for urban landscapes. More than elsewhere in the volume, spatial or temporal overlapping between contributions offers interesting comparisons, if not necessarily commonalities.

In "Hydraulic Landscapes of Roman and Byzantine Cities," Jordan Pickett seeks to outline the "hydraulic paradigm" that shaped Roman urban landscapes while facing environmental constraints that forced it to morph across space and over time. To that end, Pickett first presents a thorough survey of urban water conveyance, supply, and consumption through aqueducts across the Roman empire; he explores the many dimensions—environmental, sociotechnical, architectural—that constitute this "hydraulic paradigm." Then, Ephesus, one of the largest and archaeologically best documented Roman cities of the coast of Ionia (present-day Izmir Province, Turkey), is offered as a case study that encapsulates the complex and varying role of aqueducts in the construction of urban landscapes. Finally, he considers various scenarios of infrastructure evolution during the Byzantine era. Outright rejection or upkeep of aqueducts are two major alternatives revolving around sociopolitical choices of management systems. Pertaining to another set of equally significant factors, earthquakes or neglect caused sudden or gradual abandonment of aqueducts that entailed contrasting trajectories of settlements around them: disaggregation, nucleation, or convergence.

With "Monsoon Landscapes and Flexible Provisioning in the Preindustrial Cities of the Indian Subcontinent," Monica L. Smith revisits the relationship between city and countryside in early historic urbanism under the erratic climate of South Asia. Smith examines three case studies in which excavation and survey data from the past decades renew information about water management, food supply, and seasonality. These are the ancient sites of Kaushambi, one of the largest cities on the Ganges plain; Sisupalgarh, a walled city within the Mahanadi River delta (eastern India), northwest of which Ekamrakshetra (studied by Priyaleen Singh in this volume) would later develop; and Anuradhapura, located in the Dry Zone north of Sri Lanka. The latter, in particular, exhibits an extreme case of "low-density, agrarian-based urbanism," to use Fletcher's phrase. It was sustained by a far-reaching, intricate network of temple pools, tanks, and human-made cascades constructed after the introduction of Buddhism to Sri Lanka during the third century BCE. The hydraulic system irrigated and tied together rice fields and monasteries across the urban core and surrounding region.

Taking us farther east and a few centuries later, Jean-Baptiste Chevance investigates Mahendraparvata (approximately 20 mi², during the ninth century) in his essay on "The Phnom Kulen Capital: A Singular and Early Case of Landscape Construction in Ancient Cambodia." This urban landscape lies on top of the sacred Phnom Kulen plateau, 40 km northeast of Angkor, whose full development it shortly preceded. Early on, Mahendraparvata was abandoned, lost, and preserved from later alteration. Thanks to LiDAR technology, and the author's ground survey, excavations, and paleoenvironmental studies, it was recently recovered as a "city" whose spatial organization was dictated by water management, topography, and earthworks. It features an extensive grid of dikes, defining large square areas, with a network of ditches, canals, dams, and water tanks. Primarily built for water control and food security in a monsoon climate, this grid enabled transportation and determined the distribution of religious and secular centers. Closer study reveals the urban landscape was under constant environmental pressure. In addition to political and military factors, adverse combinations of technology, resource management, and land use soon caused abandonment of the site. It nevertheless appears as an instructive alternative to Angkor's contemporary plain-type urbanism whose historiography it complements in a momentous manner.

With "The Weave of Natural and Cultural Ecology," Priyaleen Singh brings us back to India and discusses the transition of "nature" in Ekamrakshetra, the historic temple town of Bhubaneswar, from the Middle Ages to the present. She examines how "nature" was shifted from subject to object, from animate to inanimate entity. Yet, it is not only its understanding (meanings, values), but the very attributes of "prakriti" (nature, body, matter, phenomenal universe) that changed. Of particular interest to the discussion are medieval treatises that classified land and settlements relative to water and sites. The local Ekamra Purana describes the clusters of temples, shrines, tanks, pools, wells, gardens, and fields that involved an urban ecology and economy through the collection, retention, and circulation of water. In a city where the latter is considered a medium for divine powers and a healing agent, trees and groves were to be planted as abodes for the Trimurti, for their medicinal properties, and as underground water purifiers. Worth underscoring here is Singh's use of the phrase "cultural ecology." It differs starkly from Steward's evolutionist "determination of how culture is affected by its adaptation to environment."[93] Rather, she shows ways in which human practices and nonhuman entities are interwoven within a Hindu framework of urban landscapes. Ironically, Singh's inquiry reveals that notions such as "sustainability," "mixed land use," "low-rise high-density," and "green design," which obviously had no currency in the Hindu framework, could yet be better substantiated in the past than in today's conservation plans.

Forestry

Forestry is to be taken here in both senses of forestland and its management as a counterintuitive locus for urbanism. Essays in this last section question the very notion of urbanism in two different settings: the Amazon and the rainforest belt of West Africa. Both contributors bridging remote sensing and geoarchaeology with ethnography and political advocacy, push the notion of urbanism to its limits.

In "Xingu Garden Cities: Amazonian Urban Landscapes, or What?," Michael Heckenberger shows how, in the Upper Xingu region of Brazil, forest and urbanism meshed. Mapping walled towns, dense networks of roads, and outlying settlements, Heckenberger characterizes an "Amazonian urbanism" by the dynamics of its human/nonhuman systems. Meant to nurture the forest rather than harness it, this alternative variety of preindustrial urbanism involves constellations of small-scale and diffuse settlements. The focus here is a "hierarchical galactic cluster" defined as a forest garden city, which emerges ca. 1250 CE and disappears after ca. 1650 CE. This urban type comprises plaza settlements, each spread out across some 250–400 km², with core areas (approximately 50 km²) including "walled residential centers" (20–50 ha) and a "ceremonial site or hub." Despite inevitable change over time, ethnography shows persistent practices and offers clear directions for coproducing environmental knowledge with indigenous peoples in the Amazon today and helping them better defend their rights.

Lastly, in "'when the King breaks a town he builds another': Politics, Slavery, and Constructed Urban Landscapes in Tropical West Africa," J. Cameron Monroe first presents a broad survey of recent archaeological studies of cities in West Africa. He pinpoints a variety of methodological reasons and limitations that have persistently prevented scholars from fully identifying African urban landscapes and recognizing their autochthonous character. Then, Monroe draws on his own fieldwork at Cana, an urban center of the precolonial Kingdom of Dahomey (1600–1894) in present-day Benin. Embracing multiple scales, his approach integrates various lines of archaeological and ethnohistorical evidence that illuminate how urban landscapes were locally shaped by long-distance forces, marked in large part by the transatlantic slave trade. These forces translated into clusters of earthworks, depressions, and souterrains, for shelter during slave raids, associated with dispersed shade trees (baobabs).

Conclusion

Like those of the Forestry section, the arguments developed in this volume's other essays concur in at least two respects. First, each contribution demonstrates how changing views and, whenever possible, exchanging perspectives are keys to more fully comprehending landscapes of preindustrial urbanism. Second, the methods for achieving this goal can be of many types, entwining different strands of technologies as well as a variety of theoretical frameworks. This shows how pressing it has become to challenge our preconceptions of urban landscapes. The needed shift appears all the more urgent as a postindustrial transition is hoped for in countries building "smart cities" with hybrid, digitally augmented environments; other countries, which have not yet completed their industrialization, equally have to find appropriate ways, grounded in local knowledge systems, to face climate change.

Why is this so important? Simply to escape the illusion that current views of landscape or urbanism could be considered universal, transhistorical, or politically neutral. Not only should these views no longer be exported and applied across the globe to plan the future by imposing techno-environmental frameworks onto geographical contexts that they are foreign to; they also should not be used unmediated to learn from the past and preserve it. Otherwise, this would merely amount to letting environmental injustice build into design and planning practices, just as it does into historical narratives and conceptions of time, archaeological thought, or even natural heritage policies.[94]

Now that modern nation-states are granting legal personhood to parks and rivers, isn't it time that we crossbreed science-based approaches with other techno-environmental frameworks?[95] Adopting more integrative methods, however, implies that we agree to extend historical agency to nonhumans, which, as we have seen, involves other approaches to temporalities, techniques, and materialities. In so doing, we revise late modern understandings of preindustrial urbanism and landscapes that dissociate built environments from natural landscapes. We ultimately open up current conceptions to other realities, relationships, and experiences—the prospect is to bridge remotely sensed imagery and local environmental knowledge within a vast array of past and present worldviews.

Notes

1　Because it more flexibly denotes urban character and urbanization processes (regardless of form and type), the term "urbanism" has been preferred in the volume title, as opposed to "cities," which initially featured in the symposium program. This choice moves away from professional histories of planning, however, as covered in Carola Hein, ed., *The Routledge Handbook of Planning History* (New York: Routledge, 2017).

2　One can only mention here a few recent publications from a host of different fields, which in various ways focus on relationships between landscapes and industrial or postindustrial cities: in political ecology, Erik Swyngedouw, *Promises of the Political: Insurgent Cities in a Post-Political Environment* (Cambridge, Mass.: MIT Press, 2018); in urban geography, Kevin Archer and Kris Bezdecny, eds., *Handbook of Cities and the Environment* (Cheltenham: Edward Elgar Publishing, 2016); in cultural geography, Matthew Gandy, *The Fabric of Space: Water, Modernity, and the Urban Imagination* (Cambridge, Mass.: MIT Press, 2014); and in environmental history, Martin Knoll, Uwe Lübken, and Dieter Schott, eds., *Rivers Lost, Rivers Regained: Rethinking City-River Relations* (Pittsburgh: University of Pittsburgh Press, 2017). Good reflections of current doxa, culture, debates, and theory in urban landscape ecology, planning, and design are offered, respectively, by Richard T. T. Forman, *Urban Ecology: Science of Cities* (New York: Cambridge University Press, 2014); Anita Berrizbeitia, ed., *Urban Landscape*, 4 vols. (Abingdon: Routledge, 2015); Frederick R. Steiner, George F. Thompson, and Armando Carbonell, eds., *Nature and Cities: The Ecological Imperative in Urban Design and Planning* (Cambridge, Mass.: Lincoln Institute of Land Policy, 2016); and Charles Waldheim, *Landscape as Urbanism: A General Theory* (Princeton: Princeton University Press, 2016).

3　On "urban landscapes" from the specific perspectives of archaeology and anthropology, see excellent reviews of research done over the past decades in Miriam Stark, "Early Mainland Southeast Asian Landscapes in the First Millennium BC," *Annual Review of Anthropology* 35 (2006):407–32; Monica L. Smith, "The Archaeology of Urban Landscapes," *Annual Review of Anthropology* 43 (2014):307–23; and Arlen F. Chase and Diane Z. Chase, "Urbanism and Anthropogenic Landscapes," *Annual Review of Anthropology* 45 (2016):361–76. The multifaceted notions of "anthropogenic" landscapes (urban, economic, political, and ritual) presented by these authors are variously expanded on and sometimes fruitfully distanced or even contradicted in the present volume.

4　For an introduction to the most recent (and problematic) of normative frameworks in urban heritage studies, see Francesco Bandarin and Ron van Oers, eds., *Reconnecting the City: The Historic Urban Landscape Approach and the Future of Urban Heritage* (Chichester: John Wiley and Sons, 2015).

5　Norman T. Newton, *Design on the Land: The Development of Landscape Architecture* (Cambridge, Mass.: Belknap Press of Harvard University Press, 1971) is a good reflection of the modern shaping of these notions, which still prevail in the professional field.

6　Peter J. Larkham and Michael P. Conzen, "Agents, Agency, and Urban Form: 'The Making of the Urban Landscape,'" in *Shapers of Urban Form: Explorations in Urban Morphological Agency*, ed. Peter J. Larkham and Michael P. Conzen (New York: Routledge, 2014), 3–24; and Karl Kropf, *The Handbook of Urban Morphology* (Hoboken, N.J.: John Wiley and Sons, 2017).

7　Classic works include Amos Rapoport, *The Meaning of the Built Environment: A Nonverbal Communication Approach* (Tucson: University of Arizona Press, 1990); and Spiro Kostof, *The City Shaped: Urban Patterns and Meanings through History* (London: Thames and Hudson, 1991).

8　Kevin Lynch, *The Image of the City* (Cambridge, Mass.: MIT Press, 1960); and Gordon Cullen, *Townscape* (London: Architectural Press, 1961). A comparative, art-historical genealogy of English "cityscape" (and "townscape"), French "paysage urbain," and Italian "paesaggio urbano" is proposed in Hélène Jannière and Frédéric Pousin, eds., "Paysage urbain: Genèse, représentations, enjeux contemporain," special issue, *Strates: Matériaux pour la recherche en sciences sociales* 13 (2007). On a differing, complementary context, see Celina Kress, "The German Traditions of *Städtebau* and *Stadtlandschaft* and Their Diffusion through Global Exchange," in Hein, *Routledge Handbook of Planning History*, 173–91.

9　John M. Marzluff, Eric Shulenberger, Wilfried Endlicher, Marina Alberti, Gordon Bradley, Clare Ryan, Ute Simon, and Craig ZumBrunnen, eds., *Urban Ecology: An International Perspective on the Interaction between Humans and Nature* (New York: Springer, 2008); and Dieter Schott, Bill Luckin, and Geneviève Massard-Guilbaud, eds., *Resources of the City: Contributions to an Environmental History of Modern Europe* (Aldershot: Ashgate, 2005).

10 Bruno Latour, *We Have Never Been Modern*, trans. Catherine Porter (Cambridge, Mass.: Harvard University Press, 1993).

11 John Brinckerhoff Jackson, *Discovering the Vernacular Landscape* (New Haven: Yale University Press, 1984), 3–8. References listed in note 2 offer current elaborations of such a humanistic approach.

12 See, among other recent works, contributions in Anthony F. Aveni, ed., *The Measure and Meaning of Time in Mesoamerica and the Andes* (Washington, D.C.: Dumbarton Oaks Research Library and Collection, 2015); David A. Freidel, Arlen F. Chase, Anne S. Dowd, and Jerry Murdock, eds., *Maya E Groups: Calendars, Astronomy, and Urbanism in the Early Lowlands* (Gainesville: University Press of Florida, 2017); and Edward Swenson and Andrew Roddick, eds., *Constructions of Time and History in the Pre-Columbian Andes* (Boulder: University Press of Colorado, 2018).

13 Marcus Popplow, "Technology and Technical Knowledge in the Debate about the 'Great Divergence,'" *Artefact* 4 (2016):275–85; and Francesca Bray, "Flows and Matrices, Landscapes and Cultures," *Icon* 22 (2016):8–19. See the historiographical overview in Francesca Bray and Liliane Hilaire-Pérez, "Les techniques et l'histoire globale," in *Histoire des techniques: Mondes, sociétés, cultures: XVIe–XVIIIe siècle*, ed. Guillaume Carnino, Liliane Hilaire-Pérez, and Aleksandra Kobiljski (Paris: Presses universitaires de France, 2016), 7–22.

14 On nonanthropocentric agency, see Carl Knappett and Lambros Malafouris, eds., *Material Agency: Towards a Non-Anthropocentric Approach* (Berlin: Springer, 2008). Timothy R. Pauketat, *An Archaeology of the Cosmos: Rethinking Agency and Religion in Ancient America* (New York: Routledge, 2012), 27–42, provides a review of agency theory with an eye to nonintentional actors. For an approach to artifacts and materials in associative (relational) rather than representational (symbolic) terms, see Benjamin Alberti, Andrew Meirion Jones, and Joshua Pollard, eds., *Archaeology after Interpretation: Returning Materials to Archaeological Theory* (Walnut Creek, Calif.: Left Coast Press, 2013).

15 Tim Ingold, "Toward an Ecology of Materials," *Annual Review of Anthropology* 41 (2012):427–42. See also Tim Ingold, *The Perception of the Environment: Essays on Livelihood, Dwelling, and Skill* (London: Routledge, 2000).

16 Chantal Conneller, *An Archaeology of Materials: Substantial Transformations in Early Prehistoric Europe* (New York: Routledge, 2011), 5, quoted in Ingold, "Toward an Ecology of Materials."

17 Bernadette Bensaude-Vincent and William Newman, eds., *The Artificial and the Natural: An Evolving Polarity* (Cambridge, Mass.: MIT Press, 2007).

18 Earth sciences abound with examples such as the work of Antonio Vallisneri (1661–1730), one of the first Galilean naturalists, who sought to probe the biological, (re)generative properties that were attributed to mineral ores. Francesco Luzzini, *Theory, Practice, and Nature In-Between: Antonio Vallisneri's* Primi Itineris Specimen (Berlin: Max Planck Institute for the History of Science, 2018), accessed June 2019, http://www.edition-open-sources.org/sources/9/index.html. See also Willian R. Newman, "Robert Boyle, Transmutation, and the History of Chemistry before Lavoisier: A Response to Kuhn," and Lawrence M. Principe, "The End of Alchemy? The Repudiation and Persistence of Chrysopoeia at the Académie Royale des Sciences in the Eighteenth Century," in *Chemical Knowledge in the Early Modern World*, ed. Matthew Daniel Eddy, Seymour H. Mauskopf, and William R. Newman (Chicago: University of Chicago Press, 2014), 63–80 and 96–116.

19 Justin Jennings and Edward R. Swenson, eds., *Powerful Places in the Ancient Andes* (Albuquerque: University of New Mexico Press, 2018).

20 Benjamin Alberti, "Archaeologies of Ontology," *Annual Review of Anthropology* 45 (2016):163–79.

21 Examples include: Bernard Lepetit, *The Pre-Industrial Urban System: France, 1740–1840*, trans. Godfrey Rogers (Cambridge: Cambridge University Press, 1994), originally published as *Chemins de terre et voies d'eau: Réseaux de transports et organisation de l'espace en France 1740–1840* (Paris: Éditions de l'École des hautes études en sciences sociales, 1984); Dieter Schott, "Urban Development and Environment," in *The Basic Environmental History*, ed. Mauro Agnoletti and Simone Neri Serneri (Cham, Switzerland: Springer International Publishing, 2014), 171–98; and J. W. Hanson, *An Urban Geography of the Roman World, 100 BC to AD 300* (Oxford: Archaeopress Publishing, 2016), 27–32, 88–93.

22 Johann Heinrich von Thünen, *Der isolierte Staat in Beziehung auf Landwirthschaft und Nationalökonomie* (1826; 3rd ed., Berlin: Wiegandt, 1875), 1:389–400.

23 Walter Christaller, *Central Places in Southern Germany*, trans. Carlisle W. Baskin (Englewood Cliffs, N.J.: Prentice-Hall, 1966), originally published as *Die zentralen Orte in Süddeutschland* (1933). On Christaller's often overlooked role in Nazi territorial and landscape planning, see Gert Gröning and Joachim Wolschke-Bulmahn, *Die Liebe zur Landschaft Teil III: Der Drang nach Osten. Zur Entwicklung von Landespflege im Nationalsozialismus während des Zweiten Weltkrieges in den 'einge- gliederten' Ostgebieten* (Munich: Minerva, 1987); and Mechtild Rössler, "Applied Geography and Area Research in Nazi Society: Central Place Theory and Planning, 1933–1945," *Environment and Planning: Society and Space* 7 (1989):419–31.

24 Max Weber, *The City*, trans. and ed. Don Martindale and Gertrud Neuwirth (1921; Glencoe, Ill.: Free Press, 1958); and Louis Wirth, "Urbanism as a Way of Life," *American Journal of Sociology* 44, no. 1 (1938):1–24.

25 V. Gordon Childe, "The Urban Revolution," *Town Planning Review* 21, no. 1 (1950):3–17. For recent reassessments and discussions of Childe's paradigm, see Michael E. Smith, "V. Gordon Childe and the Urban Revolution: A Historical Perspective on a Revolution in Urban Studies," *Town Planning Review* 80, no. 1 (2009):3–29; and Jason A. Ur, this volume.

26 Childe, "Urban Revolution."

27 Childe, "Urban Revolution."

28 Childe, "Urban Revolution."

29 On technology in Childe's model, see Colin Chant and David Goodman, eds., *Pre-Industrial Cities and Technology* (London: Routledge, 1999), 7–47. On the archaeology of the Fertile Crescent's urban landscapes, see Jennifer R. Pournelle and Guillermo Algaze, "Travels in Edin: Deltaic Resilience and Early Urbanism in Greater Mesopotamia," in *Preludes to Urbanism: The Late Chalcolithic of Mesopotamia*, ed. Augusta McMahon and Harriet Crawford (Cambridge: McDonald Institute for Archaeological Research, 2014), 7–34; Jason A. Ur, "Cycles of Civilization in Northern Mesopota- mia, 4400–2000 BC," *Journal of Archaeological Research* 18 (2010):387–431; T. J. Wilkinson, Graham Philip, J. Bradbury, R. Dunford, D. Donoghue, N. Galiatsatos, D. Lawrence, A. Ricci, and S. L. Smith, "Contextualizing Early Urbanization: Settlement Cores, Early States, and Agro-Pastoral Strategies in the Fertile Crescent during the Fourth and Third Millennia BC," *Journal of World Prehistory* 27 (2014):43–109; and Andrew T. Creekmore and Kevin D. Fisher, eds., *Making Ancient Cities: Space and Place in Early Urban Societies* (New York: Cambridge University Press, 2014). The notion of sur- plus is revisited in a variety of periods worldwide in Christopher T. Morehart and Kristin De Lucia, eds., *Surplus: The Politics of Production and the Strategies of Everyday Life* (Boulder: University of Colorado Press, 2015).

30 Julian H. Steward, *Theory of Culture Change: The Methodology of Multilinear Evolution* (Urbana: University of Illinois Press, 1955), 30–42. For a review of research and scholarship that followed this path from 1998 to 2008, see Stephen A. Kowalewski, "Regional Settlement Pattern Studies," *Journal of Archaeological Research* 16, no. 3 (2008):225–85. Among other fields, historical ecology has long criticized this approach for being premised on too simple a distinction between nature and culture. See Carole L. Crumley, Tommy Lennartsson, and Anna Westin, eds., *Issues and Concepts in Historical Ecology: The Past and Future of Landscapes and Regions* (Cambridge: Cambridge University Press, 2017).

31 Classics in so-called processual archaeology that embraced this approach include William T. Sanders, Jeffrey R. Parsons, and Robert S. Santley, eds., *The Basin of Mexico: Ecological Processes in the Evolution of a Civilization* (New York: Academic Press, 1979); and Joyce Marcus and Jeremy A. Sabloff, eds., *The Ancient City: New Perspectives on Urbanism in the Old and New World* (Santa Fe: School for Advanced Research Press, 2008). More recent developments in evolutionary approaches are reflected in works such as Michael E. Smith, ed., *The Comparative Archaeology of Complex Societies* (New York: Cambridge University Press, 2012); and David L. Lentz, Nicholas P. Dunning, and Vernon L. Scarborough, eds., *Tikal: Paleoecology of an Ancient Maya City* (New York: Cambridge University Press, 2015).

32 For early "neo-Marxist, hermeneutic, critical and post-structuralist" appraisals of processual archae- ology, see Ian Hodder, *Theory and Practice in Archaeology* (London: Routledge, 1992); and Timothy R. Pauketat, "Practice and History in Archaeology: An Emerging Paradigm," *Anthropological Theory* 1, no. 1 (2001):73–98.

33 John N. Miksic, "Heterogenetic Cities in Premodern Southeast Asia," *World Archaeology* 32 (2000):106–20; and Miksic, "Historical Archaeology in Southeast Asia," *Historical Archaeology* 51 (2017):471–86.

34 Miksic, "Heterogenetic Cities in Premodern Southeast Asia." See further theoretical insights in Christopher S. Beekman and William W. Baden, eds., *Nonlinear Models for Archaeology and Anthropology: Continuing the Revolution* (Aldershot: Ashgate, 2005); Stark, "Early Mainland Southeast Asian Landscapes in the First Millennium BC"; Miksic, "Historical Archaeology in Southeast Asia"; and Bisserka Gaydarska, "The City Is Dead! Long Live the City!," *Norwegian Archaeological Review* 49, no. 1 (2016):40–57.

35 On the challenges of defining city and urbanism in Byzantium's old and newly founded cities, see Luca Zavagno, *Cities in Transition: Urbanism in Byzantium between Late Antiquity and the Early Middle Ages (500–900 AD)* (Oxford: Archaeopress, 2009); Efthymios Rizos, ed., *New Cities in Late Antiquity: Documents and Archaeology* (Turnhout: Brepols, 2017); and Philipp Niewöhner, ed., *The Archaeology of Byzantine Anatolia: From the End of Late Antiquity until the Coming of the Turks* (New York: Oxford University Press, 2017). See, in this volume, Jordan Pickett on Roman and Byzantine cities and Hendrik W. Dey on medieval Rome.

36 J. David Schloen, *The House of the Father as Fact and Symbol: Patrimonialism in Ugarit and the Ancient Near East* (Winona Lake, Ind.: Eisenbrauns, 2001); Ur, "Cycles of Civilization in Northern Mesopotamia, 4400–2000 BC"; and Wilkinson et al., "Contextualizing Early Urbanization."

37 Pournelle and Algaze, "Travels in Edin."

38 George L. Cowgill, "Origins and Development of Urbanism: Archaeological Perspectives," *Annual Review of Anthropology* 33 (2004):525–49.

39 Colin Renfrew, "The City through Time and Space: Transformations of Centrality," in Marcus and Sabloff, *Ancient City*, 29–52.

40 Smith, "How Can Archaeologists Identify Early Cities? Definitions, Types, and Attributes," in *Eurasia at the Dawn of History: Urbanization and Social Change*, ed. Manuel Fernández-Götz and Dirk Krausse (New York: Cambridge University Press, 2016), 153–68. Smith organizes "urban attributes" into four categories and a number of subgroups: 1) "settlement size" (population, size, density); 2) "social impact" (economic, administrative, and religious functions) on hinterland; 3) "built environment" (defense, connective infrastructure, public space, planning principles); and 4) "social and economic features" (burials, diversity, neighborhoods, agriculture within settlement).

41 Martin V. Melosi, "Humans, Cities, and Nature: How Do Cities Fit in the Material World?," *Journal of Urban History* 36, no. 1 (2010):3–21, offers a review of "declensionist" approaches to the "nature/built environment nexus," which remains prevalent in his field to date.

42 On the rise of "metabolism" as a concept in natural and social sciences, see Marina Fischer-Kowalski, "Society's Metabolism: The Intellectual History of Materials Flow Analysis: Part I, 1860–1970; Part II, 1970–1998," *Journal of Industrial Ecology* 2, no. 1 (1998):61–78, and no. 4 (1999):107–36. Political critiques of "urban metabolism" as a capitalist framework are proposed in, among others Swyngedouw, *Promises of the Political*; and Archer and Bezdecny, *Handbook of Cities and the Environment*.

43 Essential studies covering technical, methodological, and epistemic aspects include Elizabeth Moore, Anthony Freeman, and Scott Hensley, "Spaceborne and Airborne Radar at Angkor: Introducing New Technology to the Ancient Site," in *Remote Sensing in Archaeology*, ed. James R. Wiseman and Farouk El Baz (New York: Springer, 2007), 185–216; Pournelle and Algaze, "Travels in Edin"; and Emily Hammer and Jason A. Ur, "Near Eastern Landscapes and Declassified U2 Aerial Imagery," *Advances in Archaeological Practice* (2019):1–20, doi:10.1017/aap.2018.38.

44 Douglas C. Comer, "Petra and the Paradox of a Great City Built by Nomads: An Explanation Suggested by Satellite Imagery," in *Mapping Archaeological Landscapes from Space*, ed. Douglas C. Comer and Michael J. Harrower (New York: Springer, 2013), 73–84; and Damian Evans, Christophe Pottier, Roland Fletcher, Scott Hensley, Ian Tapley, Anthony Milne, and Michael Barbetti, "A Comprehensive Archaeological Map of the World's Largest Preindustrial Settlement Complex at Angkor, Cambodia," *Proceedings of the National Academy of Sciences of the United States of America* 104, no. 36 (2007):14277–82.

45 Arlen F. Chase, Diane Z. Chase, and John F. Weishampel, "The Use of LiDAR at the Maya Site of Caracol, Belize," in *Mapping Archaeological Landscapes from Space*, ed. Douglas C. Comer and

Michael J. Harrower (New York: Springer, 2013), 187–98; and Damian Evans, "Airborne Laser Scanning as a Method for Exploring Long-Term Socio-Ecological Dynamics in Cambodia," *Journal of Archaeological Science* 74 (2016):164–75.

46 Christoph Siart, Markus Forbriger, and Olaf Bubenzer, eds., *Digital Geoarchaeology: New Techniques for Interdisciplinary Human-Environmental Research* (New York: Springer, 2018).

47 John Chapman and Bisserka Gaydarska, "Low-Density Urbanism: The Case of the Trypillia Group of Ukraine," in *Eurasia at the Dawn of History: Urbanization and Social Change*, ed. Manuel Fernández-Götz and Dirk Krausse (New York: Cambridge University Press, 2016), 81–105; and Johannes Müller, Knut Rassmann, and Mykhailo Videiko, eds., *Trypillia Mega-Sites and European Prehistory: 4100–3400 BCE* (Milton Park: Routledge, 2016).

48 Manuel Fernández-Götz, "Urbanization in Iron Age Europe: Trajectories, Patterns, and Social Dynamics," *Journal of Archaeological Research* 26, no. 2 (2018):117–62.

49 Innocent Pikirayi, "Great Zimbabwe as Power-Scape: How the Past Locates Itself in Contemporary Southern Africa," in *Cultural Landscape Heritage in Sub-Saharan Africa*, ed. John Beardsley (Washington, D.C.: Dumbarton Oaks Research Library and Collection, 2016), 89–107.

50 Akinwumi Ogundiran, "Towns and States in the West African Forest Belt," in *The Oxford Handbook of African Archaeology*, ed. Peter Mitchell and Paul Lane (Oxford: Oxford University Press, 2013), 861–73.

51 See Roland Fletcher, "Low-Density, Agrarian-Based Urbanism: Scale, Power, and Ecology," in *The Comparative Archaeology of Complex Societies*, ed. Michael E. Smith (New York: Cambridge University Press, 2012), 285–320.

52 Damian Evans and Roland Fletcher, "The Landscape of Angkor Wat Redefined," *Antiquity* 89, no. 348 (2015):1402–19.

53 Bernard-Philippe Groslier, "The Angkorian Hydraulic City: Exploitation or Over-Exploitation of the Soil?," first published in *Bulletin de l'École française d'Extrême-Orient* 66 (1979):161–202, trans. and presented by Terry Lustig and Christophe Pottier, *Aséanie* 20 (2007):133–40, 141–85.

54 On mapping and the modern historiography of Angkor, see Christophe Pottier, "Angkor et ses cartes," in *Anamorphoses: Hommage à Jacques Dumarçay*, ed. Henri Chambert-Loir and Bruno Dagens (Paris: Indes savantes, 2006), 427–42; Evans et al., "Comprehensive Archaeological Map of the World's Largest Preindustrial Settlement Complex at Angkor"; and Evans, "Airborne Laser Scanning as a Method for Exploring Long-Term Socio-Ecological Dynamics in Cambodia."

55 Evans et al., "Comprehensive Archaeological Map of the World's Largest Preindustrial Settlement Complex at Angkor."

56 Scott Hawken, "Design of Kings and Farmers: Landscape Systems of the Greater Angkor Urban Complex," *Asian Perspectives* 52, no. 2 (2013):347–67; and Miriam T. Stark, Damian Evans, Chhay Rachna, Heng Piphal, and Alison Carter, "Residential Patterning at Angkor Wat," *Antiquity* 89, no. 348 (2015):1439–55.

57 Christian Isendahl, "Agro-Urban Landscapes: The Example of Maya Lowland Cities," *Antiquity* 86, no. 334 (2012):1112–25.

58 Diane Z. Chase and Arlen F. Chase, "Caracol, Belize, and Changing Perceptions of Ancient Maya Society," *Journal of Archaeological Research* 25, no. 3 (2017):185–249; Lentz, Dunning, and Scarborough, *Tikal*; and Barbara L. Stark and Alanna Ossa, "Ancient Settlement, Urban Gardening, and Environment in the Gulf Lowlands of Mexico," *Latin American Antiquity* 18 (2007):385–406.

59 Harvey Weiss, "Megadrought, Collapse and Causality," in *Megadrought and Collapse: From Early Agriculture to Angkor*, ed. Harvey Weiss (New York: Oxford University Press, 2017), 1–31.

60 Nicholas P. Dunning, Carmen McCane, Tyler Swinney, Matthew Purtill, Jani Sparks, Ashley Mann, Jon-Paul McCool, and Chantal Ivenso, "Geoarchaeological Investigations in Mesoamerica Move into the 21st Century: A Review," *Geoarchaeology* 30, no. 3 (2015):167–99.

61 Weiss, "Megadrought, Collapse and Causality"; and Brendan M. Buckley, Roland Fletcher, Shi-Yu Simon Wang, Brian Zottoli, and Christophe Pottier, "Monsoon Extremes and Society over the Past Millennium on Mainland Southeast Asia," *Quaternary Science Reviews* 95 (2014):1–19.

62 Chase and Chase, "Caracol, Belize, and Changing Perceptions of Ancient Maya Society"; Fletcher, "Low-Density, Agrarian-Based Urbanism"; Dunning et al., "Geoarchaeological Investigations in Mesoamerica Move into the 21st Century"; and Isendahl, "Agro-Urban Landscapes."

63 Larry V. Benson, Timothy R. Pauketat, and Edward R. Cook, "Cahokia's Boom and Bust in the Context of Climate Change," *American Antiquity* 74, no. 3 (2009):467–83; Lisa J. Lucero, Roland Fletcher, and Robin Coningham, "From 'Collapse' to Urban Diaspora: The Transformation of Low-Density, Dispersed Agrarian Urbanism," *Antiquity* 89, no. 347 (2015):1139–54; Buckley et al., "Monsoon Extremes and Society over the Past Millennium on Mainland Southeast Asia"; and Weiss, "Megadrought, Collapse and Causality."

64 See Joel D. Gunn, Vernon L. Scarborough, William J. Folan, Christian Isendahl, Arlen F. Chase, Jeremy A. Sabloff, and Beniamino Volta, "A Distribution Analysis of the Central Maya Lowlands Ecoinformation Network: Its Rises, Falls, and Changes," *Ecology and Society* 22, no. 1 (2017):20, https://doi.org/10.5751/ES-08931-220120, published by the Maya working group in the Integrated History and Future of People on Earth (IHOPE) project. See also Weiss, "Megadrought, Collapse and Causality."

65 Christian Isendahl and Daryl Stump, eds., *The Oxford Handbook of Historical Ecology and Applied Archaeology* (Oxford: Oxford University Press, 2019).

66 Wendy Matthews, "Tells," in *Encyclopedia of Geoarchaeology*, ed. Allan S. Gilbert (Dordrecht: Springer Netherlands, 2017), 951–72. See also Jason A. Ur, this volume.

67 William Balée, *Cultural Forests of the Amazon: The Historical Ecology of People and Their Landscapes* (Tuscaloosa: University of Alabama Press, 2013); Clark L. Erickson, "The Transformation of Environment into Landscape: The Historical Ecology of Monumental Earthwork Construction in the Bolivian Amazon," *Diversity* 2, no. 4 (2010):618–52; and Stéphen Rostain, *Islands in the Rainforest: Landscape Management in Pre-Columbian Amazonia*, trans. Michelle Eliott (Walnut Creek, Calif.: Left Coast Press, 2013).

68 See Michael Heckenberger, this volume, as well as Jennifer Watling, José Iriarte, Francis E. Mayle, Denise Schaan, Luiz C. R. Pessenda, Neil J. Loader, F. Alayne Street-Perrott, Ruth E. Dickau, Antonia Damasceno, and Alceu Ranzi, "Impact of Pre-Columbian 'Geoglyph' Builders on Amazonian Forests," *Proceedings of the National Academy of Sciences of the United States of America* 114, no. 8 (2017):1868–73.

69 A helpful review of recent conceptual developments in ecological anthropology—now commonly adopted in landscape archaeology—is offered by Kaj Århem, "Southeast Asian Animism in Context," in *Animism in Southeast Asia*, ed. Kaj Århem and Guido Sprenger (London: Routledge, 2016), 3–30. The author comments on two different trends following the revival of the notion of animism by A. Irving Hallowell, "Ojibwa Ontology, Behavior, and World View," in *Culture in History: Essays in Honor of Paul Radin*, ed. Stanley Diamond (New York: Columbia University Press, 1960), 19–52. On the one hand, one finds Nurit Bird-David's "relational epistemology" ("'Animism' Revisited: Personhood, Environment, and Relational Epistemology," supplement, *Current Anthropology* 40 [1999]:67–91) and Tim Ingold's phenomenological approach to the environment (*Perception of the Environment*). On the other, one finds Philippe Descola's four-type structural ontology (animism, naturalism, totemism, analogism) based on four logically possible combinations of "interiority" and "physicality" (*Beyond Nature and Culture*, trans. Janet Lloyd [Chicago: University of Chicago Press, 2013]), and Eduardo Viveiros de Castro's Amerindian "perspectivism" and "multinaturalism" (implying universal culture and subject) versus Western multiculturalism (with universal nature and object) (*From the Enemy's Point of View: Humanity and Divinity in an Amazonian Society*, trans. Catherine V. Howard [Chicago: University of Chicago Press, 1992]).

70 Schloen, *House of the Father as Fact and Symbol*; see also Ur, this volume.

71 See contributions in Tamara L. Bray, ed., *The Archaeology of Wak'as: Explorations of the Sacred in the Pre-Columbian Andes* (Boulder: University Press of Colorado, 2015).

72 Alan L. Kolata, "Of Kings and Capitals: Principles of Authority and the Nature of Cities in the Native Andean State," in *The Archaeology of City-States: Cross-Cultural Approaches*, ed. Deborah L. Nichols and Thomas H. Charlton (Washington, D.C.: Smithsonian Institution Press, 1997), 245–54. See also Tom D. Dillehay, *The Teleoscopic Polity: Andean Patriarchy and Materiality* (Cham, Switzerland: Springer International Publishing, 2014); and on the integration of space and time in the urban landscape of the Cuzco Valley, see Colin McEwan, "Cognising and Marking the Andean Landscape: Radial, Concentric, and Hierarchical Perspectives," in *Inca Sacred Space: Landscape, Site, and Symbol in the Andes*, ed. Frank Meddens, Katie Willis, Colin McEwan, and Nicholas Branch (London:

Archetype Publications, 2014), 29–47; and Steve Kosiba, "Tracing the Inca Past: Ritual Movement and Social Memory in the Inca Imperial Capital," in *Perspectives on the Inca*, ed. Monica Barnes, Inés de Castro, Javier Flores Espinoza, Doris Kurella, and Karoline Noack (Stuttgart: Linden-Museum, 2015), 178–205.

73 See, among other complementary studies, Pedro Carrasco, *The Tenochca Empire of Ancient Mexico: The Triple Alliance of Tenochtitlan, Tetzcoco, and Tlacopan* (Norman: University of Oklahoma Press, 1999); Kenneth G. Hirth, "Incidental Urbanism: The Structure of the Pre-Hispanic City in Central Mexico," in Marcus and Sabloff, *Ancient City*, 273–97; and Benjamin D. Johnson, *Pueblos within Pueblos: Tlaxilacalli Communities in Acolhuacan, Mexico, ca. 1272–1692* (Boulder: University Press of Colorado, 2017). One can usefully contrast these with Sanders, Parsons, and Santley, *Basin of Mexico*, which did not reckon with the notion of *altepetl*.

74 David Carrasco, *City of Sacrifice: The Aztec Empire and the Role of Violence in Civilization* (Boston: Beacon Press, 1999); Alfredo López-Austin and Leonardo López Luján, *Monte Sagrado: Templo Mayor* (Mexico City: Instituto Nacional de Antropología e Historia, Universidad Nacional Autónoma de México, 2009); and William L. Fash and Leonardo López Luján, eds., *The Art of Urbanism: How Mesoamerican Kingdoms Represented Themselves in Architecture and Imagery* (Washington, D.C.: Dumbarton Oaks Research Library and Collection, 2009).

75 León García Garagarza, "The Aztec Ritual Landscape," in *The Oxford Handbook of the Aztecs*, ed. Deborah L. Nichols and Enrique Rodríguez-Alegría (New York: Oxford University Press, 2017), 595–604.

76 George L. Cowgill, *Ancient Teotihuacan: Early Urbanism in Central Mexico* (New York: Cambridge University Press, 2015); Susan Toby Evans, "Location and Orientation of Teotihuacan, Mexico: Water Worship and Processional Space," in "Processions in the Ancient Americas," *Occasional Papers in Anthropology at Penn State* 33 (2016):52–121; Deborah L. Nichols, "Teotihuacan," *Journal of Archaeological Research* 24, no. 1 (2016):1–74; and Matthew H. Robb, ed., *Teotihuacan: City of Water, City of Fire* (San Francisco: Fine Arts Museums of San Francisco, 2017).

77 Pedro Carrasco, *Tenochca Empire of Ancient Mexico*; and David Carrasco, Lindsay Jones, and Scott Sessions, eds., *Mesoamerica's Classic Heritage: From Teotihuacan to the Aztecs* (Niwot: University Press of Colorado, 2000).

78 Angel Palerm, *Obras hidráulicas prehispánicas en el sistema lacustre del valle de México* (Mexico City: Instituto Nacional de Antropología e Historia, Seminario de Etnohistoria del Valle de México, 1973); Margarita Carballal Staedtler and Maria Flores Hernandez, "Hydraulic Features of the Mexico-Texcoco Lakes during the Postclassic Period," in *Precolumbian Water Management: Ideology, Ritual, and Power*, ed. Lisa J. Lucero and Barbara W. Fash (Tucson: University of Arizona Press, 2006), 155–70; and Raúl García Chávez and Natalia Moragas Segura, "Historia y arqueología de la formación del 'altepetl' en la Cuenca de México durante el Posclásico Medio," *Revista española de antropología americana* 47 (2018):219–38.

79 "Chinampas are narrow, rectangular beds or platforms, which are constructed by alternating layers of lake mud and thick mats of decaying vegetation (*cespedes*) over shallow lake bottoms, or in marshy zones." Edward E. Calnek, "Settlement Pattern and Chinampa Agriculture at Tenochtitlan," *American Antiquity* 36 (1972):104–15.

80 Edward E. Calnek, "Tenochtitlan-Tlatelolco: The Natural History of a City," in *El Urbanismo in Mesoamérica/Urbanism in Mesoamerica*, ed. William T. Sanders, Alba Guadalupe Mastache, and Robert H. Cobean (Mexico City: Instituto Nacional de Antropología e Historia; and University Park: Penn State University, 2003), 1:149–202; J. Parsons, "Political Implications of Prehispanic Chinampa Agriculture in the Valley of Mexico," in *Land and Politics in the Valley of Mexico*, ed. H. R. Harvey (Albuquerque: University of Mexico Press, 1991), 17–42; Johnson, *Pueblos within Pueblos*; and Christopher T. Morehart, "The Political Ecology of Chinampa Landscapes in the Basin of Mexico," in *Water and Power in Ancient Societies*, ed. Emily Holt (New York: SUNY Press, 2018), 19–39.

81 On these territorial institutions' role in shaping the landscape, see Georges Farhat, "Manorial Economy and French Seventeenth-Century Designed Landscapes: The Formal Type by Savot (1624) and at Sceaux (1670–1690)," *Landscape Research* 40, no. 5 (2015):566–85.

82 Jean Jacquart, "Paris: First Metropolis of the Early Modern Period," in *Capital Cities and Their Hinterlands in Early Modern Europe*, ed. Peter Clark and Bernard Lepetit (Aldershot: Ashgate, 1996), 105–18; Georges Farhat, "L'urbanité au miroir de la promenade dans les parcs environnant Paris vers 1630–1670," in *Histoires de Paris (XVIe-XVIIIe siècle)*, ed. Thierry Belleguic and Laurent Turcot (Paris: Hermann, 2013), 2:49–71; Florent Quellier, "Paris is a Land of Plenty: Kitchen Gardens as Urban Phenomenon in a Modern-Era European City (Sixteenth through Eighteenth Centuries)," in *Food and the City: Histories of Culture and Cultivation*, ed. Dorothée Imbert (Washington, D.C.: Dumbarton Oaks Research Library and Collection, 2015), 273–300.

83 Anne Conchon, Hélène Noizet, and Michel Ollion, eds, *Les limites de Paris: XIIe–XVIIIe siècles* (Villeneuve d'Ascq: Presses universitaires du Septentrion, 2017).

84 Robert Muchembled, Hervé Bennezon, and Marie-José Michel, *Histoire du Grand Paris: De la Renaissance à la Révolution* (Paris: Perrin, 2009).

85 Truschet and Hoyau's map is usefully completed by François de Belleforest's description of the city and *prévôté et vicomté de Paris* in his *Cosmographie universelle de tout le monde* (Paris: Nicolas Chesneau, 1575), 175–301. On the latter, see Étienne Bourdon, "Découvrir la 'grande, excellente, et ancienne cité de Paris' dans la *Cosmographie universelle* de François de Belleforest (1575)," in *Histoire de Paris, XVIe-XVIIIe siècle*, ed. Thierry Belleguic and Laurent Turcot (Paris: Hermann, 2013), 1:407–17.

86 Focused on Paris's central market area, Françoise Boudon, André Chastel, Hélène Couzy, and Françoise Hamon, *Système de l'architecture urbaine: Le quartier des Halles à Paris*, with drawings by Jean Blécon (Paris: Éditions du Centre national de la recherche scientifique, 1977), laid the grounds for typomorphological studies of preindustrial Paris. This morphogenetic approach to urban landscapes has been recently extended to the entire city using GIS: Hélène Noizet, Boris Bove, and Laurent Costa, eds., *Paris, de parcelles en pixels: Analyse géomatique de l'espace parisien médiéval et moderne* (Saint-Denis: Presses universitaires de Vincennes and Comité d'histoire de la ville de Paris, 2013), and related, in-progress database, "ALPAGE: AnaLyse diachronique de l'espace urbain PArisien: Approche GEomatique," accessed April 2019, https://alpage.huma-num.fr. On urban transformation projects between 1580 and 1620, see the still unparalleled Hilary Ballon, *The Paris of Henri IV: Architecture and Urbanism* (Cambridge, Mass.: MIT Press, 1991).

87 Archaeological excavations conducted during the 1980s Grand Louvre works have revealed, more than 10 m deep, the long-term (presettlement to nineteenth-century) terrain and soil transformation of the city's northwestern sector between the Louvre Castle and the faubourg Saint-Honoré clay field tileries (future site of the 1564 Tuileries Palace and Garden); see Paul Van Ossel, ed., *Les jardins du Carrousel (Paris): De la campagne à la ville; La formation d'un espace urbain* (Paris: Éditions de la Maison des sciences de l'homme, 1998). On quarries, see Ania Guini-Skliar, "Les carrières parisiennes aux frontières de la ville et de la campagne," *Histoire urbaine* 8, no. 2 (2003):41–56.

88 Daniel Roche, *La culture équestre occidentale, XVIe–XIXe siècle: L'ombre du cheval*, 3 vols. (Paris: Fayard, 2008–2015).

89 Veronika Novák, "Le corps du condamné et le tissu urbain: Exécution, pouvoir et usages de l'espace à Paris aux XVe-XVIe siècles," *Histoire urbaine* 47 (2016):149–66.

90 A still provocative work, André Guillerme, *The Age of Water: The Urban Environment in the North of France, AD 300–1800* (College Station: Texas A&M University Press, 1988), originally published as *Les temps de l'eau: La cité, l'eau et les techniques; nord de la France fin IIIe–début XIXe siècle* (Seyssel: Champ Vallon, 1983), offers, from the perspective of historical anthropology, useful mappings of various hydraulic "techniques" in as many mentality-related periods of preindustrial urbanism.

91 Bernard Palissy, *Discours admirables de la nature des eaux et fontaines, tant naturelles qu'artificielles, des métaux, des sels et salines, des pierres, des terres, du feu et des émaux . . .* (Paris: Martin le Jeune, 1580); Didier Kahn, *Alchimie et paracelsisme en France à la fin de la Renaissance (1567–1625)* (Geneva: Droz, 2007); and Lawrence M. Principe, "Goldsmiths and Chymists: The Activity of Artisans within Alchemical Circles," in *Laboratories of Art: Alchemy and Art Technology from Antiquity to the 18th Century*, ed. Sven Dupré (Cham: Springer, 2014), 157–79.

92 On engineering, see Hélène Vérin, *La gloire des ingénieurs: L'intelligence technique du XVIe au XVIIIe siècle* (Paris: Albin Michel, 1993); for a recent discussion of the many varieties in sixteenth-century Aristotelianism, see Mario Sgarbi, "What Does a Renaissance Aristotelian Look Like? From

Petrarch to Galilei," *The Journal of the International Society for the History of the Philosophy of Science* 7, no. 2 (2017):226–45; on Neoplatonic philosophy and its consideration of regular polyhedrons as a means to ascend from sensitive figures to intelligible numbers, see P. M. Sanders, "Charles de Bovelles's Treatise on the Regular Polyhedra (Paris 1511)," *Annals of Science* 41 (1984):513–66; and Anne-Hélène Klinger-Dollé, *Le* De sensu *de Charles de Bovelles (1511): Conception philosophique des sens et figuration de la pensée; suivi du texte latin du* De sensu, *traduit et annoté* (Geneva: Droz, 2016).

93 Steward, *Theory of Culture Change*, 31.

94 Dipesh Chakrabarty, "Anthropocene Time," *History and Theory* 57, no. 1 (2018):5–32; Alejandro Haber, "Decolonizing Archaeological Thought in South America," *Annual Review of Anthropology* 45 (2016):469–85; and Deborah McGregor, "Mino-Mnaamodzawin: Achieving Indigenous Environmental Justice in Canada," *Environment and Society* 9, no. 1 (January 2018):7–24.

95 Jacinta Ruru, "Listening to Papatuanuku: A Call to Reform Water Law," *Journal of the Royal Society of New Zealand* 48, no. 2–3 (2018):215–24.

PART I

Earthworks

2

Space and Structure in Early Mesopotamian Cities

JASON A. UR

T HE STUDY OF PREINDUSTRIAL CITIES IS IN A PHASE OF GREAT
dynamism.[1] For a long time, early cities were viewed narrowly through the lenses
of Classical and ancient Near Eastern urbanism. In archaeology, this situation emerged
largely as a result of the great influence of V. Gordon Childe. His books and articles
established a broad model of what an early city was supposed to look like; his seminal
article on "The Urban Revolution" is the most heavily cited article in the history of the
Town Planning Review.[2] His vision of cities emphasized the "revolutionary" appearance
of relatively (for their time) large and dense settlements that housed a ruling class (and
its monuments) that extracted the production of the rural hinterland. These new urban
places were further characterized by writing systems, art and science, long-distance
trade, and the abandonment of kinship as a source of social cohesion.

At this point, the critiques of Childe have largely been accepted. First and foremost,
his characterization in "The Urban Revolution" is one of an early centralized polity—
that is, a political form rather than a settlement form. More importantly, recent scholarship has convincingly demonstrated the remarkable diversity of early urban form, and
it has argued, also convincingly, for a definition of "urbanism" that can accommodate
such diversity.[3] Indeed, for many current scholars, Childe's "classic" formulation of the
early city only really applies to the ancient Near East and the Mesopotamian examples
that inspired him.

In fact, Childe's model does not even apply to Mesopotamian urbanism, at least
not in its early stages. The diversity of urban form now recognized globally can also be
found in the earliest cities of the Tigris and Euphrates region. "The Urban Revolution"
model is not, however, useless, as it describes mature Mesopotamian cities of the third

millennium BCE, and many subsequent urban places, quite well. But these cities came about with at least a millennium of previous urban development already behind them. They represent the end of a developmental process, not the start.

This study will illustrate three early Mesopotamian urban structures. They appeared sequentially, but not necessarily in an evolutionary sequence, from the late fifth to the middle of the third millennium BCE. The first, which appears to be unique in Mesopotamian history, seems to be a Near Eastern manifestation of a "megasite," very large and low-density anomalies in the archaeological record, which in many parts of the world appeared prior to the appearance of less ambiguous urban forms. The second is a candidate for a Mesopotamian "low-density" city, a structure increasingly recognized globally but not yet in the Near East. Finally, at the time of the great Mesopotamian city-states, this study will argue that even the most geometric of settlement forms can be explained through the concept of emergence, as opposed to top-down planning.

In all of these cases, large settlements in early Mesopotamia were largely self-organized. Childe's model may have emphasized new forms of centralized government in early cities, but a critical look at the archaeological data set of sites and landscapes suggests that bottom-up processes were dominant. It would be incorrect to call them "unplanned," since all urban phenomena are planned at some scale; rather, the issue is the locus of decision-making about planning. Traditional scholarship on Mesopotamian cities assigns most agency to kings and other elites, who often claim such influence in propagandistic royal inscriptions. In the case studies presented here, emphasis has been placed on households and neighborhoods, and the ways in which decision-making at those lower levels might result in the emergent forms of the earliest Mesopotamian cities.

Geography and Chronology

The three case studies must be situated in Mesopotamian time and environmental space. The Mesopotamian landscape is dominated by two rivers, the Tigris to the east and the Euphrates to the west, which originate in Turkey, flow through northeastern Syria, and then drain through the Republic of Iraq to flow into the Persian Gulf (Figure 2.1). In the north, the landscape is variable. In the valleys, the rivers cut into floodplains, resulting in narrow bands of irrigable alluvium. Between the rivers is the arc of the Fertile Crescent, composed of broad plains where agriculture can be sustained by rainfall, although not without variability, and therefore some risk (Figure 2.2). It is in this "zone of uncertainty" that cities originated and developed.[4]

To the south, the rivers enter the southern Mesopotamian plain near Baghdad. From there to the gulf, the plain is unrelentingly flat (Figure 2.3). This lack of slope slows the rivers' flow, causing them to drop their sediment loads. As a result, the Tigris and Euphrates flow a few meters above the level of the surrounding plain, on levees a few kilometers wide. In both north and south, the environment encouraged cereal agriculture as well as sheep and goat husbandry, and it provided clay and water for mud brick architecture. The high aridity of the southern plains prevents rain-fed cultivation.

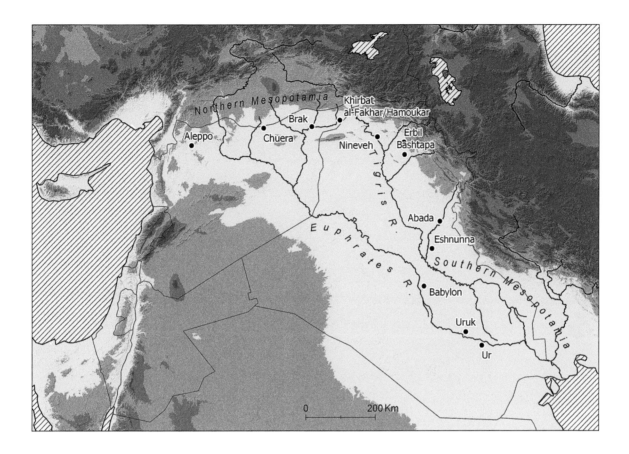

FIGURE 2.1

Mesopotamia, with sites and regions mentioned in the text. Map by Jason A. Ur.

However, the river levees enabled crop irrigation and the low surface gradient encouraged low-friction water transport. As a result, mature cities in the south grew to many times the size of their northern contemporaries.[5] In both north and south, the environmental conditions promoted the use of mud brick in most architectural forms, fired brick in some contexts, and stone in some foundations and elite constructions. Mesopotamia was the land of "cities of clay."[6]

It was in this environmental context that Mesopotamian societies emerged and evolved. The archaeological cultures of Mesopotamian prehistory consisted of small agricultural villages in the Neolithic, which by the fifth millennium BCE had spread onto the southern plains (Figure 2.4).[7] At this time, sites were characterized by a painted pottery designated as "Ubaid." At the end of this period, an anomalously large settlement emerged at Khirbat al-Fakhar, in northern Mesopotamia, the first case study.

The fourth millennium BCE was highly consequential for the evolution of Mesopotamian cities. At the start of the millennium, Mesopotamia was divided into regional cultures that still lived in small, frequently fissioning villages. By its end, the city of Uruk in southern Mesopotamia had developed large institutions, with monumental architecture, mass production of craft goods, and administrative technologies that included sealing and pictographic writing—in other words, the "classic" Childean early city. In traditional urban histories and textbooks, Uruk is often described as "the

FIGURE 2.2

The rain-fed plains of
northern Mesopotamia
in late winter. Bashtapa,
Erbil Governorate,
Kurdistan region of
Iraq, drone photograph
taken February 23,
2017. Photograph by
Khalil Barzinji.

FIGURE 2.3

An urban site on the
plains of the south:
the city of Ur. Drone
photograph courtesy of
Emily Hammer.

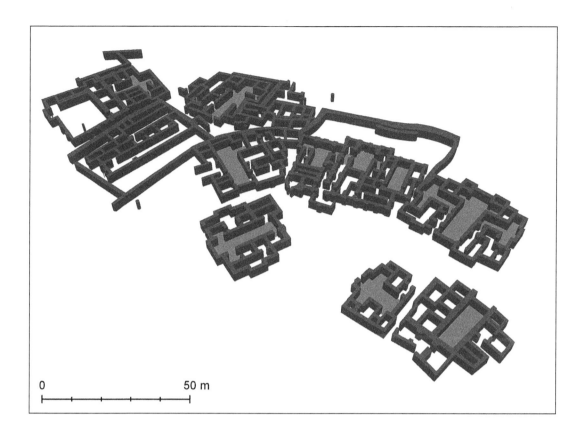

0   50 m

FIGURE 2.4

A small agricultural
village of the preurban
Ubaid period at Tell
Abada, Iraq. Based on
S. A. Jasim, "Structure
and Function in an
'Ubaid Village," in *Upon
This Foundation: The
'Ubaid Reconsidered*, ed.
Elizabeth F. Henrickson
and Ingolf Thuesen
(Copenhagen: Carsten
Niebuhr Institute, 1989),
79–90, fig. 2.

first city," emerging by 3100 BCE.[8] Recent archaeological research has demonstrated, however, that half a millennium earlier, Tell Brak, in northern Mesopotamia, had grown to urban stature, in very different forms and by a very different trajectory.

The start of the third millennium BCE saw a further regionalization. Northern settlements remained predominantly small villages. The south, on the other hand, entered a phase of hyperurbanization, in which nearly all settlements had grown larger than 40 ha. By the middle of the third millennium BCE, both north and south were characterized by the small and competing polities that were described in the Sumerian King List and that archaeologists have labeled as city-states.[9] By this point, Mesopotamian urbanism appears to have attained a mature state that most historians and archaeologists assume to have become "essential," and to have survived, more or less unchanged, in kind if not degree, through Sennacherib's Nineveh or Nebuchadnezzar's Babylon (Figure 2.5), until the coming of Alexander and new Greek-inspired urban forms.

These arguments hinge on the definition of "urbanism." In archaeology, Childe's trait list approach has been abandoned, increasingly for definitions that stress what cities do rather than what they looked like.[10] This new intellectual trend has expanded the ranks of urban places, most notably by accommodating low-density or periodically depopulated centers in the New World. The method adopted here follows a multivariate approach—in which any given settlement can be placed along many "axes of variation"—that was championed by archaeologist George L. Cowgill.[11] These axes might

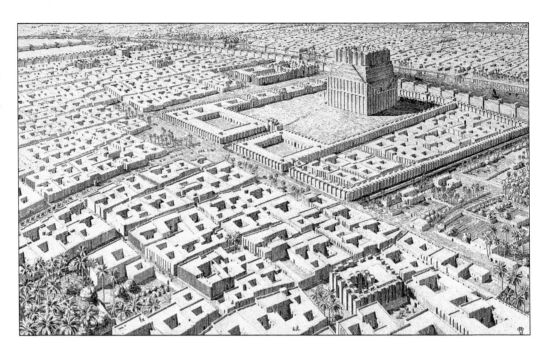

FIGURE 2.5

Reconstruction of the city of Babylon at the time of Nebuchadnezzar, typical of the "essential" form of Mesopotamian urbanism assumed for other times and places. Reproduced from Oscar Reuther, *Die Innenstadt Von Babylon (Merkes)*, Ausgrabungen Der Deutschen Orient-Gesellschaft in Babylon 3 (Leipzig: J. C. Hinrichs, 1926), tafel 1.

FIGURE 2.6

An example of historical remote sensing of archaeological sites and landscapes: a U2 aerial photograph of Tell Brak, Syria, showing its central mound, lower outer settlement, and linear trackways. U2 mission B1554 frame 200R, taken January 29, 1960. Photograph courtesy of the U.S. National Archives and Records Administration (NARA).

include obvious characteristics like size and density, but also more challenging ones, such as degrees of political centralization, religious authority, craft specialization, or wealth inequality. In the interests of critical discussion, the term will be used loosely, but mostly with reference to spatially large phenomena that have centripetal properties when their neighbors do not.

The proper study of early cities requires methodological innovation.[12] For a consideration of urban structure, excavation data are often too limited spatially and nearly always nonrepresentative of the whole. Other methods have emerged that are better suited to the large scale of investigations. The research presented here has, therefore, emphasized two extensive methods. First, remote-sensing sources can provide bird's-eye views of spatial phenomena that would be unrecognizable from the ground. Recent research has relied heavily on aerial photography and satellite imagery, especially declassified historical intelligence sources such as U2, CORONA, and HEXAGON; LiDAR data; and ground-based geophysical survey (Figure 2.6).[13] Remotely sensed imagery can identify features, but it cannot date them; it must be followed up with well-designed surface observations. Therefore, the second method is systematic archaeological surface survey. Fortunately, Mesopotamian cities erode in a manner that makes surface survey of artifacts especially fruitful. In an ideal scenario, remote-sensing analysis and survey would be followed by targeted excavation.

Proto-Urbanism at the "Megasite" of Khirbat al-Fakhar

At the end of the fifth millennium BCE, the plains of northern and southern Mesopotamia were settled by small agricultural villages. However, at least one truly anomalous settlement had developed in the north. Khirbat al-Fakhar was identified in far northeastern Syria, near the border with Iraq, in 1999. It was surveyed systematically in 2000 and subject to brief excavation in 2005.[14] It presents a challenge to several basic assumptions about urban origins: that the trajectory was outward from small village to large city; that this process was driven by improvements in subsistence agriculture; and that it occurred in a steady linear fashion. Khirbat al-Fakhar appears to contradict all of these assumptions.

At the very end of the Ubaid period, most settlements were small villages of up to two hundred persons. They grew vertically over generations. Mud brick architecture requires constant maintenance and occasional replacement, which is usually accomplished by leveling an old structure and building a new one atop its remains. As a result, the settlement grows upward through time (Figure 2.7). Vertical growth was not, however, accompanied by horizontal growth. In other words, communities remained in place, but must have been periodically riven by conflict, which resulted in settlement fission. As a result, most fifth-millennium BCE sites rarely exceed a few hectares. The plains of northern Mesopotamia are dotted with thousands of such small prehistoric mounds.

Khirbat al-Fakhar, on the other hand, took a radically different form. The site has a central core of low mounds, extending over 22 ha. Beyond this core, artifact scatters

FIGURE 2.7

A prehistoric
mounded site: Tell
Surezha, Kurdistan
region of Iraq. Drone
photograph taken
September 10, 2017.
Photograph by
Jason A. Ur.

continue outward across the fields. The total area of the scatter, including the central core, is at least 300 ha, a hundred times larger than most of the previous and contemporary sites in Mesopotamia. It is standard practice in Near Eastern archaeology to apply a ratio of one hundred to two hundred persons per hectare,[15] in which case Khirbat al-Fakhar would have been a city of 30,000–60,000 persons in 4000 BCE.

It is certainly inappropriate to assume such density, however. There are no clues about density from excavation yet, but remote sensing can offer insight. In a 1959 U2 aerial photograph, the low areas of scatter are characterized by a discontinuous light discoloration, compared to the surrounding fields (Figure 2.8). Lighter soils result from the decay of mud brick architecture, and the pattern at Khirbat al-Fakhar suggests clusters of households with unoccupied voids between them. The overall site extent was great, but density appears to have been lower than is assumed from later models.

The surface assemblage may suggest one reason for this precociousness. It includes potsherds as well as obsidian flakes, blades, and even cores in tremendous numbers over the entire extent of the site. Chemical sourcing places their origins at a source hundreds of kilometers to the north.[16] Khirbat al-Fakhar was, it would seem, a major manufacturing and distribution point for stone tools made of an exotic nonlocal material. Small-scale excavations near the site's center uncovered a residential structure, completely typical for this time period, and with evidence for the standard sedentary agropastoralist economy—but including a work space for the specialized production of obsidian blades. It seems likely, therefore, that the broad distribution of obsidian surface artifacts is hinting at a decentralized lithic industry organized at the household

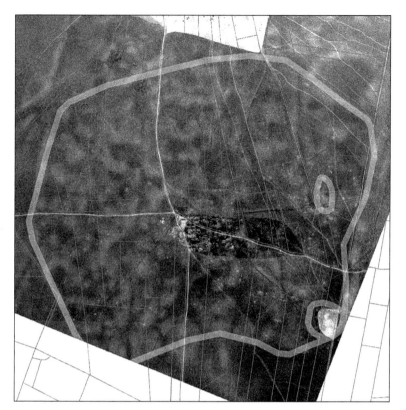

FIGURE 2.8

The low-density extensive settlement at Khirbat al-Fakhar, Syria: a) 1959 U2 aerial photograph, Mission B8648, acquired October 30, 1959; and b)interpretation showing discontinuous areas of settlement. Maps by Jason A. Ur; photograph courtesy of the U.S. National Archives and Records Administration (NARA).

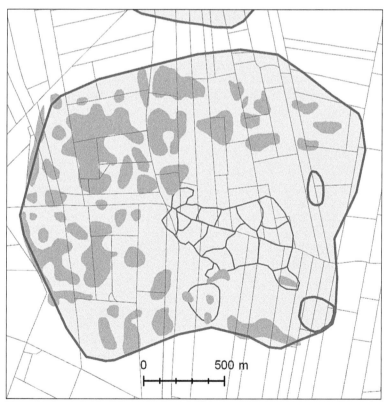

0   500 m

Space and Structure in Early Mesopotamian Cities   45

level. In other words, every household at Khirbat al-Fakhar was producing this "specialized" product.

Khirbat al-Fakhar fits very uncomfortably within the traditional Mesopotamian urban model. It was very large, but not nucleated. The intrasettlement open spaces are very anomalous. If this were a Mesoamerican site, one might assume that households or extended family blocks were separated from each other by garden plots. At the present state of knowledge, such an interpretation could stand; the climate of the fifth millennium BCE was wetter and less seasonal than in later times or at present. But small villages contemporary to Khirbat al-Fakhar show no such intrasettlement open spaces.[17] Alternatively, these vacant areas might be indicative of social distance. Khirbat al-Fakhar may have been composed of communities, more like a group of villages that happened to be semicontiguous with each other. In other words, its residents may have used space as a way of addressing or avoiding conflict. Nonetheless, people were motivated to come to this place, or to remain within it. In all likelihood, the motivation was economic: Khirbat al-Fakhar was an unambiguous center for trade and manufacturing of obsidian tools.

Although it seems very non-Mesopotamian, Khirbat al-Fakhar fits in well with other so-called megasites, or anomalous giants. These sites were large and precocious low-density settlements that have now been identified globally, but are most clearly described for the Trypillia settlements of Ukraine.[18] Megasites are diverse in many ways, but they have several properties in common. Their histories of occupation are brief, and they show a lack of connection with subsequent urban developments. At present, Khirbat al-Fakhar is unique in Mesopotamian prehistory, but this circumstance may have resulted from an overreliance on the traditional model of urbanism by archaeologists. With Khirbat al-Fakhar as an established model, we might expect that other such settlement forms may be recognized in the future.

Low-Density Urban Origins at Tell Brak

A second case study comes from Tell Brak, 80 km to the west of Khirbat al-Fakhar. Its expansion occurred a few centuries later, and it proved to be more durable. Today, the site of Tell Brak has a large central mound and a broad outer zone of settlement that is close to plain level (Figure 2.9). Its origins are unclear but are to be placed sometime prior to the mid-fifth millennium BCE, and settlement persevered as late as the early Islamic period, with some phases of abandonment over that long time span. This complex history presents great challenges to archaeological research, especially excavation. Its central mound has been under intensive investigation since the mid-1970s. In the 2000s, its outer town came under investigation, first via an intensive systematic surface collection, which documented about fifty thousand artifacts in nearly a thousand collection units across the site, and subsequently by targeted excavation.[19] The spatial distribution of chronologically sensitive artifacts from the surface collection permits the reconstruction of Brak's settlement over several millennia, and is the primary basis for the analysis of its urban structure (Figure 2.10).

The origins of the settlement are deeply buried in the core of the central mound and remain inaccessible to archaeologists. It can be assumed, however, that a small agricultural village already existed at the site in 4100 BCE, when small satellite areas of 1–4 ha began to appear in a halo around it, at a distance of 500 m (Figure 2.11a). Including the central mound, the area of this settlement was fifty-five hectares—five to ten times the size of any of its contemporaries.[20] The central mound was not collected as part of this survey because it had been so transformed by archaeological excavation, but these excavations suggest that it was already fully settled.

As at Khirbat al-Fakhar, Brak shows a pattern of settled areas with intervening vacant space. Again, this pattern might signal intrasettlement cultivation, but these discrete

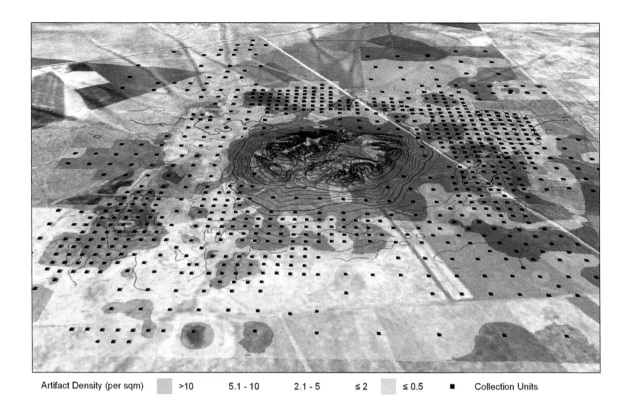

Artifact Density (per sqm) >10   5.1 - 10   2.1 - 5   ≤ 2   ≤ 0.5   ■ Collection Units

FIGURE 2.10

Surface artifact density
and collection units
across Tell Brak. Black
squares are 10 × 10 m
collection units. Map
by Jason A. Ur.

communities were also maintaining space in between them as a way of preserving social distance. As at Khirbat al-Fakhar some centuries earlier, some centripetal force was at work, but not yet a social mechanism for conflict resolution.

The two sites have some major differences, however. For one, Brak's satellite communities were more strongly isolated from one another and from the central settlement. Furthermore, Brak's satellite communities were not short-lived phenomena; they persevered and expanded. The distribution of surface artifacts of the mid-fourth millennium BCE covered 130 ha, about ten times the size of its nearest rival (Figure 2.11b).[21]

This spatial pattern of growth is unexpected. Rather than growing from a core settlement outward, Brak began as a large but dispersed constellation of core and satellite neighborhoods, with growth proceeding inward. After some three or four centuries, the end product was a dense and nucleated settlement, approaching the "classic" Near Eastern formulation described by Childe and others.

The settlement process at Brak is best interpreted through the lens of self-organization, in which individuals or communities opted in to the Brak settlement for their own reasons, but remained wary of others at the site. It was argued above that a few centuries earlier, an economic impetus drove immigration to Khirbat al-Fakhar. The impetus at Brak may have been ideological. Excavations on the high mound have documented a large structure on a monumental mud brick platform. The interior of the building was ornately decorated, and deposited within were thousands of small figurines

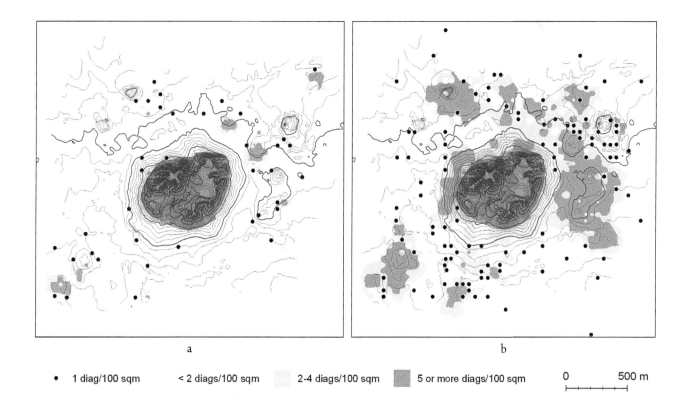

| • 1 diag/100 sqm | < 2 diags/100 sqm | 2-4 diags/100 sqm | 5 or more diags/100 sqm | 0   500 m |

that give the building its name, the Eye Temple (Figure 2.12).[22] Communities may have been inspired to immigrate to Brak to bring them closer to divine powers. In later times, divine households ("temples") were also powerful economic engines, with extensive landholdings and the ability to mobilize large numbers of workers, but it remains to be established if they served a similar role in the fourth millennium BCE. Challenging this proposal is the date of the Eye Temple; its earliest-known form appears to coincide with the late expansion of the city. Hence, it may be a result of urban cohesion, rather than part of the original impetus for immigration. Further excavation will be required to evaluate this hypothesis.

At Brak, it appears that urban institutions ultimately did develop to keep conflict in check, but the urbanization process was not a smooth one. Salvage excavations have revealed at least one, and possibly several episodes of violence. On the northern fringe of the fourth-millennium BCE city, excavations have revealed at least 230 human bodies, in various states of disarticulation.[23] These bodies were unburied and appear to have been feasted over before being discarded with other refuse at the city's edge. Given that Brak had no apparent rival, these bodies were probably the losers in the social strife that was part of the city's initial growth.

These events at Brak took place centuries before Uruk assumed the form that we know from countless textbooks, the oft-repeated "World's First City." Uruk's urban core is vividly well known on account of German research throughout the twentieth century (Figure 2.13). Extensive excavation was concentrated exclusively on the central core of

FIGURE 2.11

Distribution of surface artifacts at Tell Brak: a) Brak covered 55 ha by ca. 4100–3800 BCE; and b) Brak had grown to 130 ha by ca. 3800–3400 BCE. Map by Jason A. Ur.

FIGURE 2.12

The Eye Temple at Tell Brak. Its base platform is approximately 65 × 32 meters. Inset: Small "Eye Idol" figurines found within the Eye Temple. Courtesy of Augusta McMahon/ Tell Brak Project.

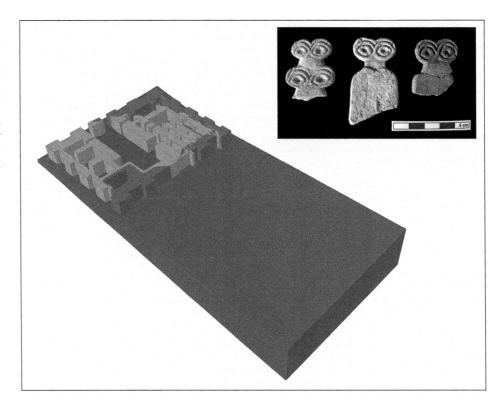

the city, where it revealed a series of enormous structures that are often described as "temples."[24] When compared to the Eye Temple from Brak, and other domestic structures from northern Mesopotamian cities, it is clear that they are dramatically different in scale, but all adhere to the same tripartite organizing principle.[25] The earliest pictographic tablets were found dumped into the fill of these buildings.

Given Childe's interest in Uruk, and its place in his urban revolution one might assume that these monumental structures sat amid a dense urban fabric of residential neighborhoods, where the majority of the city's population lived. Despite the durability of Childe's model, it has yet to be tested at Uruk itself. After nearly a century of excavation, not a single "private" (i.e., small-scale domestic, as opposed to large institutional) house of the fourth millennium BCE has been excavated at Uruk; the priorities of the excavators revolved entirely around monumental architecture. Nonetheless, it seems likely that such neighborhoods existed, given the scatter of pottery over some 250 ha.[26] Uruk's settlement history was long and convoluted, leaving a complex surface assemblage that is far more difficult to interpret than Brak's.

Uruk is a very important place for the history of urbanism, and it will continue to have a critical place in discussions of early world urbanism. We cannot forget, however, that its spatial patterning, as incompletely reconstructed by archaeology, captures its urban state at the end of the fourth millennium BCE, and most probably at the end of a centuries-long developmental sequence. The excavators privileged horizontal exposure over deep soundings, so we have a marvelous snapshot of Uruk at its height, but know nearly nothing of

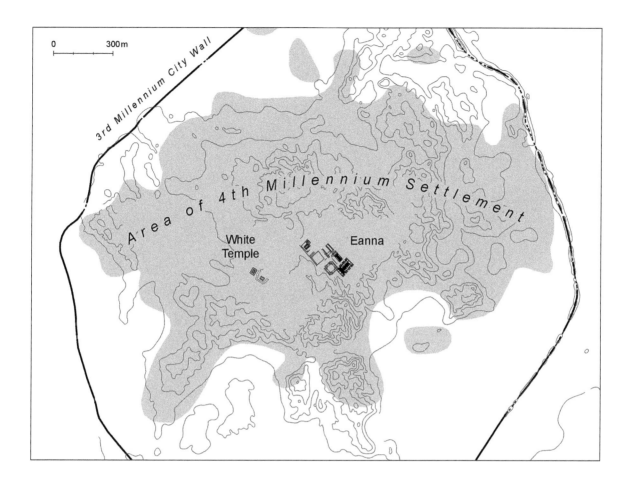

0   300m

3rd Millennium City Wall

Area of 4th Millennium Settlement

White
Temple

Eanna

its origins. The oft-reproduced plan of the city is the result of as much as a millennium of urban evolution; it cannot be used to discuss Uruk's urbanization process. It therefore remains entirely possible that Uruk's pattern of growth also proceeded from low to high density, and inward. It remains to be determined whether the earlier sequence described for Tell Brak in northern Mesopotamia was replicated at Uruk in southern Mesopotamia.

High-Density Self-Organized Cities of the Early Bronze Age

The third case study comes from the middle of the third millennium BCE, the time of the great Sumerian city-states on the southern plains. It is not an examination of an individual city, but rather a review and reinterpretation of the extensive data set of urban structure from this time. After more than a millennium of urban evolution, Mesopotamian cities had arrived at the "classic" nucleated form famously described by Childe and others.[27] They were densely occupied, with narrow streets that articulated with gates in monumental city walls. The use of cuneiform writing had expanded; it was the primary administrative tool for large institutional households, some religious and some apparently secular, that had wide landholdings and incorporated hundreds of people (Figure 2.14).

FIGURE 2.13

The site of Uruk, ca. 3100 BCE. Based on Uwe Finkbeiner, ed., *Uruk Kampagne 35–37 1982–1984: Die Archäologische Oberflächenuntersuchung (Survey)*, Ausgrabungen in Uruk-Warka Endberichte Band 4 (Mainz: Philipp von Zabern, 1991).

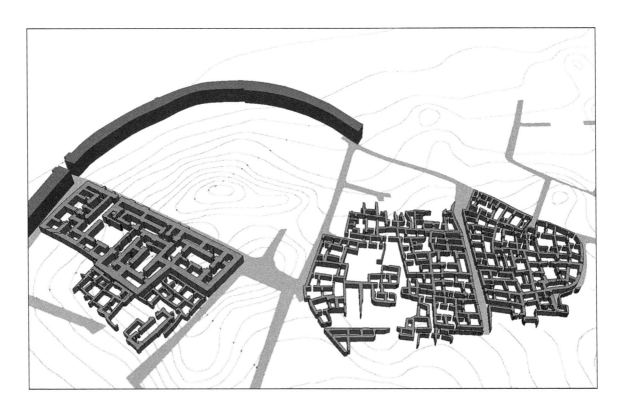

FIGURE 2.14

The "classic" form of Early Bronze Age urbanism in southern Mesopotamia: the urban fabric of Tell Asmar (ancient Eshnunna), ca. 2300 BCE. Map by Jason A. Ur.

Northern Mesopotamian Early Bronze Age cities were structurally similar in many ways, but they were fewer, smaller, and more dispersed than those of the Sumerian plains.[28] They contained similarly dense residential neighborhoods, city walls, and large institutions. Nearly all appear to have grown according to a model in which an initial small village grew outward while retaining its population at its core, which formed a central elevated part of the settlement (Figure 2.15). Growth and immigration were accommodated by adjacent areas of former cropland (the prior infields) turned into residential space.[29]

Early Bronze Age cities stretched across the lower fringes of the Fertile Crescent, from the plains around Aleppo in the west to Nineveh in the east. Until the Syrian civil war of 2011, their remains were some of the most intensively investigated sites in the Near East. Their excavators focused on elite monumental architecture, so it is, therefore, no surprise that their interpretations posit centralized planning behind urban development. Palaces, temples, and city walls all require architectural planning, but centralized planning at the level of entire neighborhoods has also been proposed.[30]

Some archaeologists even see planning and designers behind the structure of entire cities. For example, during the Early Bronze Age, several urban settlements in Syria had strongly circular plans. Geophysical surveys have revealed street patterns of outwardly radiating spokes connected by rings and culminating in circular outer walls. The excavator of Tell Chuera, the largest and best studied of these circular sites, has stated that its structure and features "are all nothing else but the result of preconceived central planning."[31]

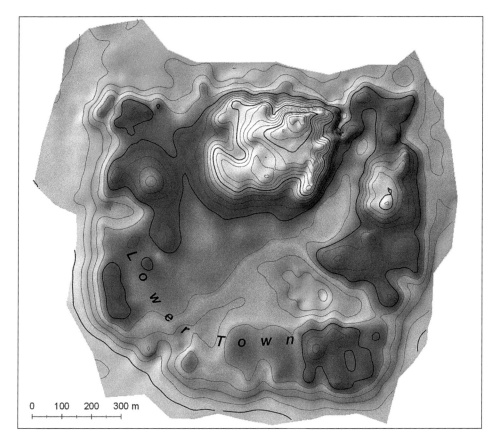

0   100   200   300 m

L o w e r   T o w n

FIGURE 2.15
Urban form in Early Bronze
Age northern Mesopotamia:
Hamoukar, Syria. The
fourth-millennium BCE
town has been located under
the high mound at north;
in the middle of the third
millennium BCE, settlement
expanded to form a lower
town to the east, south,
and west of the old mound.
Similar growth patterns can
be described at most other
Early Bronze Age cities of
northern Mesopotamia.
Contours at 1 m interval.
Map by Jason A. Ur.

Whether at the scale of the neighborhood or the entire city, these interpretations assume planners who designed and implemented major spatial changes to existing settlements. Despite the geometric regularities of Chuera and other Early Bronze Age cities, however, they were still largely the products of self-organization, although not without some top-down elite intervention. To make this argument, one must first look beyond the settlement at the broader landscape. Early Bronze Age sites of all sizes are surrounded by linear depressions that mark the former locations of trackways. These features are nearly impossible to see on the ground, but are often highly visible from space. Most frequently, tracks radiated outward from a central mound, generally for 1–3 km before fading out, although a minority do connect to other sites. Declassified intelligence satellite photographs from the 1960s and 1970s have enabled the mapping of over 6,000 km of ancient tracks across northern Mesopotamia (Figure 2.16). Almost all of them can be dated by association to the Early Bronze Age.[32]

These tracks proved to be the most critical structural element in the formation of Early Bronze Age cities, the features around which their structural regularities emerged. Farmers, herders, and animals took the shortest routes available to their fields and pastures. In doing so, they obeyed local land tenure rights; in other words, they did not cut across fields and trample crops, but rather adhered to existing tracks. When pressures from population growth necessitated the conversion of farmland into new

0   1 Km

residential land, the farmland closest to the settlement was most likely to be first, but the preexisting tracks would remain as public corridors of movement. These processes represent a set of "local rules" that would have been followed by the settlement's residents, simply by custom rather than via coercion by elite authorities.

With these rules in mind, one can imagine a scenario by which a village might have grown into a city (Figure 2.17).[33] The village's farmers cultivated land close to their settlement; beyond, its shepherds grazed animals. With population growth, immigration, or both, landowners converted arable land adjacent to the old village into areas of housing. Because they were viewed as public spaces, the former tracks through the fields were not built over, but rather became urban streets. At some point, authorities (perhaps the landowners) built a city wall, thereby formalizing what had been up to that point an emergent process driven mostly by local rules. In a few particular cases, further growth led to the conversion of more agricultural land under the same rules. The city wall would lose its defensive function and become incorporated into nearby houses. If necessary, this phase of growth beyond the old city wall might again be formally recognized with a new city wall. Following abandonment, the mud brick

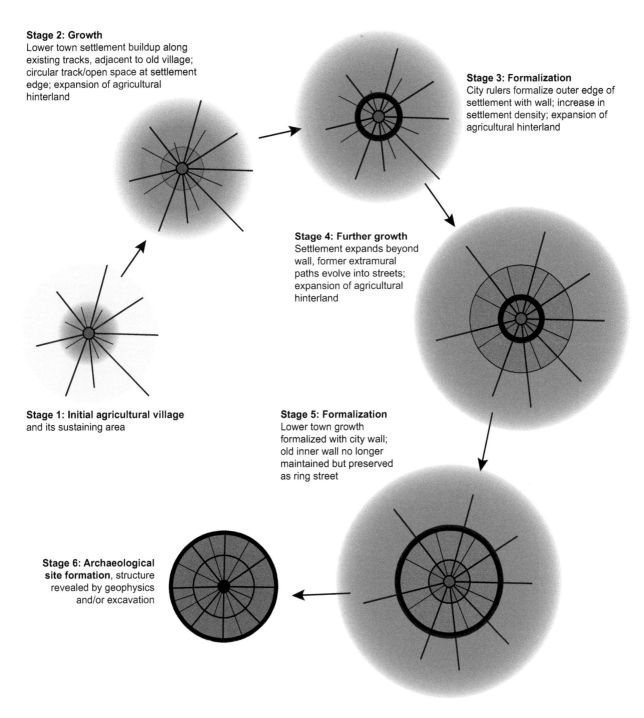

Stage 2: Growth
Lower town settlement buildup along existing tracks, adjacent to old village; circular track/open space at settlement edge; expansion of agricultural hinterland

Stage 3: Formalization
City rulers formalize outer edge of settlement with wall; increase in settlement density; expansion of agricultural hinterland

Stage 4: Further growth
Settlement expands beyond wall, former extramural paths evolve into streets; expansion of agricultural hinterland

Stage 1: Initial agricultural village and its sustaining area

Stage 5: Formalization
Lower town growth formalized with city wall; old inner wall no longer maintained but preserved as ring street

Stage 6: Archaeological site formation, structure revealed by geophysics and/or excavation

FIGURE 2.17

Schematic depiction of the self-organized evolution of a Mesopotamian city. Illustration by Jason A. Ur.

architecture of the former city would decay into an archaeological site, very similar to the pattern shown in geophysical surveys.

This developmental scenario is hypothetical; no archaeological excavation has been both broad and deep enough to demonstrate it empirically. All the local rules can, however, be demonstrated in the historical growth patterns of cities, particularly those of the Mediterranean.[34] For the Mesopotamian Bronze Age, historians and archaeologists have concentrated intensely on the elements of top-down formalization: temples and palaces, and the royal formalization of settlement growth via city walls. Such interventions by central authorities ("planners") were indeed more frequent and more structurally consequential in the Early Bronze Age than they were in earlier times. Nonetheless, the underlying self-organized character of Mesopotamian cities still dominated, if one looks closely.[35]

Conclusions:
Variability and Self-Organization in Early Mesopotamian Cities

By this point, it should be noncontroversial to state that early Mesopotamian cities were highly variable in their structure, and that these structures differed from the canonical model known from the influential writings of Childe and reproduced in textbooks and comparative studies. These conclusions are based on the last two decades of field research in northern Mesopotamia as reviewed above, but one might hope that they will spur new research on the southern plains, as research begins to reemerge after a generation's absence.

To a great degree, early Mesopotamian cities invented themselves, albeit in different ways and at different times. Powerful elites could and did make interventions in them, but these interventions were either localized, such as the construction of a temple or palace, or were reactive to emergent forces—for example, when a king commissioned a city wall around bottom-up urban growth. For "great men" to populate our archaeological narratives, one can always turn to the kings of Assyria in the first millennium BCE, who truly did commission cities, and indeed entire landscapes, sometimes more or less out of whole cloth. But such centralization of political authority just did not exist prior to that time, despite grandiose claims by rulers.[36] To extend such authority back into the Bronze Age, or into the time of urban origins, creates the sort of timeless Orientalist state that archaeologists and historians should be critiquing. Models that acknowledge a high degree of self-organization, such as the three case studies presented above, give agency to all residents of these precocious places in the formation of urban structure. Such models will, one would hope, inspire archaeologists to explore early Mesopotamian cities more holistically in the future.

Notes

1   This essay is an attempt to synthesize almost two decades of fieldwork across several projects; therefore, it comes with a long list of people to acknowledge. Khirbat al-Fakhar/Hamoukar: McGuire Gibson, Tony Wilkinson, Salam al-Quntar, Carlo Colantoni, Lamya Khalidi, and Amr al-Azm; Tell Brak: Joan and David Oates, Geoff Emberling, Augusta McMahon, Henry Wright, Philip Karsgaard, Shilan Ramadan, and Fahad Aljomaa. Permission to conduct these research projects was graciously provided by the Syrian Directorate-General of Antiquities and Museums in Damascus. Funding came from Harvard University, University of Chicago, University of Michigan, University of Cambridge, and the American Schools of Oriental Research Mesopotamian Fellowship.

2   V. Gordon Childe, "The Urban Revolution," *Town Planning Review* 21, no. 1 (1950):3–17; and V. Gordon Childe, *New Light on the Most Ancient East: The Oriental Prelude to European Prehistory*, rev. ed. (New York: W. W. Norton and Company, 1952). For the legacy of his "Urban Revolution," see Michael E. Smith, "V. Gordon Childe and the Urban Revolution: A Historical Perspective on a Revolution in Urban Studies," *Town Planning Review* 80, no. 1 (2009):3–29.

3   Two clear recent reviews are Arlen F. Chase and Diane Z. Chase, "Urbanism and Anthropogenic Landscapes," *Annual Review of Anthropology* 45 (2016):361–76; and George L. Cowgill, "Origins and Development of Urbanism: Archaeological Perspectives," *Annual Review of Anthropology* 33 (2004):525–49.

4   T. J. Wilkinson, *Archaeological Landscapes of the Near East* (Tucson: University of Arizona Press, 2003).

5   Harvey Weiss, "The Origins of Tell Leilan and the Conquest of Space in Third Millennium Mesopotamia," in *The Origins of Cities in Dry-Farming Syria and Mesopotamia in the Third Millennium BC*, ed. Harvey Weiss (Guilford, Conn.: Four Quarters, 1986), 71–108; T. J. Wilkinson, "The Structure and Dynamics of Dry-Farming States in Upper Mesopotamia," *Current Anthropology* 35 (1994):483–520; and Wilkinson, *Archaeological Landscapes of the Near East*.

6   Arlene Miller Rosen, *Cities of Clay: The Geoarchaeology of Tells* (Chicago: University of Chicago Press, 1986).

7   For reviews of Mesopotamian prehistory and its Early Bronze Age, see Peter M. M. G. Akkermans and Glenn Schwartz, *The Archaeology of Syria: From Complex Hunter-Gatherers to Early Urban Societies (ca. 16,000–300 BC)* (Cambridge: Cambridge University Press, 2003); and Susan Pollock, *Ancient Mesopotamia: The Eden That Never Was* (Cambridge: Cambridge University Press, 1999).

8   See, for example, Mario Liverani, *Uruk: The First City*, trans. Zainab Bahrani and Marc Van de Mieroop (London: Equinox, 2006); and Roger Matthews, "Peoples and Complex Societies of Ancient Southwest Asia," in *The Human Past: World Prehistory and the Development of Human Societies*, ed. Chris Scarre (London: Thames and Hudson, 2009), 432–71.

9   For reviews of settlement pattern studies, see T. J. Wilkinson, "Regional Approaches to Mesopotamian Archaeology: The Contribution of Archaeological Surveys," *Journal of Archaeological Research* 8, no. 3 (2000):219–67; and Jason A. Ur, "Patterns of Settlement in Sumer and Akkad," in *The Sumerian World*, ed. Harriet Crawford (Oxford: Routledge, 2013), 131–55.

10 Smith, " V. Gordon Childe and the Urban Revolution."

11 Cowgill, "Origins and Development of Urbanism."

12 Todd Whitelaw, "Collecting Cities: Some Problems and Prospects," in *Archaeological Survey and the City*, ed. Paul Johnson and Martin Millett (Oxford: Oxbow, 2013), 70–106.

13 For the Near East, see Jesse Casana, Jackson Cothren, and Tuna Kalayci, "Swords into Ploughshares: Archaeological Applications of CORONA Satellite Imagery in the Near East," *Internet Archaeology* 32, no. 2 (2012), http://intarch.ac.uk/journal/issue32/2/; Martin J. F. Fowler, "Declassified Intelligence Satellite Photographs," in *Archaeology from Historical Aerial and Satellite Archives*, ed. William S. Hanson and Ioana A. Oltean (New York: Springer, 2013), 47–66; Jason A. Ur, "Corona Satellite Imagery and Ancient Near Eastern Landscapes," in *Mapping Archaeological Landscapes from Space: In Observance of the 40th Anniversary of the World Heritage Convention*, ed. Douglas C. Comer and Michael J. Harrower (New York: Springer, 2013), 19–29; and Emily L. Hammer and Jason A. Ur, "Near Eastern Landscapes and Declassified U2 Aerial Imagery," *Advances in Archaeological Practice* 7, no. 2 (2019):107–26.

14 Surface collection and soundings are reported in Jason A. Ur, *Urbanism and Cultural Landscapes in Northeastern Syria: The Tell Hamoukar Survey, 1999–2001*, Oriental Institute Publications 137 (Chicago: Oriental Institute of the University of Chicago, 2010); and Salam Al Quntar, Lamya Khalidi, and Jason A. Ur, "Proto-Urbanism in the Late 5th Millennium BC: Survey and Excavations at Khirbat Al-Fakhar/Hamoukar, Northeast Syria," *Paléorient* 37, no. 2 (2011):151–75.

15 The best review of this practice remains J. Nicholas Postgate, "How Many Sumerians Per Hectare? Probing the Anatomy of an Early City," *Cambridge Archaeological Journal* 4 (1994):47–65.

16 Lamya Khalidi and Bernard Gratuze, "Late Chalcolithic Lithic Assemblage at Tell Hamoukar's Southern Extension," *Berytus* 53–54 (2010–11):15–38; and Lamya Khalidi, Bernard Gratuze, and Sophie Boucetta, "Provenance of Obsidian Excavated from Late Chalcolithic Levels at the Sites of Tell Hamoukar and Tell Brak, Syria," *Archaeometry* 51, no. 6 (2009):879–93.

17 See, for example, Tepe Gawra in northern Iraq: Mitchell S. Rothman, "Tepe Gawra: Chronology and Socio-Economic Change in the Foothills of Northern Iraq in the Era of State Formation," in *Artefacts of Complexity: Tracking the Uruk in the Near East*, ed. J. Nicholas Postgate (Warminster: British School of Archaeology in Iraq, 2002), 49–77.

18 On the Trypillia sites, see Francesco Menotti and Aleksey G. Korvin-Piotrovksiy, eds., *The Tripolye Culture Giant-Settlements in Ukraine: Formation, Development, and Decline* (Oxford: Oxbow, 2012); and Johannes Müller, Knut Rassmann, and Mykhailo Videiko, eds., *Trypillia Mega-Sites and European Prehistory, 4100–3400 BCE* (Abingdon: Routledge, 2016). For a broader discussion of "megasites" and their implications for archaeological approaches to early urbanism, see Bisserka Gaydarska, "The City Is Dead! Long Live the City!," *Norwegian Archaeological Review* 49, no. 1 (2016):40–57; and Roland Fletcher, "Anomalous Giants: Category Problems and Trajectory Analysis" (forthcoming).

19 Jason A. Ur, Philip Karsgaard, and Joan Oates, "Urban Development in the Ancient Near East," *Science* 317, no. 5842 (2007):1188; and Jason A. Ur, Philip Karsgaard, and Joan Oates, "The Spatial Dimensions of Early Mesopotamian Urbanism: The Tell Brak Suburban Survey, 2003–2006," *Iraq* 73 (2011):1–19.

20 Ur, Karsgaard, and Oates, "Spatial Dimensions of Early Mesopotamian Urbanism."

21 Ur, Karsgaard, and Oates, "Spatial Dimensions of Early Mesopotamian Urbanism."

22 Geoff Emberling, "Political Control in an Early State: The Eye Temple and the Uruk Expansion in Northern Mesopotamia," in *Of Pots and Plans: Papers on the Archaeology and History of Mesopotamia and Syria Presented to David Oates in Honour of His 75th Birthday*, ed. Lamia al-Gailani Werr, John Curtis, Harriet Martin, Augusta McMahon, and Julian Reade (London: Nabu Publications, 2002), 82–90; and Augusta McMahon, "Early Urbanism in Northern Mesopotamia," *Journal of Archaeological Research* (forthcoming).

23 Augusta McMahon, Arkadiusz Sołtysiak, and Jill Weber, "Late Chalcolithic Mass Graves at Tell Brak, Syria, and Violent Conflict during the Growth of Early City-States," *Journal of Field Archaeology* 36, no. 3 (2011):201–20.

24 See, for example, Heinrich Lenzen, "Die Architektur in Eanna in Der Uruk IV Periode," *Iraq* 36, no. 1–2 (1974):111–28.

25 For a discussion, see Jason A. Ur, "Households and the Emergence of Cities in Ancient Mesopotamia," *Cambridge Archaeological Journal* 24, no. 2 (2014):249–68.

26 Well documented by intensive surface survey, see Uwe Finkbeiner, ed., *Uruk Kampagne 35–37 1982–1984: Die Archäologische Oberflächenuntersuchung (Survey)*, Ausgrabungen in Uruk-Warka Endberichte Band 4 (Mainz: Philipp von Zabern, 1991).

27 Reviewed in Elizabeth C. Stone, "The Mesopotamian Urban Experience," in *Settlement and Society: Essays Dedicated to Robert McCormick Adams*, ed. Elizabeth C. Stone (Los Angeles: Cotsen Institute of Archaeology, 2007), 213–34; Elizabeth C. Stone, "The Organisation of a Sumerian Town: The Physical Remains of Ancient Social Systems," in Crawford, *Sumerian World*, 156–78; and Jason A. Ur, "Southern Mesopotamia," in *A Companion to the Archaeology of the Ancient Near East*, ed. Daniel T. Potts (Malden: Blackwell, 2012), 533–55.

28 Recent reviews of northern Mesopotamian cities of the Early Bronze Age include Andrew T. Creekmore III, "The Social Production of Space in Third-Millennium Cities of Upper Mesopotamia," in *Making Ancient Cities: Space and Place in Early Urban Societies*, ed. Andrew T. Creekmore III and Kevin D. Fisher (New York: Cambridge University Press, 2014), 32–73; Jason A. Ur, "Cycles

of Civilization in Northern Mesopotamia, 4400–2000 BC," *Journal of Archaeological Research* 18, no. 4 (2010):387–431; Timothy Matney, "Northern Mesopotamia," in Potts, *Companion to the Archaeology of the Ancient Near East*, 556–74; and Augusta McMahon, "North Mesopotamia in the Third Millennium BC," in Crawford, *Sumerian World*, 462–77.

29 This model is elaborated in Dan Lawrence and T. J. Wilkinson, "Hubs and Upstarts: Pathways to Urbanism in the Northern Fertile Crescent," *Antiquity* 89, no. 344 (2015):328–44; and Jason A. Ur, "Central Planning and Urban Emergence in Early Bronze Age Cities of Northern Mesopotamia," in *New Agendas in Remote Sensing and Landscape Archaeology in the Near East: Studies in Honor of T. J. Wilkinson*, ed. Dan Lawrence, Mark Altaweel, and Graham Philip (Chicago: Oriental Institute of the University of Chicago, forthcoming).

30 For an argument in favor of neighborhood planning, see Timothy Matney, Guillermo Algaze, Steven Rosen, Sumru Aricanli, and Britt Hartenberger, "Early Bronze Age Urban Structure at Titriş Höyük in Southeastern Turkey: The 1998 Season," *Anatolica* 25 (1999):185–201.

31 Jan-Waalke Meyer, "Town Planning in 3rd Millennium Tell Chuera," in *Power and Architecture: Monumental Public Architecture in the Bronze Age Near East and Aegean*, ed. Joachim Bretschneider, Jan Driessen, and Karel van Lerberghe (Leuven: Peeters, 2007), 129–42.

32 For a review of "hollow way" tracks in Mesopotamian archaeology, see Wilkinson, *Archaeological Landscapes of the Near East*. On the use of CORONA satellite photography to map "hollow ways," see Jason A. Ur, "CORONA Satellite Photography and Ancient Road Networks: A Northern Mesopotamian Case Study," *Antiquity* 77 (2003):102–15; and Ur, *Urbanism and Cultural Landscapes in Northeastern Syria*.

33 This emergent argument for Early Bronze Age urban growth is described in detail in Ur, " Central Planning and Urban Emergence in Early Bronze Age Cities of Northern Mesopotamia."

34 Spiro Kostof, *The City Shaped: Urban Patterns and Meanings through History* (London: Thames and Hudson, 1991).

35 For a thoughtful review of bottom-up versus top-down processes in Early Bronze Age cities, see Creekmore, "Social Production of Space in Third-Millennium Cities of Upper Mesopotamia."

36 Increasingly, the divergence between the rhetoric of royal claims and political reality in early Mesopotamia is being acknowledged; see especially Seth Richardson, "Early Mesopotamian History: The Presumptive State," *Past and Present* 215 (2012):3–49; and Seth Richardson, "Before Things Worked: A 'Low Power' Model of Early Mesopotamia," in *Ancient States and Infrastructural Power: Europe, Asia, and America*, ed. Clifford Ando and Seth Richardson (Philadelphia: University of Pennsylvania, 2017), 17–62. On the Neo-Assyrian engineered landscape of the first millennium BCE, see Daniele Morandi Bonacossi, "The Creation of the Assyrian Heartland: New Data from the 'Land Behind Nineveh,'" in *The Archaeology of Imperial Landscapes: A Comparative Study of Empires in the Ancient Near East and Mediterranean World*, ed. Bleda Düring and Tesse D. Stek (Cambridge: Cambridge University Press, 2018), 48–85; and Jason A. Ur, "Physical and Cultural Landscapes of Assyria," in *Blackwell Companion to Assyria*, ed. Eckart Frahm (Oxford: Wiley Blackwell, 2017), 13–35.

3

Landscape Change and Ceremonial Praxis in Medieval Rome

From the Via Triumphalis to the Via Papalis

HENDRIK W. DEY

B Y THE TWELFTH CENTURY CE, THE PRINCIPAL FOCUS OF WHAT
follows, Rome was nearly two millennia old, and had the physical remains to
prove it. At the peak of its size and power as the capital of a vast empire (second century BCE to fourth century CE), it had been the most populous city in the world. Its
last and largest circuit of walls, built in the third century CE, enclosed approximately
1,400 ha inhabited by well over five hundred thousand people.[1] The vast expanse covered
by the remains of imperial Rome, and the sheer scale and durability of its monuments
and infrastructure, powerfully informed the choices medieval Romans made about
where (and how) they lived, and how (and where) they moved through the cityscape.

Thus, medieval Rome constitutes an unusual example of the development of a premodern city. The built environment inherited from antiquity so dwarfed the capacity
of medieval Romans to master that, I suggest, the extant remains of ancient Rome, considered as a whole and as a collection of salient nodes, lend themselves well to analytical
approaches more commonly applied to the effects of geography and natural topography
on urban development. A surviving Roman bridge functioned much like a natural ford
over an otherwise impassable river; an expanse of densely packed crumbling stone and
concrete hulks might as well have been a field of boulders; a theater was a commanding
natural eminence. And like natural topography, Rome's anthropogenic topo-scape was
in constant flux, ineluctably altered and reconfigured by wind and weather, fires, floods,
earthquakes, encroaching vegetation, and so on.

A look at the evolution of two parallel streets, one inherited from the Roman period
(the Via Triumphalis) and one a medieval creation (the Via Papalis), will help to give a
sense of the range of possibilities and coping strategies available to medieval Romans

faced with the immanent legacy of the city's storied past. Complex interactions between the natural environment, the built landscape, and the capabilities and priorities of human actors combined to reshape the zone through which those streets ran over the course of Rome's medieval millennium, from the fifth century into the fifteenth. As the region of Rome through which the two streets ran, the Campus Martius, evolved into the most densely settled part of the city in the later Middle Ages, particularly from the twelfth century on, the history of these two streets is also, in a sense, the story of medieval Rome itself—of the local transformations that collectively underpinned the reconfiguration of the whole.

Before proceeding, a word on sources and methods is warranted. The study of medieval Roman architecture and urbanism depends on three main kinds of evidence, none of which is as complete or as straightforward as might be wished. The first is texts, among them narrative histories and chronicles, "guidebooks" and descriptions of the city, saints' lives and liturgical handbooks, and archival documents such as contracts for the sale and lease of real estate. It is a dauntingly large and scattered textual corpus, one that requires diligent trolling through reams of extraneous material in order to turn up the occasional nugget of topographical gold. Moreover, the usual problems with interpreting thousand-year-old texts aside, the written records are often frustratingly vague and ambiguous in their accounting of the built environment. In many cases, the presentation of local topography with cartographic precision was not the authors' intent. In others, Roman writers writing for Roman readers tended to presume a degree of familiarity with the urban surroundings that led them to omit just the sorts of details that modern scholars would most like to have.

The second type of evidence is the surviving vestiges of the medieval cityscape, including both individual buildings and infrastructure such as walls, bridges, and street networks. They are obviously of enormous importance, but they are relatively few and far between. Rome has constantly transformed since the Middle Ages, and especially after 1870, when as the capital of a newly united Italy, the sleepy papal city of approximately two hundred thousand inhabitants embarked on its metamorphosis into the sprawling modern metropolis of several millions that it is today. In the process, much of the preexisting cityscape has been covered or destroyed, and much of the rest transformed almost beyond recognition.

Finally, there is archaeology, whose great potential and considerable limitations are also largely determined by the physical parameters of the modern city. In recent decades, methodologically rigorous excavations, among them those at the Crypta Balbi and those very recently conducted during construction of the Metro C subway line (see below), have dramatically enriched and often substantially transformed the traditional picture of medieval Rome. We now know considerably more about how and where medieval Romans lived, worked, and moved through the city. But the areas susceptible to careful excavation and analysis are limited in area and casually scattered about (as digs occur only when and where feasible); and most of the medieval (and ancient) city will always remain hidden beneath the bustling sprawl of the contemporary metropolis. Further, the much more extensive excavations conducted during the later nineteenth and early twentieth centuries, in crucial areas such as the Roman Forum, are notable for the lack of attention devoted to their postclassical phases, as both the excavators and the government officials who sanctioned their work were mainly concerned with exposing the remains of ancient Rome in its full, imperial grandeur.

Thus, for all its capacity to provide genuinely new and often surprising insights into medieval Rome, archaeology mainly offers detailed vignettes, scattered windows onto a much larger urban whole whose connecting tissues typically remain lost or inaccessible to excavators. It is an essential but inevitably partial complement to the written sources and extant remains. The three kinds of evidence must be integrated in order to provide the most complete picture possible of the medieval cityscape in general, and of the two streets that concern us here, to which we now turn.

The older of the two roads, the Via Triumphalis, is very ancient. By the third century BCE, it was arguably the most important thoroughfare in Rome: the most architecturally prepossessing and the most renowned for its close association with the grandest processional ceremony the ancient city offered, the triumph. This road departed the city center via the Porta Carmentalis, a gate in the fourth-century BCE Servian Wall located at the foot of the Capitoline Hill, close to the banks of the Tiber River. From the gate, the road angled northwest across the low-lying expanse of the Tiber floodplain, traversing first the Forum Holitorium, an open marketplace for the sale of fresh produce, and then the Campus Martius, the "Field of Mars" where republican Rome's citizen-soldiers conducted exercises, voted, and were counted for the census; where horse races and other popular spectacles took place; and where occurred various religious rituals that belonged outside the pomerium, the consecrated ground of the city center. The road crossed the Tiber at the apex of the cup-handle-shaped bend in the river that envelops the Campus Martius on three sides, first via a ford and later a bridge, the Pons Neronianus. It then continued its northwestern course toward the Tyrrhenian coast and the heartland of Etruria, the confederation of Etruscan city-states centered on northern Latium and Tuscany (Figure 3.1).[2]

In 396 BCE, the Roman army that conquered the Etruscan city of Veii, the first neighboring power subjugated by Rome, departed and returned to Rome via this road. The memory of this first foreign conquest and victorious return presumably gave the street its enduring connection with triumphal processions, as well as its name: the Triumphal Way (Via Triumphalis). Although no surviving ancient source so names that portion of the road that traversed the Campus Martius, given that the Porta Carmentalis in the Servian Wall was also known as the Triumphal Gate (Porta Triumphalis), and that surviving inscriptions show that the Etruria-bound extension of the street across the Tiber was called the Via Triumphalis, I will not hesitate to use Via Triumphalis for the route in its entirety, including the nearly 2 km section between the Forum Holitorium and the Pons Neronianus that concerns us here.[3]

Over the course of the third to first centuries BCE, the period that corresponds with the conquest of most of Rome's Mediterranean empire, this section of the road, especially the first half between the Porta Carmentalis/Triumphalis and the Theater of Pompey, attracted a disproportionate share of buildings and monuments erected by the generals

FIGURE 3.1

The ancient Via
Triumphalis. 1) Pons
Neronianus; 2) Porta
Carmentalis/Forum
Holitorium; 3) Circus
Maximus; 4) Roman
Forum; and 5) Capitoline
Hill. Illustration by
Hendrik W. Dey.

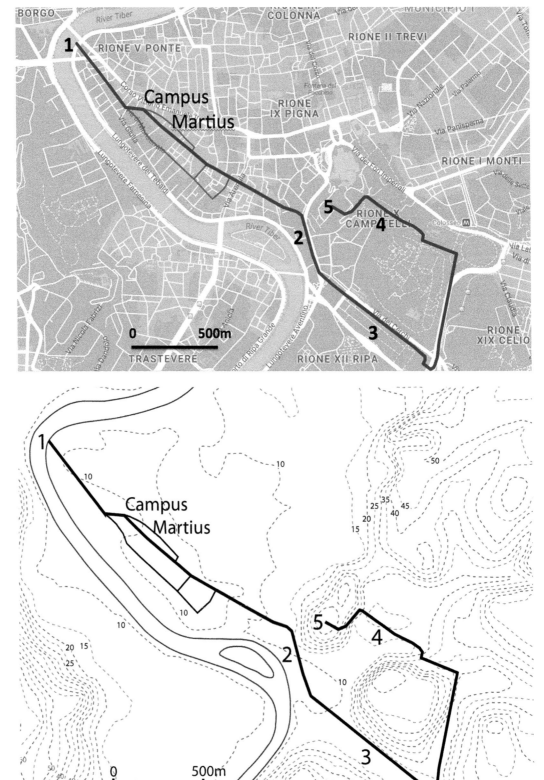

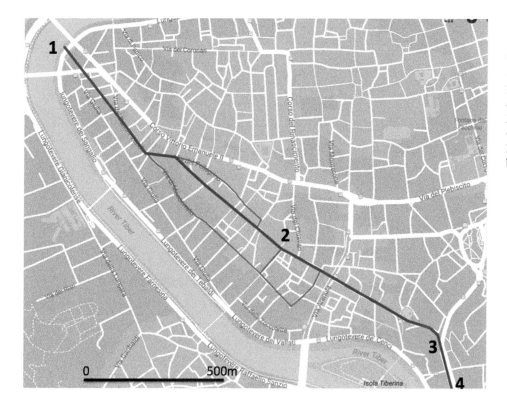

FIGURE 3.2

The Via Triumphalis in the Campus Martius. 1) Pons Neronianus; 2) Theater of Pompey; 3) Theater of Marcellus; and 4) Porta Carmentalis/Forum Holitorium. Illustration by Hendrik W. Dey.

who celebrated triumphs, and whose own triumphal processions thus passed among the monuments built by their renowned predecessors. An unusual concentration of manubial temples—temples built with the spoils of war—clustered along it; the city's first honorary arches spanned it; and in the first century BCE, Rome's first and largest stone theaters, of Pompey (dedicated 55 BCE) and Marcellus (dedicated 13 BCE), rose adjacent to its course (Figure 3.2).[4] Triumphal monuments in their own right, these theaters provided an optimal viewing platform for spectators at triumphal processions, some of which possibly wended through the theaters themselves. The colonnaded porches of the temples and the exterior arcades of the theaters were physically, visually, and stylistically connected by long, covered porticoes lining the street.[5] The result was a reasonably coherent architectonic ensemble, a monumental corridor dominated by porticoes and temple porches and theater arcades (Figure 3.3). Its monuments constituted a repository of collective memory of past victories and the physical setting for new triumphal processions, during which thousands of spectators packed the street's flanking colonnades and porticoes, raised above the roadbed on steps and sheltered from the elements.

This is not to say that all triumphal processions necessarily traversed this route; and after the fall of the Roman Republic in the late first century BCE, the emperors who thenceforth assumed the exclusive right to triumph did so less frequently than their republican predecessors.[6] Nonetheless, the route's monumentality and architectural cohesion, its collection of temples and arches and spectacle buildings, along with its connection to the main river crossing in the northern Campus Martius, ensured that

FIGURE 3.3

a) Arcade with Tuscan half-pilasters along Via Triumphalis, facing the Theater of Marcellus; and b) arcaded facade of Theater of Marcellus, with Tuscan half-pilasters. Photographs by Hendrik W. Dey.

a

b

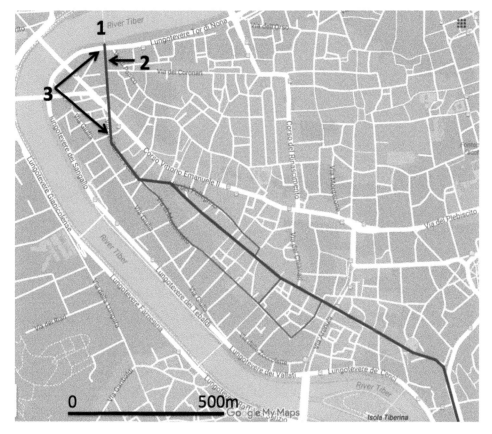

FIGURE 3.4

The Via Triumphalis and
the *porticus maximae*
after ca. 380 CE. 1) Ponte
Sant'Angelo (built in the
120s CE as Pons Aelius);
2) Triumphal Arch of
Valentinian II, Theodosius,
and Gratian; and 3) new,
final tract of the *porticus
maximae*. Illustration
by Hendrik W. Dey.

it endured as one of Rome's busiest and most architectonically distinguished streets. Its fame also helped to inspire the creation of other majestic, porticated avenues that came, starting in the first century CE, to proliferate in Mediterranean cityscapes across the empire, where they gradually became the public "stage" par excellence upon which civic and religious leaders displayed themselves to the urban multitudes.[7]

With the progressive Christianization of the empire during the fourth century, the Via Triumphalis gained anew in stature as it developed into the main link between the city center and the Vatican basilica of Saint Peter. Following the construction of the church late in the reign of Constantine (306–337), Romans, pilgrims, and visiting dignitaries alike shuttled back and forth in growing numbers along the road, which again became a privileged focus of processional ceremony, traversed by bishops and rulers on their way to and from Saint Peter's.[8] The resuscitated processional route soon received an architectural face-lift, too, via a late fourth-century intervention that shows how integral street porticoes had become to the concept of the parade route in the Roman world. New flanking porticoes were built along the final stretch of the route leading up to the Ponte Sant'Angelo (the ancient Pons Aelius), the one remaining bridge connecting the northern Campus Martius with the Vatican.[9] At the same time, in ca. 380, a triumphal arch was installed on the bridgehead, with a dedicatory inscription proclaiming that it "concluded the whole work of the greatest porticoes," the *porticus maximae* that

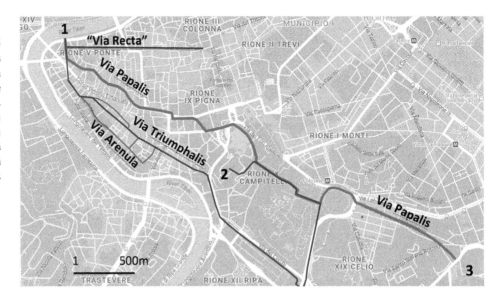

FIGURE 3.5

The Via Papalis
and other main
roads through the
Campus Martius.
1) Ponte Sant'Angelo;
2) Capitoline Hill;
and 3) Saint John
Lateran. Illustration
by Hendrik W. Dey.

evidently now stretched from the arch all the way back through the Campus Martius along the existing trunk of the Via Triumphalis (Figure 3.4).[10]

In Rome, as in many other prominent cities in the Roman world, substantial portions of this grand porticated avenue endured long after the dissolution of the Roman empire in the fifth century. As Rome contracted and crumbled during the early Middle Ages, the old Via Triumphalis remained notable for the scale of its surrounding monuments and the grandeur of its porticoes. Further, it continued to feature prominently in the ritual and liturgical life of the city. The late eighth-century Einsiedeln Itineraries show that it was still the preferred route for travelers going from Saint Peter's to the area of the Forum Holitorium and on to Rome's other great extramural shrine at Saint Paul's on the Via Ostiense; and it maintained much of its monumental cohesion: the porticoes lining the road all the way from the Theater of Pompey to the Circus Maximus (well beyond the site of the long-vanished Porta Triumphalis) feature prominently in the anonymous author's description of the route.[11] After three centuries of relative silence, the road was again described in detail in the liturgical handbook (*ordo*) compiled ca. 1143 by Benedict, a canon of Saint Peter's. His account of the grand papal procession to the Vatican on Christmas Eve traces the course of the old Triumphal Way all the way from Sant'Anastasia, by the Circus Maximus, as far as the Theater of Pompey, along a route still distinguished in places by porticoes, by surviving Roman temples, and by the looming hulks of the Theaters of Marcellus and Pompey.[12]

Almost immediately thereafter, however, it appears that the old Via Triumphalis was definitively abandoned by papal processions. Two liturgical itineraries compiled ca. 1190 that are longer and more detailed than Canon Benedict's make no mention of any continued ceremonial use of the route, neither on Christmas Eve nor at any other time of year.[13] By then, the papal processions that marked the most important occasions in Rome's ritual life, among them Christmas, Easter, and papal coronations, all returned from Saint Peter's via another road through the Campus Martius, so closely associated with papal ceremony that it took the name "Papal Way" (*via Pontificalis*, later also the *via Papalis* or *via Papae*) in the Middle Ages.

This route ran roughly parallel to the old one, only some 200–300 m to the north, all the way from the north slopes of the Capitoline Hill to the approaches to the Ponte Sant'Angelo, where it joined the final stretch of the old *porticus maximae* (Figure 3.5). It was already prominent by the time the Einsiedeln Itineraries were compiled toward the end of the eighth century, judging by the fact that two of the ten itineraries, and indeed two of the four itineraries that depart from the Ponte Sant'Angelo, proceed along it.[14] By the early eleventh century, it appears in writing as the "Papal Road";[15] and by the time of Benedict's *ordo*, ca. 1143, it already hosted papal processions on Christmas Day and Easter Monday, as well as the *possesso*, the ritual wherein a newly crowned pope returned from Saint Peter's to take official possession of his see at the Lateran Palace, processing before packed multitudes along a festively decorated itinerary spanned by dozens of temporary triumphal arches erected specially for each occasion (Figures 3.6 and 3.7).[16] By the end of the twelfth century, as noted above, this Via Papalis had, if anything, grown further in its ceremonial centrality, whereas the Via Triumphalis seems to have been wholly eclipsed in ritual terms.

Interestingly, the Via Papalis is not ancient.[17] No traces of Roman paving have turned up anywhere along its course, and it makes a series of meandering curves and sharp angles wholly uncharacteristic of main thoroughfares in the ancient Campus Martius. Further, there is no immediately apparent reason for its creation: it ran between the two main Roman roads through the Campus Martius (in addition to the Via Triumphalis, a straight street—the so-called Via Recta—ran directly west from the Vatican bridge to intersect with the Via Lata, the main route leading north out of the city), both of which remained in use throughout the Middle Ages and indeed up to the present day. It paralleled and essentially doubled the course of the Via Triumphalis, offering neither a shorter nor a more direct path from the Vatican bridge to the Capitoline Hill and the Forum beyond. It did not provide better access to especially important churches or other monuments, which, in fact, clustered more densely in the vicinity of the older road. It was often narrower than the older road, too, and its twists and turns made it slightly longer and still less practical as a parade route. Choke points at bends became so problematic during papal ceremonies that officials had to scatter coins at strategic points in order to relieve the press of people attending the *possesso* and the Easter Monday procession.[18]

Meanwhile, as of the mid-twelfth century, the Via Triumphalis remained a busy road and an equally direct connection between the Capitoline Hill/Forum and the Vatican. It also retained enough of its flanking colonnades, temples, and theaters to make it both obviously more ancient and more monumental than the Via Papalis. It had, moreover, the weight of tradition on its side: for well over a millennium, it had hosted various incarnations of Rome's most memorable and spectacular processional ceremonies.

The question, then, is why the medieval Papal Way supplanted the ancient Triumphal Way as the main processional avenue between the city center and the Vatican, replacing it entirely by the later twelfth century. What confluence of factors, environmental and human, conspired to make the Via Triumphalis less attractive as a locus of

FIGURE 3.6

Fresco, ca. 1240s, in the
St. Silvester Chapel at SS.
Quattro Coronati in Rome.
Emperor Constantine leads
Pope Silvester on horseback:
a legendary scene in the guise
of a thirteenth-century papal
procession. (When in Rome
on the occasion of a papal
coronation procession in the
later Middle Ages, the Holy
Roman Emperor served as
ceremonial papal groom,
or *strator*, for the mounted
pope in much the fashion
shown here.) Photograph
courtesy of Peter1936F /
Wikimedia Commons.

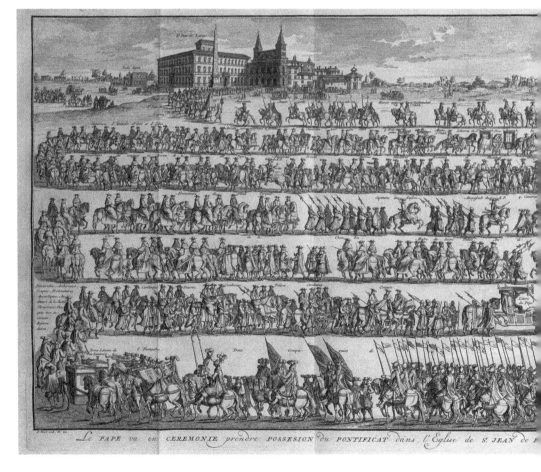

FIGURE 3.7

Coronation procession
(*possesso*) of Pope
Benedict XIII, from
St. Peter's to St. John
Lateran, in 1723. Engraving
by Bernard Picart, 1723.
Digital image courtesy
of the Getty's Open
Content Program.

processional ceremony, and prompted the creation of a new and apparently redundant medieval alternative?

Let it be said immediately that there are no definitive answers and probably no way of going about getting them, barring the future discovery of almost unimaginably rich archaeological and textual evidence. We can, however, consider some of the vast range of environmental, topographical, and social factors underlying the evolution of street networks in the Forum Holitorium and Campus Martius during the Middle Ages. The shift in processional itineraries is part and parcel of the story of the ways in which a medieval population of a few tens of thousands of people subsisted among the remains of the ancient world's largest and most populous city. By asking how and why the Via Triumphalis ceded processional pride of place to the Via Papalis, we may shed some light on the daunting choices that confronted human actors seeking to reconcile their narrow social, political, and ceremonial agendas with systemic changes in a vast urban landscape over which they exercised only limited control.

While the transformational moment that entailed the end of the Via Triumphalis as a processional artery apparently occurred in the twelfth century, the processes leading to that development have their roots much further back in the fifth and sixth centuries,

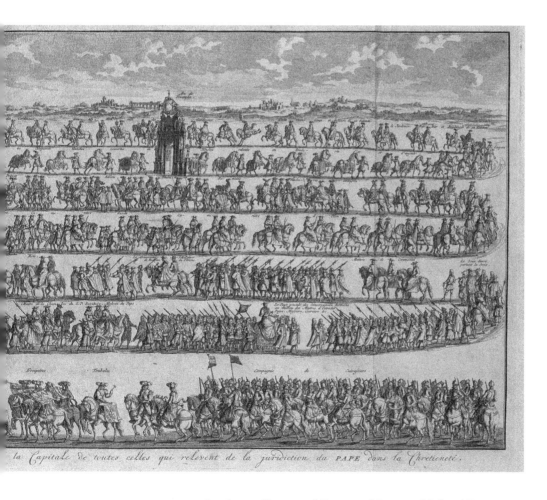

la Capitale de toutes celles qui relèvent de la jurisdiction du PAPE dans la Chretienté.

the period when "ancient" Rome disintegrated. The city in ca. 400 was still recognizably what it had been at the height of empire—its infrastructure and monuments still largely intact, its population still well over five hundred thousand. By 600, the population had declined by a full order of magnitude, to something like fifty thousand or less. With the disappearance of imperial patronage, as well as of the wealth and resources of a Mediterranean-wide empire that sustained that patronage, Rome's physical fabric declined accordingly; its inhabitants were simply too few to occupy and maintain most of what survived from antiquity.[19] All the same, life went on among the ruins and remains of imperial Rome. The material and conceptual legacy of Rome's glorious past, along with its growing importance as the hub of Latin Christianity, ensured that it survived and, in fact, remained the most populous city in Italy—even with only its few tens of thousands of inhabitants—during the early Middle Ages.

Those occupying the remains of ancient Rome confronted unique possibilities as well as challenges: rather like the survivors of catastrophe scenarios dear to modern dystopian fiction, they had considerable freedom to choose where to live and how to circulate among mostly deserted relics whose size and extent defied comprehension. Early medieval Romans faced especially acute problems and choices in the vicinity of the Via Triumphalis, and in the Campus Martius more generally, stemming from interactions between the natural environment and the built topography and infrastructure inherited from antiquity.[20]

In the Roman period as much as in the Middle Ages (and until the construction of the Tiber embankments in the late nineteenth century), Rome was frequently flooded. The lowest-lying areas along the river probably flooded every few years on average, and more traumatic events that submerged most or all of the area between the Capitoline Hill and the Vatican bridge, traversed by the Via Triumphalis and Via Papalis, may have occurred as often as once a decade.[21] From the fifth century on, the elaborate system of drains and sewers that had facilitated drainage and cleanup in the aftermath of floods gradually ceased to function, as numerous archaeologically attested instances of clogged pipes and sewers demonstrate.[22] Floodwater (and rainwater) lingered longer, and the filth and waste they left behind over vast expanses of the city defied the ability of Rome's remaining inhabitants to clean and remove. Along the Via Triumphalis, the Roman paving was submerged beneath slowly but steadily accumulating layers of riverine sediments, even as the road remained in use.[23]

The unusual concentration of monumental architecture (temples, porticoes, baths, theaters, and spectacle buildings) that occupied much of the Campus Martius presented a second challenge, likely to have been especially acute in the immediate vicinity of the Via Triumphalis. When such buildings partially or totally collapsed, as they often did during the early Middle Ages as a result of neglect, fires, and earthquakes alike, they created massive piles of rubble, many of which were never cleared. The monolithic columns that were the glory of so many Roman buildings, for example, were often too large or too damaged to be reused elsewhere, and those made of granite and other types of noncalcareous stone could not be reduced to lime, as so many ancient marbles were. The logistical difficulties of removing or even shifting column shafts that could be as long

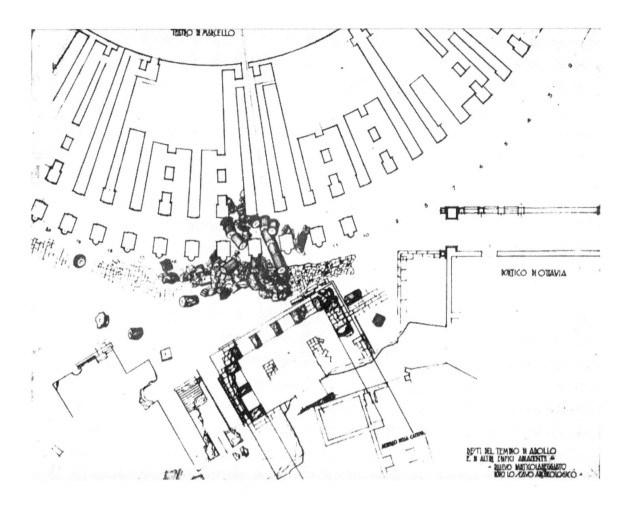

as fifty feet and weigh more than one hundred tons were such that their remains were often left where they fell, even when they fell across streets—narrow, constricted spaces that complicated the logistics of transport still more.[24] Excavations at the Theater of Marcellus, along the route of the Via Triumphalis by the Forum Holitorium, provide a representative example: at some point probably in the fifth or sixth century, almost certainly as the result of an earthquake (those of 443 and 508 are good candidates), the porch of the Temple of Apollo collapsed and several of its columns fell directly across the road. They were never removed. Instead, rubble mixed with alluvial mud accumulated (was piled up?) around them, allowing the road, raised to a higher level, to be rerouted over the fallen shafts (Figure 3.8).[25] By the time the Einsiedeln Itineraries were compiled near the end of the eighth century, and still more when Canon Benedict wrote his *ordo* ca. 1143, similar piles of rubble undoubtedly dotted the Campus Martius and encroached on many of its roads and alleyways.

Mud, dirt, and rubbish accumulated, putrid floodwater lingered, rubble piled up: these considerations may help to explain why the Via Papalis first emerged, by the eighth century, if not earlier, as an alternative to the Via Triumphalis. Although the Via Papalis was itself regularly inundated by major flooding events, it was farther from

FIGURE 3.8

Collapsed columns of the Temple of Apollo lying across the road and outer ambulatory of the Theater of Marcellus. Reproduced from Paolo Fidenzoni, *Il Teatro di Marcello* (Rome: Edizioni Liber, 1970), fig. 97.

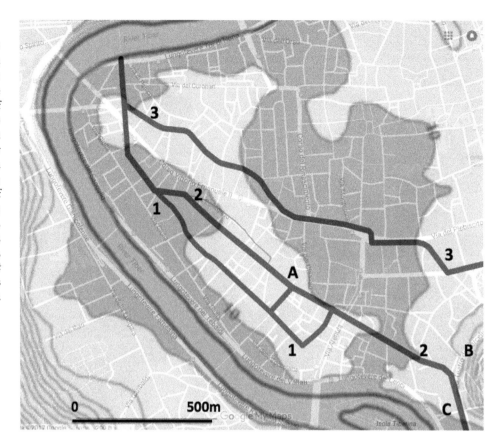

FIGURE 3.9

Main roads through the Campus Martius in the twelfth century. Darker-shaded portions indicate the approximate extent of areas inundated by a minor to moderate flooding event, with the Tiber River at approximately 12 meters above sea level. 1–1) Via Arenula; 2–2) Via Triumphalis; 3–3) Via Papalis; A) Theater of Pompey; B) Capitoline Hill; and C) Forum Holitorium. Illustration by Hendrik W. Dey, adapted from Gregory S. Aldrete, *Floods of the Tiber in Ancient Rome* (Baltimore: Johns Hopkins University Press, 2007), fig. I.7.

the Tiber, and thus somewhat less exposed to minor floods than the Via Triumphalis, whose route through the Forum Holitorium/Forum Boarium traversed a particularly low-lying area, situated moreover at a bend in the river that made it especially exposed to surging floodwater.[26] Also, as the Via Papalis did not directly abut as many towering Roman monuments as the Via Triumphalis, and was not flanked by extensive porticoes, it is less likely to have been seriously obstructed by fallen debris. According to Canon Benedict's *ordo*, in fact, by the early 1140s the papal Christmas Eve procession toward the Vatican departed from the trunk of the Via Triumphalis at or shortly before it reached the Theater of Pompey, where it turned left before again turning right onto the Via Arenula, the medieval name for another surviving Roman road that paralleled the Via Triumphalis just to the south, even closer to the Tiber (Figure 3.9).[27] Concerns with flooding clearly cannot explain the shift toward the river; partial obstruction of the ancient processional route remains as a possible motivation for the change.

In any case, it was only after Benedict's *ordo*, presumably in the period ca. 1140–90, that the popes definitively abandoned the Via Triumphalis in favor of the narrower, more winding, and less monumental Via Papalis. It bears stressing, however, that the Via Triumphalis itself did not disappear, and indeed continued to be frequented throughout the Middle Ages (and beyond). In the fourteenth and fifteenth centuries, it was among the busiest commercial streets in the city, and always remained a—or better,

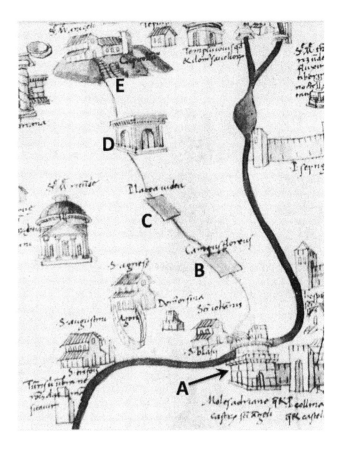

FIGURE 3.10

Detail of the Campus Martius in Pietro del Massaio's 1471 map of Rome. The one road shown closely approximates the course of the Via Triumphalis, from the Castel Sant'Angelo/Ponte Sant'Angelo (A) to the Capitoline Hill (E), via the Campo de' Fiori (B), Piazza Giudea (C), and the Porticus Octavia (D). Reproduced from Paolo A. Frutaz, *Le Piante di Roma* (Rome: Istituto di Studi Romani, 1962), 2:tav. 158.

the—principal route between the city center and the Vatican; in several fifteenth-century maps, it is, in fact, the only connection shown between the Ponte Sant'Angelo and the vicinity of Capitoline Hill (Figure 3.10). To explain why popes no longer processed even along the section between the Forum Holitorium and the Theater of Pompey, we need, therefore, to turn to the evolution of the cityscape in the twelfth century, a period when much of Rome, notably including the Forum Holitorium/Campus Martius, was profoundly transformed.

In broad terms, these transformations are the local manifestation of a wider trend common to much of Western Europe: the demographic and economic boom of the eleventh to thirteenth centuries, which resulted in a dramatic acceleration in the pace of urban life and urban development, nowhere more so than in central and northern Italy.[28] At Rome, it is precisely during the twelfth century that the most densely inhabited regions of the city center, including our area of focus in the southern Campus Martius, began to assume the contours so characteristic of later medieval cityscapes, with their continuous rows of closely packed housing crowding along narrow, winding streets.[29] Étienne Hubert's meticulous study of Roman property documents indicates that the pace of house building, along with the price of real estate and rents, began to increase dramatically from the 1120s, leading to a much denser settlement pattern in the most populous neighborhoods of the city. Whereas houses were previously scattered among gardens, orchards, vacant lots, and the crumbling hulks of ancient ruins, contiguous rows of town houses began to proliferate.[30] Thus, the skeleton of the ancient city was covered by new urban tissue that absorbed many of the landmarks, the processional routes, the urban armatures inherited from antiquity that in many cases—*faute de mieux*—had continued to define Rome's monumental and ceremonial horizons across the early Middle Ages.

These developments were especially pronounced in the sections of the Campus Martius traversed by the Via Triumphalis. Only from the eleventh and especially the twelfth centuries did this area start to become the densely inhabited nucleus of the city that it remained until the nineteenth century. Meanwhile, the expansive zone of hills in the eastern half of the old city walls, still widely if not densely inhabited in the early Middle Ages, became increasingly depopulated and often nearly indistinguishable from the surrounding countryside.[31] Various factors prompted most of Rome's growing population to settle near the Tiber. With the decay, after the ninth century, of all but one of the Roman aqueducts that had once served the inland portions of the city, proximity to the Tiber became more important than ever.[32] The water-powered gristmills that Romans depended on for their daily bread clustered along the riverbanks,[33] as of course did the city's ports, and thus also its principal markets, as we will see. Further, with the rise of the Gregorian Reform papacy from the mid-eleventh century, the wealth and international prestige of the Roman church increased considerably, along with the influx of pilgrims and other distinguished visitors from afar; pilgrims and clerics alike clustered in the neighborhood or *borgo* between Saint Peter's and the Castel Sant'Angelo, making residence in the Campus Martius just across the Ponte Sant'Angelo a more attractive proposition for local merchants, craftsmen, and hostlers, despite the regular flooding of the area.[34] Last but not least, the city's nascent communal government, proclaimed in 1143/44, established itself atop the Capitoline Hill, just above the Forum Holitorium and the initial stretch of the Via Triumphalis.[35]

Yet it was the bones of the ancient city that made the Via Triumphalis, more than any other street, the hub of the bustling quarter that the southern Campus Martius near the river became. By the twelfth century, the urban segment of the Tiber could only be crossed on three surviving Roman bridges, which thus took on an importance more akin to geographical than built features, like fords or mountain passes that channeled all movement of people and goods. In addition to the Ponte Sant'Angelo in the north, there were two crossings downstream to the south, located only about 250 m apart, which both debouched into the old Forum Holitorium and the adjacent Forum Boarium, called in the Middle Ages the Ripa Graeca for the Greek-speaking merchants and tradesmen associated with the area. These were Pons Aemilius, called the *pons maior* in the Middle Ages, and the road that traversed the Tiber Island via the Roman Pons Cestius and Pons Fabricius.[36]

Rome's main river port in the Middle Ages was the Ripa Romea, located on the far (right) bank of the Tiber in southern Trastevere, not far south of the two southern river crossings. Goods that reached Rome by sea were unloaded there and then transported into the city across the Pons Cestius/Fabricius and, especially, the Pons Maior;

the roads from both bridgeheads ran straight into the Via Triumphalis, near the Theater of Marcellus. The area between the bridgeheads and the Capitoline Hill had been a commercial entrepôt since Roman times, but again became a much busier and more crowded place from the twelfth century as Rome's resident population, its throngs of visitors, and its economy all steadily grew. This area also hosted the city's main Saturday market, which flourished after the Capitoline became the seat of communal government in the 1140s, making the region the political as well as the economic hub of the Roman commune.[37]

Three other important markets straddled the course of the Via Triumphalis itself: moving northwest toward the Ponte Sant'Angelo, these were the fish market at Sant'Angelo in Pescheria, essentially an extension of the commercial zone between the river and the Capitoline;[38] the Piazza Giudea, which in the twelfth century developed into the heart of Rome's Jewish community, previously concentrated across the river in Trastevere;[39] and the Campo de' Fiori, where horses as well as sundries were sold.[40] Still more market stalls and shops clustered along the approaches to the Ponte Sant'Angelo, just upstream of which stretched Rome's other principal port, the Ripetta, where goods shipped downriver from northern Lazio and Umbria were unloaded.[41] By the later twelfth century, then, the Via Triumphalis was the principal artery that joined all three remaining river crossings with the city's two main ports, all bustling with steadily increasing levels of activity. It was well on its way to becoming the busiest, most crowded, most stinking commercial street in the city, the route known by the fourteenth century simply as the *via mercatoria*—the market street (Figure 3.11).[42]

Had the popes of the later twelfth century attempted to follow Canon Benedict's instructions for the Christmas Eve procession from Sant'Anastasia, they would first have traversed the southern edge of the marketplace beneath the Capitoline, before arriving at the arcades of the Theater of Marcellus, which were occupied by the stalls of butchers.[43] Just beyond was the fish market at Sant'Angelo in Pescheria, which spilled across the road itself. From there, the parade would have bisected the new Jewish quarter, itself a thriving commercial district centered on the Piazza Giudea marketplace, before moving on to Campo de' Fiori, with its stables (and dung heaps), and then, finally, along the approaches to the Ponte Sant'Angelo, surrounded by still more stalls of butchers and fishmongers, merchants and craftsmen, and traders in sundry goods.

The conditions of the road in this initial period of Rome's medieval thriving can only be imagined: shop fronts and stalls that inexorably encroached on the roadway, leaving only a narrow path along which all traffic had to pass; dung from the beasts of burden that traversed it; rancid meat, fish, offal, and leavings from the other staples sold in the marketplaces along its course; waste and detritus from workshops, all mixed with the mud and filth periodically deposited—almost yearly, in some parts of the route—by flooding. The situation was probably especially grave in the later twelfth century, as municipal efforts to regulate the chaos and moderate the filth were slow to develop, and never very effective. The first mention of the *magistri aedificiorum*, the city officials tasked with keeping main streets clean and clear of obstacles, occurs in 1227, after a century of largely unchecked, unregulated demographic and commercial expansion.[44]

Landscape Change and Ceremonial Praxis in Medieval Rome   77

FIGURE 3.11
The Via Triumphalis/
via mercatoria in the
thirteenth through
fifteenth centuries:
infrastructure and
commercial spaces.
Illustration by
Hendrik W. Dey.

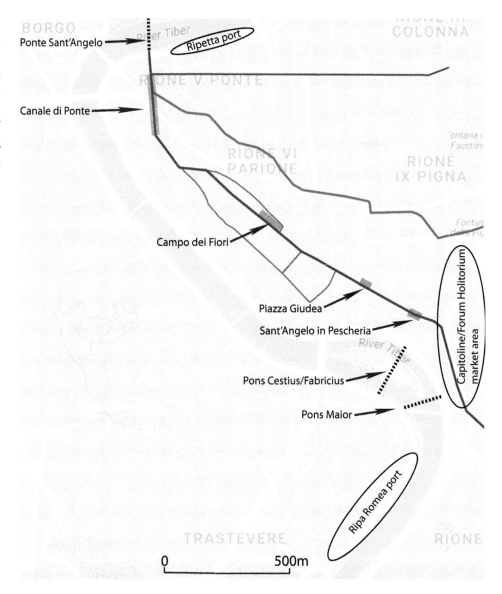

FIGURE 3.11 The Via Triumphalis/*via mercatoria* in the thirteenth through fifteenth centuries: infrastructure and commercial spaces. Illustration by Hendrik W. Dey.

The real work of turning the street back into an urban thoroughfare worthy of its name was left to popes of the later fifteenth century, Nicholas V (1447–1455) and Sixtus IV (1471–1484), who intervened radically to widen and clean it, removing the stalls and buildings that spilled out from the porticoes of the ancient *porticus maximae*, whose remains were also demolished at the time.[45]

It is understandable, then, why popes and papal officials by the mid-twelfth century might have been increasingly reluctant to direct solemn processions along the Via Triumphalis/*via mercatoria* on Christmas Eve or any other occasion, especially since an established and viable ceremonial alternative, the Via Papalis, traversed essentially the same region between the Capitoline and the Ponte Sant'Angelo. Further, there is evidence of an ambitious program of urban development undertaken on papal initiative

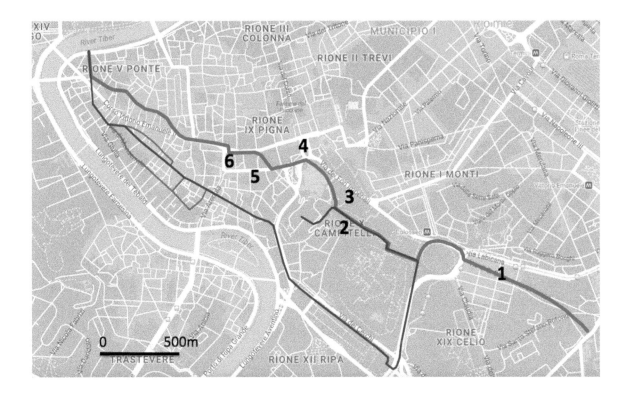

during the first half of the twelfth century that likely served, among other things, to improve the Via Papalis and enhance its capacity to host the most important processions that traversed the Campus Martius on the way to and from Saint Peter's.

Federico Guidobaldi has recently called attention to a sudden, very substantial rise in ground levels at widely scattered points across the city center that apparently began in earnest early in the twelfth century, during the long pontificate of Paschal II (1099–1118). From Largo Argentina and the Via delle Botteghe Oscure/Crypta Balbi in the west, across modern Piazza Venezia and the Forum, and on to San Clemente in the east, sudden and surprising increases of several meters plausibly or certainly occurred from the end of the eleventh century to the middle of the twelfth, in areas where levels had previously risen little since Late Antiquity.[46] Guidobaldi discusses a number of other places where similar increases occurred, but sites in the five locales in question represent over half of the examples he provides, whence it is the more remarkable that all five areas are located in the immediate vicinity of the Via Papalis, the first two along the section in the Campus Martius that parallels the Via Triumphalis, and the remaining three along the part of the route that extended to the Lateran Cathedral, the other principal pole (along with Saint Peter's) of the Easter and coronation processions, and many other processions besides (Figure 3.12).[47]

The precipitous rise in levels within, apparently, the span of a few decades or at most a few generations suggests that for some areas of the city, it may be necessary to substantially revise the traditional conception of Rome's rising ground levels as an incremental process, according to which trash, rubble, and waterborne sediment steadily and

FIGURE 3.12

Twelfth-century infill/ground-level rise in the vicinity of the Via Papalis. 1) San Clemente; 2) Roman Forum (Santi Quaranta Martiri, etc.); 3) Forum of Nerva; 4) Piazza Venezia; 5) Crypta Balbi/ Via delle Botteghe Oscure; and 6) Largo Argentina (San Nicola de Calcarari). Illustration by Hendrik W. Dey.

Landscape Change and Ceremonial Praxis in Medieval Rome   79

relatively uniformly accumulated across the centuries.[48] The best explanation for the creation of such unusually thick layers of fill within such a short span of years is intentional deposition, presumably accomplished with material obtained by razing and/or leveling the ruins of the ancient structures that undoubtedly still occupied much of the ancient city center.[49] The twelfth century apparently witnessed a coordinated effort to transform large swaths of the cityscape by rebuilding them well above the remains of the ancient city. For Guidobaldi, one primary purpose of this ambitious stab at urban remodeling was the creation of new and/or improved streets, among them the processional route between the Vatican and the Lateran, both drier than their predecessors and unencumbered by the massive piles of ancient rubble that littered the city and obstructed circulation.[50] At Largo Argentina, the Crypta Balbi, and Piazza Venezia, in particular, an additional 3 m of elevation would certainly have reduced, albeit not eliminated, the susceptibility of this low-lying portion of the Via Papalis to flooding.[51]

Recent excavations beneath the modern Via delle Botteghe Oscure, at the Crypta Balbi, open an especially revealing window onto the reconditioning of the environs of the Papal Way in the first half of the twelfth century. A long (more than 60 m) stretch along the south flank of the road was revealed in the early 2000s; meticulous stratigraphical analysis leaves no doubt about the thickness of the fill (approximately 2.6 m), its continuous extension over the full sweep of the area investigated, and its dating around the beginning of the twelfth century.[52] It is notable that the fill was evidently—intentionally—deposited in the immediate vicinity of the street itself, leaving the area farther removed from the road, to the south, at its original ground level.[53] A new row of contiguous housing typical of Rome's expanding twelfth-century residential fabric was then constructed along the raised strip of ground facing the street.[54] We see here, with unusual clarity, the creation of a new and distinctly medieval neighborhood, erected over and substantially divorced from the contours of the ancient (and early medieval) city below.

The short section of the Via Lata uncovered recently at Piazza Venezia, near the point where it intersected the Via Papalis, evolved in like manner in the later twelfth century: the roadbed was raised, and rows of new houses closely flanked it on both sides.[55] The twelfth-century increases in the level of the street appear more remarkable and anomalous in light of the fact that its level remained almost unchanged for centuries thereafter—nineteenth-century levels are only some 50 cm higher than those of the thirteenth (Figure 3.13).[56] At the Crypta Balbi, meanwhile, the Via delle Botteghe Oscure remains at almost exactly the level it reached by the thirteenth century. In both places, and undoubtedly others besides, we are evidently dealing with a concerted program of ground-scaping, the product not of gradual and aleatory processes, but rather of intense, focused human activity that imparted to the ground the contours it largely retains up to the present.

It is also noteworthy that none of the really dramatic examples of rapid and sudden infilling occurred along the Via Triumphalis, substantial portions of which have been investigated at various times. While ground levels along its course also rose above their ancient/early medieval levels, recurrent flooding along with the gradual deposition of dirt and rubbish—the old model of ground-level rise—likely do account for much

Post-medieval fill

12th/early
13th-c. layers

FIGURE 3.13

The Via Lata at Piazza
Venezia. Reproduced
from Serlorenzi,
"Le testimonianze
medievali nei cantieri
di Piazza Venezia,"
fig. 36.

or all of the increase. There is good evidence that levels at the Theater of Marcellus, for
example, were rising steadily over the course of the early Middle Ages, largely as a result
of accumulating alluvial sediment.[57] Levels also rose less suddenly and dramatically
than in Guidobaldi's case studies at the Porticus Octaviae and Sant'Angelo in Pescheria,
where the increase was only about 1 m from the eleventh to the thirteenth century.[58]
Further, the floors of the several older churches situated near this part of the Via
Triumphalis that were restored or rebuilt in the first half of the twelfth century (among
them Sant'Angelo itself, San Nicola in Carcere, Santo Stefano Rotondo, Santa Maria
in Cosmedin, and Sant'Anastasia, the starting point of Canon Benedict's Christmas
Eve procession) were not elevated anywhere near the 3–5 m characteristic of contem-
porary churches built atop the thickest strata of artificial fill (such as San Crisogono,
San Clemente, and Santa Maria in Via Lata).[59] The best conclusion is that while the
Via Papalis was artificially elevated in the early twelfth century, the Via Triumphalis
was not.

I suspect that even if Pope Paschal II and his immediate successors had wished to
transform and elevate the Via Triumphalis in the manner of the Via Papalis, they would
have found it impractical to do so, precisely because so much of its course was so densely
settled, so commercially vibrant, and so full of well-preserved ancient monuments that
were still occupied and still defined the contours of the road. In both financial and
human terms, the cost of submerging the Roman monuments, as well as the teeming
residential and commercial neighborhoods that surrounded and occupied them, would
have been prohibitive. Along the less densely settled and less monumental course of the
Via Papalis, on the other hand, popes had the chance to radically remodel the environs
of the existing street: to raze the decrepit remains of the old, to elevate the roadbed, and
to prepare the ground for the construction of new structures alongside it. They might
not have wished to restructure the Via Triumphalis, even if it had been feasible to do

so. By leaving it to continue its chaotic, damp, putrid transformation into the *via mercatoria*, they helped ensure that its mercantile reek and polyethnic bustle stayed where they were, a safe distance from the new road where they intended to process in majesty.

In sum: all indications point to the twelfth century as the crucial moment of change, the period when a denser, more compact nucleus of settlement centered on the southern Campus Martius began to supplant the diffuse, sparsely inhabited sprawl inherited from the early Middle Ages. Until then, as the Einsiedeln Itineraries and Benedict's Christmas Eve *ordo* show, the Via Triumphalis retained something of its ancient monumentality and its ceremonial functions, preserving a glimmer of late Roman urban grandeur and ceremonial praxis across the early Middle Ages until the economic and demographic resurgence of the eleventh to thirteenth centuries transformed it almost beyond recognition.[60] As Rome's swelling population collected in the Tiber floodplain from the twelfth century on, chiefly in the strip of the Campus Martius bracketed at its southeastern and northwestern extremities by the city's three surviving bridge crossings, the ancient street that connected those bridges, along with medieval Rome's two principal ports, gradually and organically transformed into an almost unbroken sequence of shops, workshops, and marketplaces. Gradually and organically: neither the popes nor, after 1143/44, Rome's communal authorities intervened to prevent merchants and craftsmen from crowding the road best suited, by virtue of natural topography and the selective survival of ancient infrastructure, for the transport and distribution of foodstuffs, raw materials, and finished goods.

Yet around the same time, in the early twelfth century, the popes launched the most profound anthropogenic reshaping of the cityscape attempted since antiquity. By raising ground levels at widely scattered locations (even if not all examples are as well documented and narrowly dated as the Via delle Botteghe Oscure/Crypta Balbi and the Piazza Venezia), they transformed parts of an early medieval road that had itself grown up gradually and organically among the mostly deserted expanse of the central Campus Martius, rendering it more suitable—higher, dryer, and less encumbered by rubble—for papal processions, including those that the Via Triumphalis no longer hosted. Here, too, however, the vestiges of the ancient city conditioned the change and informed the evolving parameters of human activity: the selective leveling and filling of damp, flood-prone depressions was made possible, and indeed desirable, by the sweep of rubble and abandoned buildings that filled much of Rome's intramural area by the twelfth century, including much of the route traversed by the Via Papalis.

Notes

1 For population estimates, see Jean Durliat, *De la ville antique à la ville Byzantine: Le problème des subsistances* (Rome: École française de Rome, 1990), 116; Elio Lo Cascio, "Le procedure di *recensus* dalla tarda reppublica al tardo antico e il calcolo della popolazione di Roma," in *La Rome imperial: Démographie et logistique; Actes de la table ronde (Rome, 25 mars 1994)* (Rome: École française de Rome, 1997), 3–76; and Nicholas Purcell, "The Populace of Rome in Late Antiquity: Problems of Description and Historical Classification," in *The Transformations of* Urbs Roma *in Late Antiquity*, ed. William Harris (Portsmouth, R.I.: Journal of Roman Archaeology, 1999), 135–61. For the Aurelian Wall, see Hendrik W. Dey, *The Aurelian Wall and the Refashioning of Imperial Rome, AD 271–855* (Cambridge: Cambridge University Press, 2011).

2 On the origins, course, and architectural evolution of this route, see Ferdinando Castagnoli, "Il Campo Marzio nell'antichità," *Memorie/Classe di scienze morali, storiche e filologiche* 8, no. 1 (1947):156; Filippo Coarelli, "Il campo Marzio occidentale: Storia e topografia," *Mélanges de l'École française de Rome, Antiquité* 89 (1977):807–46; Filippo Coarelli, *Il Campo Marzio dalle origini alla fine della repubblica* (Rome: Edizioni Quasar, 1997), 118–35; Eugenio La Rocca, *La riva a mezzaluna: Culti, agoni, monumenti funerari presso il Tevere nel Campo Marzio occidentale* (Rome: L'Erma di Bretschneider, 1984), 65–67; Eugenio La Rocca, "La processione trionfale come spettacolo per il popolo romano: Trionfi antichi, spettacoli moderni," in *Trionfi romani*, ed. Eugenio La Rocca and Stefano Tortorella (Milan: Electa, 2008), 34–55; and Maggie L. Popkin, *The Architecture of the Roman Triumph: Monuments, Memory, and Identity* (Cambridge: Cambridge University Press, 2016).

3 On the location of the republican and early imperial Porta Triumphalis, and its association with the Via Triumphalis, see Filippo Coarelli, *Il Foro Boario: Dalle origini alla fine della repubblica* (Rome: Edizioni Quasar, 1988), 363–414; and Paolo Liverani, "*Porta Triumphalis, arcus Domitiani, templum Fortunae Reducis*, arco di Portogallo," *Atlante tematico di topografia antica* 14 (2005):53–65. Regarding the name of the road across the river, several second-century CE inscriptions (*Corpus Inscriptionum Latinarum* 6, 1511 and 1512; *Corpus Inscriptionum Latinarum* 14, 3610) mention a *curator* jointly responsible for the Viae Aurelia (*nova* and *veteris*), Cornelia, and Triumphalis, all located in close proximity on the right bank of the Tiber in the *ager vaticanus*; on the identification and surviving traces of these various roads, see Paolo Liverani, *La topografia antica del Vaticano* (Vatican City: Biblioteca Apostolica Vaticana, 1999), 34–40; see also Ferdinando Castagnoli, *Il Vaticano nell'antichità classica* (Vatican City: Biblioteca Apostolica Vaticana, 1992), 29–34. Based on the presumed locations of the Porta Triumphalis and the crossing of the Tiber, the length of the intervening section is approximately 1.8 kilometers. I would not hesitate to apply the name also to the intramural extension of the road that led through the Circus Maximus, around the Palatine Hill, and through the Roman Forum to its conclusion on the Capitoline Hill, but this point need not concern us here.

4 On all these monuments, see Popkin, *Architecture of the Roman Triumph*; Coarelli, *Il Campo Marzio dalle origini alla fine della repubblica*; and Coarelli, *Il Foro Boario*.

5 For remains of these colonnades and porticoes uncovered along the route in the Campus Martius, in correspondence with the modern Vie dei Cappellari (between Vie Montoro and Vicolo del Gallo), dei Giubbonari (by San Carlo ai Catinari), di Santa Maria del Pianto, and del Portico d'Ottavia (between Vie della Reginella and di Sant'Ambrogio), see Rodolfo Lanciani, "I portici della regione IX," *Annali dell'Instituto di Corrispondenza archeologica* 55 (1883):20–21; Rodolfo Lanciani, "L'Itinerario di Einsiedeln e l'Ordine di Benedetto Canonico," *Monumenti Antichi Reale Accademia dei Lincei* 1 (1891):cols. 509–10 (the sections of colonnade known to Lanciani also appear at *Forma urbis Romae* tavv. 20–21); Guglielmo Gatti in *Bullettino della Commissione archeologica comunale di Roma* 39 (1911):87–88; and (less certainly) Edoardo Gatti in *Notizie degli scavi di Antichità* (1923):247–48. For porticoes in the Forum Holitorium, see Patrizio Pensabene, "Il 'Portichetto' tuscanico presso il tempio di Bellona e la 'Via Trionfale,'" *Bullettino della Commissione archeologica comunale di Roma* 112 (2011). Arcaded porticoes may already have been a distinguishing feature of this street by the middle Roman Republic, if Livy's *via fornicata quae ad campum erat* (22.36.8) refers to it.

6 Both points are made by recent, revisionist scholars who have sought to modify or challenge the concept of a single Via Triumphalis (e.g., Mary Beard, *The Roman Triumph* [Cambridge, Mass.: Harvard University Press, 2007], 95–102; Claudine Auliard, "La composition du cortège triomphal

dans les rues de Rome: La marque des triomphateurs," in *La rue dans l'antiquité: Définition, aménagement et devenir de l'Orient méditerranéen à la Gaule*, ed. Paschal Ballet, Nadine Dieudonné-Glad, and Catherine Saliou [Rennes: Presses Universitaires de Rennes, 2008], 69–75; Carsten Hjort Lange, review of *The Architecture of the Roman Triumph: Monuments, Memory, and Identity*, by Maggie L. Popkin, *Bryn Mawr Classical Review* 2017.1.39 [2017]); they have successfully brought nuance to the picture, but a primary ceremonial and monumental axis centered on the Via Triumphalis remains, to my mind, beyond doubt.

7   On the proliferation of such streets from the first to sixth century CE, see Giorgio Bejor, *Vie colonnate: Paesaggi urbani del mondo antico* (Rome: L'Erma di Bretschneider, 1999); and Hendrik W. Dey, *The Afterlife of the Roman City: Architecture and Ceremony in Late Antiquity and the Early Middle Ages* (Cambridge: Cambridge University Press, 2015).

8   Augusto Fraschetti, *La conversione: Da Roma pagana a Roma Cristiana* (Rome: Editori Laterza, 1999), 243–69; Augusto Fraschetti, "Dal Campidoglio alla basilica di San Pietro: Aspetti del paesaggio urbano a Roma in epoca tardoantica," in *Arte e iconografia e Roma: Dal tardoantico alla fine del Medioevo*, ed. Maria Andaloro and Serena Romano (Milan: Jaca Book, 2002), 20–22; Paolo Liverani, "Dal trionfo pagano all'adventus cristiano: Percorsi della Roma imperiale," *Anales de arqueología cordobesa* 18 (2007):385–400; and Paolo Liverani, "Interventi urbani a Roma tra il IV e il VI secolo," *Cristianesimo nella storia* 29, no. 1 (2009):12–16.

9   Since the mid-first century CE, the Via Triumphalis had crossed the Tiber on the Pons Neronianus, the bridge built by Nero (r. 54–68 CE). Soon after the building of the Aurelian Wall (ca. 271–280 CE), this bridge ceased to function, causing traffic along the road to be diverted north to cross the river via the narrower bridge originally built to connect the city center with Hadrian's mausoleum (now Castel Sant'Angelo); see Dey, *Aurelian Wall and the Refashioning of Imperial Rome*, 174–80, 304–6.

10   Dey, *Aurelian Wall and the Refashioning of Imperial Rome*, 174–80; the inscription (*Corpus Inscriptionum Latinarum* 6, 1184) reads: *Imperatores caesares ddd nnn Gratianus Valentinianus et Theodosius pii felices semper Auggg arcum ad concludendum opus omne porticuum maximarum aeterni nominis sui pecunia propria fieri ornariq. iusserunt.*

11   See Gerold Walser, *Die Einsiedler Inschriftensammlung und der Pilgerführer durch Rom (Codex Einsiedlensis 326)* (Stuttgart: Franz Steiner Verlag, 1987), 205, with Lanciani, "L'Itinerario di Einsiedeln," cols. 509–16. The so-called Einsiedeln Itineraries comprise a series of guided walks through Rome, all beginning or ending with one of the city gates, probably compiled in the 760s and then included in a ninth-century compilation found in the library of the monastery of Saint Gall in Switzerland. For an overview of the text and the discussions surrounding it, see Donatella Bellardini and Paolo Delogu, "Liber Pontificalis e altre fonti: La topografia di Roma nell'VIII secolo," in *Atti del colloquio internazionale il Liber Pontificalis e la storia materiale (Roma, 21–22 febbraio 2002)*, ed. Herman Geertman (Assen: Van Gorcum, 2003), 205–24. It survives in a ninth-century manuscript (*Codex Einsiedlensis 326*) first published by Mabillon in 1685, who christened it the *Itinerarium Einsiedlense*. Modern editions include Roberto Valentini and Giuseppe Zucchetti, *Codice topografico della città di Roma*, 4 vols. (Rome: Tipografia del Senato, 1940–53), 2:155–207; Walser, *Die Einsiedler Inschriftensammlung*, with good photographs of the whole manuscript; and Stefano Del Lungo, *Roma in età Carolingia e gli scritti dell'Anonimo augiense* (Rome: Società romana di storia patria, 2004), 23–76. Here and throughout, I use Walser's numbering of the itineraries.

12   Lanciani, "L'Itinerario di Einsiedeln," cols. 519–23. The *ordo* with the detailed description of the triumphal route is included in Benedict's *Liber Politicus*, a sort of liturgical handbook. It is published in Paul Fabre and Louis Duchesne, *Le Liber Censuum de l'Église romaine*, 3 vols. (Paris: A. Fontemoing, 1910), 2:139–77; for the route of the Christmas Eve procession, see p. 145.

13   These are the *Gesta pauperis scholaris* of Cardinal Albinus, of 1189 (Fabre and Duchesne, *Le Liber Censuum*, 2:87–137), and the *Ordo Romanus* of Cencius Camerarius, of 1192 (Fabre and Duchesne, *Le Liber Censuum*, 1:290–316).

14   The two itineraries are 1: *a porta sci Petri usque ad scam luciam in orthea* (Walser, *Die Einsiedler Inschriftensammlung*, 162–67) and 8: *a porta sci Petri usque porta asinaria* (Walser, *Die Einsiedler Inschriftensammlung*, 189–96).

15 *Regestum Farfense* 506 (anno 1017); see Ignazio Giorgi and Ugo Balzani, *Il Regesto di Farfa*, 5 vols. (Rome: Società romana di storia patria, 1879–1914), 3:217: *... per uiam communem quae est pergens ad uiam pontificalem euntium ad beatum petrum apostolum.*

16 Christmas Eve: Fabre and Duchesne, *Le Liber Censuum*, 2:145; Easter Monday: Fabre and Duchesne, *Le Liber Censuum*, 2:154. The temporary arches and the route of the *possesso* are described in most detail in the *Ordo Romanus* of Cencius Camerarius, chapters 39 and 58: see Fabre and Duchesne, *Le Liber Censuum*, 1:299 and 1:311–13, respectively; cf. Bernhard Schimmelpfennig, "Die Krönung des Papstes im Mittelalter dargestellt am Beispiel der Krönung Pius' II. (3. 9. 1458)," *Quellen und Forschungen aus Italienischen Archiven und Bibliotheken* 54 (1974):231–38; Bernhard Schimmelpfennig, "Die Bedeutung Roms im päpstlichen Zeremoniell," in *Rom im hohen Mittelalter. Studien zu den Romvorstellungen und zur Rompolitik vom 10. bis 12. Jahrhundert*, ed. Bernhard Schimmelpfennig and Ludwig Schmugge (Sigmarigen: Thorbecke, 1992), 47–61; and Chris Wickham, *Medieval Rome: Stability and Crisis of a City, 900–1150* (Oxford: Oxford University Press, 2015), 328–29.

17 Massimo Pentiricci, "La posizione della basilica di San Lorenzo in Damaso nell'Itinerario di Einsiedeln," in *Architectural Studies in Memory of Richard Krautheimer*, ed. Cecil L. Striker (Mainz: Philipp von Zabern, 1996), 127–31.

18 Cencius Camerarius, *Ordo Romanus*, chapter 39 (Fabre and Duchesne, *Le Liber Censuum*, 1:299).

19 Contributing factors to the process of rapid depopulation include the end of Rome's integrated Mediterranean economy and the imports of subsidized staples that had fed its massive population; political instability attending the end of the western empire (and thus also of Rome's role as imperial capital); wars and invasions; and famine and plague. For an overview of Rome's urban trajectory in this period, see Paolo Delogu, "Il passaggio dall'antichità al Medioevo," in *Storia di Roma dall'antichità a oggi: Roma medievale*, ed. André Vauchez (Rome: Editori Laterza, 2001), 3–40; Roberto Meneghini and Riccardo Santangeli Valenzani, *Roma nell'altomedioevo: Topografia e urbanistica della città dal V al X secolo* (Rome: Istituto poligrafico e Zecca dello Stato, 2004), 21–27 (population figures at p. 23); and Lucrezia Spera, "Roma, gli imperatori e i barbari nel V secolo," in *Potere e politica nell'età della famiglia teodosiana (395–455)*, ed. Isabella Baldini and Salvatore Cosentino (Bari: Edipuglia, 2013), 163–93.

20 On the Forum Holitorium and Campus Martius in the early Middle Ages, see Meneghini and Santangeli Valenzani, *Roma nell'altomedioevo*, 194–206; and Lucrezia Spera, "Trasformazioni e riassetti del tessuto urbano nel Campo Marzio centrale tra tarda antichità e medioevo," *Mélanges de l'École française de Rome, Moyen Âge* 126, no. 1 (2014):47–74.

21 No comprehensive study of medieval-era flooding exists; for flooding in ancient Rome, see Joël Le Gall, *Le Tibre, fleuve de Rome, dans l'antiquité* (Paris: Presses universitaires de France, 1953); and especially Gregory S. Aldrete, *Floods of the Tiber in Ancient Rome* (Baltimore: Johns Hopkins University Press, 2007).

22 Various examples in Fedora Filippi, "Nuovi dati da Campo Marzio e Trastevere," in *The Sack of Rome in 410 AD: The Event, Its Context and Its Impact*, ed. Johannes Lipps, Carlos Machado, and Philipp von Rummel (Wiesbaden: Reichert Verlag, 2013), 137–50; and Mirella Serlorenzi, "Le testimonianze medievali nei cantieri di Piazza Venezia," in *Archeologia e infrastrutture. I; Tracciato fondamentale della linea C della Metropolitana di Roma: Prime indagini archeologiche*, ed. Roberto Egidi, Fedora Filippi, and Sonia Martone (Rome: Ministero per i Beni culturali e ambientali, 2010), 135.

23 See below at nn. 56–57.

24 Federico Guidobaldi, "Un estesissimo intervento urbanistico nella Roma dell'inizio del XII secolo e la parziale perdita della 'memoria topografica' della città antica," *Mélanges de l'École française de Rome, Moyen Âge* 126, no. 2 (2014):599–601.

25 Paolo Fidenzoni, *Il Teatro di Marcello* (Rome: Edizioni Liber, 1970), 73–74, 160–61; Giuseppe Marchetti Longhi, "Il Mons Fabiorum: Note di topografia medioevale di Roma," *Archivio della Società Romana di Storia Patria* 99 (1976):18–19; and Paolo A. C. Galli and Diego Molin, "Beyond the Damage Threshold: The Historic Earthquakes of Rome," *Journal of Earthquake Engineering* 10, no. 6 (2012):section 2.4.

26 Cf. Aldrete, *Floods of the Tiber in Ancient Rome*, 35. The broad contours of Aldrete's hydrological maps of the Campus Martius in the first century (39–49) remain applicable to the situation in the Middle Ages, too, as the increase in early medieval ground levels across the area was slow and fairly uniform.

27 Fabre and Duchesne, *Le Liber Censuum*, 2:145: *deinde vadit juxta porticum Severinum, et transiens ante templum Craticule et ante insulam Militenam et drachonariorum. Et sic sinistra manu descendit at majorem viam Arenule . . .*

28 For a recent, succinct synthesis on north-central Italy, see Étienne Hubert, "Urbanizzazione, immigrazione e cittadinanza (XII–metà XIV secolo). Alcune considerazioni generali," in *La costruzione della città comunale italiana (secoli XII–inizio XIV)* (Pistoia: Centro italiano di studi di storia e d'arte, 2009), 131–45.

29 Étienne Hubert, *Espace urbain et habitat à Rome du X siècle à la fin du XIII siècle* (Rome: École française de Rome, 1990), 142–47; and Wickham, *Medieval Rome*, 158.

30 Hubert, *Espace urbain et habitat à Rome du X siècle à la fin du XIII siècle*, 134–41. For the more scattered pattern of settlement before the eleventh to twelfth centuries, see Robert Coates-Stephens, "Housing in Early Medieval Rome AD 500–1000," *Papers of the British School at Rome* 64 (1996):239–60; and Meneghini and Santangeli Valenzani, *Roma nell'altomedievo*, 31–48.

31 Hubert, *Espace urbain et habitat à Rome du X siècle à la fin du XIII siècle*, 74–96.

32 On the final repairs to Rome's aqueducts in the ninth century and their progressive decrepitude thereafter, see Robert Coates-Stephens, "Le ricostruzioni altomedievali delle Mura Aureliane e degli acquedotti," *Mélanges de l'École française de Rome, Moyen Âge* 111, no. 1 (1999):215–24; Robert Coates-Stephens, "The Water-Supply of Early Medieval Rome," *Acta Instituti Romani Finlandiae* 31 (2003):81–113; and Meneghini and Santangeli Valenzani, *Roma nell'altomedieovo*, 65–69.

33 Paolo Squatriti, *Water and Society in Early Medieval Italy* (Cambridge: Cambridge University Press, 1998), 126–59; and Meneghini and Santangeli Valenzani, *Roma nell'altomedievo*, 129–32. Ancient Romans were less dependent on the Tiber to power gristmills, as many mills were powered by aqueducts.

34 See generally Paolo Brezzi, *Roma e l'impero medievale (774–1252)* (Bologna: Cappelli Editore, 1947), 205–97; Agostino Paravicini Bagliani, "Il papato medievale, Roma e lo spazio," in *Roma e il suo territorio nel medioevo: Le fonti scritti tra tradizione e innovazione*, ed. Cristina Carbonetti, Santo Lucà, and Maddalena Signorini (Spoleto: Fondazione Centro italiano di studi sull'altomedievo, 2015), 1–22; and Wickham, *Medieval Rome*, 137–40. Specifically on the implications of these developments for the frequentation of the Via Triumphalis, see also Anna Modigliani, *Mercati, botteghe e spazi di commercio a Roma tra Medioevo ed età moderna* (Rome: Roma nel Rinascimento, 1998), 9–11 and passim.

35 Brezzi, *Roma e l'impero medievale*, 317–39; Jean-Claude Maire Vigueur, "Il comune romano," in *Storia di Roma*, vol. 2, *Roma medievale*, ed. André Vauchez (Rome: Editori Laterza, 2001), 117–57; Chris Wickham, *Sleepwalking into a New World: The Emergence of Italian City Communes in the Twelfth Century* (Princeton: Princeton University Press, 2015), 119–60; and Marco Vendittelli, "Istituzioni, società, economia a Roma tra XII e XIII secolo," in Carbonetti, Lucà, and Signorini, *Roma e il suo territorio nel medioevo*, 23–37.

36 Giuseppe Marchetti Longhi, "Il quartiere Greco-orientale di Roma nell'antichità e nel medio evo," *Atti del IV congresso Nazionale di Studi Romani*, ed. Carlo Galassi Paluzzi (Rome: Istituto di studi romani, 1938), 1:169–85.

37 Modigliani, *Mercati, botteghe e spazi di commercio a Roma tra Medioevo ed età moderna*, 29–55; and Anna Modigliani, "Mercati, botteghe e spazi di commercio nella Roma tardo-medievale," in *Mercati, arti e fiere storiche di Roma e del Lazio*, ed. R. Padovano (Padova: Esedra, 2011), 27–35; cf. Jean-Claude Maire Vigueur, *L'autre Rome: Une histoire des Romains à l'époque communale (XIIe–XIVe siècle)* (Paris: Tallandier, 2010), 38–44.

38 Modigliani, *Mercati, botteghe e spazi di commercio a Roma tra Medioevo ed età moderna*, 61–75.

39 Ibid., 57–61.

40 Ibid., 84–87, 176–97.

41 Ibid., 197–209.

42 Ibid., 145–76.

43 On the butchers (and slaughterhouses) at the Theater of Marcellus, see ibid., 78–80.

44 Pietro Fedele, "Il più antico documento dei 'Magistri aedificiorum Urbis' e 'Domna Comitissa,'" in *Miscellanea per nozze Crocioni-Ruscelloni* (Rome: Tipografia dell'unione cooperativa editrice, 1908), 147–55; and Cristina Carbonetti Vendittelli, "La curia dei magistri edificiorum Urbis nei secoli XIII

e XIV e la sua documentazione," in *Rome aux XIIIe et XIVe siècles: Cinq études*, ed. Étienne Hubert (Rome: École française de Rome, 1993), 3–42.

45 Luigi Spezzaferro, "La politica urbanistica dei Papi e le origini di via Giulia," in *Via Giulia: Una utopia urbanistica del 500*, ed. Luigi Salerno, Luigi Spezzaferro, and Manfredo Tafuri (Rome: Aristide Staderini, 1973), 36–41; Enrico Guidoni, "Les transformations du quartier Arenula et le rayonnement de l'urbanisme farnésien," in *Le Palais Farnèse*, 3 vols. (Rome: École française de Rome, 1981), 1:1 (texte), 63–68; and Modigliani, *Mercati, botteghe e spazi di commercio a Roma tra Medioevo ed età moderna*, 207. On the further development of the road in the sixteenth century, see also David Karmon, "The Destruction and Renewal of the *Via triumphalis*, 1533–1536," in *Philibert de l'Orme: Un architecte dans l'histoire: Arts—Sciences—Techniques*, ed. Frédérique Lemerle and Yves Pauwels (Turnhout: Brepols, 2016), 67–78.

46 Guidobaldi, " Un estesissimo intervento urbanistico nella Roma dell'inizio del XII secolo e la parziale perdita della 'memoria topografica' della città antica." Much of the evidence comes from late antique churches such as San Clemente, Santa Maria in Via Lata, and San Crisogono, whose floors remained near their original levels through the eleventh century, and which continued to be repaired and redecorated until shortly before they were filled in to a depth of several meters and built over in the first half of the twelfth century. In other cases, however, such as the Crypta Balbi, the Roman Forum, and Piazza Venezia, excavations have revealed more extensive sections of raised ground.

47 Largo Argentina: San Nicola de Calcarario; Via delle Botteghe Oscure: the extensive "Crypta Balbi" excavations just south of the modern road conducted from the 1980s to the present; Piazza Venezia: post-2010 excavations for the new Metro C station; Roman Forum area: Sant'Adriano; Santa Maria Liberatrice, near Santa Maria Antiqua; early medieval houses excavated in the 1990s in the Forum of Nerva; see Guidobaldi, "Un estesissimo intervento," passim.

48 Guidobaldi, "Un estesissimo intervento urbanistico nella Roma dell'inizio del XII secolo e la parziale perdita della 'memoria topografica' della città antica," 593–98.

49 This is exactly what happened in the Hadrianic auditorium recently excavated in Piazza Venezia. The massive, vaulted roof collapsed in the earthquake of 847; the resulting heaps of rubble were then leveled in the twelfth century, raising ground levels several meters above the Roman (and early medieval) levels: see Serlorenzi, "Le testimonianze medievali nei cantieri di Piazza Venezia," 149.

50 Guidobaldi, "Un estesissimo intervento urbanistico nella Roma dell'inizio del XII secolo e la parziale perdita della 'memoria topografica' della città antica," 599–603.

51 As Guidobaldi says ("Un estesissimo intervento urbanistico nella Roma dell'inizio del XII secolo e la parziale perdita della 'memoria topografica' della città antica," 598–99), most—but not all—of the other apparent cases of deep fills were also situated in especially wet and/or low-lying areas exposed to flooding, among them sites along the Via del Corso such as Santa Maria in Via Lata, and the area around San Crisogono in Trastevere.

52 Laura Vendittelli, "*Crypta Balbi*: Stato e prospettive della ricerca archeologica nel complesso," in *Roma dall'antichità al medioevo, II: Contesti tardoantichi e altomedievali*, ed. Lidia Paroli and Laura Vendittelli (Milan: Electa, 2004), 223–27; Laura Vendittelli, "La ricerca archeologica nel sito," in *Museo nazionale romano—Crypta balbi. Ceramiche medievali e moderne, I: Ceramiche medievali e del primo rinascimento (1000–1530)*, ed. Marco Ricci and Laura Vendittelli (Milan: Electa, 2010), esp. 18–19 for the levels. The excavations undertaken in connection with the new Metro C stop in Piazza Venezia reveal similar increases in ground level of similar date: see Serlorenzi, "Le testimonianze medievali nei cantieri di Piazza Venezia," 134–38, 155–57, with the synthesis of Guidobaldi, "Un estesissimo intervento urbanistico nella Roma dell'inizio del XII secolo e la parziale perdita della 'memoria topografica' della città antica," 597.

53 Guidobaldi, "Un estesissimo intervento urbanistico nella Roma dell'inizio del XII secolo e la parziale perdita della 'memoria topografica' della città antica," 590.

54 Vendittelli, " La ricerca archeologica nel sito," 18–22.

55 Serlorenzi, "Le testimonianze medievali nei cantieri di Piazza Venezia," 138.

56 Ibid., 138.

57 Fidenzoni, *Il Teatro di Marcello*, 73–74; and Marchetti Longhi, "Il Mons Fabiorum," 18–19.

58 Laura Pugliesi, "Alcune osservazioni sulle fasi più antiche della chiesa di S. Angelo in Pescheria," *Rivista di Archeologia Cristiana* 84 (2010):410–13; and Paola Ciancio Rossetto, "Portico d'Ottavia—

Sant'Angelo in Pescheria: Nuove acquisizioni sulle fasi medievali," *Rivista di Archeologia Cristiana* 84 (2008):428–35.

59 San Nicola in Carcere: the present church was built in the 1120s into, and incorporating, the remains of three Roman temples that were evidently still substantially intact at the time; see Andreina Palombi, *La basilica di San Nicola in Carcere: Il complesso architettonico dei tre templi del Foro Olitorio* (Rome: Edizioni Quasar, 2006), 25–26, 55–95. Santo Stefano Rotondo (not to be confused with the church of the same name on the Caelian; it occupied the round Temple of Hercules in the Forum Boarium): a well-known bull issued by Innocent II in 1140 specifies that the church had been "practically destroyed" (*fere distructa*) during the fighting between his partisans and those of Anacletus II in the early 1130s (Paul Fridolin Kehr, "Papsturkunden in Rom. Erster Bericht," *Nachrichten von der Königlichen Gesellschaft der Wissenschaften zu Göttingen. Philol.-hist. Kl. 1900* [1900]:166–68); the restored church maintained the same levels as its predecessor. The same is true for Sant'Anastasia, restored in the 1130s: see Peter C. Claussen, *Die Kirchen der Stadt Rom im Mittelalter 1050–1300* (Stuttgart: Steiner, 2002), 1:68; and for Santa Maria in Cosmedin, restored under Callixtus II (1119–1124): see Dale Kinney, "Rome in the Twelfth Century: *Urbs fracta* and *renovatio*," *Gesta* 45, no. 2 (2006):208–11. For San Crisogono, San Clemente, and Santa Maria in Via Lata, see Guidobaldi, "Un estesissimo intervento urbanistico nella Roma dell'inizio del XII secolo e la parziale perdita della 'memoria topografica' della città antica."

60 A process I think was repeated in other towns and cities in Western Europe (and beyond), where selective preservation of monumental topography inherited from antiquity, including processional armatures, prevailed until they were overtaken (and often dismantled or literally submerged) by new construction and denser settlement patterns beginning in the eleventh and twelfth centuries: see Dey, *Afterlife of the Roman City*, 127–220.

4

What Constituted Cahokian Urbanism?

TIMOTHY R. PAUKETAT

A MILLENNIUM AGO, SHORTLY AFTER THE START OF THE MEDIEVAL Climatic Anomaly (ca. 800–1300) and the coeval addition of maize fields to human landscapes (ca. 900), a city of 15,000–20,000 living souls in three major precincts—Greater Cahokia—coalesced along an extraordinary stretch of the Mississippi River.[1] The city was planned and built ca. 1050 on a scale never before imagined north of Mesoamerica during the precolonial era by people seldom credited with urban complexities (Figure 4.1). As an urban phenomenon, Greater Cahokia was simultaneously densely configured in places, with great monumental core areas and neighborhoods, and oddly "distanciated," with open water in between major precincts.[2] As an urbanizing force, it was in no way restricted to a city, and may have been contingent on locations hundreds of kilometers away. Lesser precincts and nodal sites, shrine complexes, and newly ruralized farmlands were emplaced across the Greater Cahokia region.[3] Religious shrines and support communities were established up and down the Mississippi River as part of a short-lived but far-flung colonial moment.[4]

In the last two decades, archaeologists have proffered two kinds of explanations about the rise and fall of this unusual complex. There are social-evolutionary scenarios that deemphasize the history-making role of the city and its people and posit instead that Cahokian society emerged gradually from maize agriculture.[5] And there are historical and phenomenological perspectives that elevate Greater Cahokia, the place, and its construction by people as agentive forces that shaped society.[6] There is utility in both arguments, but in different ways both camps have overlooked the role of nonhuman agencies and affects in the historical development of urban Cahokia, with the notable exception of one-off celestial and weather-related events.[7]

FIGURE 4.1
Greater Cahokia,
showing sites
mentioned in the
text, ca. 1050–1150.
Illustration by
Timothy R. Pauketat.

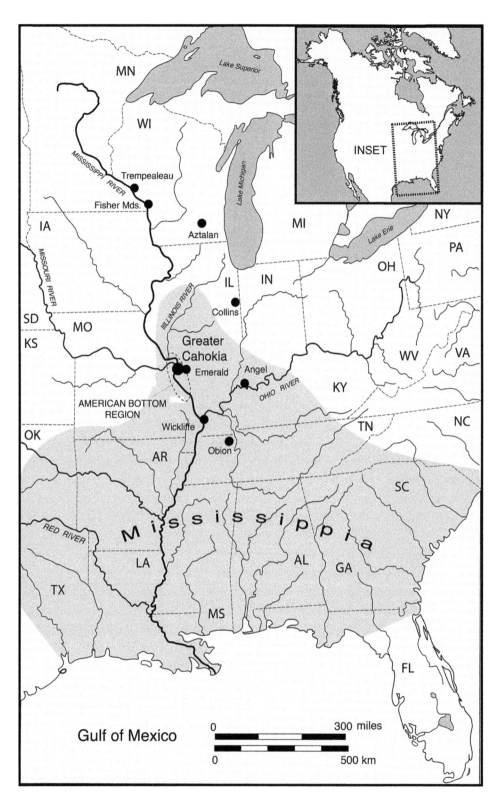

As it happens, such one-off events hint at a third perspective yet under development. That perspective adopts some elements of both previous views and moves us toward a "New Materialist" position.[8] From that third vantage point, Cahokian urbanism may be seen as rooted in the material and affective qualities of atmospheres, materials, substances, and phenomena.[9] In the present essay, a New Materialist perspective emerges particularly from observations of Greater Cahokia's other-than-human environmental, climatic, and atmospheric affects. What follows is a preliminary exploration of these other-than-human affects, especially as these intersected human bodies through earthen monuments, watery transubstantiations, maize fields, and religious architecture.

Greater Cahokia's Affective Powers

Up until 900 and the addition of maize to the local agricultural diet, the lush marshes, tree-lined backwaters, grassy terraces, and forested loess-capped bluff margins of the wide patch of floodplain—locally known as the northern "American Bottom"—had been inhabited by a relatively sparse population of Late Woodland–era forager-gardeners.[10] The landscape was teeming with biota, especially aquatic life and seasonally abundant migratory birds in oxbow lakes, sloughs, and backwater areas.[11] The human population was low.

Immediately to the east in the gently rolling, glaciated uplands of modern-day Illinois were oak-hickory forests that bordered open expanses of tallgrass prairie even farther into the interior. The prairies, said one early European visitor, were "a perfect solitude, without a living thing."[12] The closest that such solitude came to the Mississippi River along the entire central Mississippi Valley was here, just 15–24 km east of the northern American Bottom.[13] There were, as just implied, significant affective and, hence, sensorial and historical implications of the consequently vast unobstructed view of the eastern horizon near the soon-to-be city of Cahokia. Among the most significant were later to be experienced by people at a series of "shrine complexes," the largest of which was the Emerald Acropolis, its twelve flat-topped mounds surmounting an anthropogenically altered Pleistocene-era ridge (see below).

To the west, across the river, were the heavily forested Ozark uplands of modern-day Missouri, the final ripple in the geological shock wave caused when the African continental plate slammed into North America some three hundred million years ago. The uplift that resulted from this ancient collision begins just south and west of Cahokia proper, with sheer cliffs marking the river bluffs which are, in turn, composed of karstic limestone. These demarcate the edge of the floodplain and beginning of the uplands. From their summits, Cahokians cut cedar trees for use in building a monumental circle of posts, or Woodhenge, among other things. Along the river here and to the south, great cypress trees—durable, aromatic wood—were also cut and hauled to the city at significant labor costs for use as marker posts and structural timbers. Beyond the river to the southwest and into the interior of the Ozarks are heavily dissected hills, clear rocky streams, basement rocks, minerals, salts, and pine forests, all of which would soon pull Cahokians into their realm, if only by contrast to the floodplain and low-relief uplands east of the Mississippi.[14]

There, maize and the warmer, wetter weather of the tenth through thirteenth centuries may have been among the most significant historical actors helping to bring about and then sustain a new city. That Greater Cahokia might emerge where and when it did, of course, was surely not a foregone conclusion (à la social-evolutionary models). Rather, I argue that it was a result of the affective properties of all of the substantial and material components in the mix. Of various such substances/things, maize was folded into the agricultural practices of local farmers around 900, with dramatic implications for human health and agricultural labor.[15] Maize is a notoriously water-sensitive plant; the farmers tending it would closely monitor the summertime weather and, no doubt when necessary, directly engage the spiritual powers of earth, sky, and water on its behalf.

Moreover, from the moment of maize adoption, archaeological pottery assemblages in and around the American Bottom reveal that lye production, used to nixtamalize maize kernels, was under way.[16] This involved producing and then adding lye to corn in order to produce a more palatable and easily processed grain. Around the American Bottom, the production of lye necessarily involved acquiring and burning a significant quantity of limestone, available primarily from exposures around the bluffs south and west of Cahokia proper.[17] The net effect was likely critical in rearranging human bodies and cultural associations across the landscape, seemingly producing several large village complexes, of which one of the largest was that of preurban Cahokia from 900 to 1050 (Figure 4.2). This period of village growth in the American Bottom is easily recognizable to archaeologists as a distinct "Terminal Late Woodland" period.[18]

Besides those connected to nixtamalization, Susan M. Alt and I have elsewhere argued that the new relationships of people with maize, initially in the floodplain, created a novel web that also intimately bound people to a certain type of black humic soil for growing maize crops; montmorillonitic clay for making cooking pots, fish and mussels for foods; and mussel shells for tools and pottery temper.[19] These relationships were intimate, defining body and soul,[20] and seem to have been the basis for the "Mississippian" culture of this and other regions after 1050.[21]

The correlation of such cultures with a medieval climate has already been noted, but it should be kept in mind that climate for most people was most assuredly not experienced as an aggregate phenomenon, to be analyzed by farmers for what it might tell them about long-term trends. Remembered climatological knowledge for most farmers likely extended little more than a generation. Thus, Terminal Late Woodland and early Mississippian-era farmers of the tenth and eleventh centuries in the American Midwest would have experienced the onset of the Medieval Climatic Anomaly not as climate at all, but as phenomenal events—weather cells, rain, hail, thunderstorms—that had real consequences for how they might relate to the world and all of the nonhuman powers therein. Thunderclouds were understood by historic-era Native American descendants and historical neighbors of Cahokians to be actual beings that spoke to the world below through thunder.[22] No doubt similar animate entities were known to the Cahokians.

Rain, lightning, clouds, and winds were probably not inanimate phenomena either, but fundamental, inchoate, affective forces.[23] The precipitation that falls and the plant life that springs from the earth embody such causal forces. Thus, the Terminal Late

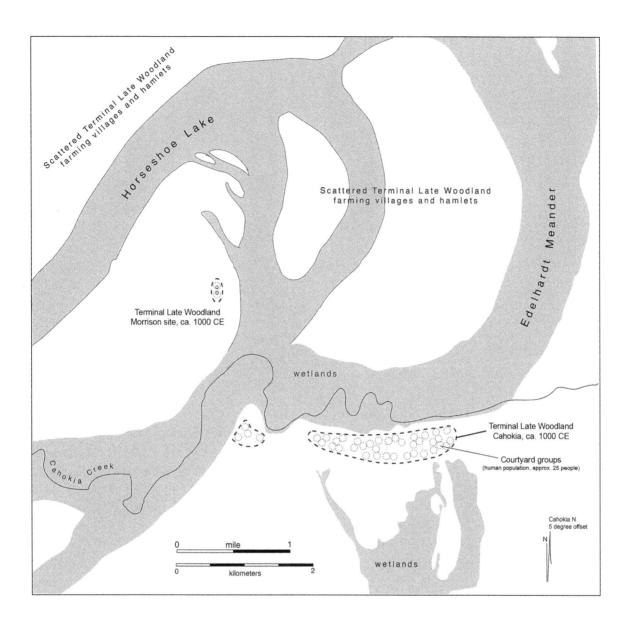

Scattered Terminal Late Woodland
farming villages and hamlets

Horseshoe Lake

Scattered Terminal Late Woodland
farming villages and hamlets

Edelhardt Meander

Terminal Late Woodland
Morrison site, ca. 1000 CE

wetlands

Cahokia Creek

Terminal Late Woodland
Cahokia, ca. 1000 CE

Courtyard groups
(human population, approx. 25 people)

0   mile   1

0   kilometers   2

Cahokia N
5 degree offset

N

wetlands

Woodland–era American Bottom—a novel sort of urbanism in the making—would have constituted a historically particular kind of mediation between people and weather or, rather, the substantial and phenomenal powers that comprised or were intimately associated with weather. That said, there are reasons to suspect that such mediations went well beyond the weather alone.

Dickens's Frogs

The eminent British author Charles Dickens happened to pass through the earthen ruins of Cahokia and its environs during his American tour in 1842. Being particularly attentive to the region's affective qualities, Dickens described an early springtime visit to St. Louis and the Looking Glass Prairie, a day's buggy ride east of the Cahokia

FIGURE 4.2

Schematic plan of the preurban Terminal Late Woodland Cahokia village site, ca. 1000. Illustration by Timothy R. Pauketat.

FIGURE 4.3

Large smoking pipe
bowl in the shape of
a bullfrog holding a
shaman's rattle (thunder)
and streamers (rain).
Photograph courtesy of
Thomas E. Emerson.

Precinct. Beginning in St. Louis, Dickens recounts that the town "had been—not to say hot, for the term is weak and lukewarm in its power of conveying an idea of the temperature. The town had been on fire; in a blaze. But at night it had come on to rain in torrents, and all night long it had rained without cessation."[24]

The next day, as his party traveled east, it passed through the ruins of both the East St. Louis and Cahokia Precincts. Dickens noted that his party "travelled at the rate of little more than a couple of miles an hour, through one unbroken slough of black mud and water." In that setting, amid the eroding earthen pyramids, he described how the "air resounded in all directions with the loud chirping of the frogs, who . . . had the whole scene to themselves."[25] Passing back through the ancient city a couple of days later, he recreated the image: "There was the swamp, the bush, the perpetual chorus of frogs, the rank unseemly growth, [and] the unwholesome steaming earth."[26]

Interestingly, Dickens's negative impression of the region and what he called its "pernicious climate" influenced a generation of twentieth-century archaeologists, some of whom concluded that, because rational human beings living under premodern conditions could not have sustained a city in the muddy Mississippi River bottoms, Cahokia must not be a city.[27] Such an atmosphere, the thinking went, may be good for maize and frogs, but not people. However, if we strip away the value judgments of Dickens and others, we can reevaluate the powerful affects associated with the atmospherics, the "steaming" earth, rain, and frogs. After all, the summertime heat and humidity of the greater St. Louis region is ideal for the growth of maize plants, especially as nourished by the humic, "black" soils of the American Bottom and quenched by the periodic "torrents" of rain. In fact, large fields of maize produce their own humidity, as any archaeologist who has worked in one can attest. Hence, for people enmeshed in relations surrounding maize agriculture, humidity may have been an affect translated to mean fertility and abundance.

So too might have been the auditory affects of the frogs that bedeviled Dickens, especially since the amphibians are most active during their springtime mating season, which is also the maize planting season. As Dickens attested, the Cahokia Precinct was centrally placed in a particularly watery portion of the American Bottom. Preurban Cahokia, in fact, was perfectly wedged between large marshes, meaning that springtime in this locality would have always entailed a perpetual chorus of frogs. Moreover, in the spring and again in the autumn, that chorus would have been superimposed by a cacophony of quacking and honking migrating waterfowl. More than the affects of people, that is, Cahokia would have been alive with the sounds of avian and amphibian beings for much of the year.

Elsewhere, researchers have made archaeological and ethnohistoric links between frogs and the moon, agricultural fertility, and maize.[28] The moon's monthly phases, from new to full, certainly might be likened to the metamorphosis of frogs, who croak loudest at the full moon. Since the latter is sometimes encircled by an atmospheric halo of light upon the approach of warm, rain-bringing weather systems,[29] it should be unsurprising that lunar-amphibian-atmospheric-hydrological-cultural-metaphorical associations were integral to Cahokia and Cahokians (Figure 4.3).

Greater Cahokia's Precincts

That new city now appears to have taken full advantage of such water- and lunar-related amphibious and atmospheric affects, beginning with the layouts of its three large, central precincts, located with a 20 km² area (Figure 4.4), and continuing outward to its shrine complexes.[30] This is clearest with the Cahokia Precinct itself, the largest of the group. Covering about 12 km², this precinct was built over an old Terminal Late Woodland village and then expanded to the north and south into the low-lying wetlands (Figure 4.5). Residential neighborhoods, each incorporating hundreds of pole-and-thatch homes and dozens of Cahokian public or ritual structures, surround major "mound-and-plaza" groups within this precinct centered on an area commonly referred to as "Downtown Cahokia."[31]

To the south, the Cahokians built a 1 km causeway that extended arrow-straight through a wetland to a prominent mortuary mound—the ridgetop-shaped "Rattlesnake Mound"—and a series of perimeter mounds arranged in a large rectangular pattern.[32] The causeway and mortuary area are thought by Sarah E. Baires to have been foundational to the precinct's design, built to assemble the living people who might walk across it with the dead souls passing from this world to the next.[33] In this portion of the expanded complex, wetlands were accentuated by the digging of large borrow pits, where sediment might be mined for use in construction projects, including the raising of the Cahokia Precinct's impressive pyramids and the leveling of its plazas.[34] Such activity seems to have recapitulated human movement along the causeway, with the

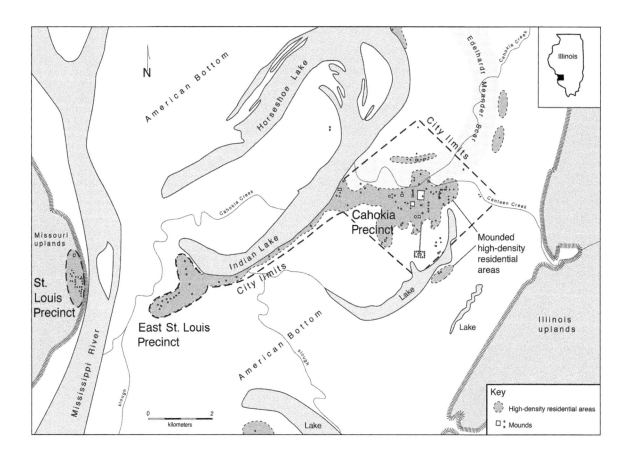

FIGURE 4.4

Plan view of Greater
Cahokia's precincts,
ca. 1100. Illustration by
Timothy R. Pauketat.

heavy black mud dug up from the pits being used to color and cap some of the largest pyramids of the living, including the great multiterraced pyramid known today as Monks Mound.[35] Great ceremonial events and festivals were held in the plazas, including feasts that fed thousands.[36] The plazas too might have been the scenes of human sacrifices viewed by as many.[37] The biggest of both kinds of ritual events, and the largest monuments to be built, date to the decades immediately following the inception of the city in ca. 1050.

Such events were carefully orchestrated, as revealed in mound construction fills. These fills consist of alternating light and dark silt and clay dug from waterlogged locations on site, perhaps used to physically narrate the creation story, where dry land was created by spirit beings from primordial waters.[38] Most were subsequently renewed or reconditioned periodically using specially processed and colored fills, to which new pole-and-thatch surmounting architecture would be added. Plazas were built similarly. The largest, the Cahokia Precinct's Grand Plaza, covered some 24 ha and fronted the south face of the great Monks Mound.[39]

The second-largest precinct, East St. Louis, was built on the banks of the same oxbow lake that runs around and through the Cahokia Precinct. Composed of some fifty earthen pyramids and a series of small built plazas, almost 10 percent of the East St. Louis complex was excavated by the Illinois State Archaeological Survey to make

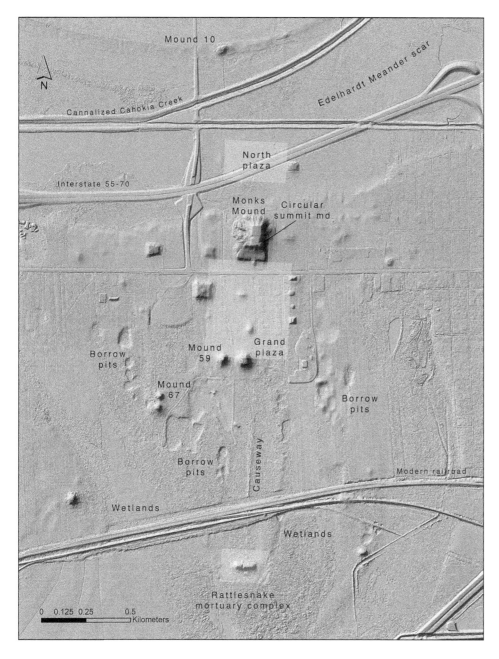

FIGURE 4.5

LiDAR plan map of the central portion of the Cahokia Precinct. Image based on Illinois State Geological Survey LiDAR data, produced by Jeffery Kruchten for the Emerald Acropolis Project; courtesy of Timothy R. Pauketat and Susan M. Alt.

way for a new Mississippi River bridge.[40] Up to one-quarter of the 1,500 pole-and-thatch constructions and reconstructions discovered were temples, council buildings, steam baths, and medicine or spirit lodges (Figure 4.6). Within them resided both people and other-than-human beings—including physical manifestations of supernatural, spiritual powers—such as "medicine bundles" thought by later descendants to be in some sense alive.[41] Minimally, such buildings highlight that the three precincts of Greater Cahokia comprised more than a city of people. This place was a living, breathing urban hybrid of people and other-than-human beings.

What Constituted Cahokian Urbanism? 97

FIGURE 4.6

Cahokian T-shaped
medicine lodge (left),
council buildings (center),
and shrine houses (right)
in one portion of the
Emerald Acropolis. 3-D
models by Alex David Jerez
Roman for the Emerald
Acropolis Project; courtesy
Timothy R. Pauketat
and Susan M. Alt.

Little is known about the third central precinct, St. Louis, as it was destroyed in the nineteenth century.[42] Built across the Mississippi River from East St. Louis on a low bluff, the St. Louis complex consisted of twenty-five earthen platforms around a spacious plaza.[43] A great mortuary mound, the twenty-sixth of the group, was built several hundred meters to the north over an opening to a cave.[44] Like others of its kind in East St. Louis and Cahokia, it was found to contain large pits or vaults full of extended human remains as it was being destroyed in 1870.

It is unknown if the other twenty-five mounds and the plaza at St. Louis were open spaces of quiet reflection or the central components of a bustling precinct of living people. Susan M. Alt argues that the entire precinct may have been both a virtual and actual portal to a Cahokian netherworld similar to the "Rattlesnake Mound" in the Cahokia Precinct.[45] If so, then St. Louis might have been a "shrine complex" occupied by few living people year-round, similar to others built by Cahokians (see below). In any event, the precinct's association with water seems obvious in its position overlooking the Mississippi River, if not also in a row of four flat-topped circular mounds at its eastern end.

Shrine Complexes

Such circular mounds are among the most prominent features at the outlying Emerald Acropolis, a recontoured hilltop in the historically famous Looking Glass Prairie some 24 km east of the city, to which it was connected by a "well-worn" avenue.[46] The major construction at this acropolis now appears to have been coincident with Cahokia's mid-eleventh-century urban expansion.[47] At that time, the hilltop was

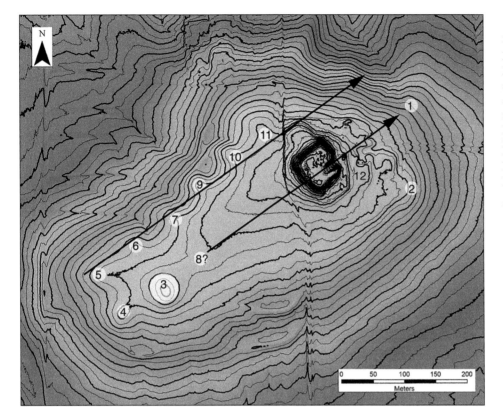

FIGURE 4.7

LiDAR map of the Emerald Acropolis and its twelve mounds aligned to a maximum northern full moonrise. Image by Jeffery Kruchten for the Emerald Acropolis Project; courtesy Timothy R. Pauketat and Susan M. Alt.

recontoured, the summit was flattened, and the geometry of the landform was sharpened. Built atop the rectilinear acropolis were eleven circular mounds arranged in rows astride and orthogonal to a twelfth mound, a large rectangular, flat-topped pyramid (Figure 4.7).

These summit features were all surrounded, in turn, by hundreds of pole-and-thatch buildings. Few of them appear to have been occupied year-round, and most were probably intended to house people during short-term ceremonial events held on the summit and sides of this hill in the middle of the open prairie. Many buildings were positioned, similar to the rows of mounds, to align with one of four prominent moonrises that happen on an 18.6-year cycle.[48] Some have small offerings left behind on or in the floors.[49] Many of these offerings were buried in water-laid silt, including the body of a young human left behind in a hole that remained when a public building's central post was removed.[50]

Reminiscent of the St. Louis Precinct, the circular buildings at the Emerald Acropolis seem to occupy the ridge crest overlooking the low-lying land around it.[51] We presume that at least eleven of these circular buildings were elevated atop the eleven circular platforms, long since reduced by modern-day plowing and bulldozing. Significantly, at the base of the hill and overlooked by the circular platforms and buildings, water yet oozes from the Emerald Acropolis throughout the year, thanks to a perched water table deep within this and nearby hills.[52] A particularly prominent seep

FIGURE 4.8

Mist-shrouded pyramidal bluffs along the Mississippi River in modern-day Minnesota, as seen from the Fisher Mounds site complex, southwestern Wisconsin. Photograph by Timothy R. Pauketat.

on the north side was also managed by Cahokians, and was later the source of refreshment for westward-moving Euro-American pioneers.[53] That is, the site's surmounting architecture and eleven of its twelve mounds appear situated to overlook water. Historically and cross-culturally, such circular constructions would have included steam baths and hothouses or, more generically, "water shrines."[54]

Constituting an integral component of Greater Cahokia's "architecture of power,"[55] such water shrines are typically found at other Cahokian nodal sites and shrine complexes, including the far-off complex at Trempealeau in Wisconsin.[56] Trempealeau and the nearby Fisher Mounds complex, some 900 km up the Mississippi, appear to have been places of pilgrimage for important Cahokians in the middle to late eleventh century, with Cahokian farmers living in dispersed farmsteads growing food to sustain the foreign Cahokians. Artifacts and radiocarbon dates suggest that the various buildings, bluff-top mounds, and shrine houses were under construction at or immediately before Greater Cahokia's mid-eleventh-century urban renovations. Additional colonial shrine complexes hundreds of kilometers north and south of Greater Cahokia are apparent as well, including the occupations of the Collins and Aztalan sites (see Figure 4.1). To the south, buildings and artifacts dating to the late eleventh century at the Carson site in Mississippi and at Reelfoot Lake in Tennessee betray similar Cahokian presences.[57]

Fisher Mounds, Aztalan, and Trempealeau are located near prominent landforms and ancient mounds and cemeteries, hinting that Cahokia's purposes in their establishment may have been a function of their proximity to spiritual power (Figure 4.8). Possibly, the Cahokian outliers were a means whereby the Cahokians centered or legitimated their new city back in the American Bottom.[58] Doubtless, there were other reasons and historical consequences. Equally clear, the foundations of other "early Mississippian" mounded complexes at Angel, Obion, and Wickliffe in the Mid-South may have earlier Cahokian roots.[59]

Sweating Bodies and Steaming Earth

Centering, in the material, substantial, and phenomenal sense I mean here, was not a mere conceptual metaphor but a repeated, physical, affective experience mediated by the city of Greater Cahokia itself. Among the components of such an affective, urban-centering process were the many steam baths in Greater Cahokia's precincts, at its out-lying nodal sites and at its shrine complexes. Inside some if not all of these nondomestic buildings, as in their historic-era counterparts, supplicants directly engaged spiritual powers through the palpable transubstantiation of water in conjunction with other materials and phenomena. Near the center of the building floors were hearths that contained rocks heated by fire (outside the room). Covered with the appropriate amount of blankets, hides, thatch, and earth, the interiors were as dark as night. Sitting within, human bodies sweated as water was poured over the hot rocks to produce the steam that filled the interiors.[60]

The intense heat inside was known to induce visions.[61] The heat and steam also alleviated bodily aches and pains and mitigated the symptoms of the common cold.[62] Hence, Greater Cahokian steam baths were places of healing, as presumably were its shrine complexes generally. More to the present point, these water shrines healed by virtue of their transformative powers. Inside, the fundamental, affective powers of water, air, earth, and fire—seen with the eyes, heard in the ears, smelled in the nose, and felt in the lungs and on the skin—might change from one state to another and translocate from one body (a pot full of water) to another (a human body). This was pure, unmitigated, other-than-human spiritual energy transferred to people by virtue of its visibility, audibility, and tangibility.[63] It was the lifeblood of Cahokian urbanism.

That this was so is attested by the genealogy of such buildings and their associated earthen platforms in the Greater Cahokia region. That is, the circular architecture appeared de novo immediately after 1050 with the urban renewal so readily evident at the Cahokia and East St. Louis Precincts.[64] As far as we know, based on the extensive excavations of several locations in the region, there were no formal or recognizable steam baths built before Greater Cahokia's mid-eleventh-century inception. Afterward, however, both large circular rotundas and small "lodges" were built in select locations within the new city, atop the Emerald Acropolis, and at other outlier "nodal" farmsteads.[65]

Spotty data on mound construction also suggest that circular platform mounds appeared at this same time, though none existed up or down the Mississippi River before the mid-eleventh century.[66] In the Cahokia Precinct, one of the largest of the circular platforms—commonly misidentified as "conical" mounds—was Mound 11, which overlooks the northern end of that precinct and, in that location, the low-lying water-logged Edelhardt meander scar. Excavations into that mound in the 1920s and 1950s revealed an internally complex structure with many stacked layers of Cahokian religious and political architectural constructions; one was a large circular steam bath.[67] Other similar prominent circular platforms, such as Mounds 59 and 67, were located in the Cahokia Precinct's southern end, overlooking large water-filled borrow pits south of the Grand Plaza.

Discussion

The general associations of circular water shrines, low-lying lands, and the Cahokia Precinct bring us back to a consideration of the potential significance of affects in the formation of Cahokian urbanism and, from there, to the theoretical questions surrounding the nature of urbanism. How important were, and are, the affective properties of some place or region in the history of urbanism?[68] How might we begin to imagine a third approach to urbanism that is both less reductionist than older social-evolutionary models and less anthropocentric than historical or phenomenological approaches?

Cahokian Ontology

With average relative humidity values in July around 85 percent, and Greater Cahokia's location in a topographic bowl more than 30 m below the bluff-lined uplands around it, the city's precincts were and still are prone to temperature inversions, stagnant air, and thick morning and evening mists. In the past, the visual effect was routine yet profound; the summits of buildings would have risen up through a shrouded surface reminiscent of the steam inside a Cahokian steam bath (Figure 4.9). Undergirded by the geology of the region, combined with the humidity, local topography, proximal water bodies, and other atmospheric and biotic affects, the city would have seemed to emerge on its own as a place of watery transubstantiation that might be experienced by people through multiple senses. This city, as an assemblage of substances and atmospherics, in some ways defined itself even before people realized it around 1050.

When people did finally realize Greater Cahokia, they did so by actively delineating the outer limits of their world at places such as Trempealeau and Fisher Mounds in the north and Carson in the south. Many peoples from these outer realms likely moved to the new city.[69] Estimates of Greater Cahokia's population in the 15,000–20,000 range demand that immigration be taken into account.[70] Perhaps 20,000–30,000 more people lived in the surrounding Greater Cahokia region,[71] where farmers resided in single-family settlements in the midst of humid maize fields arrayed around lesser Cahokian precincts and minor nodal sites studded with Greater Cahokia's official architecture.[72]

Obviously, such numbers of people had no small hand in altering the human history of the Mississippi Valley. Certainly, Cahokian rituals, such as the periodic sacrificing of people during the late eleventh and twelfth centuries, indicate a religious zeal that carried Cahokia's message to the four corners of the world as Cahokians had helped to define it. But these rituals involved both human beings and other-than-human spiritual forces, just as Greater Cahokia's steam baths did. Arguably, Greater Cahokia's religious events and monumental constructions were all—in their construction, renewal, or reanimation—a means of transferring holy powers from the cosmic realm to the human realm.[73] Certainly, all were under continual construction, as one 1950s Cahokia archaeologist noted with some astonishment.[74] This makes sense when we recognize that the materials themselves (earth, water, wood) or the transubstantiation of them (water into steam, earth from water into dry land, the sky emplaced on earth, life into death) empowered people and hence defined a Cahokian ontology. The farmers and

FIGURE 4.9

Morning mist in the
Grand Plaza of the
Cahokia Precinct.
Photograph courtesy
of Daniel Seurer.

priests of Cahokia alike were inextricably enmeshed in an urbanizing world of water, earth, celestial orbs, and atmosphere (Figure 4.10).

Perhaps a good way to illustrate this profoundly premodern ontology is to turn to the demise of Cahokia. Multiple lines of evidence suggest that, beginning as early as the mid-twelfth century, the human population—particularly upland farmers— left the region coincident with less-favorable climatic conditions. Remember, water from the sky was a virtual life force, experienced by people as weather events. If the rains stopped coming, people would have taken notice, possibly interpreting the change as an active intervention by water spirits into the realm of people. Among farmers, departure might have seemed like a reasonable or even necessary human response. There would have been political implications. At Cahokia, these seem to have included the walling off of sacred architecture and, ultimately, entire civic-ceremonial core areas.

In the lead-up to this time, ca. 1200, a walled portion of Cahokia's East St. Louis Precinct was ceremonially burned to the ground.[75] In one area, upward of seventy or more buildings were ignited, seemingly with offerings of food and tools inside. Arguably, this was the same time that a suite of other offerings were made around the region, often with the aid of fire.[76] At least one large burial mound may have been sealed and, perhaps most importantly, the religious architecture of Greater Cahokia—all the circular steam baths and hothouses among them—ceased to be built in the region.[77] Whatever and however such buildings mediated spiritual forces, that mediation ended by 1200, apparently quite deliberately and, possibly, planned years in advance.

The city of Cahokia was subsequently transformed and downsized, with all living people leaving by 1350. Yet in its moldering ruins we might yet appreciate that Cahokian

FIGURE 4.10
Rising sun behind
the principal pyramid
of the Cahokia
Precinct, as viewed
from Woodhenge.
Photograph courtesy
of Daniel Seurer.

urbanism was not simply the result of a theoretical, human exercise in urban planning (though planning was clearly present). Nor was it an undirected social-evolutionary consequence of maize agriculture (though dramatic region-wide historical change resulted).

Toward a Third Approach

Following Gilles Deleuze and Félix Guattari,[78] a series of "New Materialists" have reenvisioned the world as a fluid and permeable realm of entities, objects, and beings much as the case of Greater Cahokia suggests.[79] Manuel DeLanda has specifically considered urbanism as a kind of assemblage.[80] After all, urbanism has the virtue of being thing-like, on the one hand, and yet also ontological, on the other. This is because urbanism's fixity is to some important extent illusory, not because it is not a real thing, but because its reality is based on its affects—the properties that it exudes which, in turn, engage people, among other beings and things.[81]

We might think of other intermediate states of matter similarly. Wood and thatch, for instance, are pliable, decomposable, and aromatic. Both affect how they might be engaged or entangled in human relationships. They afford impressive vertical constructions that will not last more than a couple of human generations unless rebuilt. Water too is a fluid substance that facilitates some relationships (osmosis, for example) while imposing very real constraints on others (pedestrian movement, for example). Its fluidity is an affective quality. So is its propensity to condense as mist or steam during the warm months in the American Midwest.

There are many other affects that we might consider. Among those involved in urbanism would be sound, texture, and qualities directly or indirectly involving the sun's radiation, such as heat, luminosity, and reflectivity. Importantly, some affects impinge on, attract, or repel others, more or less. Such "intra-actions," to borrow a word from Karen Barad, give certain relational fields and objects within them vital tendencies.[82] They may change in one direction or another based solely on their internal composition or configuration, depending on the conditions at hand. At some scales of analysis, such intra-actions would be indistinguishable from the interactions between relatively inchoate entities, the boundaries themselves being difficult to discern. Again, processes happening within water, earth, and the atmosphere are among those that probably laid the Terminal Late Woodland groundwork for the appearance of Greater Cahokia in the mid-1000s.

By recognizing the fluidity and permeability of the Cahokian world, we might also identify for the first time aspects of relations with significant causal properties that often go unnoticed. For example, many archaeological studies of cities have analyzed human, urban relationships as if they happened across empty two-dimensional space. But Cahokian space was never empty. Indeed, it was always more or less pressurized and heated, pervaded by sounds, and filled with vitality. Water and water vapor, or humidity, were inescapable dimensions of Cahokian space, celebrated via the maize harvest and via its official urban architecture. Thus, climate change—the Medieval Climatic Anomaly—did not simply cause Cahokia; it was part and parcel of Cahokian urbanism.

Typical climate change scenarios usually assume that people were the unwitting victims of external forces, just as our typical approach to human agency characterizes people as always knowingly mediating nonhuman forces. However, the question that the case of Greater Cahokia brings to the fore is whether or not mediators besides people, including weather events, fronts, and storm cells, are integral to urban histories.[83] Such a theoretical third way has the advantage of paralleling Native American ontologies, where rain, water, and thunder, among other things, were often considered to be alive or imbued with spiritual energy, no doubt owing to their palpable affects.[84] Such affects, if not other-than-human forces generally, can and should be analyzed for what they do or how they assemble substances, materials, and phenomena to produce entities, beings, and things.

Thus, limestone, maize, earth, humidity, water vapor, frogs, and moonlight all were key to Greater Cahokian urbanism. All were variably entangled with human bodies. Humidity and water were palpable powers of vitality and growth. Maize and limestone entailed and enabled bodily movements. Frogs and the full moon brought rain and aligned human senses and sensibilities.[85]

Greater Cahokia was an assemblage of them all. It entangled sight, sound, breath, health, moonlight, and atmosphere. That assemblage was urban. It was also transregional, with tendrils that attached people to exotic powers and spiritual landscapes hundreds of kilometers away. And it was transdimensional, with urban experience folding together everything from soaking maize and croaking frogs to ritual steam baths.

The atmospheres within which people existed, the environments that people experienced, and the foods that people ate made them the urban beings which they became. Thus, the histories of the intra-actions and engagements of all people, places, things, materials, substances, and phenomena changed human history and humanity at and through Greater Cahokia. If Cahokian urbanism was anything, it was an ontological tangle of history and humanity.

Notes

1   Timothy R. Pauketat and Susan M. Alt, eds., *Medieval Mississippians: The Cahokian World* (Santa Fe: School for Advanced Research Press, 2015).

2   Ash Amin and Nigel Thrift, *Cities: Reimagining the Urban* (Cambridge: Polity Press, 2002).

3   Susan M. Alt, *Cahokia's Complexities: Ceremonies and Politics of the First Mississippian Farmers* (Tuscaloosa: University of Alabama Press, 2018); Thomas E. Emerson, *Cahokia and the Archaeology of Power* (Tuscaloosa: University of Alabama Press, 1997); and Thomas E. Emerson, "Reflections from the Countryside on Cahokian Hegemony," in *Cahokia: Domination and Ideology in the Mississippian World*, ed. Timothy R. Pauketat and Thomas E. Emerson (Lincoln: University of Nebraska Press, 1997), 190–228.

4   Timothy R. Pauketat, Robert F. Boszhardt, and Danielle M. Benden, "Trempealeau Entanglements: An Ancient Colony's Causes and Effects," *American Antiquity* 80, no. 2 (April 2015):260–89.

5   George R. Milner, *The Cahokia Chiefdom: The Archaeology of a Mississippian Society* (Washington, D.C.: Smithsonian Institution Press, 1998); and Mark W. Mehrer, *Cahokia's Countryside: Household Archaeology, Settlement Patterns, and Social Power* (DeKalb: Northern Illinois University Press, 1995).

6   Emerson, *Cahokia and the Archaeology of Power*; and Timothy R. Pauketat, *Chiefdoms and Other Archaeological Delusions* (Lanham, Md.: AltaMira Press, 2007); and Timothy R. Pauketat and Thomas E. Emerson, eds., *Cahokia: Domination and Ideology in the Mississippian World* (Lincoln: University of Nebraska Press, 1997).

7   Timothy R. Pauketat and Thomas E. Emerson, "Star Performances and Cosmic Clutter," *Cambridge Archaeological Journal* 18, no. 1 (February 2008):78–85; and Samuel E. Munoz, Kristine E. Gruley, Ashtin Massie, David A. Fike, Sissel Schroeder, and John W. Williams, "Cahokia's Emergence and Decline Coincided with Shifts of Flood Frequency on the Mississippi River," *Proceedings of the National Academy of Sciences* 112, no. 20 (2015):6319–24.

8   Susan M. Alt and Timothy R. Pauketat, eds., *New Materialisms Ancient Urbanisms* (London: Routledge, 2019).

9   Alt, *Cahokia's Complexities*; Sarah E. Baires, *Land of Water, City of the Dead: Religion and Cahokia's Emergence* (Tuscaloosa: University of Alabama Press, 2017); Melissa R. Baltus, "Unraveling Entanglements: Reverberations of Cahokia's Big Bang," in *Tracing the Relational: The Archaeology of Worlds, Spirits, and Temporalities*, ed. Meghan E. Buchanan and B. Jacob Skousen (Salt Lake City: University of Utah Press, 2015), 146–60; B. Jacob Skousen, "Moonbeams, Water, and Smoke: Tracing Otherworldly Relationships at the Emerald Site," in Buchanan and Skousen, *Tracing the Relational*, 38–53; Timothy R. Pauketat, Susan M. Alt, and Jeffery D. Kruchten, "The Emerald Acropolis: Elevating the Moon and Water in the Rise of Cahokia," *Antiquity* 91, no. 355 (February 2017):207–22; and Timothy R. Pauketat, *An Archaeology of the Cosmos: Rethinking Agency and Religion in Ancient America* (London: Routledge, 2013).

10 Andrew C. Fortier and Douglas K. Jackson, "The Formation of a Late Woodland Heartland in the American Bottom, Illinois ca. AD 650–900," in *Late Woodland Societies: Tradition and Transformation across the Midcontinent*, ed. Thomas E. Emerson, Dale L. McElrath, and Andrew C. Fortier (Lincoln: University of Nebraska Press, 2000).

11 William P. White, Sissel Johannessen, Paula G. Cross, and Lucretia S. Kelly, "Environmental Setting," in *American Bottom Archaeology*, ed. Charles J. Bareis and James W. Porter (Urbana: University of Illinois Press, 1984), 15–33.

12 William Oliver, *Eight Months in Illinois: With Information to Immigrants* (Carbondale: Southern Illinois University Press, 2002), 182.

13 Mary L. Simon, "Reevaluating the Evidence for Middle Woodland Maize from the Holding Site," *American Antiquity* 82, no. 1 (January 2017):140–50; and Mary L. Simon, "Reevaluating the Introduction of Maize into the American Bottom and Western Illinois," in *Reassessing the Timing, Rate, and Adoption Trajectories of Domesticate Use in the Midwest and Great Lakes*, ed. Maria E. Raviele and William A. Lovis (Midwest Archaeological Conference, Summer 2014), 97–134.

14 Thomas E. Emerson and Randall E. Hughes, "Figurines, Flint Clay Sourcing, the Ozark Highlands, and Cahokian Acquisition," *American Antiquity* 65, no. 1 (2000):79–101.

15 Mary L. Simon, "Reevaluating the Evidence for Middle Woodland Maize from the Holding Site," *American Antiquity* 82, no. 1 (January 2014):140–50.

16 Alleen M. Betzenhauser, ed., *East St. Louis Mound Complex NMRB Project: Ceramics from Pre-Mississippian Features*, Illinois State Archaeological Survey Research Report 46 (Urbana-Champaign: Prairie Research Institute, University of Illinois, 2018).

17 Timothy R. Pauketat, "Thinking Through the Ashes, Architecture, and Artifacts of Ancient East St. Louis," in *Revealing Greater Cahokia, North America's First Native City: Rediscovery and Large-Scale Excavations of the East St. Louis Precinct*, ed. Thomas E. Emerson, Brad H. Koldehoff, and Tamira K. Brennan, Studies in Archaeology 12 (Urbana: Illinois State Archaeological Survey, University of Illinois, 2018); Dale L. McElrath, Thomas E. Emerson, and Andrew C. Fortier, "Social Evolution or Social Response? A Fresh Look at 'Good Gray Cultures' after Four Decades of Midwest Research," in Emerson, McElrath, and Fortier, *Late Woodland Societies*, 3–36; and Elizabeth D. Benchley, "Mississippian Alkali Processing of Corn," *Wisconsin Archeologist* 84 (2003):127–37.

18 Andrew C. Fortier and Dale L. McElrath, "Deconstructing the Emergent Mississippian Concept: The Case for the Terminal Late Woodland in the American Bottom," *Midcontinental Journal of Archaeology* 27, no. 2 (2002):171–215.

19 Timothy R. Pauketat and Susan M. Alt, "Water and Shells in Bodies and Pots: Mississippian Rhizome, Cahokian Poiesis," in *Relational Identities and Other-than-Human Agency in Archaeology*, ed. Eleanor Harrison-Buck and Julia Hendon (Boulder: University of Colorado Press, 2017).

20 Sarah E. Baires, "A Microhistory of Human and Gastropod Bodies and Souls during Cahokia's Emergence," *Cambridge Archaeological Journal* 27, no. 2 (2016):245–60.

21 James B. Griffin, "Eastern North American Archaeology: A Summary," *Science* 156, no. 3772 (1967):175–91; and Dan F. Morse and Phyllis A. Morse, *The Archaeology of the Central Mississippi Valley* (New York: Academic Press, 1983).

22 Robert L. Hall, "The Cultural Background of Mississippian Symbolism," in *The Southeastern Ceremonial Complex*, ed. Patricia Galloway (Lincoln: University of Nebraska Press, 1989), 239–78; John G. Neihardt, *Black Elk Speaks: Being the Life Story of a Holy Man of the Oglala Sioux* (Albany: State University of New York Press, 2008); and Alfred Irving Hallowell, "Ojibwa Ontology, Behavior, and World View," in *Culture in History: Essays in Honor of Paul Radin*, ed. Stanley Diamond (New York: Columbia University Press, 1960), 19–52.

23 Hall, "Cultural Background of Mississippian Symbolism."

24 Charles Dickens, *American Notes* (London: Penguin Books, 2004), 197.

25 Ibid., 197.

26 Ibid., 203.

27 Milner, *Cahokia Chiefdom*.

28 Thomas E. Emerson, "Cahokian Elite Ideology and the Mississippian Cosmos," in Pauketat and Emerson, *Cahokia*, 190–228; Guy Prentice, "An Analysis of the Symbolism Expressed by the Birger Figurine," *American Antiquity* 51, no. 2 (1986):239–66; Pauketat, *Archaeology of the Cosmos*; and William F. Romain, "Moonwatchers of Cahokia," in Pauketat and Alt, *Medieval Mississippians*.

29 K. C. Heidorn and Ian Whitelaw, *The Field Guide to Natural Phenomena: The Secret World of Optical, Atmospheric and Celestial Wonders* (Richmond Hill, Ontario: Firefly Books, 2010).

30 Thomas E. Emerson, "Creating Greater Cahokia: The Cultural Context of the East St. Louis Precinct," in Emerson, Koldehoff, and Brennan, *Revealing Greater Cahokia*, 25–58.

31 Melvin L. Fowler, *The Cahokia Atlas: A Historical Atlas of Cahokia Archaeology*, Studies in Archaeology 2 (Urbana: Illinois Transportation Archaeological Research Program, University of Illinois, 1997).

32 William F. Romain, "Ancient Skywatchers of the Eastern Woodlands," in *Archaeology and Ancient Religion in the American Midcontinent*, ed. Brad H. Koldehoff and Timothy R. Pauketat (Tuscaloosa: University of Alabama Press, 2018), 304–41.

33 Sarah E. Baires, "Cahokia's Rattlesnake Causeway," *Midcontinental Journal of Archaeology* 39, no. 1 (2014):1–19; Baires, *Land of Water*; and Timothy R. Pauketat, Thomas E. Emerson, Michael G. Farkas, and Sarah E. Baires, "An American Indian City," in Pauketat and Alt, *Medieval Mississippians*, 20–31.

34 Susan M. Alt, Jeffery D. Kruchten, and Timothy R. Pauketat, "The Construction and Use of Cahokia's Grand Plaza," *Journal of Field Archaeology* 35, no. 2 (2010):131–46; and Rinita A. Dalan, George R.

Holley, William I. Woods, Harold W. Watters Jr., and John A. Koepke, *Envisioning Cahokia: A Landscape Perspective* (DeKalb: Northern Illinois University Press, 2003).

35 Timothy R. Pauketat, *Temples for Cahokia Lords: Preston Holder's 1955–1956 Excavations of Kunnemann Mound*, Memoirs of the University of Michigan Museum of Anthropology 26 (Ann Arbor: University of Michigan, 1993); Sarah C. Sherwood and Tristram R. Kidder, "The DaVincis of Dirt: Geoarchaeological Perspectives on Native American Mound Building in the Mississippi River Basin," *Journal of Anthropological Archaeology* 30 (2011):69–87; Timothy Schilling, "The Chronology of Monks Mound," *Southeastern Archaeology* 32 (2013):14–28; Nelson A. Reed, "Excavations on the Third Terrace and Front Ramp of Monks Mound, Cahokia: A Personal Narrative," *Illinois Archaeology* 21 (2009):1–89; and Mikels Skele, *The Great Knob: Interpretations of Monks Mound*, Studies in Illinois Archaeology 4 (Springfield: Illinois Historic Preservation Agency, 1988).

36 Timothy R. Pauketat, Lucretia S. Kelly, Gayle J. Fritz, Neal H. Lopinot, Scott Elias, and Eve Hargrave, "The Residues of Feasting and Public Ritual at Early Cahokia," *American Antiquity* 67 (2002):257–79.

37 Melvin L. Fowler et al., *The Mound 72 Area: Dedicated and Sacred Space in Early Cahokia*, Reports of Investigations 54 (Springfield: Illinois State Museum, 1999).

38 Robert L. Hall, *An Archaeology of the Soul: Native American Indian Belief and Ritual* (Urbana: University of Illinois Press, 1997).

39 Alt, Kruchten, and Pauketat, "Construction and Use of Cahokia's Grand Plaza."

40 Tamira K. Brennan, ed., *Main Street Mound: A Ridgetop Monument at the East St. Louis Mound Complex*, Illinois State Archaeological Survey Research Report 36 (Urbana-Champaign: Prairie Research Institute, University of Illinois, 2016); Tamira K. Brennan, ed., *East St. Louis Precinct Mississippian Features*, Illinois State Archaeological Survey Research Report 43 (Urbana-Champaign: Prairie Research Institute, University of Illinois, 2018); and Emerson, Koldehoff, and Brennan, *Revealing Greater Cahokia*.

41 Alleen M. Betzenhauser and Timothy R. Pauketat, "Elements of Cahokian Neighborhoods," in *Neighborhoods in the Perspective of Anthropological Archaeology*, ed. David Pacifico and L. Truex (Washington, D.C.: Archeological Papers of the American Anthropological Association, 2018).

42 John B. Marshall, "The St. Louis Mound Group: Historical Accounts and Pictorial Depictions," *Missouri Archaeologist* 53 (1992):43–79.

43 Titian Ramsay Peale, "Ancient Mounds at St. Louis, Missouri, in 1819," *Annual Report, Board of Regents of the Smithsonian Institution for the Year 1861* (Washington, D.C.: Government Printing Office, 1862), 386–91.

44 Hubert Rother and Charlotte Rother, *Lost Caves of St. Louis* (St. Louis: Virginia Publishing, 1996).

45 Susan M. Alt, "From Weeping Hills to Lost Caves: A Search for Vibrant Matter in Greater Cahokia," in Alt and Pauketat, *New Materialisms Ancient Urbanisms*, 19–39.

46 John Francis Snyder, "Certain Indian Mounds Technically Considered," in *John Francis Snyder: Selected Writings*, ed. Clyde C. Walton (Springfield: Illinois Historical Society, 1962), 230–73.

47 Pauketat, Alt, and Kruchten, "Emerald Acropolis"; and Jacob Skousen, "Pilgrimage and the Construction of Cahokia: A View from the Emerald Site" (PhD diss., University of Illinois, 2016).

48 Pauketat, Alt, and Kruchten, "Emerald Acropolis."

49 Susan M. Alt, "Putting Religion Ahead of Politics: Cahokian Origins as Viewed through Emerald's Shrines," in *Big Data and Ancient Religion in the North American Midcontinent*, ed. Brad Koldehoff and Timothy R. Pauketat (Tuscaloosa: University of Alabama Press, 2018); and Susan M. Alt, "Building Cahokia: Transformation through Tradition," in *Vernacular Architecture in the Pre-Columbian Americas*, ed. Christina T. Halperin and Lauren Schwartz (London: Routledge, 2016), 141–57.

50 Susan M. Alt, "Human Sacrifice at Cahokia," in Pauketat and Alt, *Medieval Mississippians*, 27.

51 Pauketat, Alt, and Kruchten, "Emerald Acropolis."

52 David A. Grimley and Andrew C. Phillips, eds., *Ridges, Mounds, and Valleys: Glacial-Interglacial History of the Kaskaskia Basin, Southwestern Illinois*, Illinois State Geological Survey Guidebook 41 (Urbana-Champaign: University of Illinois, 2015).

53 Snyder, "Certain Indian Mounds Technically Considered."

54 Eleanor Harrison-Buck, "Architecture as Animate Landscape: Circular Shrines in the Ancient Maya Lowlands," *American Anthropologist* 114, no. 1 (2012):64–80; and Hall, *Archaeology of the Soul*.

55 Emerson, *Cahokia and the Archaeology of Power*.

56 Pauketat, Boszhardt, and Benden, "Trempealeau Entanglements"; Timothy R. Pauketat, Robert F. Boszhardt, and Michael J. Kolb, "Trempealeau's Little Bluff: An Early Cahokian Terraformed Landmark in the Upper Mississippi Valley," *Midcontinental Journal of Archaeology* 42, no. 2 (2017):168–99; and Danielle Benden, "The Fisher Mounds Site Complex: Early Middle Mississippian Exploration in the Upper Mississippi Valley," *Minnesota Archaeologist* 63 (2004):7–24.

57 Robert C. Mainfort Jr., "The Reelfoot Lake Basin, Kentucky and Tennessee," in *Prehistory of the Central Mississippi Valley*, ed. Charles H. McNutt (Tuscaloosa: University of Alabama Press, 1996), 77–96; and Jay K. Johnson, "Cahokia Core Technology: The View from the South," in *The Organization of Core Technology*, ed. Jay K. Johnson and Carol A. Morrow (Boulder, Colo.: Westview Press, 1987), 187–206.

58 Pauketat, Boszhardt, and Benden, "Trempealeau Entanglements."

59 Elizabeth B. Garland, *The Obion Site: An Early Mississippian Center in Western Tennessee*, Cobb Institute of Archaeology Report of Investigation 7 (Mississippi State: Mississippi State University, 1992); Glenn A. Black, *Angel Site: An Archaeological, Historical, and Ethnological Study* (Indianapolis: Indiana Historical Society, 1967); and Kit W. Wesler, *Excavations at Wickliffe Mounds* (Tuscaloosa: University of Alabama Press, 2001).

60 Raymond Bucko, *The Lakota Ritual of the Sweat Lodge* (Lincoln: University of Nebraska Press, 1998).

61 Neihardt, *Black Elk Speaks*; and Joseph Epes Brown, *The Sacred Pipe: Black Elk's Account of the Seven Rites of the Oglala Sioux* (Norman: University of Oklahoma Press, 1953).

62 David Tyrrell, Irene Barrow, and J. Smith Arthur, "Local Hyperthermia Benefits Natural and Experimental Common Colds," *British Medical Journal* 298 (1989):1280–83; and Dov Ophir and Yigal Elad, "Effects of Steam Inhalation on Nasal Patency and Nasal Symptoms in Patients with the Common Cold," *American Journal of Otolaryngology* 3 (1987):149–53.

63 Paul Radin, "Religion of the North American Indians," *Journal of American Folklore* 27 (1914):335–73; and Pauketat, *Archaeology of the Cosmos*.

64 Timothy R. Pauketat, *The Ascent of Chiefs: Cahokia and Mississippian Politics in Native North America* (Tuscaloosa: University of Alabama Press, 1994); Timothy R. Pauketat, *The Archaeology of Downtown Cahokia: The Tract 15A and Dunham Tract Excavations*, Studies in Archaeology 1 (Urbana: Illinois Transportation Archaeological Research Program, University of Illinois, 1998); Timothy R. Pauketat, Mark A. Rees, and Stephanie L. Pauketat, *An Archaeological Survey of Horseshoe Lake State Park, Madison County, Illinois*, Report of Investigations 55 (Springfield: Illinois State Museum, 1998); Timothy R. Pauketat, ed., *The Archaeology of Downtown Cahokia II: The 1960 Excavation of Tract 15B*, Studies in Illinois Archaeology 8 (Urbana: Illinois State Archaeological Survey, 2013); Emerson, *Cahokia and the Archaeology of Power*; and James M. Collins, "Cahokia Settlement and Social Structures as Viewed from the ICT-II," in Pauketat and Emerson, *Cahokia*, 124–40. Follow the evidence in Alt, *Cahokia's Complexities*; Mehrer, *Cahokia's Countryside*; and Pauketat, Alt, and Kruchten, "Emerald Acropolis."

65 Emerson, *Cahokia and the Archaeology of Power*; Pauketat, *Archaeology of Downtown Cahokia II*; Pauketat, *Archaeology of Downtown Cahokia*; and Pauketat, Alt, and Kruchten, "Emerald Acropolis."

66 See Philip Phillips, James Alfred Ford, and James Bennett Griffin, *Archaeological Survey in the Lower Mississippi Alluvial Valley, 1940–1947*, Papers of the Peabody Museum of Archaeology and Ethnology 25 (Cambridge, Mass.: Harvard University, 1951).

67 Pauketat, *Temples for Cahokia Lords*.

68 Amin and Thrift, *Cities*.

69 Susan M. Alt, "The Power of Diversity: The Roles of Migration and Hybridity in Culture Change," in *Leadership and Polity in Mississippian Society*, ed. Brian M. Butler and Paul D. Welch, Center for Archaeological Investigations Occasional Paper 33 (Carbondale: Southern Illinois University, 2006), 289–308.

70 Tamira K. Brennan, Alleen M. Betzenhauser, Michael Brent Lansdell, Luke A. Plocher, Victoria E. Potter, and Daniel F. Blodgett, "Community Organization of the East St. Louis Precinct," in Emerson, Koldehoff, and Brennan, *Revealing Greater Cahokia*; and Brennan, *East St. Louis Precinct Mississippian Features*.

71 Milner, *Cahokia Chiefdom*.

72 Alt, *Cahokia's Complexities*; and Emerson, *Cahokia and the Archaeology of Power*.

73 Timothy R. Pauketat, Andrew C. Fortier, Susan M. Alt, and Thomas E. Emerson, "A Mississippian Conflagration at East St. Louis and Its Historical Implications," *Journal of Field Archaeology* 38 (2013):208–24.

74 Pauketat, *Temples for Cahokia Lords.*

75 Pauketat et al., "Mississippian Conflagration at East St. Louis."

76 Melissa R. Baltus and Sarah E. Baires, "Elements of Power in the Cahokian World," *Journal of Social Archaeology* 12 (2012):167–92.

77 Timothy R. Pauketat, "Mounds, Buildings, Posts, Palisades, and Compounds," in *The Archaeology of the East St. Louis Mound Center, Part I: The Southside Excavations,* ed. Timothy R. Pauketat, Illinois Transportation Archaeological Research Reports 21 (Urbana: University of Illinois: Urbana, 2005), 113–92.

78 Gilles Deleuze and Félix Guattari, *A Thousand Plateaus: Capitalism and Schizophrenia* (Minneapolis: University of Minnesota Press, 1987).

79 Jane Bennett, *Vibrant Matter: A Political Ecology of Things* (Durham, N.C.: Duke University Press, 2010); Manuel DeLanda, *Assemblage Theory* (Edinburgh: Edinburgh University Press, 2016); Manuel DeLanda, *A New Philosophy of Society: Assemblage Theory and Social Complexity* (London: Bloomsbury, 2006); and Karen Barad, *Meeting the Universe Halfway: Quantum Physics and the Entanglement of Matter and Meaning* (Durham, N.C.: Duke University Press, 2007).

80 DeLanda, *Assemblage Theory.*

81 N. J. Thrift, *Non-Representational Theory: Space, Politics, Affect* (London: Routledge, 2008).

82 Barad, *Meeting the Universe Halfway.*

83 Bruno Latour, *Reassembling the Social: An Introduction to Actor-Network Theory* (Oxford: Oxford University Press, 2005).

84 For a range of examples, see Hall, "Cultural Background of Mississippian Symbolism"; Jay Miller, "Changing Moons: A History of Caddo Religion," *Plains Anthropologist* 41, no. 157 (1996):243–59; and Neihardt, *Black Elk Speaks.*

85 See Miller, "Changing Moons"; Heidorn and Whitelaw, *Field Guide to Natural Phenomena*; and Thomas E. Emerson, "Materializing Cahokia Shamans," *Southeastern Archaeology* 22 (2003):135–54.

PART II

Waterscapes

5

Hydraulic Landscapes
of Roman and Byzantine Cities

JORDAN PICKETT

A POLITICAL MAP OF THE ROMAN EMPIRE AT ITS EARLY SECOND-century CE peak is a veil for its territory (Figure 5.1). This map's translucent red layer inscribes the 4.7 million km², from Spain to Syria, occupied by Roman power for the better part of seven hundred years, from approximately 150 BCE to 600 CE. This map's sea of red, however, also *conceals* the fractured environments onto which the Roman empire[1] was projected: highly variegated Mediterranean geologies[2] and hydrologies,[3] mountains and seismicity,[4] microclimates[5] and vegetation.[6] These environmental factors constrained the abilities of Romans to organize cities and hinterlands, less—quite critically—the extraordinary "techno-ideological" power of the Roman empire to engage in total transformations of landscape, not least via the engineered management of water.[7]

Environmental transformation in the Roman world became possible with the combined labor of bureaucracies and architecture, which could reproduce ways of living with water that first appeared in rainy Greece and Roman Italy alongside karst and pozzolana concrete. State-sponsored aqueducts[8] led spring water in from city hinterlands for consumption in monumental fountains and baths.[9] These structures were critical techno-ideological components in the Roman hydraulic paradigm, by which architecture and administration[10] were exported alongside conquest and militarization from Italy to the farthest Eastern Mediterranean.[11] Scholarship to date has overwhelmingly studied aqueducts as objects of engineering, impressive as they are. Archaeological narratives have traditionally been concerned with aqueducts and their build histories—foundations and restorations, alongside service disruptions or terminations caused by wars and earthquakes—with less attention to their long-term evolution or their role

FIGURE 5.1

A political map of the Roman empire, ca. 114 CE, with cities and sites mentioned in this essay.
1) Alexandria; 2) Amorium; 3) Anazarbos; 4) Aphrodisias; 5) Aspendos; 6) Athens; 7) Banias;
8) Barbegal; 9) Basilica Therma; 10) Bet She'an; 11) Butrint; 12) Caesarea Maritima; 13) Chersonesus;
14) Constantinople; 15) Corinth; 16) Dara; 17) Ephesus; 18) Hierapolis; 19) Hippos; 20) Ingelheim;
21) Jerash; 22) Knossos; 23) Kourion; 24) Larissa; 25) Mokissos; 26) Myra; 27) Nicopolis ad Istrum;
28) Olynthus; 29) Orcistos; 30) Ostia; 31) Pella; 32) Pergamum; 33) Perge; 34) Petra; 35) Pliska;
36) Preslav; 37) Priene; 38) Pylos; 39) Ramla; 40) Rome; 41) Sagalassos; 42) Samos; 43) Side;
44) Sirmium; 45) Stobi; 46) Therma/Myrikion; 47) Thessaloníki; 48) Tiberias; 49) Troy; 50) Tylissos;
51) Venice. Map by Jordan Pickett; site content projected on political and elevation data from Ancient
World Mapping Center (http://awmc.unc.edu/wordpress/map-files) / Creative Commons.

within the wider Roman urban environment or society. This essay briefly outlines an environmental history of Roman aqueducts and urban water management that has emerged from recent scholarship in order to elucidate the nature of the Roman hydraulic paradigm and to explain how that paradigm encouraged particular environmental and city-hinterland relationships that were ultimately unsustainable.

The Hydraulic Paradigm for Aqueducts and Water for Roman Cities

The hydraulic or techno-ideological framework for Roman imperial-era water should be located within the Roman administrative category for cities, the Latin *civitas* or Greek *polis*. *Civitates* or *poleis* (pl.) were qualified often but not exclusively as population

FIGURE 5.2
Kırkgöz, one
of twenty-two
aqueduct bridges
outside Side
in Pamphylia,
southern Turkey.
Photograph by
Jordan Pickett.

centers. More important was their primary role as locations for municipally organized
tax collection, and as central places for the exchange of agricultural products drawn
from their hinterlands, connected by paved roads and coast-hopping ships.[12] The *polis*
was, secondarily, a monumentalized space for local ritual and elite self-representation
through benefactions both religious and secular, with a standardized typology of public
buildings[13] whose donors were commemorated with portrait sculpture and inscriptions
in stone or mosaic.[14]

Architecturally, Roman *poleis* became as familiar and predictable as American suburbs thanks to a highly standardized "tool kit" of public buildings and connective tissue,
constructed with a material minimum of localized differentiation.[15] Cities throughout
the empire—from Spain to Syria—became functionally and visually interchangeable,
sharing rectilinear roads with porticoes and arched gates punctuating towered walls.
Columned temples (or later, churches) stood alongside those buildings for assembly
and entertainment: forums and baths, theaters and hippodromes. Water's supply, distribution, consumption, and drainage[16] was accommodated in giant, vaulted public
baths[17] and multitiered public fountains,[18] replete with sculptural displays[19] that advertised both immense volumes of potable water and the distant hinterland springs from
which they came, carried via aqueducts into cities (Figure 5.2).[20]

≈

After disagreements about which water sources were best for consumption during the
Classical and Hellenistic periods (fifth to first centuries BCE)—compare Plato's love

for springs[21] with Hippocrates's preference for fresh rainwater[22]—Roman authors such as Columella,[23] Pliny the Elder,[24] and Athenaeus[25] found consensus when they denigrated drinking water from wells and cisterns to favor consumption of spring water instead. Springs, collected at their sources before confluence with larger stream and river systems, became the universally preferred source for Roman drinking water; this was a habit enabled and propagated by aqueducts. (Perhaps surprisingly, abundant surface water from rivers or lakes was only rarely used to feed aqueducts.)[26] Reluctant or forced consumption of water from wells and cisterns was linked by ancient observers to the decisions[27]—via a variety of administrative and fiscal mechanisms—that initiated Roman aqueduct construction.

A few words about the technological history and context of Bronze and Iron Age aqueducts, which were not at all like the later Roman ones.[28] The earliest Bronze Age aqueducts were simple, unpressurized, open-flow systems with channels and terra-cotta pipes—relatively short, just 1–5 km long—that first appear in connection with palace and sanctuary contexts around 1700 BCE, such as the Minoan palace at Knossos on Crete,[29] and slightly later at Mycenaean Pylos[30] and Tylissos.[31] After a long absence in the historical record, open-flow aqueducts reappear suddenly in the Archaic period from ca. 600 to 400 BCE—for the limited supply of communities rather than palaces, in tandem with cisterns and wells—for instance, on the Aegean island of Samos,[32] at Athens in Greece,[33] in the cities of Greek Sicily,[34] and in western Anatolia at Priene.[35]

≈

More technologically sophisticated than open-flow systems are those aqueducts that depend on inverted siphons, which carry water across valleys through pipelines under pressure, by the principle of water rising to its own level.[36] Inverted siphons also appear ca. 500–400 BCE on a fairly small scale at Olynthus in Greece,[37] before their installation in 200–150 BCE—again for palace and sanctuary—at the Antiochid palace at Pergamum,[38] and in Rome to supply the Republican Temple of Jupiter on the Capitoline Hill.[39]

From these brief remarks, it is important to emphasize that, before the first century CE, early aqueducts were small in scale and technologically simple, with narrow rock-cut tunnels or pipelines just a few kilometers long. Pre-Roman aqueducts were always used in combination with wells and cisterns for ground- and rainwater, and such early aqueducts were most frequently directed to royal and religious buildings for display. Dora Crouch demonstrated that most pre-Roman cities in the Mediterranean were preferentially built on karst/carbonate-surface geologies.[40] If local springs were not available, shallow bedrock held the promise of a water table accessible via wells. Otherwise, precipitation was readily captured in cisterns that were organized at the level of households, rather than neighborhoods.[41]

The critical accomplishment of Roman bureaucracy and engineers was, therefore, the ability to upscale and proliferate Archaic/Classical and Hellenistic water technologies—to create new and substantially larger water-supply systems that could quench developing tastes for spring water's display and consumption in Roman cities of tens of thousands, by even the meanest citizen, in the most inhospitably arid Eastern Mediterranean environments, where bountiful springs could not be found within fifty or one hundred kilometers.[42]

Roman aqueducts were constructed with various financial mechanisms by contracted labor, corvée, or soldiers, who employed a combination of rock-carved, cut-and-cover channels with masonry-built sections to move water from its source at springs across topography and into cities.[43] Following the contours of Roman military and urban expansion, aqueducts were typically designed at the same time as a city's roads and gates. At least 1,600 Roman aqueducts were constructed in the nine centuries from 300 BCE to 600 CE.[44]

The longest and most complex Roman systems—at Constantinople[45] or Rome[46]—peaked at approximately 250 km in length, with dozens of striding, arcaded stone bridges and the capacity to deliver between 50–100 million l of water per day (Figures 5.3 and 5.4). Side's aqueduct, in southern Anatolia, represents a reasonably average system: 30 km long with tunnels and bridges, delivering on the order of 10–20 million l of water per day.[47] A detailed study of construction logistics for the Side aqueduct estimated that this system's construction—including materials requisition, transport, and labor for erection—could have required 500 persons working full-time, 365 days a year, for three years.[48]

The provision of such incredible volumes of water created very particular and often precarious environmental relationships within and between Roman cities and hinterlands. Aqueducts promoted increases in population density because city dwellers no longer needed to take responsibility for their own household's water autonomy via wells and cisterns, as was typical in the Classical and Hellenistic periods.[49] The Roman shift away from Hellenistic water autonomy at the family level can be related to urban densification after the first century CE, especially via multistory apartment blocks called *insulae* that provided space for both shops and housing (often in squalid conditions).[50] In *insulae* and other forms of high-density housing (such as barracks), tenants lacked their own roofs and courtyards, obviating the choice for domestically organized rainwater collection into cisterns via gutters, or digging wells. Very few Roman houses had direct connections to the water mains of aqueducts—around 10 percent at Pompeii, for instance. But as today, those with access consumed disproportionate quantities of water for continuously running courtyard fountains and private baths.[51] Rather, most Roman city dwellers took their water from public fountains either directly themselves or indirectly, with the service of water carriers (*aquarii*) who sold fountain water from ceramic jars in the streets.[52] After the construction of aqueducts in many Roman cities, water portfolios demonstrably narrowed: cisterns and wells were decommissioned and replaced by fountains, resulting in greater dependency on aqueduct-fed spring water to meet basic needs.[53] Reliance on aqueducts for subsistence-level water supplies necessitated substantial and continuous Roman investments for upkeep (in the form of money, labor, and bureaucracy) while also amplifying attendant risks in the event of neglect,[54] drought,[55] or invasion.[56]

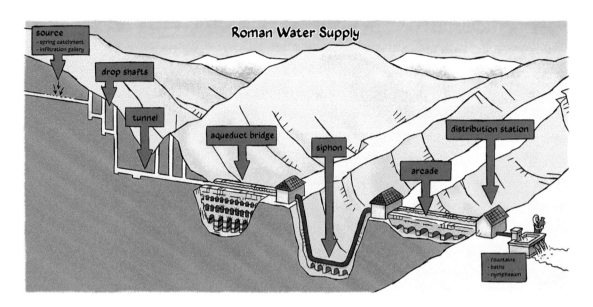

FIGURE 5.3

Graphical overview of Roman aqueduct system components, from spring to city. Image courtesy of Roger Klaasen.

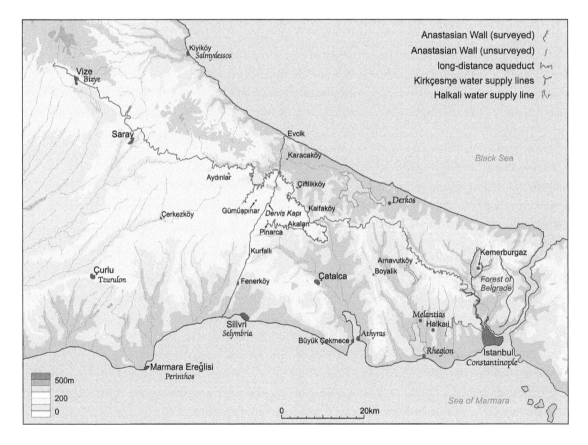

FIGURE 5.4

The aqueduct supplying Constantinople. Image courtesy of Jim Crow.

FIGURE 5.5
Coin from Butrint/ Buthrotum, showing the *arcuatio* or arcade of the city's aqueduct. Drawing by Jordan Pickett, after Marvin Tameanko, *Monumental Coins: Buildings and Structures on Ancient Coinage* (Iola, Wis.: Krause Publications, 1999); see n. 20.

Roman aqueducts naturalized a city's ownership of distant, hinterland springs by appropriating their flows for city fountains and baths, which were vitally important for state ideologies and popular conceptions of urban life in the empire (Figure 5.5).[57] Aqueducts concealed the geological and sociotechnical processes that created urban water supplies, as liquid trickled from springs into fountains to produce the miracle or *thauma* of spring water flowing where it did not naturally belong, for instance in otherwise dry cities or atop mountain sanctuaries of the gods.[58] This technological development—which progressively bound cities in resource dependency to their hinterlands via invisible networks of pipes that separated water consumption from its rural sources—was a critical step toward what Karl Marx called the "fetishization of commodities," excepting the important fact that money was rarely involved. Roman water was mostly provided gratis to the public via fountains, with supplies diverted from the water mains to private houses primarily on the basis of office and rank, and only secondarily with purchased subscriptions.[59]

During the high Roman empire, from the first to third centuries CE, water from aqueducts was preferentially used for display (in fountains and baths) and for consumption (via fountains). There were relatively limited applications for urban production, primarily due to regulations which prohibited activities that created fire risks (and noxious smells) within city walls.[60]

On the other hand, the flow of water in Roman aqueducts was well adapted as a source of motive power in mills, especially but not exclusively after the fourth century CE.[61] Water carried through millraces was not polluted: it continued down the line for consumption and use elsewhere. Water-powered mills were—like the inverted siphon—a technological advance born in the Hellenistic period (fourth to first centuries BCE) that was inherited and upscaled by the Romans. Under their vision, water-powered mills proliferated across the Mediterranean for a variety of applications, most notably in cities for grinding grain into flour and for sawing stone. We have widespread archaeological evidence for the installation of water mills, about sixty from across the empire altogether,[62] many of which were placed on the lines of urban aqueducts. For instance, a cascade of water-powered flour mills excavated at Rome and known from literary and archaeological sources was powered by the Aqua Traiana as it poured down the Janiculum Hill.[63] These installations also appear in provincial towns such as Barbegal, outside Arles in southern France, where an aqueduct powered a cascade of eight water mills, producing 4.5 tons of flour per day—enough for bread to feed approximately ten thousand people, apparently used not for the local community but to supply military needs.[64] Stone saws were another application for late antique water mills: geared saw blades turned by aqueduct waters have been excavated in urban artisanal areas at Ephesus[65] and Jerash[66] in northern Jordan.

Urban aqueducts were occasionally used, both legally and illegally, to irrigate urban and suburban gardens. Yet demand for grain (and olives or wine) in Rome or Constantinople far exceeded local availability of water and fields. To satisfy the public's appetite, agricultural commodities were shipped in via state-sponsored or state-subsidized deliveries then called *annona*,[67] along with what is today called "virtual water."[68] Compared to grains and cereals, fruits and vegetables required more water and more labor. They were also less conducive to sale after long-distance transport, and thereby necessitated the creation of local networks for irrigation and trade.[69] Urban aqueducts were one source for this water and—by virtue of their proximity to city markets—helped to create lucrative opportunities for urban and suburban gardeners. No surprise then that Roman legal codes repeatedly complained about illicit diversions of aqueduct water for irrigation, and noted that illegally irrigated gardens were subject to confiscation.[70] On the other hand, surveys from Italy and Aphrodisias (in western Anatolia) indicate that suburban irrigation could also be well integrated with aqueduct systems in configurations where rural and urban needs were complementary and supplied by the same source.[71]

Here we should also note the variation in irrigation requirements for different regions and crops. The vast majority of east Roman agricultural areas, excepting the driest portions of Syria and the Levant, received more than 200 mm in annual precipitation.[72] Those regions receiving less than 200 mi of yearly rain required irrigation for even the most drought-resistant cereals, such as barley. In these parched areas, for instance around Petra in modern Jordan, Roman and especially late antique settlements adapted sophisticated Nabataean/pre-Roman methods of runoff irrigation.[73]

Case Study: Ephesus

The complex environmental relationships that aqueducts created in Roman cities are neatly encapsulated in a case study of Ephesus in western Anatolia. One of the largest ancient Roman cities, it is also one of the best archaeologically documented today, thanks to more than a century of careful study by Austrian excavations.[74]

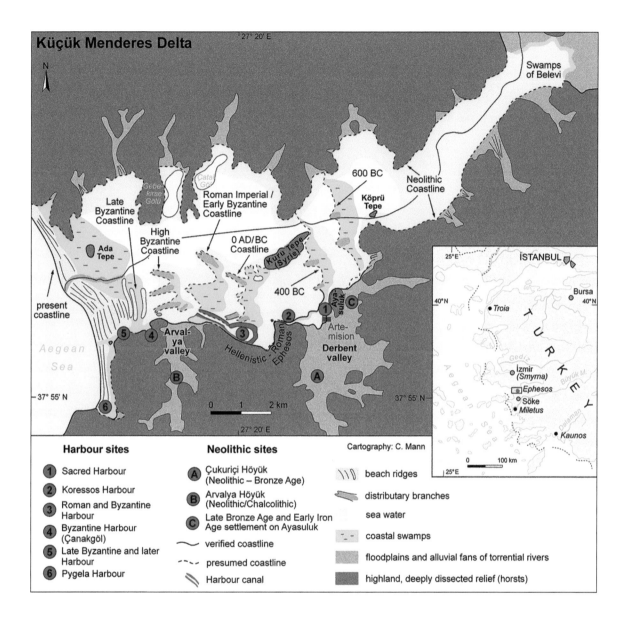

Figure content:

Küçük Menderes Delta

27° 20' E

Swamps of Belevi

600 BC

Neolithic Coastline

Köprü Tepe

Roman Imperial / Early Byzantine Coastline

Late Byzantine Coastline

High Byzantine Coastline

0 AD/BC Coastline

Çatal Gö...

Gebe kirse Gölü

Ada Tepe

present coastline

Aegean Sea

Kuru Tepe (Syrie)

400 BC

Aya suluk

Arvalya valley

Hellenistic – Roman Ephesos

Arte- mision

Derbent valley

37° 55' N

0   1   2 km

27° 20' E

İSTANBUL

25°E

40°N

Bursa

Troia

İzmir (Smyrna)

Ephesos

Söke

Miletus

Kaunos

40°N

T U R K E Y

Aegean

Gediz

Büyük M.

Dalaman

Cartography: C. Mann

0   100 km

25°E

Harbour sites
1. Sacred Harbour
2. Koressos Harbour
3. Roman and Byzantine Harbour
4. Byzantine Harbour (Çanakgöl)
5. Late Byzantine and later Harbour
6. Pygela Harbour

Neolithic sites
A. Çukuriçi Höyük (Neolithic – Bronze Age)
B. Arvalya Höyük (Neolithic/Chalcolithic)
C. Late Bronze Age and Early Iron Age settlement on Ayasuluk

— verified coastline

- - - presumed coastline

Harbour canal

beach ridges

distributary branches

sea water

coastal swamps

floodplains and alluvial fans of torrential rivers

highland, deeply dissected relief (horsts)

The development of Ephesus was constrained on all sides by water: an important port, the Aegean Sea lies immediately to its west. To the north is the delta of the Little Maeander River, also called the Küçük Menderes or Caystros, whose rapid alluviation gradually pushed the coastline west and encouraged the progressive western displacement of the city's center (Figures 5.6 and 5.7).[75] Around 200 BCE, Lysimachus moved the city from its center around the Artemision temple on the coast/alluviated river plain to the site that tourists visit today,[76] set in a westward saddle between two small mountains, above an aquifer trapped between layers of crystalline marble and micaceous slate.[77] Water was drawn from this aquifer via wells throughout the city; wells of Hellenistic date have been excavated in the lower agora, for instance.[78] The city's population growth and densification in the following centuries was facilitated by any

FIGURE 5.6

Historical alluviation in the Caystros River Valley, with Ephesus indicated. Image courtesy of Friederike Stock and Helmut Brückner.

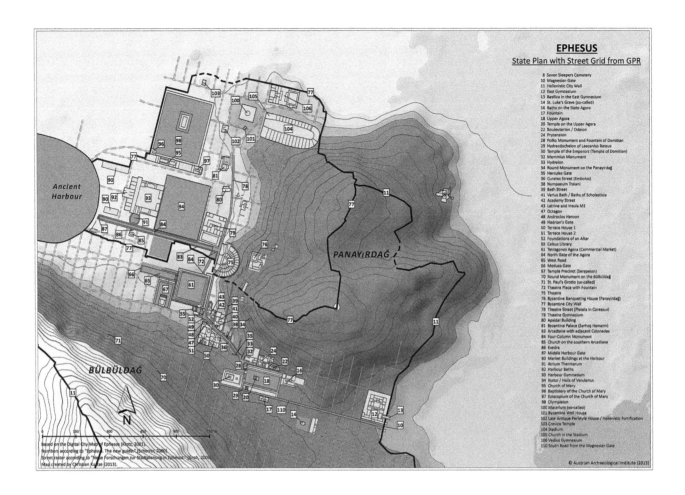

The following is the legend text from the map:

EPHESUS
State Plan with Street Grid from GPR

8 Seven Sleepers Cemetery
10 Magnesian Gate
11 Hellenistic City Wall
12 East Gymnasium
13 Basilica in the East Gymnasium
14 St. Luke's Grave (so-called)
16 Baths on the State Agora
17 Fountain
18 Upper Agora
20 Temple on the Upper Agora
22 Bouleuterion / Odeion
24 Prytaneion
28 Pollio Monument and Fountain of Domitian
29 Hydreodocheion of Laecanius Bassus
30 Temple of the Emperors (Temple of Domitian)
32 Memmius Monument
33 Hydreion
34 Round Monument on the Panayırdağ
35 Hercules Gate
36 Curetes Street (Embolos)
38 Nymphaeum Traiani
39 Bath Street
41 Varius Bath / Baths of Scholasticia
42 Academy Street
43 Latrine and Insula M1
47 Octagon
48 Androclos Heroon
49 Hadrian's Gate
50 Terrace House 1
51 Terrace House 2
52 Foundations of an Altar
55 Celsus Library
61 Tetragonos Agora (Commercial Market)
64 North Gate of the Agora
65 West Road
66 Medusa Gate
67 Temple Precinct (Serapeion)
70 Round Monument on the Bülbüldağ
71 St. Paul's Grotto (so-called)
72 Theatre Place with Fountain
75 Theatre
76 Byzantine Banqueting House (Panayırdağ)
77 Byzantine City Wall
78 Theatre Street (Plateia in Coressus)
79 Theatre Gymnasium
80 Apsidal Building
81 Byzantine Palace (Şerhoş Hamamı)
83 Arcadiane with adjacent Colonades
84 Four-Column Monument
86 Church on the southern Arcadiane
86 Exedra
87 Middle Harbour Gate
90 Market Buildings at the Harbour
91 Atrium Thermarum
92 Harbour Baths
93 Harbour Gymnasium
94 Xystoi / Halls of Verulanus
95 Church of Mary
96 Baptistery of the Church of Mary
97 Episcopium of the Church of Mary
98 Olympieion
100 Macellum (so-called)
101 Byzantine Well House
102 Late Antique Peristyle House / Hellenistic Fortification
103 Crevice Temple
104 Stadium
105 Church in the Stadium
106 Vedius Gymnasium
110 South Road from the Magnesian Gate

© Austrian Archaeological Institute (2013)

Based on the Digital City Map of Ephesus (Klotz, 2001).
Numbers according to "Ephesus. The new guide" (Scherrer, 2000).
Street raster according to "Neue Forschungen zur Stadtplanung in Ephesos" (Groh, 2006).
Map created by Christian Kurtze (2013).

FIGURE 5.7

Labeled plan of structures in Ephesus. Image by OeAW-OeAI/ Christian Kurtze.

of six aqueducts: two short-distance, low-output aqueducts in the pre-Roman period, and four long-distance, high-output aqueducts added by 150 CE.[79] As these aqueducts were brought online, older wells and cisterns became obsolete, were infilled, and went out of use: the city's approximately two hundred thousand people became dependent on its aqueducts.

Ephesian aqueducts carried water for the city's standard architectural "tool kit": no fewer than six massive vaulted bath complexes and at least ten public fountains or nymphaea, where most city dwellers took their water (Figure 5.8).[80]

The so-called Fountain of Trajan, or Nymphaeum Traiani, is illustrative of city-hinterland relationships established by aqueduct construction (Figure 5.9).[81] The nymphaeum's closure panels on the street-side basin are worn from centuries of heavy use as hands, ropes, and buckets withdrew water. The ornate architecture above the large water basin—a facade of columns and aediculae—serves no utilitarian purpose but rather provides an artfully framed space for sculptured portraits of the patron, the local magistrate and priest Claudius Aristion, with his family, who subsidized the aqueduct.

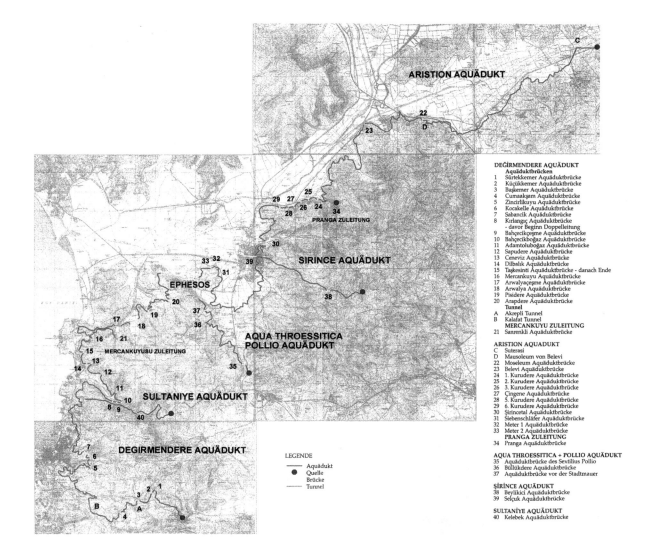

The portraits of Aristion's family were displayed alongside the imperial family, an index of their importance for the community and the empire writ large. The Nymphaeum Traiani's sculptural ensemble was centered on a heroic portrait of Trajan, with water springing forth below his feet, seemingly at his command.[82] The personification of the river Caystros, whose tributary springs (50 km distant) had been diverted into the Aristion aqueduct, appeared throughout the city's coinage.[83]

Similarly, baths at Ephesus were densely populated sculptural environments that advertised the capabilities of emperors and local elites to move huge quantities of earth, stone, and water.[84] Ephesian baths were, simultaneously, tremendous consumers of timber for heating. Extrapolating from a recent scientific study of a similarly scaled bath (at nearby Sagalassos), we can understand how the provision of timber for Ephesian baths could create immense pressure on regional forests: six operational baths at Ephesus would have demanded some 12,000–17,000 tons of timber per year (the equivalent of

FIGURE 5.8

Aqueducts at Ephesus. Image courtesy of Gilbert Wiplinger for OeAW-OeAI.

FIGURE 5.9

Fountain of Trajan
(Nymphaeum
Traiani) at Ephesus,
in anastylosis.
Photograph by
Jordan Pickett.

2–3 km² of dense forest), without accounting for the demands of cooking fuel, pottery kilns, or any other activities, in a city of perhaps 200,000 at its peak.[85] Without careful management, forest resources in many Roman cities were potentially pushed to the limits of sustainability by the fuel demands of public baths.

Issues of sustainability at Ephesus extended to water. In a city where aqueducts provided on the order of 30–50 million l of water per day, the imperial city was devoid of water storage. A recent study of the harbor has indicated that the continuous flow-through of the aqueducts was critical for maintenance of the artificial Roman harbor, without which Ephesus quickly became a swampy sediment trap.[86]

Endless flows of water into imperial Roman Ephesus were interrupted by a series of earthquakes in the later third and fourth centuries, which prompted a substantial reconfiguration of the city's water system at the beginning of the fifth century, coincident with the introduction of Christian monumental architecture.[87]

We can observe important changes in water supply, distribution, and consumption patterns at Ephesus after the early fifth century. Water-powered mills were installed in new productive areas in the city's former monumental core, adjacent to new administrative complexes suggestive of their importance and, perhaps, official oversight.[88] Baths were closed and adapted to new purposes. The massive Vedius Gymnasium by the hippodrome and two smaller baths (the Scholastikia bath on the Embolos and the Upper Agora baths) were restored and maintained, but others were abandoned or repurposed. Portions of the East Bath were reused as a church and cemetery,[89] while the vast palaestra of Constantine's Harbor baths (the so-called Verulanus Hall) was subdivided for housing.[90] New, immense public cisterns and water-storage installations were created for the first time since the first century in order to capture both rainwater and aqueduct overflow. Aqueduct-fed fountains were built, too, even as numerous new wells for groundwater were sunk throughout the city, in both public and private contexts, expanding the city's water portfolio.[91] Water was also diverted from obsolescent temples to new consumers in late antique Ephesus, including churches and artisanal areas. For instance, water mains that had fed into the Temple of Hadrian's precinct were repurposed for baths, latrines, fountains, and productive installations around the episcopal complex at the Church of Saint Mary.[92]

Roman aqueduct and water-distribution systems remained operational at Ephesus until sometime in the seventh or eighth century, albeit with the aforementioned revisions that reflected fundamental changes in the city's relationships with water. Limited sections of the Değirmendere aqueduct at Ephesus—stretching 50 km into its southern hinterland—were, however, maintained until perhaps the tenth century for the Roman-Byzantine coastal settlement at Anaia/Kadıkalesi, with a new diversion to the Genoese/Venetian coastal settlement created in the fourteenth century, before its seventeenth-century repair for an Ottoman caravansary at Scala Nova.[93]

The Afterlives of Roman Aqueducts

While preexisting Roman aqueducts and distribution systems at Ephesus were creatively adapted during Late Antiquity, surviving in modified form and adapted in sections until the seventeenth century, aqueducts in other cities were phased out under various circumstances at much earlier dates.

The evolution of Roman water systems does not parallel political history, but rather should be understood as a bundle of developmental options that played out from the third to eighth century, driven by local circumstances and exigencies in the shadow of larger-scale cultural and religious shifts. During this long period, the traditional Roman hydraulic paradigm fell apart everywhere. Where spring-water–fed aqueducts and endless water for leisure and display in baths and fountains had previously been prioritized, an expanded palette of ground- and rainwater options came to replace them. Simultaneously, the administrative and architectural category of the city or *polis* expanded during Late Antiquity: the Roman *polis* shed its infrastructural requirements for aqueducts, massive baths, and aediculated fountains. Increasingly, we find instead in Byzantine *poleis* the conservative architecture of hot springs,[94] water-powered mills,[95] ornate wells,[96] and water storage (Figures 5.10 and 5.11). Late antique or Byzantine cisterns were no longer the miniscule, twenty- to thirty-square-meter tanks under the management of households—as was so typical during the Hellenistic period or earlier Roman empire. Cisterns became, instead, works of cutting-edge, monumental architecture aggrandized by elites,[97] the church,[98] and emperors.[99] The modular brick- and stone-vaulted forms of Late Antique cisterns mirror contemporary innovations in church

FIGURE 5.10

Byzantine puteal/wellhead from Venice. Harvard Art Museums / Fogg Museum, Gift of Denman W. Ross, 1917.146. Imaging Department © President and Fellows of Harvard College.

architecture after the fifth century, as the timber roofs of basilicas began to be replaced with stone vaults; some of the earliest pointed arches in the history of architecture may be found in seventh- and eighth-century cisterns in Cyprus and Palestine.[100] Aqueducts remained too after the seventh century, especially in important Byzantine ports and provincial capitals (see below), but their uses were more diversified and they were no longer requisite for ideological and institutional definitions of the city.

This shift is perhaps best illustrated by an overview of the six outcomes or endgames for Roman aqueducts as they evolved between the third and eighth century.

Outright Rejection of Aqueducts

Spring water from aqueducts was the most desirable source for potable water during the imperial Roman period. But the diversification and pursuit of alternative water sources during Late Antiquity is nowhere more visible than in those cities that retained administrative status and continued to function as *poleis* or provincial capitals *without* aqueducts. Nicopolis ad Istrum in Bulgaria is a good example—sacked and mostly destroyed in the 450s, it was reoccupied as the metropolitan capital of the province of Moesia after the sixth century, albeit without municipal buildings or restoration of its four aqueducts.[101] Comparable examples of Late Antique provincial capitals without aqueducts include Larissa in Thessaly,[102] Mokissos in Cappadocia,[103] and Amorium in Phrygia.[104] After the seventh century, a new military organization of Roman provinces called *themes*

FIGURE 5.11

The Basilica Cistern at Constantinople, built during the reign of Justinian (527–565 CE). Photograph by Ralf Steinberger / Creative Commons.

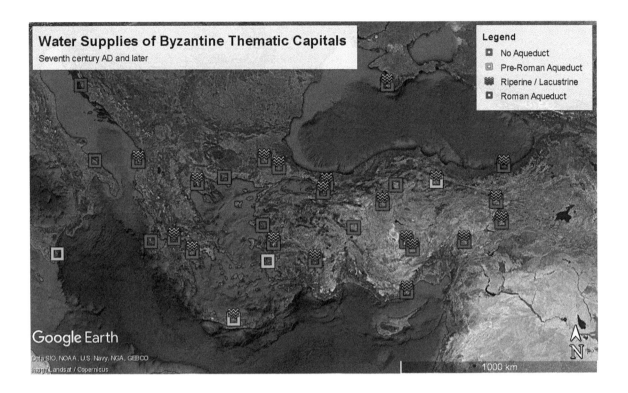

Water Supplies of Byzantine Thematic Capitals
Seventh century AD and later

Legend
☐ No Aqueduct
☐ Pre-Roman Aqueduct
🌊 Riperine / Lacustrine
☐ Roman Aqueduct

Google Earth

Data SIO, NOAA, U.S. Navy, NGA, GEBCO
Image Landsat / Copernicus

1000 km

FIGURE 5.12

Water resources
in the so-called
thematic capitals,
post-seventh
century CE. Image
by Jordan Pickett.

emerged; examination of arrangements for water supply in this system's thirty-three *thematic* capitals reveals a comparable pattern. Roughly a third of the *thematic* capitals maintained their preexisting Roman aqueducts (mainly around ports), another third had aqueducts but abandoned them, and the last third never had aqueducts to begin with, but instead relied upon naturally available sources from lakes and rivers, wells or cisterns (Figure 5.12).

Outright Continuity of Aqueducts

While Roman cities captured by the Umayyads in the Levant after 636 almost universally maintained their aqueducts, the picture in the remaining Byzantine territories centered on Constantinople was considerably more uneven. Abandonment rates were very high, but Byzantine cities with functioning aqueducts after 600 include Thessaloníki,[105] Chersonesus in the Crimea,[106] Ephesus,[107] and Myra, among others. Myra—the capital of the province of Lycia, a critical navy base, and an international pilgrimage destination—is illustrative in that it demonstrates how maintained Byzantine systems tended to be very simple, short-distance, open-channel, and often pre-Roman gravity systems without siphons, bridges, or other such technical vulnerabilities, in port locations that had unusual state, military, and/or religious importance.[108]

Catastrophe and Sudden Abandonment

Archaeologically attested examples of aqueducts suddenly rendered dysfunctional by catastrophes such as earthquakes are surprisingly rare. But this may, in many places,

be due to a lack of visibility in the archaeological evidence. Aspendos in south Turkey is, however, a very clear example of aqueducts' seismic vulnerability.[109] The aqueduct at Aspendos was a double-inverted siphon—among the most technically sophisticated of aqueducts—built in the late second or early third century. But it functioned for less than seventy-five years before it was ruined by earthquake (Figure 5.13). Seismic damage at Aspendos was repaired not with a restoration of the system, but with technical simplifications (as also at Pergamum) wherein renovation eliminated inverted siphons.[110] Alternatively, earthquake-damaged aqueducts were sometimes given up because others still functioned (as at Ephesus). Earthquake damage to aqueducts did not usually precede wider settlement abandonment, if sometimes it did portend lower-intensity occupation organized around cisterns and wells. On the other hand, sudden abandonment of aqueducts can be better related to defensive insecurity, particularly in the borderlands affected by sixth- and seventh-century invasions, for instance at Stobi[111] or Sirmium[112] in the Balkans, or at Anazarbos[113] and Side[114] near the Arab frontier.

Gradual Abandonment
In cities such as Banias,[115] Caesarea Maritima,[116] or Troy,[117] we can observe the gradual abandonment of aqueducts due to neglect and lack of repair. Archaeologically this is attested by the deposition of sediments—especially calcium carbonate or sinter, as well as ceramics and alluvium in the aqueducts' channels—which gradually diminished system flow-through at places such as Perge and Bet She'an.

FIGURE 5.13

The short-lived, double-inverted siphon aqueduct at Aspendos, built in the second to third centuries CE and felled by earthquake shortly thereafter. Photograph by Jordan Pickett.

Disaggregation

Disaggregation was the denucleation of settlements to smaller spring sources in a city's hinterland. We encounter precisely this process at Phrygian Hierapolis, where settlement after earthquakes in the 680s fragmented the monumental core toward villages at the springs that had supplied the city's aqueducts.[118] Comparable examples of settlement disaggregation as a consequence of failing urban water systems come from Kourion in Cyprus[119] and Corinth in the Peloponnese.[120]

Nucleation or Convergence

Nucleation or convergence of settlements around locations with maintained aqueducts or plentiful natural water resources was another option for settlement resilience after antiquity. Tiberias in Palestine, for example,[121] grew by leaps and bounds after the Umayyad conquest, even as nearby cities such as Hippos[122] and Pella[123] were abandoned. Such growth at Tiberias may be explained at least in part by the maintenance of aqueducts there, in addition to abundant supplies from the Sea of Galilee[124] and the added attraction of natural hot spring baths; the Umayyads also made Tiberias a provincial capital.[125]

Conclusions and Comparisons

The evidence assembled in this brief essay broadly describes consequences for the trajectory by which Rome and Byzantium progressively disinvested from aqueducts as an administrative, architectural, and ideological prerequisite for cities.[126] Causality for this phenomenon is more diffuse and difficult to explain. Critical, no doubt, were increasingly constrained finances after the loss of Roman territories in Western Europe during the fifth century; the Balkans and Mesopotamia in the sixth century; and the Levant, Egypt, and North Africa following the Islamic conquests of the 630s. Depopulation of cities, coincident with increased focus on rural investments after the seventh century, may also be a factor. Crucially, continued investment in aqueducts at some urban locations—at what are thought of as very late dates (for example, Constantinople, Antioch, and Thessaloníki after the eighth century)—demonstrates that the repair of systems was *not* beyond the technical reach of late Roman or Byzantine engineers. Climate change, also, appears to be a red herring, with similar outcomes in areas such as Anatolia and the Levant with rather different climate histories.[127] Organic Byzantine alternatives to the Roman hydraulic paradigm emerged in the infrastructural space created by older, preexisting Roman water systems. This occurred in cities such as Ephesus, as demonstrated above, even when the Byzantine state chose to extend resources for aqueduct repair from the capital, Constantinople, into the provinces.[128] Besides necessity as the mother of invention, a broad range of religious and cultural stimuli can also be implicated in this shift, as indicated for instance by the Jewish Mishnah's more positive attitudes toward groundwater,[129] or the Christian and Islamic aggrandizement of holy wells.[130] Strategic retrenchment or disinvestment from aqueducts is reflected by the continued, selective maintenance of aqueducts for palaces, ports, capitals, and pilgrimage centers. New paths were charted elsewhere by the imperial and institutional aggrandizement of alternative water supplies, such as wells and cisterns, which were so denigrated and marginalized in the earlier imperial period. At the same time, during this critical era from the sixth to eighth century, Roman-style aqueducts emerge as ideologically and pragmatically valued components of court life in neighboring polities, such as early medieval Italy,[131] Carolingian Francia,[132] Abbasid Iraq and Egypt,[133] and the nascent Bulgarian state at its new capitals in Pliska and Preslav.[134] Curiously, the aggrandizement of groundwater resources in post-Roman territories was, excepting qanats, microscale: ornately carved wellheads or puteals reappear during the sixth and seventh centuries,[135] precisely contemporary with the emergence of macroscale, monumental stepwell complexes in India, but representing an entirely different architectural tradition for groundwater embellishment.[136]

The export of a distinctively Roman hydraulic paradigm from the temperate, water- and timber-rich Italian peninsula to the farthest, arid reaches of the empire necessitated the perpetuation of a particular set of environmental and ideological relationships between hinterland and monumentalized urban cores. These norms—characterized by spring water carried by aqueducts for display and consumption—were outside the realm of sustainability in much of the Roman empire, and arguably constituted a technological overreach. That is, Roman aqueducts enabled conspicuous forms of water and timber consumption that could not be supported by adjacent hinterlands, especially when provincial administrations progressively devalued Roman notions of *urbanitas*.[137] At the same time, typical Roman water-consumption patterns created skeletons of infrastructure during the imperial period (first to third centuries) that could be reappropriated and modified for more locally determined, flexible forms of water consumption during and after Late Antiquity (fourth to seventh centuries). Taken altogether, the range of evidence promotes the perspective that, though many of the empire's aqueducts had been felled by sudden catastrophe, disrepair, or gradual abandonment, the Roman empire began to abandon the aqueduct as an ideological or architectural prerequisite for cities, if not by Justinian's time then certainly by the seventh century, along with those environmental relationships that had been promoted by aqueducts during the period of the high empire, and pursued alternative pathways instead.

Notes

1 Fundamental for fractured Mediterranean landscapes is Nicholas Purcell and Peregrine Horden, *The Corrupting Sea: A Mediterranean History* (Oxford: Blackwell, 2000).

2 Dora Crouch, *Geology and Settlement: Greco-Roman Patterns* (Oxford: Oxford University Press, 2003).

3 For Mediterranean surface geology, see Kristine Asch, *The 1:5 Million International Geological Map of Europe and Adjacent Areas: Development and Implementation of a GIS-Enabled Concept*, Geologisches Jahrbuch Sonderheft SA 3 (Hannover: Bundesanstalt für Geowissenschaften und Rohstoffe, 2003).

4 J. R. McNeill, *The Mountains of the Mediterranean World* (Cambridge: Cambridge University Press, 1992); and for seismicity, see Gianfranco Vannucci, Silvia Pondrelli, Andrea Argnani, Andrea Morelli, Paolo Gasperini, and Enzo Bosci, "An Atlas of Mediterranean Seismicity," supplement, *Annals of Geophysics* 47, no. 1 (2004):247–306.

5 For an overview of precipitation in the historical Mediterranean, see Martin Finné, Karin Holmgren, Hanna S. Sundqvist, Erika Weiberg, and Michael Lindblom, "Climate in the Eastern Mediterranean, and Adjacent Regions, during the Past 6000 Years—A Review," *Journal of Archaeological Science* 38, no. 12 (2011):3153–73; for precipitation in the contemporary Mediterranean, see Christian Töttrup and Ulf Helldén, "Long Term NOAA-AVHRR GIMMS-NDVI-Rainfall Relationships and Trends 1981 to 2003 for Entire DeSurvey Area of Interest," *FP6, DeSurvey IP, Sub-deliverable 1.5. 1.17 (1), Deliverables Data Base* (2007), accessed July 9, 2017, https://lup.lub.lu.se/search/ws/files/5982796/960123.pdf.

6 M. C. Peel, B. L. Finlayson, and T. A. McMahon, "Updated World Map of the Köppen-Geiger Climate Classification," *Hydrology and Earth System Sciences Discussions* 4, no. 2 (2007):439–73, here at fig. 8.

7 For the technology of aqueducts, see Alfred Trevor Hodge, *Roman Aqueducts and Water Supply*, 2nd ed. (London: Duckworth, 2002).

8 Nicholas Purcell, "Rome and the Management of Water: Environment, Culture, and Power," in *Human Landscapes of Classical Antiquity*, ed. Graham Shipley and John Salmon (London: Routledge, 1996), 180–212.

9 See nn. 17–19 below.

10 Werner Eck, "Die Wasserversorgung im römischen Reich: Sozio-politische Bedingungen, Recht und Administration," in *Die Wasserversorgung Antiker Städte* (Mainz: Phillip von Zabern, 1987), 49–102, provides an overview of the administrative processes that governed the construction and maintenance of Roman urban water systems in Italy and across the empire; for Italy, note also Paolo Squatriti, *Water and Society in Early Medieval Italy, AD 400–1000* (Cambridge: Cambridge University Press, 1998).

11 Arid areas inevitably presented the most trouble for the Roman hydraulic paradigm. Salutary are regional case studies from North Africa including Andrew Wilson, "Water Management and Usage in Roman North Africa: A Social and Technological Study" (DPhil thesis, Oxford University, 1997); from hyperarid Arabia and Nabataea, see John Peter Oleson, *Humayma Excavation Project*, vol. 1, *Resources, History, and the Water-Supply System*, ASOR Archaeological Reports 15 (Boston: American Schools of Oriental Research, 2010); and for the coastal Levant, see David Amit, Joseph Patrich, and Yizhar Hirschfeld, eds., *The Aqueducts of Israel*, JRA Supplement 46 (Portsmouth, R.I.: Journal of Roman Archaeology, 2002).

12 For Roman cities as centers for administration, taxation, and exchange, see Arnold H. M. Jones, *The Later Roman Empire 284–602: A Social, Economic, and Administrative Survey*, 2nd ed. (Baltimore: Johns Hopkins University Press, 1986).

13 For cities as spaces of elite and imperial self-representation, see Franz Alto Bauer, *Stadt, Platz, und Denkmal in der Spätantike: Untersuchung zur Ausstattung des öffentlichen Raums in den spätantiken Städten Rom, Konstantinopel, und Ephesos* (Mainz: Von Zabern, 1996).

14 Ramsay MacMullen, "The Epigraphic Habit in the Roman Empire," *American Journal of Philology* 103, no. 3 (1982):233–46.

15 For the replication of Roman urbanism across territory, see William MacDonald, *The Architecture of the Roman Empire*, vol. 2, *An Urban Reappraisal* (New Haven: Yale University Press, 1986), 130–31.

16 For drainage and sanitation, see Ann Kolowski-Ostrow, *The Archaeology of Sanitation in Roman Italy* (Chapel Hill: University of North Carolina Press, 2015).

17 For the architecture and typology of Roman baths, see Inge Nielsen, *Thermae et Balnea* (Aarhus: Aarhus University Press, 1993); and Fikret Yegül, *Baths and Bathing in Classical Antiquity* (New York: Architectural History Foundation, 1992); for epigraphy and social history of baths, see Garrett Fagan, *Bathing in Public in the Roman World* (Ann Arbor: University of Michigan Press, 1999).

18 For a functionalist, archaeological study of Roman fountains and their water supplies, see Julian Richard, *Water for the City, Fountains for the People: Monumental Fountains in the Roman East; An Archaeological Study of Water Management*, Studies in Eastern Mediterranean Archaeology 9 (Turnhout: Brepols, 2012).

19 For an art-historical approach to sculptural installations at Roman fountains, see Brenda Longfellow, *Roman Imperialism and Civic Patronage: Form, Meaning, and Ideology in Monumental Fountain Complexes* (Cambridge: Cambridge University Press, 2011).

20 Sculptural installations at baths and fountains included personified rivers alongside patrons and notables; coins also included similar imagery of river personifications alongside representations of fountains and aqueducts. See Marvin Tameanko, *Monumental Coins: Buildings and Structures on Ancient Coinage* (Iola, Wis.: Krause Publications, 1999).

21 Plato, *Critias* 110–12.

22 Hippocrates, *Airs, Waters, Places* 8.8.

23 Columella, *de Re Rustica* 1.5.1, trans. Harrison Boyd Ash, Loeb 361 (London: William Heinemann, 1941), 59–61.

24 Pliny tells us, regarding cisterns, that "he is surprised that some physicians [following the Hippocratic tradition] highly recommend water from cisterns ... [because] there is no kind of water which contains more slime or more numerous insects of a disgusting nature." *Natural History* 31.21–22, trans. William Henry Samuel Jones, Loeb 418 (London: William Heinemann, 1963), 394–99.

25 See Athenaeus, *Deipnosophistae* 2.35A–47E, trans. Charles Burton Gulick, Loeb 204 (London: William Heinemann, 1927), 152–209 (and quoting here 2.42C–D at 183–84), for a long discussion of the relative value of water versus wine, which describes a number of springs and their waters, and preserves many otherwise lost sources.

26 Hodge, *Roman Aqueducts and Water Supply*, 69.

27 Among many comparable notices, see Philostratus, *Lives of the Philosophers and Sophists*, trans. Wilmer Cave Wright, Loeb 134 (London: William Heinemann, 1921), 142–43, who describes how Herodes Atticus intervened on behalf of the city of Troy, before the Emperor Hadrian, in order to obtain funds that underwrote construction of the aqueduct at that city, after observing that Troy was "ill-supplied with baths, and that the inhabitants drew muddy water from their wells, and had to dig cisterns to catch rain water."

28 For a general overview of the earliest aqueducts, set in a broad history of ancient water technologies, see Steven Mithen, *Thirst: Water and Power in the Ancient World* (Cambridge: Cambridge University Press, 2012), 75–103.

29 James Walter Graham, *The Palaces of Crete* (Princeton: Princeton University Press, 1987), 219.

30 Georgios P. Antoniou, "Architecture and Evolution of the Aqueduct of Pylos," *Proceedings of the 3rd IWA Specialized Conference on Water and Wastewater Technologies in Ancient Civilizations* (Istanbul: IWA Publishing, 2012), 410–19.

31 Larry W. Mays, ed., *Ancient Water Technologies* (Dordrecht: Springer, 2010), 7–15.

32 Hermann J. Kienast, *Die Wasserleitung des Eupalinos auf Samos*, Samos 19 (Bonn: Deutsches Archaeologisches Institut, 1995).

33 Renate Tölle-Kastenbein, *Das archaische Wasserleitungsnetz für Athen und seine späteren Bauphasen* (Mainz: Von Zabern, 1994).

34 Crouch, *Geology and Settlement*, 27–112.

35 Dora Crouch, *Water Management in Ancient Greek Cities* (Oxford: Oxford University Press, 1993), 158–67.

36 For the technology of inverted siphons, see Giorgio Temporelli and Fiorina De Novellis, "Hydraulic Engineering of Inverted Siphons in Roman Age: A Review," *Water Science and Technology Water Supply* 10, no. 3 (2010):445–52.

37 Crouch, *Water Management in Ancient Greek Cities*, 71–75.

38 Günther Garbrecht and Heinrich Fahlbusch, "Die Wasserversorgung von Pergamon," *Istanbuler Mitteilungen* 54 (2004):185–195.

39 Thomas Ashby, *The Aqueducts of Ancient Rome* (Oxford: Clarendon Press, 1935), 152.

40 See n. 2 above.

41 Karst and domestic organization of cisterns and wells in pre-Roman territories: see Crouch, *Geology and Settlement*, 11–12 and 82, respectively.

42 Overview of Roman aqueducts in a historical and technological context: Andrew Wilson, "Hydraulic Engineering and Water Supply," in *Oxford Handbook of Engineering and Technology in the Classical World*, ed. John Peter Oleson (Oxford: Oxford University Press, 2008), 285–318.

43 Hodge, *Roman Aqueducts and Water Supply*, 93–125, for construction.

44 See the incomplete if substantial data set available via ROMAQ: The Atlas Project of Roman Aqueducts, accessed July 7, 2017, http://www.romaq.org/the-project/aqueducts.html.

45 James Crow, Jonathan Bardill, and Richard Bayliss, *Water Supply of Byzantine Constantinople*, Journal of Roman Studies Monographs 11 (London: Society for the Promotion of Roman Studies, 2008).

46 Still fundamental is Ashby, *Aqueducts of Ancient Rome*.

47 Klaus Grewe, "Die römische wasserleitung nach Side (Turkei)," *Antike Welt* 25, no. 2 (1994):192–203.

48 Michael Engels, Matthias Hupperich, Ralf Müller, and Michael Olberding, "Die Wasserleitung von Side: Eine Betrachtung aus bautechnischer Sicht" (Dipl. diss., Lehrstuhl und Institut für Baumaschinen und Baubetrieb, 1983).

49 Efforts to calculate population based on aqueduct output vis-à-vis city area and other factors have, however, remained highly tentative; see J. A. Lloyd and P. R. Lewis, "Water Supply and Urban Population in Roman Cyrenaica," *Libyan Studies* 8 (1977):35–40; and R. P. Duncan-Jones, "Aqueduct Capacity and City Population," *Libyan Studies* 9 (1978):51.

50 James Packer, *The Insulae of Imperial Ostia*, Memoirs of the American Academy in Rome 31 (Rome: American Academy in Rome, 1971); and James Packer, "Housing and Population in Imperial Ostia and Rome," *Journal of Roman Studies* 57, nos. 1–2 (1967):80–95. On sanitary conditions and hygiene in *insulae* and Roman high-density housing, see the classic study by Alex Scobie, "Slums, Sanitation, and Mortality in the Roman World," *Klio* 68, no. 2 (1986):399–433.

51 Rick Jones and Damian Robinson, "Water, Wealth, and Social Status at Pompeii: The House of the Vestals in the First Century," *American Journal of Archaeology* 109, no. 4 (2005):699.

52 For *aquarii* at Rome, see Gerda de Kleijn, *Water Supply of Ancient Rome: City Area, Water, and Population* (Amsterdam: Gieben, 2001), 110n44.

53 Ostia and Pompeii are good examples of this process, whereby cisterns and wells were decommissioned after aqueduct construction; see Maria Antonietta Ricciardi, *La civiltà dell'acqua in Ostia antica* (Rome: Fratelli Palombi, 1996), 1:78–87; and Duncan Keenan-Jones, "Somma-Vesuvian Ground Movements and the Water Supply of Pompeii and the Bay of Naples," *American Journal of Archaeology* 119, no. 2 (2015):208–9.

54 See the remarkable sixth-century testimony of Choricius reproduced and discussed by Philip Mayerson, "Choricius of Gaza on the Watersupply System of Caesarea," *Israel Exploration Journal* 36, nos. 3–4 (1986):269–72.

55 On urban violence centered on fountains during times of drought, see, for instance, Theophanes, *Chronographia* AM 6055 (CSHB 43.366), trans. Cyril Mango and Roger Scott, *The Chronicle of Theophanes Confessor: Byzantine and Near Eastern History AD 284–813* (Oxford: Clarendon Press, 1997), 349.

56 For aqueducts used as pressure points by besieging armies, there are many accounts, including Ammianus Marcellinus, *Res Gestae* 21.12.17, trans. John Carew Rolfe, Loeb 315 (London: William Heinemann, 1940), 151.

57 Jordan Pickett, "Water in Byzantium," in *Proceedings of the 23rd International Congress of Byzantine Studies, Belgrade 22–27 August 2016: Round Tables*, ed. Bojana Krsmanović and Ljubomir Milanović (Belgrade: AIEB, 2016), 835–39.

58 On aqueducts as *thauma* or marvels, see Maria Kaika, *City of Flows: Modernity, Nature, and the City* (New York: Routledge, 2005).

59 For the commodification of water, see principally Marx, *Capital* 1.4; and Maria Kaika and Erik Swyngedouw, "Fetishizing the Modern City: The Phantasmagoria of Urban Technological Networks," *International Journal of Urban and Regional Research* 24, no. 1 (2000):120–38. On the gratis provision of Roman water, a fifth-century rescript preserved in the Codex Iustinianus (*CJ* 11.42/43.7) says "it would be execrable that the houses of this fair city [Constantinople] should be provided with purchased water." Rather, water was provided on the basis of rank (e.g., as described in the later fourth century, *Codex Theodosianus* 15.2.3) following a formal request or grant. In the earlier imperial period, Frontinus, Martial, and Statius refer to this process for obtaining rights to water privileges in, respectively, *De aquis Urbis Romae* 105, *Silvae* 3.1.61–64, and *Epigrammata* 9.18.

60 See, for example, the sixth-century source Julian of Ascalon, discussed by Besim Hakim, "Julian of Ascalon's Treatise of Construction and Design Rules from Sixth-Century Palestine," *Journal of the Society of Architectural Historians* 60, no. 1 (2001):10–13, but note that these regulations are regularly contradicted by archaeological evidence of urban artisanal and craft activity, especially in late antique cities, including glass- and metalworking.

61 For the imperial development of mill technologies, see especially Andrew Wilson, "Machines, Power, and the Roman Economy," *Journal of Roman Studies* 92 (2002):1–32.

62 For an introduction, see Örjan Wikander, "The Water-Mill," in *Handbook of Ancient Water Technology*, ed. Örjan Wikander, Technology and Change in History 2 (Leiden: Brill, 2000), 371–400. Water mills appear in Vitruvius, *De Architectura* 5.5.2, but do not seem to have overtaken animal-powered mills until late antiquity, when declining labor availability made the initial investment more attractive (2,000 denarii for a water mill versus 1,250 denarii for an animal mill, according to Diocletian's price edict). Water mills have an extensive history in Byzantium, known especially from monastic and legal literature that indicates they were built by households and in common by communities. See Dionysios Stathakopoulos, "Between the Field and the Plate: How Agricultural Products Were Processed into Food," in *Eat, Drink, and Be Merry (Luke 12:19)—Food and Wine in Byzantium*, ed. Leslie Brubaker and Kallirroe Linardou (Aldershot: Ashgate, 2007), 27–38.

63 Andrew Wilson, "The Water-Mills on the Janiculum," *Memoirs of the American Academy in Rome* 45 (2000):219–46.

64 Gül Surmelihindi, Philippe Leveau, Christoph Spötl, Vincent Bernard, and Cees Passchier, "The Second Century CE Roman Watermills of Barbegal: Unraveling the Enigma of One of the Oldest Industrial Complexes," *Science Advances* 4, no. 3 (2018):1–8.

65 Jacques Seigne, "A Sixth-Century Water-Powered Sawmill at Jerash," *Annual of the Department of Antiquities of Jordan* 46 (2002):205–13.

66 Fritz Mangartz and Stefanie Wefers, *Die byzantinische Steinsäge von Ephesos: Baubefund, Rekonstruktion, Architekturteile*, Monographien des Römisch-Germanischen Museums 86 (Mainz: Römisch-Germanischen Zentralmuseums, 2010). Note also the intriguing funerary relief discovered at Phrygian Hierapolis (modern-day Pamukkale): Tullia Ritti, Klaus Grewe, and Paul Kessener, "A Relief of a Water-Powered Stone Saw Mill on a Sarcophagus at Hierapolis and Its Implications," *Journal of Roman Archaeology* 20 (2007):139–63.

67 Michael McCormick, *Origins of the European Economy: Communications and Commerce, c. 700–c. 900* (Cambridge: Cambridge University Press, 2001), 86–114.

68 B. Dermody, R. P. H. van Beek, E. Meeks, K. Klein Goldewijk, W. Scheidel, Y. van der Velde, M. F. P. Bierkens, M. J. Wassen, and S. C. Dekker, "A Virtual Water Network of the Roman World," *Hydrology and Earth System Sciences* 18, no. 12 (2014):5025–40.

69 Purcell and Horden, *Corrupting Sea*, 220–24.

70 On illegal tapping of water from aqueducts, see Frontinus, *De aquis Urbis Romae* 75–76, 97, 112–15. On illegal tapping of water from aqueducts for irrigation: *CTh* 15.2.4 = *CJ* 11.43.2; *CTh* 15.2.7 = *CJ* 11.43.4.

71 Robert Thomas and Andrew Wilson, "Water Supply for Roman Farms in Latium and South Etruria," *Papers of the British School at Rome* 62 (1994):139–96; and Angela Commito and Felipe Rojas, "The Aqueducts of Aphrodisias," in *The Aphrodisias Regional Survey*, ed. Christopher John Ratté and Peter D. De Staebler, Aphrodisias 5 (Mainz: Philipp von Zabern, 2012), 285–86.

72 On two-hundred-millimeter isohyet, see Michael Decker, *Tilling the Hateful Earth* (Oxford: Oxford University Press, 2009), 12–15, map 1.

73 See Oleson, *Humayma Excavation Project*, 417–92.

74 For an overview, see Sabine Ladstätter and Andrea Pülz, "Ephesus in the Late Roman and Early Byzantine Period: Changes in Its Urban Character from the Third to the Seventh Century AD," *Proceedings of the British Academy* 141 (2007):391–433.

75 Friederike Stock, Anna Pint, Barbara Horejs, Sabine Ladstätter, and Helmut Brückner, "In Search of the Harbours: New Evidence of Late Roman and Byzantine Harbours of Ephesus," *Quaternary International* 312 (2013):57–69.

76 John C. Kraft, Helmut Bückner, Ilhan Kayan, and Helmut Engelmann, "The Geographies of Ancient Ephesus and the Artemision in Anatolia," *Geoarchaeology* 22, no. 1 (2007):121–49.

77 Wolfgang Vetters, "Ein Beitrag zur Hydrogeologie von Ephesos," in *Cura Aquarum in Sicilia: Proceedings of the Tenth International Congress on the History of Water Management and Hydraulic Engineering in the Mediterranean Region Syracuse, May 16–22, 1998*, ed. Gemma C. M. Jansen (Leiden: Stichting BABESCH, 2000), 85–92.

78 Peter Scherrer and Elisabeth Trinkl, *Die Tetragonos Agora in Ephesos: Grabungsergebnisse von archaischer bis in byzantinische Zeit: Ein Überblick: Befunde und Funde klassischer Zeit*, Forschungen in Ephesos 13/2 (Vienna: Österreichischen Akademie der Wissenschaften, 2006).

79 Gilbert Wiplinger, "Die Wasserversorgung von Ephesos in byzantinischer Zeit," in *Ephesos in Byzantinischer Zeit*, ed. Falko Daim and Sabine Ladstätter (Mainz: Römisch-Germanisches Zentralmuseum, 2011), 103–24.

80 Johanna Auinger and Elisabeth Rathmayr, "Zur spätantiken Statuenausstattung der Thermen und Nymphäen in Ephesos," in *Statuen in der Spätantike*, ed. Franz Alto Bauer and Christian Witschel, Kunst im ersten Jahrtausend 23 (Wiesbaden: Reichert Verlag, 2007), 237–69.

81 Ursula Quatember, *Nymphaeum Traiani in Ephesos*, Forschungen in Ephesos 11/2 (Vienna: Österreichischen Akademie der Wissenschaften, 2011).

82 Brenda Longfellow, *Roman Imperialism and Civic Patronage: Form, Meaning, and Ideology in Monumental Fountain Complexes* (Cambridge: Cambridge University Press, 2011), 77–95.

83 Stephan Karwiese, "*Polis Potamon—Stadt der Flüsse*: Die Gewässer auf den ephesischen Münzen," in *Cura Aquarum in Ephesus*, ed. Gilbert Wiplinger, Babesch Annual Papers on Mediterranean Archaeology Supplement 6 (Leuven: Peeters, 2006), 17–22.

84 Johanna Auinger, "The Sculptural Decoration of Ephesian Bath Buildings in Late Antiquity," in *Archaeology and the Cities of Asia Minor in Late Antiquity*, ed. Ortwin Dally and Christopher Ratté, Kelsey Museum Publication 6 (Ann Arbor, Mich.: Kelsey Museum of Archaeology, 2011), 67–80.

85 Ellen Janssen, Jeroen Poblome, Johan Claeys, Vincent Kint, Patrick Degryse, Elena Marinova, and Bart Muys, "Fuel for Debating Ancient Economies: Calculating Wood Consumption at Urban Scale in Roman Imperial Times," *Journal of Archaeological Science: Reports* 11 (2017):592–99.

86 Hugo Delile, Janne Blichert-Toft, Jean-Philippe Goiran, Friederike Stock, Florent Arnaud-Godet, Jean-Paul Bravard, Helmut Brückner, and Francis Albarède, "Demise of a Harbor: A Geochemical Chronicle from Ephesus," *Journal of Archaeological Science* 53 (2015):202–13.

87 For reconfiguration of water distribution in late antiquity, with extensive references: Jordan Pickett, "Temples, Churches, Cisterns, and Pipes: Water in Late Antique Ephesus," in *De Aquaeductu Atque Aqua Urbium Lyciae Pamphyliae Pisidiae*, ed. Gilbert Wiplinger, Babesch Annual Papers on Mediterranean Archaeology Supplement 27 (Leuven: Peeters, 2016), 297–312.

88 Pickett, "Temples, Churches, Cisterns, and Pipes," 299–302.

89 Auinger, " Sculptural Decoration of Ephesian Bath Buildings in Late Antiquity," 76–79.

90 Sabine Ladstätter and Ephesos Excavations, *Wissenschaftlicher Jahresbericht des Österreichischen Archäologischen Instituts* [*JÖAI*] 2012 (2013):23–27.

91 For instance, Hermann Vetter, "Das Regierungsviertel," in "Grabungen in Ephesos von 1960–1969 bzw. 1970," *Jahresbericht des Österreichischen Archäologischen Instituts* 50 (1972/1975):Beibl. 229–300, here at 249, describes the late antique conversion of the Hestiasaal in the Prytaneion (an imperial-period public building on the Upper Agora), for use as a cistern.

92 Pickett, "Temples, Churches, Cisterns, and Pipes," 307–8.

93 Gilbert Wiplinger, "Der Değirmendere Aquädukt von Ephesos und seine Zukunft," in *Historische Wasserleitungen 2011—Gestern—Heute—Morgen*, ed. Gilbert Wiplinger, Babesch Annual Papers on Mediterranean Archaeology Supplement 24 (2013):109.

94 During late antiquity, numerous sites with hot springs were elevated to the status of *polis* with a bishop: see Therma/Myrikion in Galatia, via Klaus Belke and Marcell Restle, *Galatien und Lykaonien*, Tabula Imperii Byzantini 4 (Vienna: Verlag der Österreichischen Akademie der Wissenschaften, 2004), 208; or Basilica Therma in Cappadocia via Friedrich Hild and Marcell Restle, *Kappadokien (Kappadokia, Charsianon, Sebasteia, und Lykandos)*, Tabula Imperii Byzantini 2 (Vienna: Verlag der Österreichischen Akademie der Wissenschaften, 1981), 157.

95 An inscription from Orcistos in Phrygia records the settlement's petition for status as *polis*, in part because of its many water mills: André Chastagnol, "L'inscription constantinienne d'Orcistus," in *Mélanges de l'École française de Rome, Antiquité* 93, no. 1 (1981):384–402.

96 Alberto Rizzi, *Vere da pozzo di Venezia: I puteali pubblici di Venezia e della sua laguna*, 3rd ed. (Venice: Filippi editore, 2007).

97 Note, for example, cisterns in Constantinople, with testimonia discussed by Raymond Janin, *Constantinople Byzantine: Développement urbain et repertoire topographique*, 2nd ed. (Paris: Institut français d'études byzantines, 1964), 198–215.

98 Late antique cisterns are commonly found in association with the public areas of churches; at Dara, see Zachariah of Mytilene, *Historia Ecclesiastica 7.6, Chronicle of Pseudo-Zachariah Rhetor: Church and War in Late Antiquity*, trans. Geoffrey Greatrex, Liverpool Translated Texts for Historians 55 (Liverpool: Liverpool University Press, 2011), 247–51; for the archaeology, Gunnar Brands, "Ein Baukomplex in Dara-Anastasiopolis," *Jahrbuch für Antike und Christentum* 47 (2004):153–54.

99 Most famously, the Basilica Cistern built by Justinian at Constantinople, as described by Procopius, *de Aedificiis* 1.11.12–15, trans. H. B. Dewing with Glanville Downey, *Buildings*, Loeb 343 (London: William Heinemann, 1940), 91–93; and with commentary Jordan Pickett, "Water and Empire in the *de Aedificiis* of Procopius," *Dumbarton Oaks Papers* 71 (2017):95–125.

100 See Charles Anthony Stewart, "Architectural Innovation in Cyprus," *Architectural History* 57 (2014):11–18; and Myriam Rosen-Ayalon, "The White Mosque of Ramla: Retracing Its History," *Israel Exploration Journal* 56 (2006):67–83. Important also are the innovative forms of the massively multistory, modular column-and-vault cisterns of late Roman or Byzantine Alexandria (e.g., el-Nabeh), which share design elements with cisterns in Constantinople (e.g., Binbirdirek): Judith McKenzie, *The Architecture of Alexandria and Egypt c. 300 BC to AD 700* (New Haven: Yale University Press, 2007), 24–25 and 218–20.

101 Andrew Poulter, *Nicopolis ad Istrum: A Roman, Late Roman, and Early Byzantine City; Excavations 1985–1992*, Journal of Roman Studies Monograph 8 (London: Society for the Promotion of Roman Studies, 1995), 6, 45–46.

102 The city is primarily known through salvage excavations, as expertly summarized by Olga Karagiorgou, "Urbanism and Economy in Late Antique Thessaly (3rd–7th Century AD): The Archaeological Evidence" (DPhil thesis, Oxford University, 2001), 38–39, for the cisterns that comprise the city's water infrastructure known to date.

103 Albrecht Berger, "Viranşehir (Mokisos), eine frühbyzantinische Stadt in Kappadokien" *Istanbuler Mitteilungen* 48 (1998):366, for lack of an aqueduct.

104 Eric A. Ivison, "Amorium in the Byzantine Dark Ages (Seventh to Ninth Centuries)," in *Post-Roman Towns, Trade and Settlement in Europe and Byzantium*, ed. Joachim Henning (Berlin: Walter de Gruyter, 2007), 2:25–59.

105 Thessaloníki: for the long-lived aqueduct, see Despina Makropoulou, Sofia Akrivopoulou, and Vassiliki Kaltapanidou, *The Hortiati Aqueduct: Consolidation and Conservation*, Hellenic Ministry of Culture and Sports, 9th Ephorate of Byzantine Antiquities (Thessaloníki: Ministry of Culture, 2014), 11–13. There are various textual testimonia that may indicate continued functionality for the city's water system during the later medieval period, for instance, Theodore the Studite's visit to baths at the cathedral in 795, *Epistles* I.3 (*PG* 99.917D).

106 Chersonesus: Alla I. Romančuk, *Studien zur Geschichte und Archäologie des byzantinischen Cherson*, Colloquia Pontica 11 (Leiden: Brill, 2005), 50 and 102–3, for medieval functionality of older Roman aqueduct system, no longer used for baths and display but for fish-salting, instead.

107 Ephesus: Pickett, "Temples, Churches, Cisterns, and Pipes."

108 James Morganstern, *Fort at Dereağzı and Other Material Remains in Its Vicinity: From Antiquity to the Middle Ages*, Istanbuler Forschungen 40 (Tübingen: Wasmuth, 1993), 90.

109 Paul Kessener, "The Triple Siphon at Aspendos and Its Bridges," in *Archäologie der Brücken* (Regensburg: Verlag Friedrich Pustet, 2011), 77–83.

110 Günther Garbrecht, "Erdbeben in der Wasserversorgungsgeschichte Pergamons," in *Wasserhistorische Forschungen*, vol. 1, *Schwerpunkt Antike*, ed. Christoph Ohlig (Siegburg: Deutsche Wasserhistorische Gesellschaft, 2003), 127–28.

111 The cathedral's pipe-fed baptistery provides critical evidence that Stobi's water system was still intact before it was abandoned coincident with the Slavic invasions of the latter sixth century, and thereafter robbed for its metal; see James Wiseman, "Stobi in Yugoslavian Macedonia: Archaeological Excavations and Research, 1977–78," *Journal of Field Archaeology* 5, no. 4 (1978):410–11; and James Wiseman, "The City in Macedonia Secunda," in *Villes et peuplement dans l'Illyricum protobyzanti: Actes du colloque de Rome (12–14 mai 1982)*, Collection de l'École française de Rome 77 (Rome: École française de Rome, 1984), 309, fig. 15.

112 Sirmium's aqueduct was adapted to feed domestic and artisanal or craft installations in the area of a former imperial palace during the fifth and sixth centuries, before near-total abandonment of the settlement in the latter sixth or seventh centuries coincident with the Slavic invasions. See Edward L. Ochsenschlager and Vladislav Popovíc, "Excavations at Sirmium, Yugoslavia," *Archaeology* 26, no. 2 (1973):87.

113 A new aqueduct was built at Anazarbos around 516 or 517, not long before the apparent dislocation of the settlement during the seventh century coincident with Persian and Arabic incursions into the area; see *Inschriften Griechischer Städte aus Kleinasien* 56.1.22–24; Hansgerd Hellenkemper and Friedrich Hild, *Neue Forschungen in Kilikien,* Veröffentlichungen der Kommission für die Tabula Imperii Byzantini 4 (Vienna: Verlag der Österreichischen Akademie der Wissenschaften, 1986), 129.

114 The line of the aqueduct and new reservoirs were incorporated into city walls, built in the seventh or eighth century, shortly before Side's abandonment: see Clive Foss, "Attius Philippus and the Walls of Side," *Zeitschrift für Papyrologie und Epigraphik* 26 (1977):172–80; and Christian Gliwitsky, "Die Kirche im sog. Bischofspalast zu Side," *Istanbuler Mitteilungen* 55 (2005):376; on the walls and for the reservoirs H1 and H2, see Arif Mufid Mansel, *Die Ruinen von Side* (Berlin: De Gruyter, 1963), 171.

115 For ceramics filling the aqueduct channel before fifth-century settlement abandonment, see Andrea Berlin, "The Archaeology of Ritual: The Sanctuary of Pan at Banias/Caesarea Philippi," *Bulletin of the American Schools of Oriental Research* 315 (1999):42–43.

116 Sinter buildup in Caesarea Maritima's Channel C aqueduct reduced its flow-through by 75 percent: see Diane Everman, "The Water Supply of Caesarea Maritima: A Historical Study" (PhD diss., University of Maryland, 1997), 161.

117 For discussion of the disaggregation of the Roman city core toward smaller perennial water sources (e.g., at Spring Caves), see Charles Brian Rose, *The Archaeology of Greek and Roman Troy* (Cambridge: Cambridge University Press, 2014), 274.

118 Compare Giuseppe Scardozzi, "Ricognizioni archeologiche nel territorio di Hierapolis: Gli acquedotti, le cave di materiali lapidei, gli insediamenti rurali, i tumuli funerari," in *Hierapolis V: Le attività delle Campagne di Scavo e Restauro 2004–2006*, ed. Francesco D'Andria, M. Piera Caggia, and Tommaso Ismaelli (Istanbul: Ege Yayınları, 2012), 116–17, on aqueduct operationality; and Giuseppe Scardozzi, "Integrated Methodologies for the Archaeological Map of an Ancient City and Its Territory: The Case of Hierapolis in Phrygia," in *Satellite Remote Sensing: A New Tool for Archaeology,* ed. Rosa Lasoponara and Nicola Masini (Dordrecht: Springer, 2012), 151.

119 A. H. S. Megaw, ed., *Kourion: Excavations in the Episcopal Precinct* (Washington, D.C.: Dumbarton Oaks Research Library and Collection, 2007), 560–61, concerning the abandonment of the aqueduct-dependent Roman city in preference for the site of its Bronze Age predecessor, near modern Episkopi, which has a high water table for wells and easy access to the river Korusi.

120 Compare Mark Landon, "Beyond Peirene: Toward a Broader View of Corinthian Water Supply," in *Corinth, the Centenary: 1896–1996*, ed. Charles K. Williams II and Nancy Bookidis, Corinth 20 (Princeton: American School of Classical Studies at Athens, 2003), 43–62; and David K. Pettegrew, "The End of Ancient Corinth? Views from the Landscape," in *Archaeology and History in Roman, Medieval and Post-Medieval Greece: Studies on Method and Meaning in Honor of Timothy E. Gregory,* ed. William R. Caraher, Linda Jones Hall, and R. Scott Moore (Aldershot: Ashgate, 2008), 259, on settlement dispersal.

121 Zalmon S. Winogradov, "The Aqueduct to Tiberias," in Amit, Patrich, and Hirschfeld, *Aqueducts of Israel*, 295–305.

122 The basalt pipes of Hippos's aqueduct were disassembled, floated over the Sea of Galilee, and reassembled for the Caliph Mu'awiya's fortified palace complex/*qasr* near Tiberias at al-Sinnabra. See Yardenna Alexandre, "Tel Bet Yerah, the Inverted Siphon Pipeline," *Hadashot Arkheologiyot* 125 (2013), accessed July 7, 2017, http://www.hadashot-esi.org.il/report_detail_eng.aspx?id=3336&mag_id=120.

123 Anthony McNicoll, Robert Houston Smith, John Basil Hennessy, Timothy F. Potts, Linda E. Villiers, and Alan G. Walmsley, *Pella in Jordan 1: An Interim Report on the Joint University of Sydney and the College of Wooster Excavations* (Canberra: Australian National Gallery, 1982), 123–26.

124 Consumption of lake water at Tiberias from the medieval sources: see Guy Le Strange, *Palestine under the Moslems* (London: Watt, 1890), 334–35.

125 For hot spring baths at Tiberias, see David Stacey, Ariel Berman, and Ayala Lester, "Excavations at Tiberias, 1973–1974: The Early Islamic Periods," *Israel Antiquities Authority Reports*, n.s., 21 (2004):3–10.

126 The contemporary literature related to this shift is explored in extenso in Pickett, "Water and Empire in the *de Aedificiis* of Procopius."

127 Adam Izdebski, Jordan Pickett, Neil Roberts, and Tomasz Waliszewski, "The Environmental, Archaeological and Historical Evidence for Regional Climatic Changes and Their Societal Impacts in the Eastern Mediterranean in Late Antiquity," *Quaternary Science Reviews* 136 (2016):189–208.

128 Constantine V hoarded labor and capital resources when he restored Constantinople's aqueduct in 765: see the detailed account of Theophanes, *Chronographia* AM 6258 (CSHB 43.680), in Mango and Scott, *Chronicle of Theophanes Confessor*, 608.

129 Herbert Danby, *The Mishnah: Translated from the Hebrew with Introduction and Brief Explanatory Notes* (Peabody, Mass.: Hendrickson Publishers, 1993), Moed Erubin 2.1, 122–23, for distinctions between public and private wells.

130 Famous is the Zamzam Well at Mecca; note also the Holy Well at Hagia Sophia allegedly built by the Emperor Justinian. For the latter, see Albrecht Berger, *Accounts of Medieval Constantinople: The Patria*, Dumbarton Oaks Medieval Library 24 (Cambridge, Mass.: Harvard University Press, 2013), 4.22 and 4.26, 260–67. See also Shimon Gibson and David M. Jacobson, *Below the Temple Mount in Jerusalem: A Sourcebook on the Cisterns, Subterranean Chambers and Conduits on the Haram al-Sharif*, BAR International Series 637 (Oxford: British Archaeological Reports, 1996).

131 Bryan Ward-Perkins, *From Classical Antiquity to the Middle Ages* (Oxford: Oxford University Press, 1984), 132–34 and passim, with reference to the primary sources from Italy; note also Squatriti, *Water and Society in Early Medieval Italy*, 18.

132 For Carolingian palace aqueducts, see Holger Grewe, "Die Ausgrabungen in der Königspfalz zu Ingelheim am Rhein," in *Splendor palatii. Neue Forschungen zu Paderborn und anderen Pfalzen der Karolingerzeit*, Deutsche Königspfalzen 5; Veröffentlichungen des Max-Planck-Instituts furs Geschichte 11.5 (Göttingen: Vandenhoeck and Ruprecht, 2001), 155–74.

133 On the arcaded Tulunid aqueduct for Cairo, see Tarek Swelim, *Ibn Tulun: His Lost City and Great Mosque* (Cairo: American University in Cairo Press, 2015), 42–44. Control of running water was also critical for the automatons or mechanical devices that played important roles in late ancient court diplomacy, such as the famous water clock given by Harun al-Rashid to Charlemagne in 807: see recently Elly Rachel Truitt, *Medieval Robots: Mechanism, Magic, Art, and Nature* (Philadelphia: University of Pennsylvania Press, 2015), 19–26. Note, too, the testimony of a handbook by the late ninth-century Baghdadi merchant Pseudo-Jahiz, who records that hydraulic engineers were at that time among the most coveted skilled laborers arriving from Byzantium (in addition to agronomists, marble workers, and eunuchs); see Ch. Pellat, "Ğāhiẓiana, I: Le Kitāb al-Tabaṣṣur bi-l-tiğāra attribué à ğāḥiẓ," *Arabica* 1, no. 2 (1954):159.

134 Andrey Aladzhov notes new water mains and drainage systems at Pliska, in addition to a bath with hypocaust, all dating from the eighth to tenth century; water mains from this period were also discovered at Preslav: see Andrey Aladzhov, "The Byzantine Empire and the Establishment of the Early Medieval City in Bulgaria," in *Byzanz—Das Römerreich im Mittelalter. Teil 3: Peripherie und Nachbarschaft*, ed. Falko Daim and Jorg Drauschke (Mainz: Römisch-Germanisches Zentralmuseum, 2010), 129.

135 For ornate Byzantine puteals or wellheads at Venice, see n. 96.

136 The stepwells at Jhilani and Manjushri are dated to 550–575 and ca. 650, respectively: see Michael Meister, Madhusudan Dhaky, and Krishna Deva, eds., *The Encyclopedia of Indian Temple Architecture, North India*, vol. 2, pt. 1, *Foundations of North Indian Style, AD 350–650* (Delhi: Pradeep Mehendiratta for the American Institute of Indian Studies, 1988), 21–22.

137 *Poleis* were no longer the central vehicles for tax collection after state centralization during the late third and early fourth centuries; Leo VI's *Novella 46* terminated the *polis*'s utility as an administrative category altogether by ending city councils from 886 to 899. For commentary on shifts in the administrative and architectural valence of the Roman-Byzantine *polis*, see John Haldon and Leslie Brubaker, *Byzantium in the Iconoclast Era c. 680–750* (Cambridge: Cambridge University Press, 2011), 547–48.

6

Monsoon Landscapes and Flexible Provisioning in the Preindustrial Cities of the Indian Subcontinent

MONICA L. SMITH

THE MONSOON BELT OF ASIA PRESENTS A DRAMATIC LANDSCAPE OF annual environmental change that includes long, hot summers followed by seasonal deluges of rain. Although challenging to manage, this punctuated variability nonetheless provides distinct opportunities for high agricultural productivity (Figures 6.1 and 6.2). In the Indian subcontinent, the annual anticipation of high water can be characterized as "normal floods," through which people strategically utilize routine and expected high-water events as part of the regular agricultural cycle.[1] Over the past three thousand years, the resultant dynamic feedback loop of labor and landscape in the region has enabled urban centers to become stable points of economic interaction, both at their inception and throughout their long centuries of occupation.

In the Indian subcontinent as elsewhere, the world was wholly rural prior to the development of urbanism. Starting with the purposeful cultivation of plants and tending of domestic animals ten to twelve thousand years ago worldwide, farmers and pastoralists produced food within natural parameters of topography, elevation, heat, cold, and moisture. Climate (as a long-term phenomenon measured along a gradient of decades) and weather (the day-to-day expression of natural conditions) were closely monitored but could not be altered by human agents.[2] Interspersed with factors of climate and weather were other dynamic environmental systems that adversely affected human food-production strategies, such as insects, fungi, and crop-raiding mammals and birds.

The advent of cities resulted in a radical restructuring of the countryside.[3] Although the fringes of ancient cities would have been interdigitated with farmland and villages,

FIGURE 6.1

Women planting rice,
India. Photograph by
Neil Grant / Alamy
Stock Photo.

FIGURE 6.2

Farmers preparing
fields in staggered
plantings during the
monsoon. Photograph
by Daniel J. Rao /
Alamy Stock Photo.

cities' central areas were densely occupied with inhabitants engaged in nonfarming pursuits such as specialized craft production, middle management and administration, and full-time ritual employment. As a result, urban households depended upon rural producers to supply them with needed goods including food and fuel. From the rural perspective, the emergence of cities brought both new opportunities and new constraints. Each household in rural settlements continued to produce and utilize its own resources at a high level of self-sufficiency, but the presence of cities encouraged an increase in rural production and provided the opportunity to support and augment rural standards of living by engaging with market economies and commodity (or "cash") crops. Yet cities in the past—as they do in the present—primarily grew through immigration as a process that drew labor away just at the moment that rural places needed more workers to supply urban food needs.

People living in the countryside were attracted to cities for work that had no rural analogue, such as the urban institutions of temples and palaces that needed both educated administrators and employees for mundane tasks including construction, maintenance, and the transportation of raw materials and finished goods.[4] Cities often also had manufacturing centers that drew in both skilled craftsmakers and low-skilled workers who labored at routine tasks such as cleaning and maintaining work spaces. For those who were less industrious, or who had physical limitations, cities had institutions and venues where people who had been limited to simple tasks in the countryside could now make a living through an expanded repertoire of activities including petty crime, begging, and charitable donations.

A recognition of the vicissitudes of the urban-rural dynamic compels us to focus on urbanism not as a point-specific phenomenon, but as one that implicates entire landscapes and causes shifts in every aspect of food production and consumption behavior. Archaeological evidence affirms that there were many agentive forces throughout urbanizing landscapes, and that inhabitants' adaptations and innovations resulted in changes to population centers of all sizes. In Mesopotamia, for example, Tony J. Wilkinson and colleagues have turned the long-held trope of the "Fertile Crescent" on its head, noting that annual factors of uncertainty in productive capacity should instead lead us to call the region the "Fragile Crescent."[5] In the Maya region, a greater understanding of human strategies related to cultivation and water conservation are transforming simplistic narratives of catastrophic drought as a causative factor in the Maya "collapse" into a more nuanced understanding of long-term human resilience.[6]

In the Indian subcontinent, human investments in agricultural lands through the management of water and soil fertility had outcomes whose effects were continually augmented for thousands of years with an impact that continues to the present day.[7] The subject of urbanism also is of continued interest at both the social and the governmental level, given the growth of individual cities in the subcontinent; in India alone, there are forty-seven cities with one million or more residents, and urbanism is growing at the same rate as the population, indicating that cities will continue to increase in size.[8]

Urbanism in South Asia

The earliest urbanism in the Indian subcontinent dates to the Indus (Harappan) period of the mid-third millennium BCE, focused on the Indus River in Pakistan and in the western portion of India. Urban centers were few in number (current estimates suggest the presence of four to six such settlements, located at a minimum of 300 km apart).[9] The distribution of distinct elements such as pottery, stone seals, and beads suggests that the Indus cultural area was more than ten times larger than the geographic area of contemporary civilizations in Egypt and Mesopotamia.[10] As a large and dispersed material phenomenon, the Indus may represent a distended cultural system rather than a political configuration such as a "state" or other territorial political unit. The cities themselves faded out by about 1800 BCE, probably due to a combination of earthquakes, river shifts, population dynamics, and migration that favored a return to a dispersed village-level settlement pattern that thereafter prevailed for a thousand years.

Sometime after about 1000 BCE, people again began to gather into large settlements in the Indian subcontinent, although none of the known Harappan cities were reoccupied. Research on the origins of these new urban centers is made difficult by the fact that many of them were continuously occupied afterward and into the present day, making archaeological investigations of the earliest habitation levels difficult. We do know that by the middle of the first millennium BCE, there was a dense network of nearly one hundred sites that we can identify as "urban" stretching from present-day Afghanistan to Bangladesh and throughout peninsular India (Figure 6.3).[11] People coalesced into cities throughout the subcontinent and in a variety of environmental and topographic zones. The archaeological remains from these settlements indicate widespread cultural contact, with some cities being as close as 20 km apart.

Urban growth was integrated with other significant cultural developments, including the widespread manufacture of iron that, along with forest clearance through fire, enabled people to transform heavily vegetated areas into agricultural fields.[12] The growth of cities also was interwoven with significant changes in religious practice. The dominant Vedic ritual tradition of the preceding era is known through the *Rig Veda* and other hymns that extolled priestly hierarchies and elaborate sacrifices. By the sixth century BCE, these practices were augmented and in some cases challenged and supplanted by new religious traditions including Buddhism, Jainism, and lesser-known sects such as the Ajivikas.[13] Followers of these new religious traditions abstained from killing animals and promoted meditative practices that focused on self-actualization through individual inputs. New communities of practitioners also sprang up, often located in the countryside and endowed by royal patrons as well as donations from visiting pilgrims.

Rural landscapes of Buddhism and other religious traditions served as productive centers of agriculture and as educational institutions that enhanced urban life not only through the production of food, but through the production of theories about cultural and social life that thereafter permeated the intellectual circles of urban centers. Religious pilgrims traveled from cities to ritual centers and back again, with movement

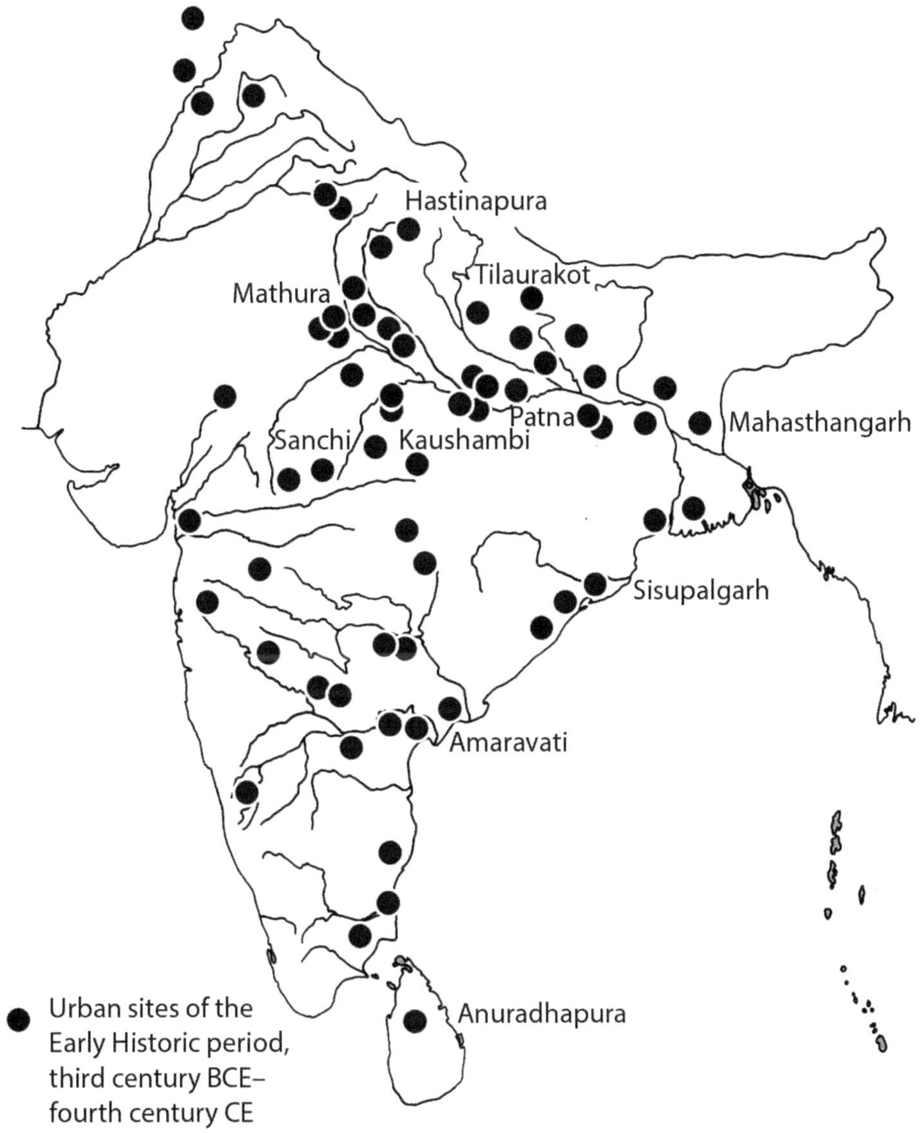

FIGURE 6.3

Map showing sites
mentioned in text. Map
by Monica L. Smith.

Hastinapura

Tilaurakot

Mathura

Sanchi Kaushambi Patna Mahasthangarh

Sisupalgarh

Amaravati

● Urban sites of the
Early Historic period,
third century BCE–
fourth century CE

Anuradhapura

and migration dictated by seasonality. In fact, Buddhist and Jain religious places were created because of the dramatic oscillations of rainfall and dryness that characterize the subcontinent: "The practice of taking temporary shelter from the rain led to the formation of stable and permanent monasteries."[14]

The Social and Environmental Power of the Monsoon

The monsoon is a rainy season of several months, resulting in a weather pattern of dry seasons interspersed with wet seasons. Although the monsoon is most commonly associated with South and Southeast Asia, monsoons occur in many parts of the world, providing seasonal change and both opportunities and restrictions on agricultural production, travel, migration, craftmaking, and warfare (see, for example, the chapter by Jean-Baptiste Chevance on Phnom Kulen).

In the Indian subcontinent, the monsoon is a powerful poetic trope as well as an annual punctuation of environmental change. Although there are both winter and summer rainy seasons over much of the subcontinent, it is the summer monsoon, which occurs after a period of intense heat, that is the most ardently anticipated. The sense of relief after a relentless summer season is a factor that not only animates today's Bollywood film industry but can be seen in the earliest written records of the subcontinent. In the words of a Sanskrit play nearly two thousand years old, heavy gray monsoon clouds are compared to the dark bodies of elephants, weighty and ponderous in their trumpeting: "Clouds, harnessed in the lightning's gleams, like charging elephants dash by; at Indra's bidding, pour their streams until with silver cords it seems that earth is linked with sky . . ."[15]

Although the monsoons occur regularly in each annual cycle, there is considerable variation from year to year in the onset of the first rains, as well as variability in the subsequent amplitude and duration of rainfall. Even during the monsoon season, it does not rain all day every day, and there can be days in which there is no rain at all. Our present-day records of fluctuation are not unique; historians and environmental scientists have used historical records of flooding in the Nile Valley of Egypt, as well as sedimentary cores, to demonstrate that monsoonal variability was experienced by the ancient inhabitants of the Indian subcontinent.[16]

Adaptability to the monsoon was an essential component of agricultural practice in the Indian subcontinent; as noted in B. K. Paul's work, the term "normal flooding" provides an opportunity to evaluate the way in which water excess was a normal, expected, and welcome part of the agricultural cycle, as well as a factor of climate that agriculturalists, both ancient and modern, have handled in a routine and matter-of-fact way.[17] Indeed, the understanding of annual excesses provided by nature is an important corrective to the prevailing view that scarcity is the defining trope of the natural world and of human-environmental dynamics. In our haste to view climate and environments as adversarial to human efforts, we rarely think about, or even acknowledge, the ways in which the environment is abundant (or "giving," in the words of Christopher R. Moore and Christopher W. Schmidt).[18]

In the case of the Indian subcontinent, farmers strategically used the abundance of rainfall deposited through the monsoon to produce an abundance of food, primarily in the form of rice. Rice is a labor-intensive grain crop, but is ideally suited to the subcontinent's soils and annual episodes of rainfall; the exact timing of the earliest rice agriculture is debated, but it is clear that rice production increased dramatically by the first millennium BCE in tandem with the growth of urbanism.[19] Rice is distinct among the world's grain domesticates in its tolerance for water, and it can be grown continuously, crop after crop, without a fallow period, even under traditional means of cultivation.[20] The ability of rice to provide both biologically necessary calories and aesthetically and socially pleasing volume is striking; actualized on a daily basis, rice presents abundance even during the act of cooking in which a small amount of dry grain renders a large pot of food in a short amount of time.

The archaeological study of the Buddhist monastic site of Sanchi in central India provides an excellent illustration of the way in which people undertook rice cultivation within an intensively managed agricultural landscape starting in the third century BCE. Working with her colleague John Sutcliffe, Julia Shaw has proposed that the religious establishment at Sanchi was able to organize labor for both cultivation and water management to produce grain in a quantity that could be used to support local populations including religious personnel and pilgrims, as well as the inhabitants of surrounding settlements such as the nearby urban center of Vidisha located ten kilometers away.[21]

At Vidisha and other urban centers, inhabitants managed their supplies through a variety of mechanisms including markets, itinerant vendors, individually brokered relationships of mutual obligation and patronage, and redistributions from religious and civic institutions. Early South Asian leaders in both monasteries and urban centers were likely to have been relatively busy with construction and administration, as well as occasional territorial expansions, and likely lacked the time and capacity to monitor the production of food.[22] Given the many factors of adjustment necessary to take advantage of the day-by-day and year-by-year expression of the monsoons, a diversified approach to provisioning that relied at least in part on entrepreneurial initiative in rural locations and on a village-by-village basis would have been a more reliable mechanism for urban consumers to meet their nutritional needs.

The study of the relationships among urban food networks, rural agricultural hinterlands, and religious institutions enables archaeologists to bridge three realms of inquiry that often are separated in archaeological analysis. Although it has long been acknowledged that ancient state leaders had close ties to theology through claims to divinity and through the construction of labor-intensive monuments that commingled royal power with divine sanction, the effect of religious activities at nonelite levels has only recently been examined with an eye toward understanding the social and economic effects of religious communities as part of routine economic activities including food provisioning.[23] The integration of ritual and urban economic spheres indicates that population centers were supplied by complex, continually adjusted networks of provisioning in which knowledge and expertise were distributed throughout the supply chain from rural producers to urban consumers.

South Asian Urban Centers

The following comparisons make use of archaeological and historical data about three cities of the first millennium BCE in the Indian subcontinent. Kaushambi is located along the Yamuna River, a wide tributary of the Ganges; Sisupalgarh is located along India's eastern coastal plain on the banks of the Daya River within the Mahanadi River delta; and Anuradhapura is located in the northern lowlands of Sri Lanka. Their utility as comparative examples also stems from the fact that the sites themselves are, or were until recently, not obscured by modern habitation. As a result, there is an opportunity to see and experience the sites as population centers, as well as to assess the topography and environmental diversity of the surrounding productive hinterlands that would have supplied food to the cities.[24]

Kaushambi, Sisupalgarh, and Anuradhapura also are well inland and surrounded by agriculturally productive zones, which reduces the complexities encompassed by the study of port sites that could have been sustained in part by long-distance waterborne commerce. All three sites also have evidence for religious activities within their urban precincts.[25] Finally, all of these sites have monumental encircling ramparts, indicating the presence of large populations that would have been needed to create the surrounding walls and which provide good proof of densely occupied urban spaces.[26] At all three sites, stratigraphic excavations show that populations were present prior to the beginning of urbanism, indicating a long period of in-place development rather than the imposition of a city by political command. Although there are dozens of urban archaeological sites known from the first millennium BCE, few sites have had comprehensive surveys to supplement the excavations; however, Kaushambi, Sisupalgarh, and Anuradhapura have each had some hinterland investigations that provide further details for models of food provisioning.

Kaushambi

Kaushambi is among the largest first-millennium BCE cities in the subcontinent, located along the banks of the Yamuna River (a major tributary of the Ganges River) in the northern central plains of India (Figure 6.4). The riverside site was occupied by the seventh century BCE with a core area marked by ramparts measuring 6.4 km in length and enclosing an area of 250 ha; the ramparts were constructed after the initial period of occupation, suggesting an incremental growth of population before the period of wall construction.[27] Kaushambi contains evidence for hundreds of years' worth of occupation and several excavations were undertaken in the twentieth century that revealed evidence for a large administrative building, a monastery, roadways, and residences amid a city whose population size has been estimated at 24,000 individuals.[28]

The site is graced with a monumental stone pillar with an inscription ascribed to the third-century BCE Gangetic ruler Ashoka, who ruled from the city of Pataliputra (modern Patna), 380 km to the east down the Yamuna River. The site has other evidence for long-distance contacts in the form of trade goods such as beads, whose raw materials came from as far away as present-day Afghanistan, 1,500 km to the west. The city was known in the contemporary literature as a focal point of trade and of Buddhist activity, with its wealth indicated by the "growth of the rich and the well-to-do middle class, who, inspired by the idea of piety and devotion, wanted to acquire religious merit by taking part in building stupas, viharas and images through donations."[29] The wealth of its inhabitants is also seen in housing that included multiroom courtyard dwellings within the city walls.

A regional survey undertaken by George Erdosy has documented the presence of a range of site sizes representing a halo of towns and villages outside the ramparts of Kaushambi's city core (Figure 6.5).[30] Many of these hinterland sites have evidence for

FIGURE 6.4

Kaushambi eastern rampart, view to the north. Photograph by Monica L. Smith.

elaborate sculptures and architectural investments in both Buddhism and other religious traditions, and some sites had extensive evidence of craft-making activities in shell, iron, and stone.[31] Religious establishments would have required the work of numerous surrounding villages to support resident personnel and pilgrims with food and other donations. The production of water-intensive crops was documented by ancient visitors to the site, such as the seventh-century CE Buddhist pilgrim Hiuen-Tsang (Xuanzang), who noted that the principal crops in the countryside around Kaushambi were sugarcane and rice.[32]

Erdosy notes four different ecological zones within twenty kilometers of the site of Kaushambi. On the basis of twentieth-century traditional farming practices, he observes that the diversity of soils would have been able to support a variety of agricultural endeavors, with the alluvial soils along the riverbanks useful for growing winter-crop wheat and the interior uplands suitable for rice and pulses. Erdosy also notes the existence of other important environmental products, such as thatching grass that he observed still growing in the uncultivated parts of the alluvial strip that parallels the Yamuna River. The presence of many different cultivars, including both rice and wheat as staple starches, demonstrates that choice-making was precipitated from the

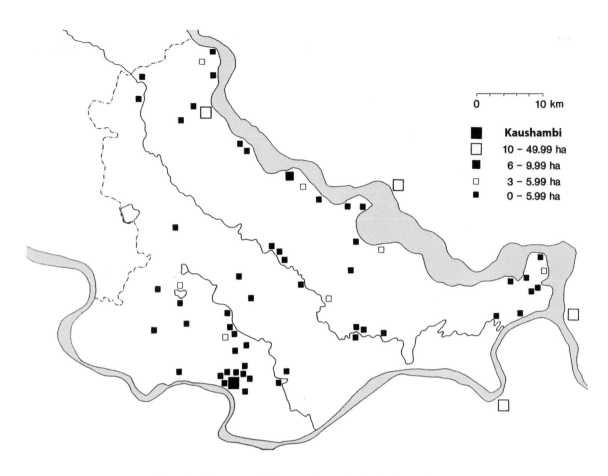

FIGURE 6.5

Distribution of sites in the
hinterlands of Kaushambi,
100 BCE–300 CE. Reproduced
from George Erdosy,
*Urbanisation in Early Historic
India*, BAR International
Series 430 (Oxford:
British Archaeological
Reports, 1988), 83.

initial act of cultivation all the way through the final act of consumption, with wheat and rice necessarily requiring different preparations and cooking techniques. Moreover, the growth of rural settlements over time included the budding off of new village sites in regions that were converted from forestland to agriculture.[33]

The Gangetic floodplain receives an annual abundance of water during the monsoons, but the timing of the onset and the periodicity of rainfall within the monsoon season is variable. Erdosy suggests that the "fluctuation in rainfall, along with localized differences in soils and topography, the general lack of minerals, and the existence in the past of forests in the interior, is the most important ecological characteristic" of the area in and around Kaushambi.[34] In addition to variations in the timing, onset, and amplitude of "normal floods," there were occasional catastrophic changes from which local farmers and urban residents could not easily recover. Religious documents suggest that the ancient city of Kaushambi received a population boost after the nearby city of Hastinapura was abandoned after a flood.[35] Kaushambi was also vulnerable to flooding given that its walls encircled the site on only three sides, with the fourth side consisting of the river itself. The river thus represented both opportunities and risks, offering the routine certainty of easy transport and the occasional vulnerability of floodwaters.

Sisupalgarh

Located on the eastern Indian coastal plain on the outskirts of the modern city of Bhubaneswar, Sisupalgarh is a walled settlement whose ramparts measure 1.1 km in length on each side, enclosing an area of 134 ha whose population is estimated at 25,000 people (Figure 6.6).[36] Among all the walled settlements of the Early Historic period, Sisupalgarh is by far the most regular in its outline, suggesting a particularly precise delineation of the urban perimeter; like Kaushambi, the earthen ramparts were begun after the area was already inhabited and constituted an act of circumvallation that would have instantly produced urban "insiders" and "outsiders" (Figure 6.7).[37] A sense of administrative precision is seen inside the settlement as well, where there is evidence for regularly spaced major thoroughfares running at ninety-degree angles to the linear ramparts. The site also has a central ritual precinct of monumental pillars and a large formal water reservoir, as well as residences of variable size and architectural investment, ranging from substantial houses with laterite block foundations to smaller structures made with reused bricks (Figure 6.8).

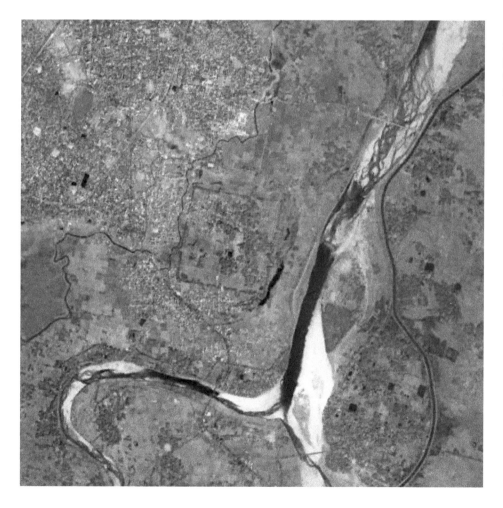

FIGURE 6.6

Sisupalgarh (center of image) with Daya River to the east and south. © Google Earth.

Assessments of Sisupalgarh's rural hinterlands and regional settlements are hampered by the medieval and modern sites in the vicinity that obscure ancient remains.[38] It is no longer possible to undertake the kinds of surveys that Erdosy conducted in the relatively open hinterlands of Kaushambi, but the preservation of religious institutions and other outlying settlements provides evidence for diverse rural activities at Sisupalgarh. Two nearby sites have Buddhist vestiges: Dhauli hill (3 km south of Sisupalgarh) has an Ashokan inscription and an elaborate carving of an elephant on one of its foothills, and Aragarh (18 km southwest) has a substantial Buddhist stupa (reliquary mound) at the top of the hill and a commanding view of the surrounding agricultural plain.[39] Udayagiri is a Jain site with extensive rock-cut caves located 9 km northwest of Sisupalgarh, with an inscription of patronage from the first-century BCE ruler Kharavela.

For the ancient inhabitants of Sisupalgarh, the religious sites of Dhauli and Udayagiri provided opportunities for monumental architecture as a visible investment of time and labor resulting in value-added, emotionally laden hinterlands. Throughout the Indian subcontinent, we know that royal patrons often supported more than one religious group, and that ideology, architecture, and iconography overlapped between Buddhist and Jain traditions.[40] Ordinary people also engaged in a multiplicity of religious

FIGURE 6.8
Central bunded
reservoir at Sisupalgarh,
on the interior of the
rampart. Photograph by
Monica L. Smith.

Monsoon Landscapes and Flexible Provisioning in the Preindustrial Cities of the Indian Subcontinent   155

FIGURE 6.9

Contemporary seasonal variation in crops as seen from the northeastern corner of the ancient rampart of Sisupalgarh (top: May 2002; bottom: January 2003). Photographs by Monica L. Smith.

activities, and city-based populations had an expectation of movement from urban centers out to pilgrimage places and back again.[41] Even people who lived their whole lives in their natal villages in the hinterlands of cities had experiences of movement, both as they moved around (sometimes voluntarily, for pilgrimage, and sometimes involuntarily, due to flooding that displaced them) and as other people moved toward and away from them. In eastern India, in addition to the religious sites, there were settlements that were visibly replete with architectural referents to Sisupalgarh as the dominant city. The recently discovered sites of Talapada and Lathi, which each measure 25 ha, have square ramparts that were too modest in height to have served as a defensive perimeter but that nonetheless adhered to the same perfectly rectilinear model with clear overtones of emulation and connectivity.[42]

Geographical and environmental data can be used to model the productive capacity of Sisupalgarh's surrounding region, in which year-by-year variability provided the environmental parameters for strategic investments of time, labor, and crop selection (Figure 6.9). Starting in the second millennium BCE, the region's farmers increasingly relied on rice and pulses that are still grown in the region today.[43] Farmers in this eastern part of the subcontinent coped not only with the range of responses demanded by anticipated annual "normal floods" but also with the damaging effect of occasional unpredictable oceanic cyclones that could overwhelm local productive infrastructure and inflict heavy damage on crops. The intense amount of work required to grow rice—including field preparation, sowing, weeding, harvesting, and threshing—would have required a substantial labor force, a factor that perhaps drew people out from the city on a periodic basis to engage in seasonal farm labor.[44] Thus the experiences of movement from place to place that were undertaken for ritual purposes were mirrored in the experiences of movement undertaken for agricultural and economic purposes, enabling people to become familiar with production locales, transport routes, and alternative sources of supply for desired agricultural and nonagricultural commodities.

Anuradhapura

The archaeological site of Anuradhapura is located in the northern portion of the island of Sri Lanka. This region, geographically known as the Dry Zone, experiences a sharp juxtaposition of water scarcity in the dry season with water abundance in the rainy season, a factor that makes successful ancient cultivation noteworthy compared to the modern view that the Dry Zone is economically unproductive.[45] Research led by Sri Lankan and British archaeologists has included excavation in the urban core and surveys in the outlying ancient settlement zone, measuring a 50 km radius around the ancient city, to catalog rural sites and to investigate the relationship between the city and its surrounding rural and monastic settlements (Figure 6.10).[46]

The cultivation of rice in this region relies on a significant amount of landscape management, primarily through the capture of water into human-made reservoirs with gates that are opened and closed to regulate the flow of water. At the city of Anuradhapura, excavations indicated that the earliest settlement began ca. 840–460 BCE, but that the earliest signs of rice consumption came from the subsequent phases of occupation

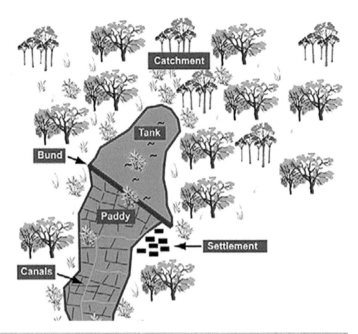

FIGURE 6.10

Hinterlands of Anuradhapura, showing a mosaic of land and water uses. Reproduced from Krista Gilliland, Ian A. Simpson, William Paul Adderley, Christopher Ian Burbidge, Alan J. Cresswell, David C. W. Sanderson, Robin Alexander Evelyn Coningham, Mark Manuel, Keir Magalie Strickland, Prasanta Gunawardhana, and Gamini Adikari, "The Dry Tank: Development and Disuse of Water Management Infrastructure in the Anuradhapura Hinterland, Sri Lanka," *Journal of Archaeological Science* 40 (2013):1013.

around 400 BCE.[47] In addition to the presence of rice grains, there was proxy evidence for a watery landscape, as seen in the bones of water-dwelling fauna such as turtles and monitor lizards in the settlement excavations.[48] The adoption of intensive rice agriculture in the countryside around Anuradhapura was coincident with two other significant developments: an increase in population and the construction of a substantial moat-and-rampart city perimeter that enclosed the 100 ha urban core.[49]

Starting ca. 400 BCE, the population density within the city walls was matched by an increase in hinterland populations who intensified their farming processes to match the demands of irrigated rice agriculture through the construction of reservoirs, canals,

FIGURE 6.11

Basawakkulama
tank, Anuradhapura.
Photograph by
Amalka Wijesuriya.

and moated sites (Figure 6.11).[50] Although the inception of this agricultural management strategy appears to have been autochthonous and highly localized, the landscape
was soon afterward augmented by the implantation of religious sites. Buddhist monas-
ticism, introduced to Sri Lanka in the third century BCE, quickly became integrated
into the productive landscape of urbanism, as seen in the close physical association of
Buddhist sites with landscape features such as reservoirs, "indicating exchange between
monastery and laity, with monastic oversight."[51] But the tightening networks of agriculture, urban consumption, and religious control were not static and the landscape
continued to evolve over the course of its thousand-plus years of intensive occupation

Tissawava tank
near Isurumuniya,
Anuradhapura.
Photograph courtesy
of the American
Institute of Indian
Studies, 74860.

FIGURE 6.13
Dematamal Viharaya,
Anuradhapura.
Photograph by
Amalka Wijesuriya.

(Figures 6.12 and 6.13). People living in the countryside continued to upgrade their landscapes, including the transformation of some swidden lands to irrigated fields even after the city of Anuradhapura reached its maximum size in the early first millennium CE.[52]

How Were Urban Landscapes "Flexible"?

Human agency and choice-making take place within environmental constraints and opportunities, with natural parameters constituting a series of opportunities (what James J. Gibson has called "affordances").[53] The acquisition of food constitutes the ultimate connection of people with their environments: everything about food production, from the planting of crops to their harvest, packaging, and transportation, reflects myriad decisions. People strategically invested time into landscapes, whether through labor-intensive field preparations for rice paddies or through an opportunistic sowing of other crops along riverbeds as monsoon waters gradually receded.[54] Interspersed with the management of soil, water, temperature, and weather are the social parameters of food preference and desirability. Resilience and sustainability are encoded into daily, seasonal, and lifetime decisions to grow particular types of crops through the modification of landscapes to maximize production and to reduce risk. Those decisions can be planned many months in advance according to the expectations of a known number of able-bodied members of a household or the size of landholdings to which a farmer or pastoralist has access. Nonetheless, those decisions can be revisited continually in the face of actual conditions from season to season and from day to day.

Flexible farming strategies are exercised at a variety of timescales: far in advance of agricultural activities; immediately in advance of such activities; and in response to shortfalls that require recalibration of individual and household labor investments. Although some aspects of urban environments such as topography or latitude are unchangeable once a city has grown into existence, other aspects of the landscape can be modified. In the Indian subcontinent, landscape-scale projects such as dams, reservoirs, and canals serve as an "anticipatory agricultural infrastructure."[55] Other types of work represent just-in-time configurations, such as the premonsoon acts of plowing and the construction of field bunds; the latter result either from heaping up earth or cutting down terrain to form markers that also retain water and that can be easily breached to let water flow into or out of a particular field. Labor also is expended for trade and transportation to bring food supplies into cities.

Transportation, which encompasses both human labor and environmental capacity, is another important factor in urban provisioning. In the Indian subcontinent, commodities ranging from food to fuel to raw materials would have been moved most readily by human and animal "foot-power," although the difficulties of road travel would probably have favored human transport over oxcarts.[56] In any case, transportation was likely to have been tailored to the types of commodities that moved toward urban consumers, in which both the food crops and the mechanisms of transport were scalable. Vegetables, fish, dairy products, tree crops, spices, and other lightweight or time-sensitive comestibles that were the result of household-level production moved at different scales compared to bulk commodities such as rice and pulses.[57] The full extent of ancient water transport is unknown, but contemporary Early Historic iconography of ships confirms that watercraft were known in the subcontinent. Further, the placement of many Early Historic urban centers alongside rivers suggests that waterways were an important component of urban design and placement.

Flexibility in provisioning—as evidenced by labor, transportation, and the type of commodity—was integrated into the entirety of the "landscapes of movement" that anchored social networks into physical spaces of urban connectivity.[58] These movements included peoples' daily commutes from the city into the countryside for agricultural work and the delivery of agricultural products, whether by city dwellers themselves making a round-trip to rural places, or by rural vendors coming in and out of the city. Movements also would have constituted seasonal treks to the countryside and back, whether to rural places of agricultural production farther afield than a daily walk from the city, or in and out of pilgrimage centers. And there were annual or life-stage migrations of people from their natal villages to new households because of marriage, apprenticeship, or adoption.

Another important factor of flexibility is the division of labor among different social groups. In the Indian subcontinent, the concept of the caste system affected production and consumption capacities. First, the existence of a hierarchical system of expected work activities meant that some groups might have been particularly pressed to engage in manual field labor. However, the presence of a caste system also results in a series of mutual dependencies of a kind that would have made it possible for people living in cities to claim access to resources not through monetary means alone, but through hereditary relationships of obligation. Reciprocal obligations of material transfer occurred in the form of the *jajmani* system, in which producers provided direct supplies to consumers.[59] The presence of coinage in Early Historic archaeological sites indicates that there was a monetized economy, but monetized exchanges were supplements rather than replacements for the *jajmani* system.

Closely related to factors of caste as crosscutting social structures is the phenomenon of gender. We cannot evaluate the gendered division of farm labor from archaeological remains, but we can utilize contemporary texts that suggest expectations for gendered labor and forms of movement in the Early Historic period.[60] Iconographic depictions illustrate that women were highly visible in the public sphere; inscriptions confirm that women also were patrons of rural religious institutions.[61] Early Buddhist literature dating back to the mid-first millennium BCE provides insights on the differential performative aspects of ritual by women and men, and other religious textual traditions that contained gender-specific activities continued to be transmitted, such as the pre-Buddhist Vedic ritual texts, which probably survived in part because the mores and expectations expressed therein continued to resonate with contemporary populations. The Sangam literature of southern India, starting around the third century BCE, consists of lengthy descriptive poems about economy and society, describing women and men performing distinct kinds of work and enjoying different kinds of leisure. One can suggest, based on urban analogies elsewhere, that economic opportunities may have differentially drawn in women from the countryside to the city, with follow-on effects on the availability of labor for rural food production.[62]

Discussion

People living in ancient South Asian cities made use of flexible networks of provisioning that were, in turn, dependent on local farmers' abilities to manage and mitigate parameters of natural variability. While monsoons are predictable in the sense that they are expected every year, the arrival of rainwater is not like an irrigation tap whose volume can be controlled and velocity predicted. The terminology of excess water in the Indian subcontinent includes not only the idea of "normal floods" but also an understanding of the gradations of water abundance that include "nuisance floods," which resulted in gradually rising waters and had deleterious effects on structures and stored food stocks, and "catastrophic floods," which could reshape landscapes very dramatically.[63]

Incremental rainwater floods and powerful storms have different effects on the landscape, but both types of destruction can be patchy rather than all-encompassing, with local expressions of destruction mitigated by topography, the presence of trees, and the timing of floods relative to the agricultural cycle. When damage to standing crops did occur, people used networks of interaction opportunistically to bring in grain and other supplies from greater distances in order to make up for local losses. Changes in resource provenance were perhaps not even noticed by city dwellers except in terms of quality or price. For those urban dwellers who relied on a market mechanism or other form of redistribution for their food, there was relatively little point in knowing the exact provenance of ingredients (just as we purchase fruits and vegetables with scant notice of whether they are locally in season or come from the opposite hemisphere). Through globalization, we have accelerated the process of being able to pull in a hinterland of food production, a concept that nonetheless goes back to the beginning of urbanism. One excellent piece of evidence for the tenacity and resilience of the urban form in the Indian subcontinent is that despite the documented existence of warfare, cyclones, earthquakes, floods, and other disruptors, archaeological excavations show that cities were continuously occupied, perhaps because the experience of annual variability provided a physical mechanism and psychological buffer to more significant interruptions as well.

The physical landscapes of rural and urban places provided a spatial and tangible expression of the use of labor to enhance flexible provisioning. People in rural areas terraformed the landscape to accommodate "normal floods" and to guard against "nuisance floods." The terraforming of cities in the form of ramparts may have had some effects against water in places like Kaushambi, and to a certain extent at Sisupalgarh as well, although the presence of gates right on the water would suggest that ancient residents were not particularly worried about seasonal flooding entering the city. On the contrary, the slope of the ramparts and the terraforming of the interior of urban settlements may have constituted a form of water management, providing drinking and other daily-use water that passed through shared, intermediary spaces and hence was out of the exclusive or direct control of many residents.[64]

FIGURE 6.14

Man creating a rice
field boundary.
Photograph by Frank
Bienewald / Alamy
Stock Photo.

Just as household architecture was renewed on an annual basis, so too was the landscape of agricultural productivity. Wet-rice agriculture is predicated on the widespread
availability of water, but the presence of water that scours the landscape means that
bunds and other demarcations of ownership and investment often are reconstructed
from one year to the next (Figure 6.14). The markers of jurisdiction can be very subtle, as
we experienced when excavating at the gateway of the site of Talapada in the hinterlands
of Sisupalgarh. One of our workers asked us not to move a certain stone that served as
a property marker just beyond one of our excavation areas. There were many stones of
similar size and shape in the immediate vicinity, so we asked him to point it out. He
went to a stone that was the same size as the others, with no particular distinguishing characteristics. The ephemeral nature of this marker indicates the extent to which
boundary-making and property management was a social phenomenon rather than a
physical one. For the farmer and his neighbors, the boundary stone was just as authori-
tative as if it had been a formal construction marked by a tall edifice or proprietary sign.

In the past as in the present, agricultural productivity was encoded into the materiality of the landscape at a variety of scales. Rural-urban dynamics can be modeled in
terms of the concept of "functionality," in which people used each component of the
landscape in order to produce distinctly different types of desired goods and foods.[65]
But as Alan L. Kolata has emphasized,[66] the resultant rural-urban dynamic constitutes
a socially integrated continuum. This dynamic sense of sociability can be added to a
recognition that urban landscapes were the scenes of a constant ebb and flow of people.
Flexible provisioning is just another type of movement around a landscape in which
people were constantly in motion as laborers, soldiers, pilgrims, and traders, even if
settlements themselves were permanent.[67]

In their sense of motion and emotion, the monsoon landscapes of South Asia have similarities to other case studies presented in this volume's symposium antecedent. Christophe Pottier identifies three elements in the Angkorian landscape—which was also a rice-growing terrain—that resonate with the presentation of the Indian subcontinent found here.[68] First of all, he notes that there were both smaller sites and domestic/village shrines around Angkor, indicating the extent to which small-scale investments in place-making were evident in the hinterlands of the urban site. Although we are particularly struck by the grandeur of Angkor's largest monuments, we should remember that for individuals living in rural areas there was perhaps less emotional attachment to the largest temples compared to the quotidian venues of local religion. Such factors of investment also would have emanated from an intimate knowledge of the landscapes' capacities for production under variable conditions of seasonal weather and long-term climate. Secondly, Pottier mentions that the act of making rice fields, multiplied over many square kilometers of land, had the effect of slowing the downstream flow of water, a factor of large-scale landscape terraforming that was the result of many small-scale and localized decisions (a point also raised in Chevance's chapter). Finally, the dynamics of the Angkorian landscape fluctuated dramatically between the dry season and the rainy season in ways that remind us that people in cities, no less than residents of the countryside, responded to marked changes in seasons as a lived part of the urban experience.

Conclusion

Regionally informed research projects in the Indian subcontinent provide the opportunity to understand urbanism not merely as a phenomenon linked to densely populated cities, but one in which residents were actively engaged with the surrounding countryside in order to address basic needs in increasingly sophisticated ways. In the Indian subcontinent in the first millennium BCE, the use of flexible networks of provisioning enabled urban residents not only to mitigate fluctuations in annual water availability but also to buffer themselves from food-provisioning shortfalls resulting from other conditions such as pests and droughts. Pest infestations are a leading source of crop destruction, and management systems known from elsewhere in the monsoon belt indicate the extent to which pest control is both planned for in "typical" years and subject to mitigation under conditions of excessively heavy pest loads.[69] Drought is a rather different landscape condition than floods because it is an incremental, longitudinal process, the manifestation of which can stretch out over several years and have long-lasting effects on plants and animals within a landscape.[70] Drought is not a sudden-onset condition in the same way as floods and pest invasions; it requires some ideological flexibility in planning for, mitigating, and recovering from prolonged periods of aridity. On the other hand, although drought is incremental, it can be addressed through the same range of scalar solutions as those for water abundance.[71] From both an economic and a social perspective, once a flexible network was established it was a multipurpose entity that not only addressed one type of difficulty but provided a mechanism for multivariate urban problem-solving.[72]

Beyond the case studies of Kaushambi, Sisupalgarh, and Anuradhapura, research at other sites in the Indian subcontinent is revealing the intricacies of rural-urban integration in the ancient past. Work at Mahasthangarh in Bangladesh has combined excavations in the walled urban center with rural surveys and excavations that illustrate the urban center as a landscape phenomenon closely interwoven with religious practices.[73] In Nepal, intensive investigation of the Buddha's birthplace at Lumbini has been accompanied by excavations at the nearby urban center of Tilaurakot.[74] And in the hinterlands of the urban center of Vidisha, the study of Buddhist landscapes has provided primary data for both the mechanics of urban provisioning and the theory of landscape management in the Early Historic period.[75] These projects have provided evidence for the connections that extend religious structures into the city and urban-derived elements of social organization into the countryside.

Cities, as places of concentrated populations that depended on extensive hinterlands of food provisioning, prompted a significant reorganization of the landscape into "rural" and "urban" sectors. These social factors were integrated into the specific dynamics of different global urban landscapes. In the Indian subcontinent, the monsoon is an annual threshold moment of physicality and affect, perceived by individuals and experienced on the landscape scale. The dramatic fluctuation of the monsoon environment provides a case study for the evaluation of seasonal dynamics in the rural-supporting landscapes of ancient cities. In the Early Historic period, there were many concurrent changes, including the development of territorial states, integrative religious traditions such as Buddhism, and cities as densely concentrated population centers. The dramatic effects of water management provide a rubric against which we can evaluate environmental fluctuations in other ancient global cases, where seasonality affected food production as well as the manufacture and transportation of people, animals, and goods.[76] The abundance of water as a landscape phenomenon also illuminates the limits of human control of the local environment, and emphasizes that nature has agency in its capacity to significantly enhance as well as to disrupt patterns of human activities.

Acknowledgments

Many thanks go to John Beardsley and Georges Farhat for their invitation to the symposium "Landscapes of Pre-Industrial Cities" at Dumbarton Oaks, and to my fellow attendees for their stimulating presentations and commentary. My utmost appreciation goes to Professor R. K. Mohanty, codirector of the research projects at Sisupalgarh, Talapada, and Ostapur. Research support has been provided by the National Science Foundation; National Geographic Society; Wenner-Gren Foundation; Ahmanson Foundation; American Institute of Indian Studies; Department of Anthropology and Faculty of Arts and Sciences, University of Pittsburgh; and the Academic Senate, Department of Anthropology, and Cotsen Institute of Archaeology, University of California, Los Angeles. I would like to also thank Ian Simpson for kindly sharing the image and granting permission to reproduce Figure 6.10.

Notes

1 For the idea of "normal floods," see B. K. Paul, "Perception of and Agricultural Adjustment to Floods in Jamuna Floodplain, Bangladesh," *Human Ecology* 12, no. 11 (1984):3.

2 For an insightful discussion of the human perception and responses to climate as a long-term variation and weather as a year-by-year phenomenon, see Jane I. Guyer, "Farmers' Rainfall Anticipation: Incidence and Patterns in Western Nigeria; Advantages of Focus and Problems of Extrapolation in Case Studies," *Research in Economic Anthropology* 35 (2015):135–53.

3 The concept of "rurality" as a component of urban development has been raised by Norman Yoffee ("Political Economy in Early Mesopotamian States," *Annual Review of Anthropology* 24 [1995]:284) and George L. Cowgill ("Origins and Development of Urbanism: Archaeological Perspectives," *Annual Review of Anthropology* 33 [2004]:527). In general, the relationship between the advent of plant and animal domestication and the development of cities has long been a subject of scholarly inquiry. In the 1930s, V. Gordon Childe articulated the two developments as one of a "neolithic revolution," in which people adopted domesticates as a component of settled village life, followed several thousand years later by the "urban revolution," characterized by a restructuring of economic relationships of full-time craft specialization, civic administration, and architectural intensification that underwrote urban economies and accelerated the production of manufactured goods (see, e.g., *Man Makes Himself* [London: Watts, 1936]). While Childe's concept in its broad outlines has been almost universally accepted for its recognition of the need for agricultural production as a precursor to urban development, there are some detractors among urban planners who have advocated for a "cities first" model, in which it is argued that prior to urbanism there was no rationale for an agricultural village economy. This view was initially proposed by Jane Jacobs (e.g., *The Economy of Cities* [New York: Vintage, 1969]) and recently revived by Peter J. Taylor, *Extraordinary Cities: Millennia of Moral Syndromes, World-Systems and City/State Relations* [Cheltenham: Edward Elgar, 2013]). Although the "cities first" concept has been vigorously disallowed by archaeologists (most recently by Michael E. Smith, Jason Ur, and Gary M. Feinman, "Jane Jacobs' 'Cities First' Model and Archaeological Reality," *International Journal of Urban and Regional Research* 38, no. 4 [July 2014]:1525–35), there is a kernel of truth to the way in which urban demands cause an intensification of rural agricultural practices.

4 About the middle class as a dynamic force for urban development, see Monica L. Smith, "Urbanism and the Middle Class: Co-Emergent Phenomena in the World's First Cities," *Journal of Anthropological Research* 74, no. 3 (2018):299–326; and Monica L. Smith, *Cities: The First 6,000 Years* (New York: Viking, 2019).

5 Tony J. Wilkinson, Graham Philip, Jenny Bradbury, Robert Dunford, Danny Donoghue, Nikolaos Galiatsatos, Dan Lawrence, Andrea Ricci, and Stefan L. Smith, "Contextualizing Early Urbanization: Settlement Cores, Early States, and Agro-Pastoral Strategies in the Fertile Crescent during the Fourth and Third Millennia BC," *Journal of World Prehistory* 27 (2014):43–109. Wilkinson et al. further offer the provocative comment that urban systems in northern Mesopotamia might have thrived because of, rather than in spite of, environmental risks.

6 See, for example, Diane Z. Chase and Arlen F. Chase, "Caracol, Belize, and Changing Perceptions of Ancient Maya Society," *Journal of Archaeological Research* 25 (2017):185–249.

7 For a discussion of the concept of "landesque capital" in the southern Indian context, see Kathleen D. Morrison, "Capital-esque Landscapes: Long-Term Histories of Enduring Landscape Modifications," in *Landesque Capital: The Historical Ecology of Enduring Landscape Modifications*, ed. N. Thomas Håkansson and Mats Widgren (Walnut Creek, Calif.: Left Coast Press, 2014), 49–74.

8 "City Census 2011," accessed August 16, 2019, https://www.census2011.co.in/city.php; and "India," World Bank Group, accessed August 16, 2019, https://data.worldbank.org/country/india.

9 For Indus cities and cultural configuration, see Rita P. Wright, *The Ancient Indus: Urbanism, Economy, and Society* (Cambridge: Cambridge University Press, 2010).

10 This observation of the Indus cultural area size is made in Robin Coningham and Ruth Young, *The Archaeology of South Asia: From the Indus to Asoka, c. 6500 BCE–200 CE* (New York: Cambridge University Press, 2015), 178.

11 Upinder Singh, *A History of Ancient and Early Medieval India* (Delhi: Pearson Longman, 2008); and Monica L. Smith, "The Archaeology of South Asian Cities," *Journal of Archaeological Research*

14, no. 2 (2006):97–142. The definition of "urban" has resulted in a great deal of discussion among archaeologists; for this chapter, an urban center is defined as an entity of diverse economic activities and relatively large population density compared to the surrounding hinterlands, i.e., settlements that would have encompassed more than 50 ha and 10,000 people. In many cases, the absolute site of Early Historic urban centers is unknowable, however, because of subsequent medieval and modern occupations that have obscured the Early Historic antecedents. Raymond Allchin suggests that the largest Early Historic settlement was at Pataliputra (now under the modern city of Patna) with an estimated size of more than 240 ha ("Patterns of City Formation in Early Historic South Asia," *South Asian Studies* 6, no. 1 [1990]:163–73). However, L. A. Waddell provided an even more generous assessment of "a long parallelogram about nine miles (14.5 km) in length" on the basis of the writing of the ancient Greek ambassador Megasthenes and in reference to Waddell's own excavations around the site (*Excavations at Pātaliputra [Patna]: The Palibothra of the Greeks* [Calcutta: Bengal Secretariat Press, 1903], 20).

12 Researchers have emphasized, however, that the predominant vegetation type of the Ganges was savanna rather than forest (e.g., Rakesh Tewari, "Myth of Dense Forests and Human Occupation in the Ganga Plain," *Man and Environment* 29, no. 2 [2004]:102–16), and that in any case fire was likely to have been much more effective in clearing forests than iron tools; see A. Ghosh, *The City in Early Historic India* (Simla: Institute of Advanced Studies, 1973).

13 Singh, *History of Ancient and Early Medieval India*.

14 Kazi K. Ashraf, *The Hermit's Hut: Architecture and Asceticism in India* (Honolulu: University of Hawai'i Press, 2013), 2.

15 Raja de Mogadha Sudraka, *The Little Clay Cart (Mṛicchakaṭika): A Hindu Drama, Attributed to King Shudraka*, trans. Arthur William Ryder (Cambridge, Mass.: Harvard University Press, 1905), 9:83–84.

16 Ranabir Chakravarti, "Agricultural Technology in Early Medieval India (c. AD 500–1300)," *Medieval History Journal* 11, no. 2 (2008):229–58. Eleanor Kingwell-Banham has noted that generalized patterns of monsoon intensity on the subcontinental level had variable local expressions ("Early Rice Agriculture in South Asia: Identifying Cultivation Systems Using Archaeobotany" [PhD diss., Institute of Archaeology, University College London, 2015], 36).

17 Paul, "Perception of and Agricultural Adjustment to Floods in Jamuna Floodplain," 3.

18 Christopher R. Moore and Christopher W. Schmidt, "Abundance in the Archaic: A Dwelling Perspective," in *Abundance: The Archaeology of Plenitude*, ed. Monica L. Smith (Boulder: University Press of Colorado), 48.

19 Peter Civáň, Sajid Ali, Riza Batista-Navarro, Konstantina Drosou, Chioma Ihejieto, Debarati Chakraborty, Avik Ray, Pierre Gladieux, and Terence A. Brown, "Origin of the Aromatic Group of Cultivated Rice (*Oryza sativa* L.) Traced to the Indian Subcontinent," *Genome Biology and Evolution* 11, no. 3 (2019):832–43; Dorian Q. Fuller, "Pathways to Asian Civilizations: Tracing the Origins and Spread of Rice and Rice Cultures," *Rice* 4 (2011):78–92; Eleanor Kingwell-Banham, "Early Rice Agriculture in South Asia"; and Monica L. Smith, "The Archaeology of Food Preference," *American Anthropologist* 108, no. 3 (2006):480–93.

20 D. J. Greenland, *The Sustainability of Rice Farming* (New York: CAB International, 1997).

21 Julia Shaw, *Buddhist Landscapes in Central India: Sanchi Hill and Archaeologies of Religious and Social Change, c. Third Century BC to Fifth Century AD* (Walnut Creek, Calif.: Left Coast Press, 2007); and Julia Shaw and John Sutcliffe, "Ancient Irrigation Works in the Sanchi Area: An Archaeological and Hydrological Investigation," *South Asian Studies* 17 (2001):55–75.

22 The environmental positioning of religious institutions as productive engines of agricultural management was also seen in later Indian contexts, including the medieval period in which temples received grants from rulers and, in turn, coordinated the production of rice; see, for example, Burton Stein, "The Economic Function of a Medieval South Indian Temple," *Journal of Asian Studies* 19, no. 2 (1960):163–76. Melinda Zeder has suggested that urban leaders' control of food lay not in the management of the minutiae of production, but in the control of food once it actually got to the city ("Food Provisioning in Urban Societies: A View from Northern Mesopotamia," in *The Social Construction of Ancient Cities*, ed. Monica L. Smith [Washington, D.C.: Smithsonian Institution Press, 2003], 159); a similar argument for the Maya region has been offered by K. Anne Pyburn, "Pomp and Circumstance

Before Belize: Ancient Maya Commerce and the New River Conurbation," in *The Ancient City: New Perspectives on Urbanism in the Old and New World*, ed. Joyce Marcus and Jeremy A. Sabloff (Santa Fe: School for Advanced Research Press, 2008), 247–72.

23 For example, Mesopotamia has a vast literature on temple redistribution as part of the economy, in which the relationships of urban consumption to rural production include statistics on relative inputs of labor and supervision; see Robert K. Englund, "Hard Work—Where Will It Get You? Labor Management in Ur III Mesopotamia," *Journal of Near Eastern Studies* 50, no. 4 (1991):255–80.

24 Note that while topography has remained steady, hydrological regimes have in some cases been significantly modified since ancient times due to modern dams upstream, as is the case with Sisupalgarh. The amplitude of all the watercourses in the Mahanadi River delta has been moderated by the twentieth-century Hirakud Dam, which impounds rainwater that provides flood protection during the monsoon and irrigation water in the dry season (D. Nagesh Kumar and M. Janga Reddy, "Ant Colony Optimization for Multi-Purpose Reservoir Operation," *Water Resources Management* [2006] 20:879–98). As a result, there is a limit to the use of ethnographic observations about farming practices as a model for reconstructing ancient patterns of coping with seasonal change; such observations do, however, assist with understanding rainfall-associated patterns of agriculture and decision-making for which analogies can also be found in highland areas unaffected by dams; see Deepak K. Mishra, "Production and Exchange Relations in Rain-Fed Agriculture: The Case of Rice in Odisha," *RGTW Working Paper* 12 (June 2015).

25 The placement of ritual architecture within the urban core at these and other sites such as Saheth-Maheth and Taxila is in apparent contradiction to the textual prescriptions that Buddhist sites should be only on the outskirts of cities.

26 As also discussed by Suzanne Preston Blier for West African cities ("Walls That Speak: Landscape Factors in Early West African Urban Centers" [paper presented at "Landscapes of Pre-Industrial Cities," Garden and Landscape Studies symposium, Dumbarton Oaks Research Library and Collection, Washington, D.C., 2017]), the walls of South Asian urban sites appear to have had a multipurpose function as economic, social, and military perimeters (see Monica L. Smith, "Urban Social Networks: Early Walled Cities of the Indian Subcontinent as 'Small Worlds,'" in Smith, *Social Construction of Ancient Cities*, 269–89).

27 G. R. Sharma, *Excavations at Kauśāmbī 1949–50*, Memoirs of the Archaeological Survey of India 74 (Delhi: Archaeological Survey of India, 1969); and G. R. Sharma, *The Excavations at Kauśāmbī 1957–59: The Defences and the Śyenaciti of the Puruṣamedha* (Allahabad: Institute of Archaeology, 1960); for a summary, see K. S. Ramachandran, "Kaushambi," in *Encyclopedia of Indian Archaeology*, ed. A. Ghosh (New Delhi: Munshiram Manoharlal, 1989), 2:212–15. While Sharma suggested that the initial ramparts were constructed ca. 1025 BCE and within a century after the site's initial occupation, B. B. Lal's subsequent investigations indicated that the ramparts were likely to be sixth century BCE or later ("Are the Defences of Kauśāmbī Really as Old as 1025 BC?," *Puratattva* 11 (1979–80):88–95, reprinted in *Kauśāmbī Revisited*, ed. B. B. Lal [New Delhi: Aryan Books, 2017], 33), while K. K. Sinha proposed that the site as a whole could be dated to the seventh century ("Stratigraphy and Chronology of Early Kauśāmbī—A Reappraisal," in *Radiocarbon and Indian Archaeology*, ed. D. P. Agrawol and A. Ghosh [Bombay: Tata Institute of Fundamental Research, 1973], 31–238, reprinted in Lal, *Kauśāmbī Revisited*, 57–62).

28 For population estimates, see George Erdosy, *Urbanisation in Early Historic India*, BAR International Series 430 (Oxford: British Archaeological Reports, 1988), 72; in a footnote on p. 75 he adds that with the suburbs, the population of Kaushambi could be estimated at thirty-two thousand.

29 Aruna Tripathi, *The Buddhist Art of Kauśāmbī (from 300 BC to AD 550)* (New Delhi: D. K. Printworld, 2003), 314.

30 Erdosy, *Urbanisation in Early Historic India*, 59.

31 Ibid. See Tripathi, *Buddhist Art of Kauśāmbī*, for an extensive catalog of sites and artifacts bearing religious motifs in and around Kaushambi.

32 Xuanzang, *Si-Yi-Ki Buddhist Records of the Western World*, trans. Samuel Beal (1884; London: Routledge, 2000), 1:235.

33 Erdosy, *Urbanisation in Early Historic India*, 75.

34 Ibid., 35.

35 Ibid., 7.

36 B. B. Lal, Rabindra Kumar Mohanty, and Monica L. Smith, "Sisupalgarh," in *History of Ancient India*, vol. 3, *The Texts, Political History and Administration till c. 200 BC*, ed. Dilip K. Chakrabarti and Makkhan Lal (New Delhi: Aryan Books International, 2014), 620.

37 Initial excavations were undertaken in 1947 by B. B. Lal, "Sisupalgarh 1948: An Early Historical Fort in Eastern India," *Ancient India* 5 (1949):62–105, and again from 2005 to 2009 by an international team: Rabindra Kumar Mohanty and Monica L. Smith, *Excavations at Sisupalgarh* (New Delhi: Indian Archaeological Society, 2008); and Monica L. Smith and Rabindra Kumar Mohanty, "Archaeology at Sisupalgarh: The Chronology of an Early Historic Urban Centre in Eastern India," in *South Asian Archaeology and Art 2012*, ed. Vincent Lefèvre, Aurore Didier, and Benjamin Mutin (Turnhout: Brepols, 2016), 2:683–95.

38 For a discussion of recent growth trajectories in the region, see Priyaleen Singh's contribution on medieval and contemporary Bhubaneswar in this volume.

39 Sunil Kumar Patnaik, "Dhauli—Aragarh Culture Complex: A Study of Recent Archaeological Investigations," *Purānveshana: Indian Journal of Archaeology and Tradition* 1, no. 2 (2018):51–64.

40 Robin Coningham, "The Archaeology of Buddhism," in *Archaeology and World Religion*, ed. Timothy Insoll (London: Routledge, 2001), 61–95.

41 Monica L. Smith, "The Phenomenology of Neighborhoods in the Early Historic Period of the Indian Subcontinent (3rd Century BCE–4th Century CE)," in "Excavating Neighborhoods: A Cross-Cultural Exploration," ed. David Pacifico and Lise A. Truex, special issue, *Archeological Papers of the American Anthropological Association* 30, no. 1 (2019):62–70.

42 Tilok Thakuria, Tosabanta Padhan, Rabindra Kumar Mohanty, and Monica L. Smith, "Google Earth as an Archaeological Tool in the Developing World: An Example from India," *SAA Archaeological Record* 13, no. 1 (2013):20–24.

43 Eleanor Kingwell-Banham, Emma Karoune née Harvey, Rabindra Kumar Mohanty, and Dorian Q. Fuller, "Archaeobotanical Investigations into Golbai Sasan and Gopalpur, Two Neolithic-Chalcolithic Settlements of Odisha," *Ancient Asia* 9, no. 5 (2018):1–14, https://doi.org/10.5334/aa.164.

44 Monica L. Smith and Rabindra Kumar Mohanty, "Monsoons, Rice Production, and Urban Growth: The Microscale Management of Water Abundance," *Holocene* 28, no. 8 (2018):1325–33.

45 Bjørn Axelsen, "How Dry Is Sri Lanka's Dry Zone? Some Comments on Agricultural Potential, Perception and Planning," *Norsk Geografisk Tidsskrift—Norwegian Journal of Geography* 37, nos. 3–4 (1983):197–209.

46 Robin Coningham, *Anuradhapura: The British-Sri Lankan Excavations at Anuradhapura Salgaha Watta 2*, vol. 1, *The Site*, BAR International Series 824 (Oxford: Archaeopress, 1999); Robin Coningham, *Anuradhapura: The British-Sri Lankan Excavations at Anuradhapura Salgaha Watta 2*, vol. 2, *The Artefacts*, BAR International Series 1508 (Oxford: BAR Publishing, 2006); Robin Coningham and Prishanta Gunawardhana, *Anuradhapura*, vol. 3, *The Hinterland*, BAR International Series 2568 (Oxford: BAR Publishing, 2013); and Krista Gilliland, Ian A. Simpson, William Paul Adderley, Christopher Ian Burbidge, Alan J. Cresswell, David C. W. Sanderson, Robin Alexander Evelyn Coningham, Mark Manuel, Keir Magalie Strickland, Prasanta Gunawardhana, and Gamini Adikari, "The Dry Tank: Development and Disuse of Water Management Infrastructure in the Anuradhapura Hinterland, Sri Lanka," *Journal of Archaeological Science* 40 (2013):1012–28.

47 Coningham, *Anuradhapura*, 1:126–27.

48 Ibid., 1:127.

49 Ibid., 1:127.

50 Gilliland et al., "Dry Tank."

51 Ibid., 1026.

52 Ibid., 1025.

53 James J. Gibson, *The Ecological Approach to Visual Perception* (New York: Taylor and Francis, 1986).

54 Seetha N. Reddy, "On the Banks of the River: Opportunistic Cultivation in India," *Expedition* 33, no. 3 (1991):18–26.

55 Tom D. Dillehay and Alan L. Kolata, "Long-Term Human Response to Uncertain Environmental Conditions in the Andes," *Proceedings of the National Academy of Sciences of the United States of America* 101, no. 12 (2004):4328.

56 Roadways would have been passable by domestic animals or elephants bearing packs, but long-distance cart travel was likely to have been difficult, as it was still in the nineteenth century according to British colonial documents. For a delightful discussion of animal transport, see Julian Baker, "Trans-Species Colonial Fieldwork: Elephants as Instruments and Participants in Mid-Nineteenth-Century India," in *Conflict, Negotiation, and Coexistence: Rethinking Human-Elephant Relations in South Asia*, ed. Piers Locke and Jane Buckingham (New Delhi: Oxford University Press, 2016), 115–36. The factor of difficult road travel probably prompted the development of railways as an alternative; road conditions in India are still a major dampening factor on agricultural provisioning of cities.

57 For an insightful treatment of urban vegetable logistics, see Bianca Ambrose-Oji, "Urban Food Systems and African Indigenous Vegetables: Defining the Spaces and Places for African Indigenous Vegetables in Urban and Peri-Urban Agriculture," in *African Indigenous Vegetables in Urban Agriculture*, ed. Charlie M. Shackleton, Margaret W. Pasquini, and Axel W. Drescher (London: Earthscan, 2009), 1–33.

58 The concept of "landscapes of movement," articulated by James E. Snead, Clark L. Erickson, and J. Andrew Darling in a volume of the same name (*Landscapes of Movement: Trails, Paths, and Roads in Anthropological Perspective*, ed. James E. Snead, Clark L. Erickson, and J. Andrew Darling [Philadelphia: University of Pennsylvania Museum of Archaeology and Anthropology, 2009]), can also be traced to the long history of phenomenology in anthropological literature including works by Keith Basso (*Wisdom Sits in Places: Landscape and Language among the Western Apache* [Albuquerque: University of New Mexico, 1996]); Christopher Tilley (*A Phenomenology of Landscape: Places, Paths, and Monuments* [Oxford: Berg, 1994]); and Matthew Johnson ("Phenomenological Approaches in Landscape Archaeology," *Annual Review of Anthropology* 41, no. 1 [2012]:269–84).

59 In fact, the opportunities for reciprocal interactions of mutual dependency are also important to envisage for other regions of the world, given that coined money is a very late development in human history relative to the advent of urbanism. The earliest coinage was in the seventh century BCE in the Mediterranean (David M. Schaps, "War and Peace, Imitation and Innovation, Backwardness and Development: The Beginnings of Coinage in Ancient Greece and Lydia," in *Explaining Monetary and Financial Innovation: A Historical Analysis*, ed. Peter Bernholz and Roland Vaubel [Cham, Switzerland: Springer, 2014]:31–51). Urban economies prior to that time had standards of value such as cowries or cacao pods, but no recognizable units of manufactured currency, a lacuna in what might otherwise be a very obvious development; this means that the entirety of Mesopotamian civilization and Egyptian civilization were economies of barter, reciprocal obligation, and command redistribution, or some combination of the three.

60 Singh, *History of Ancient and Early Medieval India*. In theory, one could evaluate gendered divisions of labor through human skeletal analysis, which would reveal differential work injuries and stresses. But due to ancient practices of cremation, there are few human skeletal remains from the Early Historic period.

61 Iconography from Buddhist monastic sites such as Sanchi, Bharhut, and Amaravati show women engaged in worship and in the iconography in general; these sites also received patronage of Buddhist nuns as well as other categories of donors (Romila Thapar, "Patronage and the Community," in *The Powers of Art: Patronage in Indian Culture*, ed. Barbara Stoler Miller [Delhi: Oxford University Press, 1992], 19–34). At the ancient city of Mathura, donors to the Jain stupa at Kankali Tila were "mainly the wives of various tradesmen and craftsmen" (Barbara Stoler Miller and Richard Eaton, "Introduction," in Miller, *Powers of Art*, 5).

62 Cf. Jeanne Marie Penvenne, "Seeking the Factory for Women: Mozambican Urbanization in the Late Colonial Era," *Journal of Urban History* 23, no. 3 (1997):342–79.

63 For the concept of "nuisance floods," see Sheena Panja, Arun K. Nag, and Sunando Bandyopadyay, *Living with Floods: Archaeology of a Settlement in the Lower Ganga Plains, c. 600–1800 CE* (Delhi: Primus, 2015), 52; and Jakub Kocanda and Kati Puhakka, "Living with Floods along the Karnali River: A Case Study of Adaptive Capacity in the Rajapur Area, Nepal" (MA thesis, Lund University, 2012).

64 Rabindra Kumar Mohanty and Monica L. Smith, "Water Management Systems in the Early Historic Fortified Cities in Kalinga," *Abstracts of the 50th Anniversary Conference of the Indian Society for Prehistoric and Quaternary Studies* (Varanasi, 2017), 83–84.

65 For a discussion of the functional model, see J. Cameron Monroe, "Cities, Slavery, and Rural Ambivalence in Precolonial Dahomey," in *The Archaeology of Slavery: A Comparative Approach to Captivity and Coercion*, ed. Lydia Wilson Marshall, Center for Archaeological Investigation Occasional Paper 41 (Carbondale: Southern Illinois University, 2015), 193–94.

66 Alan L. Kolata, "The Autopoietic City: Landscape, Science, and Society in the Pre-Industrial World" (paper presented at "Landscapes of Pre-Industrial Cities," Garden and Landscape Studies symposium, Dumbarton Oaks Research Library and Collection, Washington, D.C., 2017).

67 Jason Ur's lyrical opening to his discussion of early urbanism emphasizes that movement characterized our collective human history prior to the development of cities ("The Birth of Cities in Ancient West Asia," in *Ancient West Asian Civilization: Geoenvironment and Society in the Pre-Islamic Middle East*, ed. Akira Tsuneki, Shigeo Yamada, and Ken-ichiro Hisada [Singapore: Springer, 2017], 133–47). However, urbanism only brought a fixity of architecture, enabling people to still move around landscapes of various sizes ranging from the open spaces of the agricultural landscape to the urban built environment in which there were vertical as well as horizontal pathways to follow.

68 Christophe Pottier, "Uncovering Ancient Landscapes in Angkor" (paper presented at "Landscapes of Pre-Industrial Cities," Garden and Landscape Studies symposium, Dumbarton Oaks Research Library and Collection, Washington, D.C., 2017).

69 An important and seminal discussion of landscape planning and localized management can be found in J. Stephen Lansing, *Priests and Programmers: Technologies of Power in the Engineered Landscape of Bali* (Princeton: Princeton University Press, 1991).

70 Mark Svoboda, Doug Lecomte, Mike Hayes, Richard Heim, Karin Gleason, Jim Angel, Brad Rippey, Rich Tinker, Mike Palecki, David Stooksbury, David Miskus, and Scott Stephens, "The Drought Monitor," *Bulletin of the American Meteorological Society* (August 2002):1181–90.

71 Hydrologists studying floods are specifically interested in their effects relative to risk management so that they can plan infrastructure strength on the basis of the largest range of floods that have been experienced in the past. Because detailed meteorological record-keeping has only existed for about the past century, hydrologists rely on historical records (where they are available) and geological studies of paleoflood deposits, which are the only way to ascertain the magnitude of floods on the 10^2- or 10^3-year scale, as discussed by Vishwas S. Kale, Lisa L. Ely, Yehouda Enzel, and Victor R. Baker, "Geomorphic and Hydrologic Aspects of Monsoon Floods on the Narmada and Tapi Rivers in Central India," *Geomorphology* 10 (1994):157–68. Particularly in the Americas, where written records do not extend earlier than the sixteenth century, the assessment of paleofloods is essential in order to ascertain the landscape effects of a one-thousand-year flood.

72 The capacity for multivariate problem-solving is probably a main reason why cities became, despite their inherent challenges, a viable form of population center.

73 Md. Shafiqul Alam and Jean-François Salles, eds., *France-Bangladesh Joint Venture Excavations at Mahasthangarh First Interim Report 1993–99* (Lyon: Department of Archaeology, Dhaka, and Maison de L'Orient et de la Méditeranée Jean Pouilloux, 2001); and Jean-François Salles, ed., *Mahasthan II: Fouilles du Rempart Est: Études archéologiques* (Turnhout: Brepols, 2015).

74 C. E. Davis, R. A. E. Coningham, K. P. Acharya, I. A. Simpson, J. Tremblay, R. B. Kunwar, M. J. Manuel, K. C. Krishna Bahadur, and B. Bidari, "Re-Investigating Tilaurakot's Ancient Fortifications: A Preliminary Report of Excavations Through the Northern Rampart (Nepal)," *Ancient Nepal* 190 (2016):30–46.

75 Shaw, *Buddhist Landscapes in Central India.*

76 See, for example, the discussion of medieval Scandinavian port towns and the effects of the winter season on both local productivity and long-distance travel: Axel Christophersen, "Performing Towns: Steps Towards an Understanding of Medieval Urban Communities as Social Practice," *Archaeological Dialogues* 22, no. 2 (2015):109–32.

7

The Phnom Kulen Capital

A Singular and Early Case of
Landscape Construction in Ancient Cambodia

JEAN-BAPTISTE CHEVANCE

L IGHT DETECTION AND RANGING (LIDAR) TECHNOLOGY HAS RECENTLY been applied in Angkor and other capitals or archaeological complexes in Cambodia, thanks to two consecutive and complementary archaeological projects undertaken in 2012 and 2015.

Angkor attracted the attention of most researchers, whereas scholars tended to neglect Phnom Kulen (Figure 7.1).[1] An elongated plateau situated approximately 25 mi to the northeast of Angkor, Phnom Kulen was a late Khmer Rouge stronghold that was difficult to access until the early 2000s, when we first started to survey the area. Since the 1920s, Phnom Kulen has been identified with Mahendraparvata, one of the earliest capitals of the Khmer empire from the beginning of the ninth century.

This essay introduces the preliminary LiDAR results on Phnom Kulen, including a previously unseen but large urban settlement that required important landscape modifications, including water-management features (Figure 7.2).[2] Combined with the outcomes of previous and complementary excavation campaigns, it introduces this early, ephemeral, and vast settlement. The essay presents a historiographic clarification, then offers a brief summary of the knowledge on Mahendraparvata prior to the LiDAR operation. The third section aims to detail the urban network of Phnom Kulen's ancient city as well as its organization. Finally, the essay presents the city's interactions with the natural environment and the impact of such large-scale landscape modification on the site's natural resources.

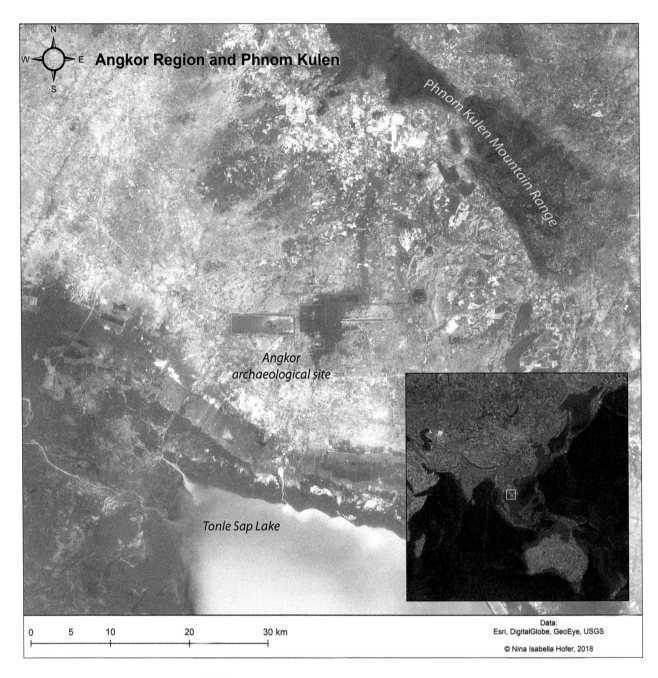

FIGURE 7.1

Map of the Angkorian region with the Phnom Kulen range. Data from Esri, DigitalGlobe, GeoEye, USGS; and Nina Isabella Hofer, 2018.

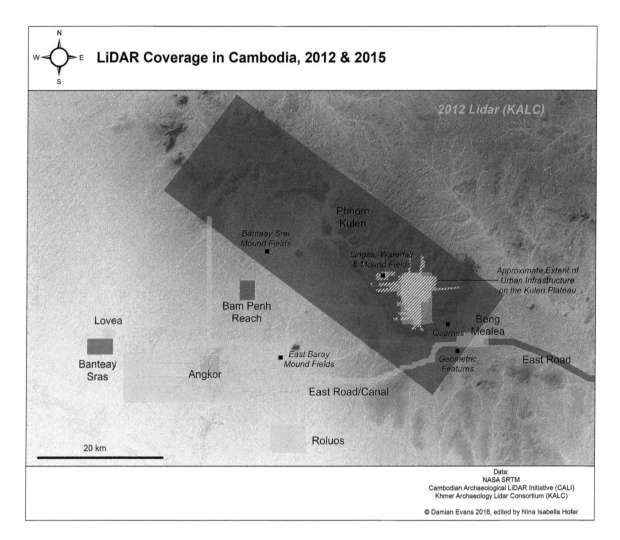

Data:
NASA SRTM
Cambodian Archaeological LiDAR Initiative (CALI)
Khmer Archaeology Lidar Consortium (KALC)

© Damian Evans 2016, edited by Nina Isabella Hofer

FIGURE 7.2

Detailed map of the Angkorian region in northwest Cambodia, showing the main coverage blocks
for the 2012 and 2015 Airborne Laser Scanning campaigns and noting features mentioned in the text.
Background elevation courtesy of NASA Shuttle Radar Topography Mission; Damian Evans, "Airborne
Laser Scanning as a Method for Exploring Long-Term Socio-Ecological Dynamics in Cambodia,"
Journal of Archaeological Science 74 (October 2016):164–75; Khmer Archaeology LiDAR Consortium;
and Cambodian Archaeological LiDAR Initiative, edited by Nina Isabella Hofer, 2018.

The "Rediscovery" of Angkor and the Khmer Civilization

The Khmer civilization, which spread across Southeast Asia from the ninth to the
fifteenth century, is mostly known for its main capital, Angkor, which was occupied without interruption during that period. Angkor, the vast, low-density capital
of the Khmer Kingdom, sprawled over nearly 400 mi² and may have housed hundreds of thousands of people. A primarily administrative and religious center for a
kingdom that dominated most of mainland Southeast Asia by the eleventh century,

Angkor was the largest preindustrial city on earth and remains the world's largest archaeological site.

The Angkor period is commonly understood to have started in 802, as evidenced by ancient inscriptions, particularly the Sdok Kak Thom stela (K.235). A self-proclamation by Jayavarman II as the universal-king was made from Kulen Mountain (Phnom Kulen), which overlooks the vast alluvial plain where Angkor would emerge in the following centuries.[3] Other epigraphic sources also indicate that along with initiating the *devaraja* cult, Jayavarman II confirmed himself as the great unifier, drawing Cambodia's disparate polities together and establishing the Khmer empire at the end of the eighth century, before settling on Phnom Kulen and the Angkor region.[4] Successive kings during the Angkorian era, and particularly from the tenth and eleventh centuries, referred to themselves as successors with more or less direct lineage to Jayavarman II, and inscriptions often mentioned Mahendraparvata, the Sanskrit name of the Phnom Kulen settlement.[5] By extension, Phnom Kulen became the birthplace of the Angkorian period (802–1432) and the Khmer empire, even though several major pre-Angkorian sites such as Sambor Prei Kuk (seventh century) predate this capital.

Despite mentions by Portuguese and Spanish missionaries during the sixteenth century, the Western "discovery" of Angkor and more generally that of the Khmer civilization was possible thanks to the first explorers, mostly French, during the 1860s, within the framework of the French Protectorate of the time. The first inventories by these "researcher-adventurers," such as Étienne Edmond Lunet de Lajonquière, Louis Delaporte, and Étienne Aymonier, were published in the early twentieth century.[6] These publications were contemporary with the creation of the French School of Asian Studies, École française d'Extrême-Orient (EFEO), founded in 1898 as the "Mission archéologique d'Indo-Chine." Its main goal was to organize the inventory and preservation of the cultural heritage of Indochina. In 1907, EFEO was assigned responsibility for the conservation of the Angkor archaeological site.

From that point in time, the study of Khmer civilization was mostly focused on three angles of approach: its monumental architecture, which would lead to numerous restorations; Angkorian art history, with the study of sculpture, architectural decoration, and classification of Khmer styles (from the late sixth century to the post-Angkorian styles of the fourteenth century); and epigraphy, with the transcription and publication of numerous inscriptions. Studies were, therefore, mostly oriented toward social elites, religious architecture, and religion, whereas common life and the territorial approach were neglected. Other sites and clusters of temples, constituting ancient capitals or important religious complexes spread over the empire, were documented during the first explorations as well as through these three perspectives.

This dynamic would remain mostly unchanged for the following sixty years, with a few exceptions.[7] On the Phnom Kulen plateau, the archaeological mission of Pierre Dupont and Philippe Stern in the 1930s[8] and surveys from Jean Boulbet and Bruno Dagens in the 1960s[9] constitute the only investigations undertaken in this area. Research was interrupted by tragic civil conflict in Cambodia, which lasted for more than twenty years, from the 1970s to the 1990s. Since the mid-1990s, due to recent studies combined with new technologies, the approach has covered a much larger territorial scale.[10] Remote-sensing techniques (aerial pictures, satellite and radar images) coupled with surveys, excavations, and paleoenvironmental studies have considerably enriched our perception of the Angkorian archaeological landscape and the settlements around religious sites. Nonmonumental and hydraulic features, agrarian spaces, production sites, and road networks provide new insights on the habitat and its density, the landscape's use and organization, and the economic interactions between the main religious monuments.

The Capital of Mahendraparvata

From the first Khmer studies at the beginning of the twentieth century, scholars have progressively identified the Phnom Kulen plateau as Mahendraparvarta and as one of the earliest capitals in the region, where Jayavarman II resided and ruled the Khmer empire for some time at the beginning of the ninth century.[11] Phnom Kulen was also confirmed as a capital by its concentration of temples, which are architecturally homogeneous.[12] There are a few remaining examples of these monuments on the plateau, dating from the early ninth century; they are mostly single brick towers, with similar architectural decoration.[13] One of these temples stands out as a typical marker of a Khmer empire capital: the mountain-temple or pyramid of Rong Chen. Its morphology replicates Mount Meru, symbolizing the center of the universe in Hindu mythology. Rong Chen's five-level pyramid is built on the highest point of this part of the mountain, and it constitutes the first mountain-temple built on a natural mountain in ancient Cambodia. This architectural prototype was to evolve and expand greatly during the Angkorian period, illustrated by later major, sophisticated examples such as the Pre Rup, Angkor Wat, and Bayon temples.

Alongside this architectural type, the principal features characterizing an Angkorian capital are the royal palace, satellite temples, and reservoirs. It was only a few years ago that we were able to identify the site of Banteay as the royal palace and the capital's center of secular power, thanks to its rectangular shape, size, orientation, and architectural remains.[14] Field surveys revealed organized earthen dikes and platforms. Three excavation campaigns unearthed associated traces of wooden buildings, laterite gutters, and brick sidewalks and buildings, all of which indicate a complex site. This research provided radiocarbon dating, numerous roof-tile fragments, and earthenware ceramics; it clarified the dating of Banteay's construction, occupation, and abandonment, which corresponds roughly to the reign of Jayavarman II (770–835). Additionally, this recent discovery allowed us to detect a spatial correlation between its center of secular power and religious sites, notably the mountain-temple. However, the resulting map mainly showed several sites of different sizes, with only a glimpse of any interorganization. Another particularity of Phnom Kulen is its hosting of sites that are linked to a later and different occupation of the massif: rock shelters installed by hermits, some of which became meditation centers and were occupied from the tenth to the sixteenth century.[15]

FIGURE 7.3
Carved riverbed of the one
thousand lingas (phallic
representations of Shiva)
in Phnom Kulen, March
2006. Photograph courtesy
of Jean-Baptiste Chevance
/ Archaeology and
Development Foundation.

Associated with these occupations are the famous carved riverbed of Kbal Spean and
its one thousand lingas. These spectacular transformations of Phnom Kulen's main rivers, with multiple representations of Shiva and Vishnu, bring a sacred dimension to the
water before it reaches the Angkorian region (Figure 7.3).

The Urban Network of Mahendraparvata

The natural features of the landscape should first be acknowledged. Rivers have eroded
the Angkorian region's Jurassic- and Cretaceous-aged sandstone to form this major
geological feature. Oriented northwest–southeast and measuring 9 × 15 ½ mi, Phnom
Kulen rises abruptly to a maximum of 1,600 ft above the plain, with margins marked on
all sides by steep escarpments and boulders (Figure 7.4). This strongly distinguishes
it from the Angkor region, which was generally characterized by a flat landscape with
religious sites surrounded by artificial groups of earth mounds, raised for habitation, or
long axes marked by earthen dikes and associated canals. The sandstone plateau is also
the origin of the regional watershed. Subject to Southeast Asia's strongly contrasting
seasons, the permanent water flow and relative altitude of the mountain create a micro-
climate and an environment conducive to settlement.

The most significant discovery of the recent LiDAR campaigns is the presence of a grid organizing the landscape, subdivided into squares of approximately 4,900 ft per side (Figure 7.5). This network is constituted of parallel earthen dikes (four oriented north–south and six oriented east–west), spaced at regular distances and marking the main axes of the capital. Most of the dikes are perfectly oriented to the cardinal directions and cover the southern part of the Kulen massif almost entirely. Only the axis leading to the royal palace does not fit within the grid. Traversing the entire plateau, it marks the importance of this site, which is associated with secular power. Extremely difficult to see in this irregular topography, with its forested environment, these dikes do not rise more than 3 ⅓ ft and extend over miles (Figure 7.6). These axes are, in some sections, materialized by excavated linear features. Some other sections of the network are missing, probably because of erosion or because they were never completed. The total area covered by the grid measures 2 ⅘ × 3 ¾ mi, for a total of approximately 10 ½ mi², with its longest axes being 6 ⅕ mi north–south and 9 ⅓ mi east–west. The spacing between these parallel dikes varies from 200 to 260 ft, a distance quite unrealistic for consideration as a road width. The top of these parallel dikes could rather be considered as the communication network of the ancient city.

The previously known archaeological sites composing this urban settlement (mountain-temple, royal palace, temples) now appear very clearly integrated within this network. The orientation of some of them is more coherent: traditionally open to the

FIGURE 7.4

Southern escarpment of the Phnom Kulen plateau, with a view toward Angkor, April 2015. Photograph courtesy of Jean-Baptiste Chevance / Archaeology and Development Foundation.

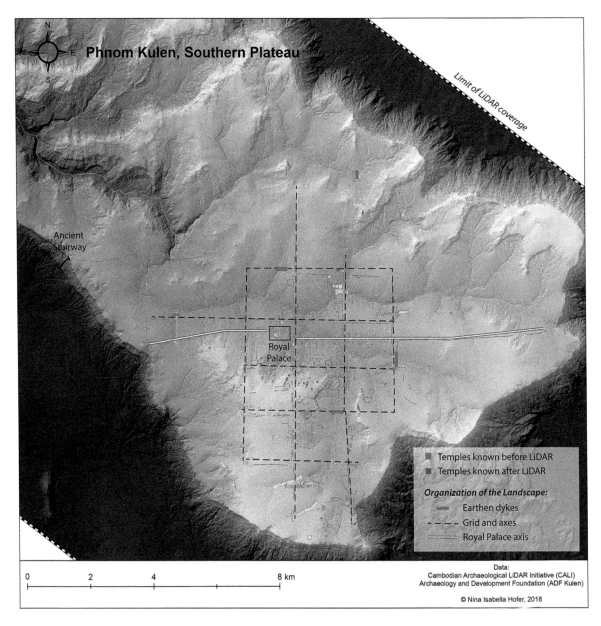

FIGURE 7.5

Map of the grid organizing the landscape of the southern Phnom Kulen plateau, subdivided into squares of approximately 4,900 ft per side. The dotted and white lines correspond to the main axis (mostly made of two parallel earthen dikes). The thick red line corresponds to the previously known earthen dikes, which block valleys and create reservoirs. Cambodian Archaeological LiDAR Initiative/ Archaeology and Development Foundation, mapping by Nina Isabella Hofer, 2018.

east, a few temples opening to the west are now obviously linked to the network's main axes. Additional unfinished temples have also been discovered.

This network acted as a base for the spatial organization of other archaeological features that lined its axes: platforms; plots defined by smaller earthen dikes with, in some cases, associated ponds; secondary dikes; canals; and embankments (Figure 7.7). Clearly, the concentration of these features determined the location of the settlements of the ancient city's population. They "fill" the empty spaces between the previously known religious sites and bring new light to daily life, the organization of the landscape, and its use by the population. The density of these features, more important in the center of the urban network, allows us to think that it was occupied first, with the edges developed later. Moreover, the main axes of the city lead to empty spaces without any traces of urbanization, or in the best cases, isolated features. It seems that the urbanization process was conceived first through organizing space on a large scale by establishing the grid, using several axes to define squares or "neighborhoods," and then occupying them. Within the defined squares, settlements were established with less well-oriented earthen dikes to subdivide spaces. Ponds seem to have had an importance as well, despite the proximity of streams, probably in order to mitigate drought during the dry

FIGURE 7.6

Archaeologist Sakhoeun Sakada standing on an earthen dike from one of the city's main east–west axes, January 2016. Photograph courtesy of Jean-Baptiste Chevance / Archaeology and Development Foundation.

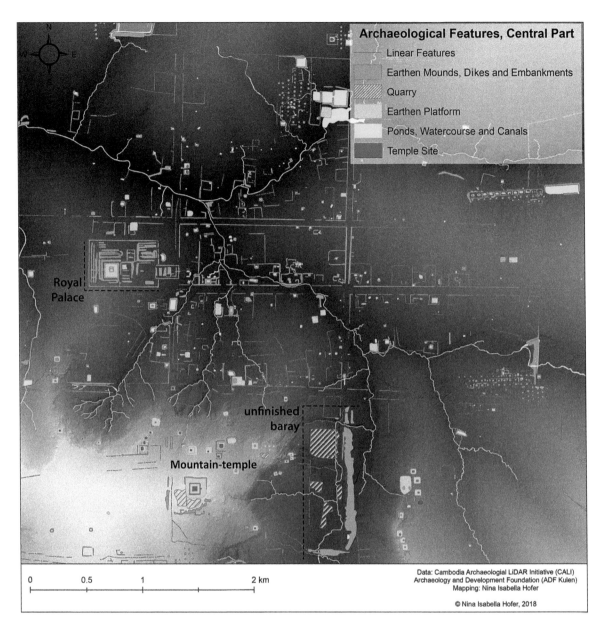

Royal Palace

unfinished baray

Mountain-temple

Data: Cambodia Archaeologial LiDAR Initiative (CALI)
Archaeology and Development Foundation (ADF Kulen)
Mapping: Nina Isabella Hofer

© Nina Isabella Hofer, 2018

FIGURE 7.7

Central part of the grid showing the density of archaeological features lining its axes (platforms, plots defined by smaller earthen dikes, associated ponds, secondary dikes, canals, and embankments); dams and reservoirs are in valleys. The largest axis, planned to be oriented north–south, was unfinished, with its center corresponding to the eastern axis of the mountain-temple. Cambodian Archaeological LiDAR Initiative/Archaeology and Development Foundation, mapping by Nina Isabella Hofer, 2018.

season and for domestic use. There are not many platforms, as opposed to Angkor. In Phnom Kulen, it was not necessary to raise land to protect it from flooding during the monsoon, the topography being radically different from the flat Angkorian plain.

Following the digitization of the features revealed by the LiDAR data by type (dikes, mounds, ponds), weeks of pedestrian surveys were undertaken to identify and register those that are most significant. These features, which are extremely hard to distinguish, require a GPS with the downloaded LiDAR data and a trained eye to recognize them in dense vegetation. Further on, the most representative were selected for excavation by single or multiple trenches, focusing on one type of feature per campaign and, in some cases, opening two types of features per trench (plot and axis, axis and pond, etc.).

The 2014 and 2016 excavation campaigns investigated two platforms (KL023, KL0138), several axes (KL0136, KL0341, KL0343), and one plot (KL0236). Radiocarbon dating, artifacts, and stratigraphy, all showing a single level of occupation, indicate that this city was briefly occupied, probably for a few decades during the ninth century. This corroborates the observations made of a royal palace that had been occupied for a relatively short period[16] and, more generally, of an ephemeral capital. As most of the civil constructions were made of perishable materials (wood and thatched roofs), in the framework of these archaeological diagnoses, only the interpretation of the stratigraphy and the cultural remains (mostly ceramics) are able to narrow the context. Written history merely consists of a few inscriptions and those found in Phnom Kulen date from the later Angkorian period.[17]

The LiDAR campaign over Mahendraparvata also revealed numerous groups of earth mounds, totaling more than 360.[18] These unusual features were only previously known from two sites in Angkor. Their interaction with the general grid indicates that they may have been superimposed onto the ancient city later. The 2013 excavation campaign indicated that they could indeed be from the tenth century. Their function is still unclear but could correspond to a forgotten religious ritual. Their importance on Phnom Kulen is particularly significant, since it is the highest concentration known so far: of the twenty-five known groups of earth mounds in Cambodia and Thailand, fifteen are located in Phnom Kulen. Other similar sites were also found in the ancient capital of Sambor Prei Kuk, the Angkor region, and Phanom Rung in modern Thailand.

The Interaction between the Urban Network and the Natural Environment

The natural characteristics (geography, hydrology, etc.) of Phnom Kulen present constraints and advantages for the sophisticated and geometrical grid that organized this capital. They dictated the layout of the settlements, and the builders of the Phnom Kulen capital, despite the implementation of a strict geometric design, adapted to and modified their natural environment with ingenuity. This urban planning was not only designed to highlight the location of the religious and secular centers (Rong Chen and Banteay) but also to address issues related to water control and reservoirs, as well as food security.

This network's interaction with its natural environment reveals a sophisticated system. The dikes, dams, and canals, some of which were previously known,[19] are ingenious parts of the urban network. The dams are placed in valleys, allowing them to be crossed perpendicularly and requiring less construction for the best efficiency (see Figure 7.5). They retain water, creating reservoirs with, in some cases, very substantial capacities. Scholars have questioned their function in the past. The absence of structures to control the release of impounded water was interpreted as evidence for their use as flood-prevention devices, rather than for agricultural water storage, for which it was claimed there was insufficient capacity.[20] It was proposed that these features were not built to irrigate areas downstream, but only to constitute water reservoirs. In fact, our recent field surveys have revealed indications of possible sluice gates in the channels going through or next to the main dams. LiDAR has also revealed numerous smaller, successive dams located in secondary valleys. We believe that they were used for storage, an advantage for a large population. Some reservoirs must have constituted important reserves for fish in a location that is quite far from Tonle Sap Lake. In some other cases, the dams may also have been built to irrigate some parts of the valleys downstream and occasionally upstream. In any case, the technical systems relevant to environmental control and their survival were forgotten, and further studies should determine their functioning.

Two of the principal hydraulic features are particularly interesting. In the main southern valley of the massif, all the rivers follow the natural slope, which is northward. They reach a dam, which was supposed to mark the southern part of a reservoir three-fifths of a mile long, which is closed on its eastern side by a monumental dike, Thnal Mrech, known as the location of later ceramic kilns. LiDAR has revealed a parallel north–south cut in the bedrock corresponding to the western edge of the reservoir and confirmed the east–west parallel quarries, used to extract material and raise the surrounding dikes. Built by excavating the valley, the reservoir was never finished, but it was planned in a location where it would have been possible to collect the maximum volume of water. The center of this reservoir also corresponds to the eastern axis of the mountain-temple, the religious center of the city (see Figure 7.7).

At the other end of the same valley, a channel three-fifths of a mile long diverts water to the south, through higher lands and even to the sandstone bedrock. This feature was regulated by dams and sluice gates, bringing water to the southern tip of the massif. Down on the plain and close to the Angkorian quarries (known to be the sources of the sandstone blocks used to build the Angkor temples), an east–west dike blocked the water flow and allowed for the transportation of the blocks toward the network of dikes and channels leading to Angkor (Figure 7.8). This channel could, therefore, be a later modification of the original hydraulic system, created to facilitate the extraction of the blocks during the expansion of the Angkorian capital.

Efficiently located ponds were known on Kulen previous to the LiDAR campaigns. Built with three to four earthen dikes, they directly capture water from a source and, in some cases, are arranged in tiers to follow the local topography. To capture stream water, other features were adapted to the natural hydraulic network, with channels, ponds, or small dikes diverting their courses to irrigate smaller areas.

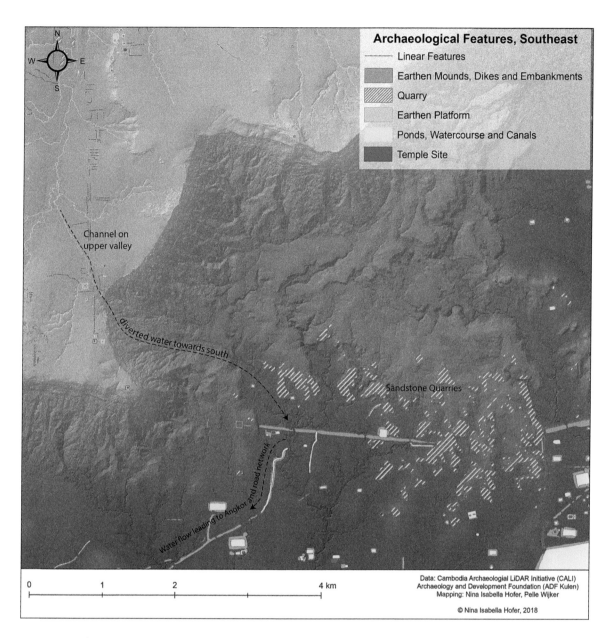

FIGURE 7.8

Southeast tip of the Kulen plateau with its slope and the area featuring the lower quarries. A probable later channel diverts water from the upper valley toward the south—to the southern tip of the massif, down onto the plain, and to the sandstone quarries. In the lowland area, two dikes retained the water flow to facilitate the transportation of blocks toward the network of dikes and channels, leading to Angkor. Cambodian Archaeological LiDAR Initiative/Archaeology and Development Foundation, mapping by Nina Isabella Hofer and Pelle Wijker, 2018.

With the natural fortress constituted by the topography of the mountain, the location of this capital at the origin of the local hydraulic network is a clear advantage with regard to settling the population and ensuring both physical protection and provision of natural resources for food security. The general settlement of this urban network is another example of the Khmers' ability to adapt to the topography of the plateau. In order to avoid a steep slope on the main axes, the builders chose a location where the slope was minimal. It is also likely that the main sites (such as the mountain-temple and the royal palace) were the benchmarks for establishing this network. Generally, this would require a very good knowledge of the entire topography and hydrology of the mountain. The organized urban landscape must have been structured within a geometrical entity (the entire southern part of the plateau), with a dense population and, very probably, a correspondingly large scale of deforestation. However, these signs are barely distinguishable on the ground today, as the forest has regrown, the archaeological features marking this grid are very subtle or shallow, and the plateau presents an irregular topography.

Impact on Natural Resources

LiDAR has provided new insights about the landscape's organization and its related settlements. But questions remain regarding the food supply for this population. No traces of small dikes surrounding ancient terraces for flooded rice fields have been revealed. Taking into account erosion, we can suppose that remains would have been visible for at least a few of them. Slash-and-burn or swidden agriculture, which does not require any modification of the landscape and is still used by the current population on Kulen, could have been the main mode of cultivation.

However, erosion has to be considered, as a recent study indicates that such an important example of urban planning in this particular environment must have had a significant impact on the area's natural resources. A sedimentological and paleobotanical analysis of a sedimental core from one of the ancient reservoirs shows "discrete periods of significant soil mobilisation within the catchment, either from the surrounding low hills or from the dyke [of the reservoir] itself."[21] The thickness of the coarse sand layers from the mid-valley area may represent very large volumes of material, as well as significant periods of soil erosion and deposition. They may correspond to particularly "intense summer monsoon rainfall events, high-energy floods related to the release of water from smaller upstream reservoirs, or periods of clearing on slopes proximal to the reservoir related to slash-and-burn agriculture or building activity."[22] It could also correspond to the production of ceramic items on the neighboring site, Thnal Mrech, which would have required large amounts of clay, water, and wood; some kilns at Thnal Mrech date from the tenth to the eleventh centuries.[23]

The episodic deposition of medium to coarse sand into the reservoir began in the mid-ninth century and ended in the late eleventh century. This suggests that the settlement on Phnom Kulen "was not only spatially extensive but temporally enduring, and sufficiently intensive to trigger extensive soil mobilisation within the catchment over

FIGURE 7.9

Excavation at site KL0341: lower layers of sediment in a pond, indicating successive periods of charcoal and deposition layers, March 2016. Photograph courtesy of Jean-Baptiste Chevance / Archaeology and Development Foundation.

approximately 250 years from the middle of the ninth century."[24] This indicates intensive land use, but further studies need to determine if this phenomenon was general or particular in the vicinity of the water catchment. During the eleventh and twelfth centuries, the reservoir was colonized by vegetation, reflecting some form of change in its operation. It could be linked to changes in water management and settlement organization in Angkor during the twelfth century, and more precisely to the creation of the southern channel in the same valley, excavated to provide water for the transportation of sandstone blocks from the quarries in the foothills of Kulen toward Angkor.

The Phnom Kulen Capital   187

Excavations in other, smaller ponds belonging to this original network have revealed successive periods of charcoal and deposition layers, probably providing evidence of slash-and-burn activities (KL0341, KL0342) (Figure 7.9). Even though these layers have not yet been dated, they show evidence of erosion. They also reveal changes in the utilization of these sites and the presence of a population after the abandonment of the capital as the seat of power.

Conclusion

Questions still remain as to the abandonment of this capital, and different causes may be proposed. The pacification of the political context and the control taken by Jayavarman II over a smaller, independent kingdom could explain why the court did not further require the Kulen area as a natural fortress. In times of peace, access to the Kulen capital from the Angkorian plain is quite problematic in itself, with the steep cliff surrounding the massif representing a constraint to entry from the surrounding lowlands.

The ancient laterite stairway (Pleu Cere), one-third of a mile long, is isolated from the city grid and seems to be a later Angkorian addition. This is also the case with a group of three temples far from the capital's center (dating from the tenth to the twelfth centuries), the "River of One Thousand Lingas," Kbal Spean, probably the numerous nearby earth mounds, and finally the rock shelter sites. These sites illustrate a later concentration of activities on the western part of the plateau.

The environmental and urban interactions, natural resource management, and, more generally, land use suggest that they might have contributed to some extent to the abandonment of Mahendraparvata. The deforestation required in setting up this important urban network and, more importantly, maintaining its population (burning wood for fuel) must have had a short-term impact on the plateau's natural environment. Considering slash-and-burn agriculture as the principal cultivation mode used on these poor and sandy soils, its extension and related low yields must have been even less sustainable for a large population.

It is hard to determine if the environmental changes made this urban settlement obsolete, or if the consolidation of power in the Angkor region was more decisive in abandoning it to Angkor's benefit. However, a certain relevance to the current period can be observed and we can speculate that a similar phenomenon is repeating itself with some equivalent consequences (Figure 7.10). For the last fifteen years, a significant and accelerated level of deforestation has been observed in the exact same area. The growing population of farmers is eradicating Phnom Kulen National Park's forestland by changing from the shifting cultivation of rain-watered upland rice to permanent cashew plantations. These agricultural practices, combined with encroachments upon and illegal logging within the national park, are severely threatening its natural resources and biodiversity. Climate change indicators such as deregulated seasons, longer droughts, and heavier and shorter rain periods are accelerating soil erosion and also impeding the locals' cultivation, yields, and access to markets.

FIGURE 7.10

A plot of forest recently
cleared and burned on
Phnom Kulen for upland
rice and permanent
plantations of cashew trees,
April 2016. Photograph
courtesy of Sakhoeun
Sakada / Archaeology and
Development Foundation.

Remote-sensing techniques, and particularly LiDAR, are astounding tools for detecting structures and modifications to the landscape. However, they must be completed through repeated surveys, excavations on key sites, the unearthing of materials that allow dating, and paleoenvironmental studies to allow further interpretation. LiDAR in itself cannot date the features, but gives the great advantage of a global, detailed vision of the landscape's layout. It is particularly beneficial for cultures that evolved in tropical climates, with thick forests often covering important features.

LiDAR technology revealed this ambitious, spectacular, early, and yet incomplete urban network. It was created ex nihilo, with very few traces of previous installations; it was quickly abandoned as the seat of power, thus preserving it from further important modification. As opposed to the Angkorian agrarian plain, where a succession and superimposition of features (spectacular architectural remains as well as agrarian, hydraulic, and settlement features) created a complex picture, which is harder to interpret, the early example of Mahendraparvata is unique in Khmer civilization. It represents a snapshot of a great and extremely geometrically organized city from the ninth century, with very few later modifications. In the context of the Angkorian civilization, the extended grid, organizing the urban settlements on a large scale and its dense center, constitutes a regional organization, as opposed to clusters of agrarian communities, such as those scattered across the flat plain of Angkor.

Nevertheless, a few elements indicate that the capital was definitively abandoned as the seat of royal power during the ninth century, that later occupations with different functions occurred, and that some of them, combined with erosion (ceramic kilns, repetitive slash-and-burn practices, mound fields), came to disturb the original, ambitious urban organization.

Mahendraparvata also represents a unique example of an engineered, urban landscape in a constraining environment—and it shows the ability of the ancient Khmers to adapt to it. However, issues related to intense farming, food supply, and deforestation might have posed a threat to a permanent and important population in such an environment. Further studies will allow ascertainment of these last points. More comparative studies with pre-Angkorian sites such as Oc-Eo and the West Baray region in Angkor could give indications regarding the origin of the spatial grid. Finally, this urban model allows for understanding of the further evolution of the Angkorian era, where patterns of such design can be seen, such as in Angkor Thom, by giving us an early example of an open urban layout. Later models in Angkor have been disturbed by successive additions, and Mahendraparvata appears to be even more unique in this regard.

Acknowledgments

This research is part of the Phnom Kulen Program initiated by the Archaeology and Development Foundation (ADF), in collaboration with the Authority for the Protection and Management of Angkor and the Region of Siem Reap (APSARA). The LiDAR acquisitions were consecutively undertaken within the framework of the Khmer Archaeology LiDAR Consortium (KALC, with ADF being one of the eight partners), Cambodian Archaeological LiDAR Initiative (CALI) of the École française d'Extrême-Orient (EFEO), and funded by the European Research Council (ERC). The author is grateful to Damian Evans, who initiated the projects and shared data, and to the Mohamed S. Farsi Foundation, which funded the Kulen acquisition in 2012. Nina Isabella Hofer, Stéphane De Greef, Prey Sovann, Akphivath Vitou, Norng Many, Hem Mike, and Sakhoeun Sakada have provided help with the interpretation and verification of data in the office and in the field. We thank the valuable comments of the reviewers as well as the Dumbarton Oaks Garden and Landscape Studies team for this opportunity.

Notes

1 Khmer Archaeology LiDAR Consortium and Cambodian Archaeological LiDAR Initiative 2013; Damian H. Evans, Roland J. Fletcher, Christophe Pottier, Jean-Baptiste Chevance, Dominique Soutif, Boun Suy Tan, Sokrithy Im, Darith Ea, Tina Tin, Samnang Kim, Christopher Cromarty, Stéphane De Greef, Kasper Hanus, Pierre Bâty, Robert Kuszinger, Ichita Shimoda, and Glenn Boornazian, "Uncovering Archaeological Landscapes at Angkor Using LiDAR," *Proceedings of the National Academy of Sciences of the United States of America* 110, no. 31 (July 2013):12595–600, https:// doi.org/10.1073/pnas.1306539110; and Damian Evans, "Airborne Laser Scanning as a Method for Exploring Long-Term Socio-Ecological Dynamics in Cambodia," *Journal of Archaeological Science* 74 (October 2016):164–75, http://dx.doi.org/10.1016/j.jas.2016.05.009.

2 Damian Evans, "Putting Angkor on the Map: A New Survey of a Khmer 'Hydraulic City' in Historical and Theoretical Context" (PhD diss., University of Sydney, 2007).

3 George Coedès and Pierre Dupont, "Les stèles de Sdŏk Kăk Thoṃ, Phnoṃ Sandak et Práḥ Vihār," *Bulletin de l'École française d'Extrême-Orient* 43 (1943):56–154; and Pierre Dupont, "Étude sur l'Indochine ancienne: 2. Les débuts de la royauté angkorienne," *Bulletin de l'École française d'Extrême-Orient* 46, no. 1 (1952):118–76.

4 Claude Jacques, "Études d'épigraphie cambodgienne: 7. Sur l'emplacement du royaume d'Aninditapura, 8. La carrière de Jayavarman II," *Bulletin de l'École française d'Extrême-Orient* 59 (1972):193– 205, 205–20.

5 Jean-Baptiste Chevance, "Inscriptions du Phnom Kulen: Corpus existant et inscriptions inédites, une mise en contexte," *Bulletin de l'École française d'Extrême-Orient* 100 (2014):201–30.

6 Étienne Edmond Lunet de Lajonquière, *Inventaire descriptif des monuments du Cambodge*, vol. 1, Publication de l'EFEO 4 (Paris: Ernest Leroux, 1902); Étienne Edmond Lunet de Lajonquière, *Inventaire descriptif des monuments du Cambodge*, vol. 2, Publication de l'EFEO 8 (Paris: Ernest Leroux, 1907); Étienne Edmond Lunet de Lajonquière, *Inventaire descriptif des monuments du Cambodge*, vol. 3, Publication de l'EFEO 9 (Paris: Ernest Leroux, 1911); Étienne Edmond Lunet de Lajonquière, *Inventaire descriptif des monuments du Cambodge, 1: Carte archéologique de l'ancien Cambodge, 2: Carte du groupe d'Angkor par Buat et Ducret*, Publication de l'EFEO 9 (Paris: Ernest Leroux, 1911); Louis Delaporte, *Les monuments du Cambodge. Études d'architecture khmère publiées d'après les documents recueillis au cours des missions qu'il a dirigé au Cambodge en 1873 et en 1882–83 et de la mission complémentaire de M. Farault en 1874–75*, 3 vols. (Paris: Ernest Leroux, 1914–24); Étienne Aymonier, *Le Cambodge. Tome I: Le royaume actuel* (Paris: Ernest Leroux, 1900); Étienne Aymonier, *Le Cambodge. Tome II: Les provinces siamoises* (Paris: Ernest Leroux, 1901); and Étienne Aymonier, *Le Cambodge. Tome III: Le groupe d'Angkor et l'Histoire* (Paris: Ernest Leroux, 1904).

7 For Victor Goloubew's aerial surveys in the 1930s, see Victor Goloubew, "Reconnaissances aériennes au Cambodge," *Bulletin de l'École française d'Extrême-Orient* 36 (1936):465–77; Victor Goloubew, "Chronique. Rapport de mission au Cambodge," *Bulletin de l'École française d'Extrême-Orient* 36, no. 2 (1936):630–34; and Victor Goloubew, "La collaboration de l'Aéronautique et de la Marine indochinoises aux travaux de l'École française d'Extrême-Orient," *Cahiers de la société de géographie de Hanoï* 31 (1936):5–39. For Bernard-Philippe Groslier's stratigraphical excavations and studies in the 1950s and 1960s, see Jacques Dumarçay and Paul Courbin, *Documents graphiques de la Conservation d'Angkor 1963–1973—La fouille du Sras-Srang*, Mémoire archéologique de l'EFEO 18 (Paris: École française d'Extrême-Orient, 1988); and Bernard-Philippe Groslier, "La Cité hydraulique angkorienne: Exploitation ou surexploitation du sol?," *Bulletin de l'École française d'Extrême-Orient* 66 (1979):161–202.

8 Pierre Dupont, "Chronique. Rapport de mission au Cambodge," *Bulletin de l'École française d'Extrême-Orient* 36, no. 2 (1936):630–34; Pierre Dupont, "Chronique. Cambodge, Mission au Cambodge, recherches archéologiques sur le Phnom Kulen à Angkor et à Battambang," *Bulletin de l'École française d'Extrême-Orient* 37, no. 2 (1937):666–73; Pierre Dupont, "Les monuments du Phnom Kulen: I, Le Prasat Nak Ta," *Bulletin de l'École française d'Extrême-Orient* 38, no. 1 (1938):199– 207; Pierre Dupont, "Chronique. Mission au Cambodge, recherches archéologiques sur le Phnom Kulen: II, Le prasat Nak Ta, Krus Prah Aràm Rôn Cen, Prasat Damrei Krap," *Bulletin de l'École française d'Extrême-Orient* 38, no. 2 (1938):426–35; Philippe Stern, "Chronique. Mission Stern-de Coral," *Bulletin de l'École française d'Extrême-Orient* 36, no. 2 (1936):629–30; Philippe Stern, "Le

style du Kulên (décor architectural et statuaire)," *Bulletin de l'École française d'Extrême-Orient* 38, no. 1 (1938):111–49; Philippe Stern, "Hariharâlaya et Indrapura," *Bulletin de l'École française d'Extrême-Orient* 38, no. 1 (1938):175–97; and Philippe Stern, "Travaux exécutés au Phnom Kulên (15 avil–20 mai 1936)," *Bulletin de l'École française d'Extrême-Orient* 38, no. 1 (1938):151–73.

9 Jean Boulbet and Bruno Dagens, "Les sites archéologiques de la région du Bhnam Gulen (Phnom Kulen)," special issue, *Arts Asiatiques* 27 (1973):68, photographs and maps.

10 Evans, "Putting Angkor on the Map"; Damian Evans, Christophe Pottier, Roland Fletcher, Scott Hensley, Ian Tapley, Anthony Milne, and Michael Barbetti, "A Comprehensive Archaeological Map of the World's Largest Preindustrial Settlement Complex at Angkor, Cambodia," *Proceedings of the National Academy of Sciences of the United States of America* 104, no. 36 (2007):14277–82; Evans et al., "Uncovering Archaeological Landscapes at Angkor Using LiDAR"; and Christophe Pottier, "Carte Archéologique de la Région d'Angkor. Zone Sud" (PhD diss., Université Paris III—Sorbonne Nouvelle, 1999).

11 Aymonier, *Le Cambodge. Tome I*, 428; Aymonier, *Le Cambodge. Tome III*, 470–71; George Coedès, "Les inscriptions de Bat Cum (Cambodge)," *Journal Asiatique*, 2nd ser., 10, no. 12 (1908):213; Louis Finot, "Sur quelques traditions indochinoises," *Bulletin de la Commission Archéologique de l'Indochine* (1911):23–25; Henri Parmentier, *L'Art khmèr primitive*, 2 vols., Publication de l'EFEO 21–22 (Paris: École française d'Extrême-Orient, 1927), 341–42; Philippe Stern, *Le Bayon d'Angkor et l'évolution de l'art Khmer, étude et discussion de la chronologie des monuments khmers*, Annales du musée Guimet (Paris: Paul Geuthner, 1927), 162–66; George Coedès, "Études Cambodgiennes: 19. La date du Bàyon, 20. Les capitales de Jayavarman II," *Bulletin de l'École française d'Extrême-Orient* 28, nos. 1–2 (1928):81–112, 113–23; George Coedès, "Études Cambodgiennes: 21. La tradition généalogique des premiers rois d'Angkor d'après les inscriptions de Yasovarman et de Rajendravarman," *Bulletin de l'École française d'Extrême-Orient* 28 (1928):122; and Henri Parmentier, "Complément à l'Art Khmer primitif," *Bulletin de l'École française d'Extrême-Orient* 35, nos. 1–2 (1935):1–116.

12 Stern, "Chronique"; Stern, "Le style du Kulên," 115; Stern, "Hariharâlaya et Indrapura"; Stern, "Travaux executés"; Dupont, "Chronique. Rapport de mission au Cambodge," 629–31; Dupont, "Chronique. Cambodge, Mission au Cambodge, recherches archéologiques sur le Phnom Kulen," 665–73; Dupont, "Les monuments du Phnom Kulen," 199–207; Dupont, "Chronique. Mission au Cambodge, recherches archéologiques sur le Phnom Kulen," 426–35; Goloubew, "Reconnaissances aériennes au Cambodge"; Goloubew, "Chronique"; Goloubew, "La collaboration de l'Aéronautique et de la Marine"; and George Coedès, "Le fondateur de la royauté angkorienne et les récentes découvertes archéologique au Phnom Kulen," *Cahiers de l'École française d'Extrême-Orient* 14 (1938):40–48.

13 Jean-Baptiste Chevance, "Le Phnom Kulen à la source d'Angkor, nouvelles données archéologiques" (PhD diss., Université Paris III—Sorbonne Nouvelle, 2011), 1:369.

14 Jean-Baptiste Chevance, "Banteay, Palais Royal de Mahendraparvata," *Aséanie* 33 (June 2014):279–330.

15 Jean-Baptiste Chevance, "Pœng Tbal et Pœng Eisei, ermitages angkoriens méconnus du Phnom Kulen," *Aséanie* 32 (December 2013):11–76.

16 Chevance, "Banteay."

17 Chevance, "Inscriptions du Phnom Kulen."

18 Evans, "Airborne Laser Scanning as a Method for Exploring Long-Term Socio Ecological Dynamics in Cambodia."

19 Erik Hansen, "Cambodge, Aménagement du Phnom Kulen" (Paris: UNESCO, September 1969).

20 W. J. Van Liere, "Traditional Water Management in the Lower Mekong Basin," *World Archaeology* 11, no. 3 (1980):265–80.

21 Dan Penny, Jean-Baptiste Chevance, David Tang, and Stéphane De Greef, "The Environmental Impact of Cambodia's Ancient City of Mahendraparvata (Phnom Kulen)," *PLoS ONE* 9, no. 1 (2014):e84252, doi:10.1371/journal.pone.0084252.

22 Penny et al., "Environmental Impact of Cambodia's Ancient City of Mahendraparvata."

23 Yukitsugu Tabata and Chhay Visoth, "Preliminary Report of the Excavation of the Anlong Thom Kiln Site, Cambodia," *Journal of Southeast Asian Archaeology* 27 (2007):63–69; and Yukitsugu Tabata, "Some Aspects of the Anglong Thom Kiln Site," *Journal of Southeast Asian Archaeology* 28 (2008):61–74.

24 Penny et al., "Environmental Impact of Cambodia's Ancient City of Mahendraparvata."

8

The Weave of Natural and Cultural Ecology

Ekamrakshetra—
the Historic Temple Town of Bhubaneswar, India

PRIYALEEN SINGH

THE TRAJECTORY OF URBAN PLANNING AND RELATED LANDSCAPE design in India is a reflection of the changing relationship between human beings and nature over time, demonstrating an intricate weave of natural and cultural ecology and producing a distinctive landscape. Many of these urban landscapes, though fragmented, still survive. This essay, by addressing the changing perceptions of and engagement with nature over time, as reflected in shifting urban landscapes, focuses on the seventh-century temple town of Bhubaneswar and its evolution over centuries. It seeks to highlight the multiple attributes and interpretations of elements of nature—beyond their purely utilitarian functions in the urban environment, developing Bhubaneswar as a significant cultural landscape. The narrative emphasizes that while landscapes shape cultures, cultures also shape landscapes, and in imparting new meanings to natural elements, result in distinct cultural ecologies. This, in the case of Bhubaneswar, produced a sacred landscape where the hydrology and geomorphology of the region seamlessly connected with temples, tanks, associated rituals, and festivals, which, in turn, sanctified the natural landscape within which they were set (Figure 8.1). The essay concludes by contrasting the preindustrial landscape of Old Bhubaneswar with New Bhubaneswar, planned in the twentieth century, to offer perspectives on the many ways in which the past might intelligently inform the present, and thus help to better position both human beings and urban developments in relation to nature and natural resources.

FIGURE 8.1

Brahmeswara temple
complex, with tank.
Photograph by
Priyaleen Singh.

Changing Patterns of Engaging with Nature
in the Urban Indian Context: An Overview

In tracing the nature-culture connection in the Indian subcontinent, the Vedas, composed in the first millennium BCE as an attempt to understand the phenomenon of
nature, have been interpreted by many scholars as books of ecology rather than of
ritual.[1] This understanding evolved into the classification of the five natural elements,
or *panchbhutās*, as *prithvi* (earth), *āp* (water), *tejās* (fire), *vāyu* (air), and *ākāsha* (sky),
as an explanation of the existence of life. Texts such as Arthashastra and Amarakosha,
written as early as 300 CE, furthered this comprehension and provided more tangible
expressions by scientifically classifying landscapes as *urvāra* (fertile), *usāra* (barren),
nadimātrka (land watered by river), and *devamātrka* (land watered by rain).[2] This was
then manifested in medieval texts such as Mansārā and Māyāmātā, which theorize
urban planning by tabulating settlements, and forts in particular, into *giridurga* (mountain fort), *jaladurga* (water fort), and *pankhādurga* (marshy fort).[3]

This knowledge and respect for nature and natural resources expresses itself in both
physical and metaphysical forms in all scales of urban planning and design. The city of
Varanasi in the northern plains of India epitomizes this. With its tangible and intangible connection with land and water, as a city it reaches out to embrace, both literally

and metaphorically, the river Ganges, a river that embodies both celestial and earthly vitality. As a personification of health and abundance, the Ganges guides a religious geography through the various territorial definitions of the *panchkoshi* or pilgrimage routes, which include ponds, tanks, and other geographic features. A similar concept of sacred space woven around the Vaishnava culture was to evolve much later in the sixteenth century in the cultural landscape of the Braj region, where a number of woods, groves, and ponds formed important landmarks in the pilgrimage circuit.[4] This interaction with water and vegetation is also very visible in the seventeenth-century cities of Delhi and Agra, where the Mughals created an urban landscape of leisure comprising riverfront garden districts. At a more intimate scale, the courtyard typology of housing was adopted as an architectural form in all regions and in all periods in Indian history, often with a tree and tank in the central open space, which helped modulate the climate and also ensured a daily interaction with these natural elements.

This urban landscape underwent a transformation in the colonial period in the nineteenth century due to very different responses to and understandings of nature and its elements. Nature was demystified and, with parallel narratives of colonization, industrialization, and capitalism, which by their inherent logics implied exploitation of natural resources, new norms for physical spatial planning were introduced, some of them based on several theories related to health and hygiene that were developing in eighteenth-century industrializing England.[5] Changed recreational patterns and new forms of colonial leisure informed by a new aesthetic, namely the picturesque or landscape as scenery, also resulted in a wholly new Indian urban landscape with racecourses, cricket clubs, gymkhanas, and public parks.[6]

Urban planning in postcolonial, independent India, through the "master plan" approach, changed the landscape further. Cities were planned with "zoning" as the principal concept to create settlements with distinctly demarcated areas for work, residence, and recreation. This was in complete contrast to the traditional planning principles, wherein mixed land use and related open space systems had ensured that water and vegetation were woven into people's daily experiences. In undermining traditional urbanism, historic settlements, which originally reflected a symbiotic relationship between the natural and human-made environment, were reduced to slums, defying the basic standards of hygiene and health.[7]

Today, design with nature has come a long way from being a "subject" replete with social meanings and intents to a superficial "object," at times ready for sale and conspicuous consumption. Elements of nature are not just being sold, but are also used as devices for marketing or as packaging materials for the promotion of various habitats.[8]

The Preindustrial Cultural Landscape of Ekamrakshetra

Bhubaneswar, the capital of the state of Odisha, is unique as a case study, as it offers an opportunity to study this trajectory of changing attitudes to design with natural elements: its old town dates to the seventh century CE, still survives in large parts as a preindustrial landscape, and coexists with the new city of Bhubaneswar planned in the mid-twentieth century. Ancient texts such as Ekamra Purana, Ekamra Chandrika, and Svanadri Mahodaya describe in detail the components of the historic settlement,[9] offering descriptions of important temples and tanks, as well as the legends and festivals associated with them. This narrative, when superimposed on the morphology of the surviving urban fabric, provides insights into the life and spatial planning of the town in preindustrial times.

Bhubaneswar derives its name from the city's chief deity, the Lingaraj: the Lord of the Three Worlds, or Tribhuvaneshvara. Excavations at Sisupalgarh, five kilometers to the southeast, take the origin of the old city to the fourth century BCE and also lend credence to the belief that the city of Tosali, the regional administrative capital of Emperor Ashoka, might have been situated in the neighborhood of Dhauligiri, 8 km south of Bhubaneswar. Political events in the region after the Mauryan period (ca. 180 BCE) become diffuse. The interval between the fall of the imperial Kushan and the rise of the Gupta dynasty in the fourth century CE is a well-documented period in history, as north India took a distinct turn toward Brahmanic Hinduism under Gupta rule. With the revival of Brahmanism in the fifth century CE, Bhubaneswar gradually developed into a temple city under the active patronage of the royal dynasties of the period. It was in the seventh century CE that Kalinga, the ancient name of Odisha, entered a period of hectic building activity. However, there is evidence to indicate that in the intervening centuries, Bhubaneswar remained an important cultural and religious center for Buddhists, Jains, and Hindus. The people connected with the worship, ritual, and management of the temples started to live here, laying the foundation for the town of Ekamrakshetra. Mentioned in ancient Sanskrit literature as Ekamrakshetra or "mango forest," named after the mango groves in the area, Old Bhubaneswar developed around the Lingaraj temple that stood under a mango tree.[10] The golden era in the cultural history of this area begins at the end of the sixth century CE, when the region remained under the administrative control of the Sailodbhavas (575–700 CE), Bhaumakaras (736–940 CE), Somavamsis (885–1100 CE), Gangas (1100–1435 CE), Suryavamsis (1435–1540 CE), and the Chalukya dynasty (1559–1568 CE). In all instances, the royal patronage of religion resulted not so much in mass conversion of the people, but in a royal obsession with building temples to new gods. The Ganga kings' patronage of Vaishnavism notwithstanding, their rule ushered in a period of great syncretism during which Saivism and Vaishnavism, the two great traditions of Hinduism, coexisted. As a result of this prolific building activity, the temples of Bhubaneswar today help interpret the history of the region. These temples present the best of the north, the Nagara style of architecture, and the south, the Dravidian style, attesting to the craftsmanship of local artisans in blending the two manners to produce a distinctive art of Odisha. Literary and epigraphic evidence also proves beyond a doubt the importance of Ekamrakshetra as a center of pilgrimage from at least the eighth and ninth centuries CE. Pilgrims visited Ekamrakshetra, and continue to do so today, on their way to Srikshetra or Jagannatha at Puri, which is one of the *chaturdhāmas*, or most sacred place in India.[11]

Topographically, Bhubaneswar lies on the western fringe of the coastal plain of Odisha. On the northeast, east, and southeast edges of the town flow the Kuakhai,

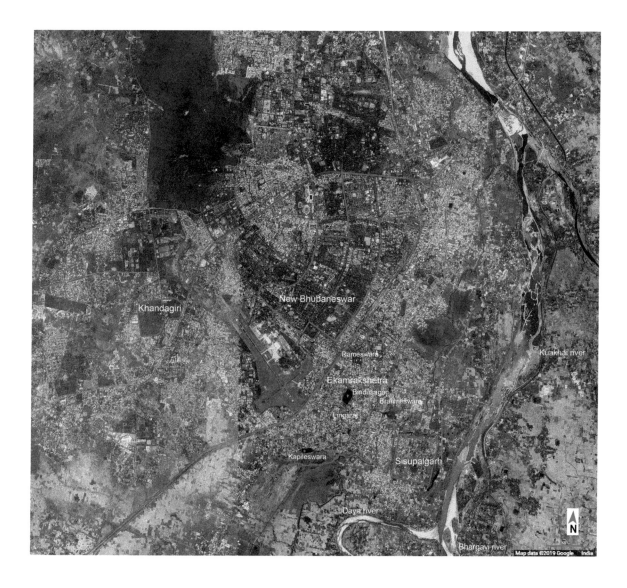

Bhargavi, and the Daya, minor tributaries of the river Mahanadi. To the north, west, and south are numerous hillocks and forests. In the low-lying areas, Sisupalgarh fort was built on the riverbank (Figure 8.2). Although this place was well suited for a fort, it was most probably abandoned due to frequent devastation caused by floods, which led to the settlement moving to the uplands. Bhubaneswar sits on the edge of the lateritic plateau and erosion over centuries shaped the landscape into gentle valleys. Geologically, the Bhubaneswar region belongs to the Gondwana supercontinent, one of the oldest and most stable landmasses in the world. Abounding in building stones such as laterite and sandstone, the geology helped to give the architecture of Bhubaneswar its distinctive character. The ancient master builders selected sandstone, more difficult to quarry but easier to shape and sculpt, for the magnificent temples that formed the settlement's core; they used laterite, softer but coarser, for the vernacular architecture and the outer walls and temple enclosures as well as the tanks attached to them (Figure 8.3).

FIGURE 8.2

Ekamrakshetra and the surrounding landscape. © Google.

Located at the junction of laterite, in the foothills of the Eastern Ghats, and coastal alluvial deposits, the lack of a perennial surface-water source might have posed the most serious problem in the past, possibly preventing the growth of the settlement on the plateau. However, subterranean springs on the fringe of the lateritic plateau, such as at Khandagiri and Kedargouri, provided the prime source of water for habitation, playing a major role in shaping the settlement. This is amply illustrated by the clustering of temples with their tanks in close proximity to these water sources (Figure 8.4). Most of the

LEGEND

1. Bindusagar
2. Lingaraj Temple
3. Aisaneswara Temple
4. Langaleswara Temple
5. Papanasini Temple
6. Chitrakarini Temple
7. Bhavani Sankara Temple
8. Mohini Temple
9. Markandeswara Siva Temple
10. Yameswara Temple

11. Bakresvara Temple
12. Nilakantheswara Temple
13. Vaitala Temple
14. Balunkeswara Temple
15. Gosagareswara Temple
16. Asthashambu Siva Temple
17. Taleswara Temple
18. Pataleswara Temple
19. Nageswara Temple

20. Parasuramesvara Temple
21. Muktesvara Temple
22. Raja Rani Temple
23. Kedar Gouri Temple
24. Daiteswara Temple
25. Duara Basini Temple
26. Ananta Vasudev Temple
27. Shukuteswara Temple
28. Dakara Bivisaneswara Temple

☐ TEMPLE COMPLEX

▢ TEMPLE TANKS

▲
N

⊢___ 100 m ___⊣

subterranean springs are found in this belt and most of the temples are huddled around these sources of water. Since the geographical extent of these springs is very limited, as they arise out of a common geological fault structure, it can be conjectured that the planners of the town were well informed of this fact and that they applied their traditional wisdom in siting the settlement very strategically around this zone.

Ekamrakshetra as a sacred site made tangible and intangible connections with water. The settlement revolved around the Lingaraj temple and the adjoining Bindusagar, a tank known to have been excavated in 1000 CE by King Varaha Keshari, but which according to legend was formed by collecting a drop from all the sacred waters on earth

FIGURE 8.4

Historic core of Ekamrakshetra, the temple town of Bhubaneswar. © Google.

FIGURE 8.5
Bindusagar tank.
Photograph by
Priyaleen Singh.

and in heaven (Figure 8.5). Extending over an area measuring 396 × 213 m, it is the largest tank in Bhubaneswar. Its depth varies, with an average of 3 m. In its northeast corner is a channel under a stone covering, designed to feed in water from adjoining areas, and it is additionally fed by many natural springs at its bottom. In the center is an island of 33.5 m², protected by stone revetments, with a small temple in its northeast corner.[12] In the Hindu conception of creation, the symbolisms in water are many.[13] Water precedes creation and reabsorbs it, and is thus associated with both dissolution and evolution, implying both death and rebirth.[14] Physical purification that leads to spiritual rejuvenation is another recurrent water metaphor. In the Vedas, water is the great cleanser, second only to *Agni*, or Fire, the Great Purifier, as explicitly stated in the Rig Veda hymn, "Waters have healing powers, they drive disease away; they have a balm for all, let them make medicines."[15] These expressions explain the presence of innumerable temples built close to sources of water, as well as the concept of sacred landscapes in the Indian subcontinent, best illustrated in the cluster of holy places in the upper reaches of the Ganges and Yamuna, two highly revered rivers. The association of pilgrimage centers with water can also be seen in the number of sacred spots that lie on riverbanks, at confluence of rivers, or on the seacoast. Explaining the concept of pilgrimage in her seminal work on the Hindu temple, Stella Kramrisch defined *tirthā* as a sacred place of pilgrimage on the bank of a river, sea, tank, or lake. The meaning of the word is a ford, or a passage, where the current of the river of life may be forded, leading to inner realization as the pilgrim crosses over to the other shore.[16] When the believer reaches her pilgrimage point, whether it is the Ganges or other tanks or rivers, higher or lower in attributed levels of purity, she conducts an elaborate series of rituals. As a result, all temples have water bodies in the form of ponds and tanks built within for ritual purposes.[17] Water is also considered one of the mediums through which a transfer of power can be effected. Water, which has been poured over an idol, when drunk by worshippers, conveys to them the power of the deity.[18] Apart from ritual bathing in sacred waters, personifications of the life-giving powers of water abound in Hindu mythology and religious iconography.[19] Its maternal, procreative aspect is often symbolized by the Ganges and Yamuna Rivers as female divinities adorning the temple doorways and guarding the sanctuary within.

The importance of water can also be gauged from many ancient texts, such as the Puranas, which explain the construction of water tanks, pools, and wells. Lawbooks of the period also prescribe stringent punishments for those who cause any damage to water reservoirs built for the welfare of the community.[20]

In consonance with these beliefs, in the context of Ekamrakshetra, the Brahma Purana, a text dating to the seventh century CE, states: "He who undertakes the pilgrimage to this *tirthā* and performs due ceremonies, liberates his twenty-one generations and goes to the heaven of Shiva. One may bathe in the Bindusagar any day and if he has the *darshan* [vision], he goes to Shiva's heaven. The Ekamra is the Shivkshetra, as sacred as Kashi and one who takes a bath here will certainly attain liberation."[21] A pilgrimage to Bhubaneswar thus began with a bath in Bindusagar, followed by a visit to the Lingaraj temple. In medieval times, over seven thousand small shrines with sacred groves surrounded the tank (Figure 8.6). Ponds and tanks were an integral part of the temple complexes elsewhere in the settlement too, many with perennial sources of water and used by local residents and pilgrims alike. Gouri tank, adjacent to the Kedar Gouri temple, is another celebrated tank about one kilometer east of Bindusagar. To the west of this complex there is another perennial spring called Dudhakunda, meaning milk tank, and its waters are believed to have medicinal properties. To the east of Kedareswara temple there is another tank called Kedarkunda, which is also spring fed. Mukteswara tank is another tank located behind the temple of Mukteswara, just north of Kedar Gouri temple (Figure 8.7).[22] In the presence and use of all tanks, the sacred and the secular came together, with the local people using these tanks extensively for their daily needs. Along with tanks, wells were another source of water and punctuated all the public open spaces, streets, and courtyards.

The sacred geography of Bhubaneswar was determined primarily by these temples and tanks. The Ekamra Purana describes in its four parts and fifty-one chapters all the *tirthās*, temples, and legends, as well as the importance of each shrine found at Ekamrakshetra. These temples fall into eight groups or *ashtaāyatanās*, eight sacred areas existing as clusters of holy ponds and shrines. The *pradakshinā* or circumambulation route through the associated rituals and festival paths knitted them together, lending meaning and legibility to the spatial form. Since Ekamra Purana describes the *ashtaāyatanās*, it is correct to assume that these eight clusters of temples and ponds were already considered sacred places before the text's date. While the Ekamra Purana

FIGURE 8.6

Temple complex
on the banks of
the Bindusagar.
Photograph by
Priyaleen Singh.

describes the important places of the *ashtaāyatanās* separately, the Svarnadri Mahodaya
and Ekamra Chandrika describe the monuments of each *āyatanā* as groups of monuments. These texts also discuss auspicious days in the year, suitable for worshipping
the deities in each *āyatanā*.[23] To date, the ritualistic connections between the Lingaraj
and other temples exist, with many of the monuments described in the *ashtaāyatanās*
surviving.[24] Lingaraj, as the chief deity residing in the Lingaraj temple, was a key figure
in the lives of the community, with the people engaging in temple activities on a daily
basis. The role of the temples in society and its economy is the most important aspect of
the cultural ecology of Old Bhubaneswar. In medieval times, the temples catered to the
socioreligious needs of a large section of people and also functioned as a link among the
king, the founder of the temple, and the rest of the population through various festivals
and functions organized in honor of the deities. The construction of the temples was
also considered to be a very significant and pious social service. At the same time, temples represented the wealth and social power of the founder and were also a medium of
spreading and consolidating royal influence. Temples were also maintained by various
endowments from individuals who at times donated plots of land.[25] The accumulation
of these donated lands made the temples the largest landowner in Bhubaneswar. A large

FIGURE 8.7
Mukteswara temple
complex. Photograph
by Priyaleen Singh.

number of agricultural laborers were employed to cultivate these lands, the produce of
which fed the temple kitchen and yielded income to sustain other occupations related
to the temple management. These jobs included musicians, drummers, and singers
associated with rituals; gardeners supplying flowers grown in the monastery gardens as
offerings; potters providing earthen pots to the temple kitchen for the *prasādam* (ben-
ediction) offered in the form of food given to devotees (Figure 8.8); and basket weavers
weaving baskets from palm leaves for the same purpose (Figure 8.9). Temple festivals

FIGURE 8.8

Earthen pots for
the *prasādam*
stacked in a
courtyard adjoining
the Lingaraj
temple complex.
Photograph by
Priyaleen Singh.

guided the community life too. The beginning of the cultivation and harvest started with offerings to the ruling deity of the temple. In fact, the temples of Odisha were the epitome of social and cultural life as one can also trace the origin of its dance, drama, literature, and music to the various religious festivities and temples.

The structure of the open space systems of the preindustrial settlement can be deciphered through a study of the town as it survives today, with many of its historic elements (such as temples and tanks) intact. As important markers in the landscape, they impart an understanding of the town's medieval texture and help to explain concepts of preindustrial living. The open space systems of Bhubaneswar appear to be primarily informed by and structured around its temples and associated tanks, which are also intertwined with the sacred groves and gardens attached to monasteries.[26] In accordance with the traditional concept of *panchavati*,[27] where five of the most useful trees of the region were planted in private and public spaces, most monastic gardens have papaya, mango, coconut, *bel* (*Aegle marmelos*), and guava trees, which sustain both the monasteries and the local population. Bhubaneswar has no large central recreational green, but the area around the Lingaraj temple and the Bindusagar tank continues today as the town's focal point, with a range of activities found in any public open space in India. It also accommodates functions closely associated with temple rituals such as the

FIGURE 8.9
Palm-leaf baskets
marketed for the
prasādam. Photograph
by Priyaleen Singh.

sale of flowers, earthen lamps, incense sticks, green and dry coconuts, and banana-leaf offerings (Figure 8.10).

Courtyards and terraces are private open spaces attached to dwellings and are residential, recreational, and work spaces. The street as an open space is also important as a semipublic realm. With mutually shading walls ensuring a climate-friendly design, the *otlas* or platforms along the streets are interactive community open spaces (Figure 8.11). The street is also an important work space (Figure 8.12). Bhubaneswar has

FIGURE 8.10

Offerings being
sold in the square in
front of the Lingaraj
temple complex.
Photograph by
Priyaleen Singh.

FIGURE 8.11

Otlas or platforms
along streets, as an
interface of private
and public realms.
Photograph by
Priyaleen Singh.

FIGURE 8.12

The street as a
workplace: basket
weavers at work.
Photograph by
Priyaleen Singh.

no landscaped space large enough to be called a town-level park. The green image of the town is accentuated, however, by the presence of a central green agricultural belt, running through its heart, which was traditionally part of the temple land, cultivating rice for the temple kitchen. In catching the surface runoff from surrounding areas, it originally helped to recharge the tanks and water bodies.[28] Even after heavy monsoon showers today, the land becomes dry within a very short period of time due to the high rate of percolation because of the lateritic bed. This water seeps through to tanks and water bodies, recharging them and helping to augment the natural water supply of the region. Visually, the Lingaraj temple—with its spire, it was the tallest structure in the landscape—was and continues to be a major organizing element for both small and large open spaces (Figure 8.13). As a landmark visible from most open spaces and major roads, it helps to orient the resident and pilgrim alike.

As with water, the tree in the Indian landscape resonates with many meanings and symbolisms. In Indian thought, the tree figures as the total cosmos, with its branches likened to the heavens, the lower branches or the surface of the ground where it grows akin to the plane of the earth, and the roots plunging into the subterranean levels as hells.[29] The branches and roots are thought of as the superior and inferior states of

FIGURE 8.13

View of the Lingaraj
temple spire from
the surrounding
settlement.
Photograph by
Priyaleen Singh.

existence. In another interpretation, the trunk is considered the world axis that centers
and supports multiple worlds, and is the source of all riches and felicities.[30] As a result,
the planting of trees acquired the status of a religious rite conferring merit on the person planting them, with religious texts further sanctifying this act. Quoting from the
Puranas, "A person who plants a tree, that gives flowers, fruit and shade, helps the
release of his ancestors from any sin that they may have committed."[31] Tree cults were
widespread in India, where each settlement had its sacred tree or grove (Figure 8.14).

FIGURE 8.14

The worship of the
sacred fig tree *Ficus
religiosa*. Photograph
by Priyaleen Singh.

Especially sacred were the peepal (*Ficus religiosa*) and banyan (*Ficus benghalensis*).
Peepal was also regarded as the dwelling place of the Hindu trinity: Brahma the
Creator, Vishnu the Protector, and Mahesh the Destroyer; thus, it was strictly prohibited to use its wood as fuel. These species are venerated to this day and no temple
exists without such trees within its complex. Trees were religiously planted, protected,
and cared for by the inhabitants of Ekamrakshetra. Species like banyan and peepal not
only provided shade in a hot climate, but as modulators of public space helped to define

FIGURE 8.15

Trees as modulators
of public open
space, outside
the Kedar Gouri
temple complex.
Photograph by
Priyaleen Singh.

gathering places, the overall dimensions of which relate to the spread of the tree. Many still survive, guiding the open spaces in their spatial form (Figure 8.15). The sacred garden or grove was also an extension of these ideas. Planting of trees as groves is represented in the sacred books of Hinduism as an act of merit from which follows wealth, power, and longevity.[32] In the Varaha Purana, the planter of a group of trees is promised heavenly bliss: "He never goes to hell who plants an Asvattha, or a Pichumarda, or a Banyan, or ten Jasmines, or two pomegranates, a Panchamra or five mangoes."[33] The planting of *panchavati* or five sacred trees in a garden was encouraged to earn salvation. The Skanda Purana recommends a "*vilva* in the centre, and four others on four sides, four banyans in four corners, twenty five Asokas in a circle, with a myrobalan on one side, as the constituents of a great *panchavati*."[34] Traditional wisdom encouraged planting species such as *kuchila* (*Strychnos nux-vomica*), neem (*Azadirachta indica*), and *chiraiguri* (*Vitex peduncularis*) close to water tanks in Bhubaneswar since they all had medicinal properties, some of which are known to improve the water quality. *Chiraiguri* is a medicinal plant whose extract may be used to cure malaria; *kuchila*[35] is used as a remedy for dysentery, fever, and cholera, and purifies water over a radius of 1 km.[36] There were several other design gestures toward recognizing the value

FIGURE 8.16

Tulsi (*Ocimum sanctum*) on a pedestal at the threshold of a house. Photograph by Priyaleen Singh.

FIGURE 8.17

Traditional stone sculptor at work. Photograph by Priyaleen Singh.

The Weave of Natural and Cultural Ecology   211

FIGURE 8.18
A temple
accommodated
in a traffic island.
Photograph by
Priyaleen Singh.

of plants, such as the tulsi (*Ocimum sanctum*) pedestal on the courtyard's threshold (Figure 8.16). The use of these natural elements was not merely as functional entities but as symbols of well-being, life, and, by extension, happiness. Through the religious valorization of these design interventions, by attributing an element of divinity to the natural world, the endeavor invoked its blessings and protective power. As nature was not separate from culture, nonhuman entities were anthropomorphized and established as cultural icons.

≈

Bhubaneswar retains its identity as a temple town: through its temple-based economy, with a relatively intact urban form, and through traditional crafts like stone sculpting (Figure 8.17), albeit catering to a new clientele of tourists. But the landscape is slowly transforming. With unplanned urbanization and ecologically unsustainable development decisions, the quality of life is being undermined. The central green belt which sustained the temple economy is now an open drain for the sullage from encroaching residential buildings. New road networks are creating barriers to the natural flow of stormwater. Many of the temples are now buried under these roads, which have reduced

the temples to traffic islands (Figure 8.18). Tanks, which were once the lifeline of the population, are crumbling, polluted, and eutrophic (Figure 8.19), even as some people continue to use them, considering their waters sacred. There are proposals to fill many of these abandoned tanks and convert them into parking spaces for the burgeoning number of vehicles belonging to the local population, pilgrims, and tourists, an action which will further adversely impact the ecology.

Many of the temple complexes originally sitting within sacred groves have become archaeological sites and major tourist destinations, with the single vocabulary of lawns replacing the groves of trees (Figure 8.20). As fenced sites, some with ticketed entries, these temples and related spaces, which were intricately linked with the lives of the people, now sit as museum artifacts, completely alienated from the people inhabiting the settlement. As part of the beautification of these spaces, some of which now function as sites for cultural performances for tourists, ornamental species like *Mussaenda*, *Canna*, *Delonix regia*, and *Bombax malabarica* have replaced the palette of indigenous plant material.

But perhaps the biggest change in the landscape and one that continues to impact Bhubaneswar the most was the planning of the city of New Bhubaneswar adjoining it.

FIGURE 8.19
The neglected state of the Rameswara tank. Photograph by Priyaleen Singh.

FIGURE 8.20
"Landscaping" in
the Mukteswara
temple complex.
Photograph by
Priyaleen Singh.

Postindependence Urban Planning Paradigms
and the Landscape of New Bhubaneswar

With India gaining independence in 1947, Bhubaneswar was established as the capital
of the state of Odisha. At the time, there was intense debate on the nature of the relationship between the old town and the new capital city, including which planning principles and architectural styles to adopt.[37] It was finally agreed that the old town would
be preserved as a national historic and cultural site of major importance, its temples
and tanks restored and maintained, and strict controls put on further construction. The
recommendation that the old town be "preserved," however, provided a partial rationale for maintaining it as a separate entity from the capital. It was, therefore, not on the
agenda of the administrators or planners, who were focusing on the new city. In fact, it
ensured that New Bhubaneswar turned its back, literally, to the old town, with the newly
introduced railway line defining the edge between the two settlements. The planning
principles, which included patterns of design with natural resources like vegetation and
water, were derived entirely from Western planning concepts of the time, with land-use
control—which marked a distinct central administrative zone, residential zone, and
recreational zone—considered the chief means of controlling urban form and growth.
The result was a city very different in its spatial expression from the old town and from

most existing Indian cities, with neighborhood units planned in a hierarchical manner, defined by a gridiron road network (Figure 8.21).

FIGURE 8.21
Roads in New Bhubaneswar. Photograph by Priyaleen Singh.

The landscape of New and Old Bhubaneswar is a study of contrasts. Old Bhubaneswar or Ekamrakshetra had its physical form based on animate rather than inanimate forms of energy, resulting in a city of human scale, planned for pedestrian movement—unlike New Bhubaneswar, where vehicular transportation was the key to the planning and dispersal of various land uses. Because of its relatively high density and compact form, open spaces in Old Bhubaneswar encouraged multiple uses, blurring boundaries of work, recreation, and residence, in the process also ensuring greater economy in the use of time, energy, and land. In New Bhubaneswar, zoning meant a Central Business District surrounded by administrative offices, clearly defined residential quarters, and monofunctional recreational spaces in the form of large parks. In contrast, traditional open spaces in Old Bhubaneswar still exist in the form of tanks, *chowks* or squares, and groves, providing a range of opportunities for interaction with natural features (Figure 8.22). Terraces and courtyards are also a major component of this open space system. Through their multifunctionality, they are very adaptable in their spirit and content. The master plan of New Bhubaneswar, on the other hand, like master plans for all cities in India, recognizes only green spaces as open spaces, with the ubiquitous

nomenclature of tot lots, neighborhood parks, and city-level district parks. The often
criticized banality of modern town planning is frequently due to this absence of a multiplicity of meanings; the modern planner seeks order and coherence, generating a functionally segregated land-use plan. These plans are undifferentiated from place to place,
and much like flattening a hilly site, they flatten the social contours which give a particular place its identity.[38]

In Old Bhubaneswar, the relationship between culture and nature continues to
form the symbolic geography of the area. Temple tanks and groves, besides constituting the "genius of the place" and giving meaning to the landscape, also ensure that
nature is integrated with the everyday life and experience of the people. This experiential aesthetics is in contrast to the one experienced in New Bhubaneswar; while its
green areas are concentrated along wide roads, roundabouts, and medians, many are
fenced off to prevent access to them and exist only for visual appreciation (Figure 8.23),
an example of imagemaking clearly overshadowing more real ecological demands.
There is an emphasis on planting ornamental and exotic species such as gulmohur
(*Delonix regia*) and simal (*Bombax malabarica*) along the roads, which provide little
relief to the users. This is in sharp contrast to Old Bhubaneswar, where the "informal

sector" finds relief from the heat in the shade of trees planted in public open spaces, ensuring that they are well cared for, as opposed to green swaths edging the roads lying unused and unattended.

One of the more insidious results of this new pattern of planning has been the demise of the street as an open space. In the old town, the streets serve a variety of formal and informal community needs as an interface between the public and private realms. However, in the new town there exist no such streets: roads exist as collector

roads, distributor roads, arterial roads, or simply as primary, secondary, and tertiary roads, a nomenclature common to all master plans. These roads are also used for fewer activities, often for only parking and vehicular movement.

Another aspect of the master plan approach involves "standards" and "bylaws." Standards have often been misinterpreted as a measure of the quantity at the expense of the quality of open space. So even as the quantum of green space increases, it does not necessarily help improve the habitat due to limited access to these open spaces. In historic towns, there was a "moral code of conduct" in the use of open space—that is, in respecting thresholds of public and private domains, public space was not encroached upon, to the benefit of all. Today, bylaws invariably demand setbacks of all buildings from the boundaries of individual plots, resulting in strips of open space enveloping the built mass, which is a complete inversion of the courtyard typology of housing. The loss of the courtyard additionally implies the loss of a work space, one that also captured the sights and smells of nature. In recent years, with urbanization pressure on limited buildable land, a new typology in the form of multistory flats is replacing single-story dwellings in both the new and old town. These dwellings, however, are disliked because of minimal outdoor space, balconies being no real substitute for courtyards, and the complete absence of terraces, which in traditional housing was both an outdoor room and a work space also offering opportunities to connect with elements of nature. And in adopting names such as "Lake View Homes," in the absence of any lake or any view, these apartments clearly suggest a yearning for nature (Figure 8.24).

The Rationale for Conservation of Historic Urban Landscapes

In making a case for conservation of the preindustrial landscape of Old Bhubaneswar today, it needs to be underscored that the value of these urban landscapes lies not in their visual imagery, but rather in the way that they once performed. Old Bhubaneswar illustrates that the central feature of the precolonial or preindustrial settlement planning was its complementary relationship with nature and an experiential aesthetics, encapsulating the metaphysical and the physical, its resultant form displaying a synergy among the various elements of nature and culture. As Old Bhubaneswar, the city of one thousand temples, is preparing a nomination dossier as a World Heritage City in the UNESCO World Heritage List, it is important that this aspect be recognized in its statement of Outstanding Universal Value. A dossier which primarily focuses on the imagery of its temple architecture and does not include in its ambit the spatial and cultural aspects will only help to promote its visual image as a tourist destination, but without the soul and spirit of its culture.

To conclude, while settlements such as Old Bhubaneswar retain their original morphological patterns indicative of systems of preindustrial living, they also display the ability to reinvent themselves to allow for modern-day living. Living historic towns and cities, in fact, embody many of the concepts expressed in terms such as "sustainable," "eco-friendly," "mixed land use," "low-rise high-density," "pedestrianization," and "green design," all of which are now entering the vocabulary of an alternative discourse in architecture and planning of new settlements. A healthy and vibrant engagement with nature is integral to all these concepts. In the change from a feudal to a capitalist world order, there was an eco-philosophical shift from eco-theology to a technocratic view of nature, which also impacted how natural resources were viewed and incorporated in urban settlement design. Settlements like Bhubaneswar offer an opportunity to develop an alternative socialist ecology perspective which would encourage a different way of engaging with nature and celebrating it. In this framework and in a secular world, connecting with nature might be described as "worshipful"—compared to "religious" in preindustrial landscapes—a concept that encourages valuing nature for a better quality of life. Conceptually, it also implies that in framing conservation plans for historic settlements with distinct local cultures like Bhubaneswar, it is imperative to ensure that local natural ecosystems are conserved as well.

Notes

1 Marta Vannucci, *Ecological Readings in the Veda* (New Delhi: D. K. Printworld, 1994); Braj Bihari Chaubey, *Treatment of Nature in the Rigveda* (Hoshiarpur: Vedic Sahityasadan, 1970); and Kapila Vatsyayan, ed., *Prakriti: The Integral Vision*, 5 vols. (New Delhi: IGNCA, 1995).

2 Nirmal Kumar Bose, *Culture and Society in India* (Calcutta: Asia Publishing House, 1967).

3 Prabhakar V. Begde, *Ancient and Medieval Town Planning in India* (New Delhi: Sagar Publications, 1977).

4 Alan W. Entwistle, *Braj Centre of Krishna Pilgrimage* (Groningen: Egbert Forsten, 1987); and Behula Shah, "The Pilgrimage of the Groves: Restructuring the Meaning of a Sixteenth-Century Hindu Landscape," *Arnoldia* 64, no. 4 (2006):39–41.

5 Hill stations, such as Shimla and Ooty, used as summer retreats, were developed in response to nostalgia for an England left behind. However, settlements in the plains were characterized by low-density developments; large park areas; and broad, tree-lined roads, which gave access to a system of large compounds, each containing a bungalow. This morphology was echoed in the planning of the imperial capital in New Delhi. The basic territorial unit of the colonial culture was the bungalow sitting in an open space, in complete contrast to the indigenous built form of *havelis*, or houses with courtyards, an example of introverted planning.

6 Anthony King, *Colonial Urban Development* (London: Routledge and Kegan Paul, 1976).

7 Old Delhi illustrates this best: Shahjahanabad, a Mughal city planned by Emperor Shahjahan in the seventeenth century, was built for his nobility and court as the capital city of Hindustan. It was declared a slum in the first master plan for Delhi in 1960.

8 For example, builders offer a range of housing and residential apartments with names like Green Meadows, Forest Greens, and Charmwood Village that were built in the suburbs of cities like Delhi and Bengaluru, habitats which appear to have all the trappings of nature but with no respect for the cultural and ecological contexts within which they sit.

9 It is believed that Ekamra Purana is the earliest and was composed between 950 and 1150 CE, in Karuna Sagar Behera, *The Lingaraja Temple of Bhubaneswar, Art and Cultural Legacy* (New Delhi: Aryan Books International, 2008), 5.

10 Behera, *Lingaraja Temple of Bhubaneswar*, 1, 3.

11 Nirmal Kumar Bose, *Canons of Orissan Architecture* (Calcutta: R. Chatterjee, 1932); and Krishna Chandra Panigrahi, *Archaeological Remains at Bhubaneswar* (Delhi: Kitabmahal, 1961).

12 Behera, *Lingaraja Temple of Bhubaneswar*. Religious connotations of water are explained in the Padma Purana, Siva Purana, and Brahma Purana, texts composed in the fifth century CE.

13 See Jutta Jain-Neubauer, ed., *Water Design: Environment and Histories* (Mumbai: Marg Foundation, 2016).

14 Mircea Eliade, *Sacred and the Profane: The Nature of Religion* (New York: Harcourt, Brace, and World, 1957).

15 Rig Veda verse X137 in Vatsyayan, *Prakriti*, 6.

16 Stella Kramrisch, *The Hindu Temple*, 2 vols. (Calcutta: University of Calcutta, 1946).

17 Morna Livingston, *Steps to Water: The Ancient Stepwells of India* (New York: Princeton Architectural Press, 2002).

18 J. Abbott, *The Keys of Power: A Study of Indian Ritual and Belief* (London: Methuen, 1932), 168.

19 Veronica Ions, *Indian Mythology* (Feltham: Newnes Books, 1983).

20 Ram Sharan Sharma, *Light on Early Indian Society and Economy* (Bombay: Manaktalas, 1966).

21 Ravi Kalia, *Bhubaneswar: From a Temple Town to a Capital City* (Delhi: Oxford University Press, 1994), 4.

22 INTACH listing, 1990, unpublished report.

23 INTACH, *Ekamrakshetra Heritage Project* (unpublished report; Delhi, 1989), 17–18. The concept of *ashtaāyatanās* (eight zones) derives from the need to, after bathing, have the *darshan* (vision) and blessings of eight deities: Shiva, Parvati, Chanda, Kartikeya, Ganesha, Nandi, Kalpavriksha, and Savitri. According to the Ekamra Chandrika, the first *āyatanā* consists of the following monuments: Bindusarovara, Anantavasudeva, Devi Padhara, and Tirthesvara. The second *āyatanā* consists of Kapilakunda, Papanasinikund, Maitresvara, Varunesvara, Venukichaka, Isanesvara, Punarisana, and Yamesvara. The monuments of the third *āyatanā* are Ganga Yamuna Kunda, Gangesvara,

Yamunesvara, Devipada, Lakshmisvara, Kotitirthasarovara, Kotisvara, Svarnajalesvara, Sampur-najalesvara, Suresvara, Siddhesvara, Muktesvara, and Siddha Kunda. In the fourth *āyatanāare* Kedaresvara, Gaurikunda, Gouridevi, Kedarakunda, Shanta Siva, Daityes'vara, Disisvaridevi, and Indresvara (Rajarani). Monuments in the fifth *āyatanā* are Brahma Kunda, Brahmesvara, Gokarnesvara, and Utpalekesvara. In the sixth *āyatanā* are Meghatirtha, Megheswar, Bhaskaresvara, and Kapalamochanesvara. In the seventh *āyatanā* are Atavutirtha, Atavukesvara, Uttaresvara, and Bhimesvara. The eighth *āyatanā* includes Ramakunda, Ramesvara, Laksmanesvara, Bharatesvara, Satruganesvara, Gosahagresvara, Paradearesvara, and Gohrada.

24 INTACH, *Ekamrakshetra Heritage Project*, 19–20. Prathamastami is considered to be the first of fourteen festivals in the annual ritual cycle of Lord Lingaraj. On this day, the procession of the deity Lingaraj, along with other subordinate deities, is taken to Mitreswar temple, situated to the west of the temple compound near the Kapilanath. In the precinct of the Mitreswar temple, the subordinate deities are bathed in the waters of the Papanasini tank. Later, the deity returns to the procession, passing by the Kali shrine on the way. Pusyaviseka is the third festival in the annual ritual cycle and occurs on the day of the full moon during the month of Puspa (December–January). On this day, prior to the Bhoga Mandapa food offering, water brought from Bindusagar in 108 new earthen jugs is poured on the deity during the great bath ritual. Asokastami is the most important festival of Lord Lingaraj and continues for a week in the town. During this period, the deity and his companions visit the Ramesvara temple on a wooden chariot drawn by devotees. This festival occurs in the month of Chait (March–April). The car is constructed according to the measurements of the Megheswar temple. Akshaya Tritiya (Sandal Festival) occurs in the month of Baisakh (April–May). On this day, the subordinate deities of Lingaraj, Parvati, and Basudeva, as well as Kapilanath, the presiding deity of Kapileswara temple, are displayed for twenty-two evenings on a wooden barge in Bindusagar.

25 Susan Seymour, ed., *The Transformation of a Sacred Town: Bhubaneswar* (Boulder, Colo.: Westview Press, 1980).

26 Of the twenty-two monastic establishments existing today in Bhubaneswar, five were founded in the medieval period between the seventh and fifteenth centuries, ten were founded between 1918 and independence in 1947, and seven were founded after 1947. See Priyaleen Singh, "Changing Attitudes to Design with Nature: The Urban Indian Context" (PhD diss., University of York, 1998).

27 Bansi Lal Malla, *Trees in Indian Art Mythology and Folklore* (New Delhi: Aryan Books International, 2000); and Banwari, *Panchavati: Indian Approach to Environment* (Delhi: Shri Vinayak Publications, 1992).

28 Piyush Das, *Memory of a Stream: Gandhabati* (Ghaziabad: Copal Publishing, 2016).

29 Adrian Snodgrass, *The Symbolism of the Stupa* (Delhi: Motilal Banarasidass, 1992), 180.

30 One of the earliest representations of vegetation in Indian sculpture is the *kalpavriksha* of Besnagar, which has been dated to the third century BCE. It represents the mythical wish-fulfilling tree which produced food, drinks, and ornaments. At the root of the tree are pots, bags of money, and a conch exuding coins. The tree is meant to symbolize plenty and abundance, amply suggested by the exceeding luxuriance of thickset leaves, each one rendered individually and robustly. The *kalpavriksha* or wish-fulfilling tree is also described in the Jatakas as feeding, clothing, and attending to the needs of passersby seeking shade. It is graphically represented in Bharhut showing hands carrying food and water issuing from the clumps of boughs.

31 Sadashiv Ambadas Dange, *Glimpses of Puranic Myth and Culture* (Delhi: Ajanta Publishers, 1987), 158.

32 Kailash Malhotra, Yogesh Gokhale, Sudipto Chatterjee, and Sanjiv Srivastava, *Sacred Groves in India: An Overview* (New Delhi: Aryan Books International, 2007); and Vasudha Narayanan, "Water, Wood, and Wisdom: Ecological Perspectives from the Hindu Traditions," *Daedalus* 130, no. 4 (Fall 2001):179–206.

33 Varaha Purana, chapter 172, verse 39, quoted in Werner Y. Wolff, *Open Space Planning in India* (Bern: Lang, 1990), 555.

34 Sankar Sen Gupta, ed., *Tree Symbol Worship in India* (Calcutta: Asia Publishing House, 1965), 126.

35 *Strychnos nux-vomica* is a deciduous tree rich in two alkaloids: strychnine $C_{21}H_{22}N_2O_2$ (present in seeds, roots, bark, and leaves) and brucine $C_{23}H_{26}N_2O_4$.

36 See INTACH, *Ekamrakshetra Heritage Project*.

37 See Kalia, *Bhubaneswar*. Given the iconic imagery of Bhubaneswar as a temple city, there was a case made to borrow elements of temple architecture and use them in the new buildings of the capital. But Otto Koenigsberger, the German planner hired by the Indian government to advise on the new city, maintained that as the new India was intended to be a secular state, there was no place for temple architecture in the capital. He was prepared, however, to include important religious monuments of the old town in his master plan in order to form interesting viewpoints at the ends of main roads.

38 A. G. K. Menon in INTACH, *Ekamrakshetra Heritage Project*, 19.

PART III

Forestry

9

Xingu Garden Cities

Amazonian Urban Landscapes, or What?

MICHAEL HECKENBERGER

It is in the soul that architecture exists.
  —Ralph Waldo Emerson

URBANISM IS NOT WHAT TYPICALLY COMES TO MIND FOR MOST people when they consider the history or ecology of indigenous Amazonia. The Amazon is generally viewed as the paradigmatic case of primitive tribal societies living in small, relatively autonomous villages. The rise of preindustrial cities, at least, is rarely seen as relevant to the world's largest forest, except negatively—lacking the harbingers of civilization. The meteoric rise of archaeological research over the past two decades has rapidly changed these views. This research documents vast cultural landscapes in many parts of the tropical forest, including large, densely settled and regionally integrated social formations, some of which fall within the range of small- to medium-sized urban societies in other world regions, particularly those in other forested regions. Still lacking, however, are detailed case studies of how settled, regional, and hierarchical societies were organized in their maximal form or, in other words, what exactly might constitute an "Amazonian urbanism."

Long seen as a natural laboratory, today threatened by mechanized frontier development, urbanism, and global climate change, the Amazon supported much larger populations and technological innovations than previously thought. Recent studies reveal regional planning, environmental engineering, and landscape modification no less remarkable or sophisticated than those of small- to medium-sized urban polities in other regions in the preindustrial world. These highlight human agency and social dynamics in coupled human-natural systems, including the place of contemporary

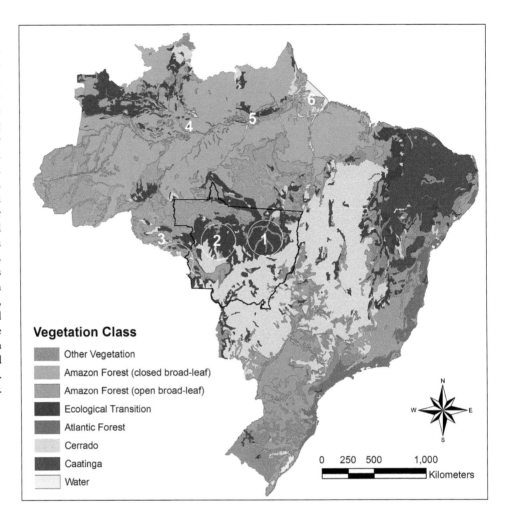

FIGURE 9.1

Map of Brazil, showing major vegetation classes. Regions of late Pre-Columbian large regional populations in the southern Amazon, including Upper Xingu basin (1), Upper Tapajós basin (2), and eastern Upper Madeira (Guaporé) basin (3), and along the Amazon River, including middle Amazon (Manaus, 4), middle-lower Amazon (Santarém, 5), and Marajó Island (6). There is a notable concentration of large, regionally organized societies associated with the southern transitional forest areas (1–3), which forms a discrete ecological region distinctive from the broad-leaved evergreen Amazon forests and open woodland and savanna areas of the Cerrado. Map by Michael Heckenberger.

indigenous peoples and cultural heritage in debates about the Amazonian past. Many Pre-Columbian societies differ dramatically from historically known tribes, known largely within the ethnographic present of the twentieth century, although nothing like a full-blown city ever seems to have emerged there, much less the apparatus of bureaucratic states. This variation does prompt us to consider the question: What was urbanism in its smallest and most diffuse preindustrial forms, including urbanized landscapes without singular cities?

This essay considers what constitutes Pre-Columbian Amazonian urbanism, in terms of settlement organization, regional integration, and the associated urban ecology of these regional social formations in complex-coupled human-environmental systems. The discussion focuses on late Pre-Columbian settlement and land use in the Upper Xingu region, defined as the headwater basin of the Xingu River, one of the largest of the southern tributaries of the Amazon River (Figure 9.1). At the apogee of regional demography and built environment, between 1250 and 1650 CE, archaeological research identified integrated, hierarchical clusters, composed of multicentric ("galactic") networks of walled towns and satellite villages. These were connected by well-developed road systems, which

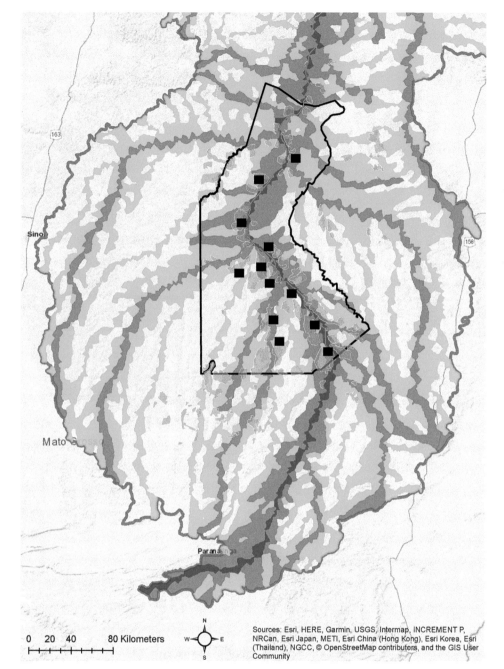

FIGURE 9.2
Headwater basin of the Xingu
River, showing hydrology by
major (dark blue) and minor
(light blue) rivers, with areas
of banded forest associated
with recent forest fires and
correlating with distribution
of known Pre-Columbian
clusters (black squares).
Additional Pre-Columbian
clusters are suggested by
indigenous knowledge of dark
earth sites and earthworks in
the Território Indígena do
Xingu (black line). Projeto
Etnoarqueológico Kuikuro
(AIKAX).

document highly standardized systems of spatial organization and engineering across
much of the basin, an area of over 50,000 km² (Figure 9.2). Specifically, it considers (1) the
nature of large prehistoric settlements, in terms of size and density, functional variation,
and structural elaboration; (2) the politico-ritual integration of communities in clusters,
based on sociopolitical and ritual activities in walled towns and village nodes, all linked
by a well-planned system of roads; and (3) the broader landscapes managed and constructed near settlements in forest, wetland, and agricultural areas.

Amazonian Urbanism: Definitions and Themes

Recent studies in archaeology and historical ecology document great variation in indigenous resource management strategies, including large, regionally organized geopolitical systems along the Amazon River and in the southern transitional forests, among other areas. The meteoric rise of archaeological research over the past two decades reveals dynamic human-natural systems, including long-term human occupations throughout the Holocene and the influence of large, settled, and regionally organized late Pre-Columbian populations in some areas. These areas are characterized by large settlements (20–50 ha, or more), high regional site densities, supralocal sociopolitical integration, and substantial human intervention and engineering of forest environments. The semi-intensive land management practiced by these regionally organized complex societies created extensive production and extraction landscapes, which had far-ranging indirect impacts on biodiversity and regional population distributions. Nonetheless, most scholars eschew the notion of indigenous Amazonian urbanism, instead portraying most of the region as a paradigmatic case of small-scale nonurban social formations, the so-called tropical forest tribe or small-scale chiefdoms and loose confederacies, which typically did not live in enduring settlements, much less cities. The question remains: Did these societies constitute some form of early urbanism?

What Is Amazonian Urbanism?

Whether there were cities in ancient Amazonia obviously hinges on what is meant by "city" or "urban," as opposed to some earlier, intermediate, or alternative form of settlement or sociopolitical organization. In most world areas, discussions revolve around the appearance and variation of certain key features or traits of cities, such as large settlement size, structural or monumental elaboration within towns and cities, and certain technologies, rather than how they were organized or how they integrated large regional populations. We might instead ask: What were the processes of urbanism or urbanization, notably in complex areas that lack full-blown cities, including networks of towns and villages? Certainly, settlement patterns in ancient Amazonia diverged from the ethnographic model of small, nonpermanent, and autonomous villages, but where does the village end and the city begin? What is urbanism in its smallest, most diffuse, and non-Western—in this case Amazonian—forms, or is some other term more appropriate to describe them?

In his overview of the city, Ulf Hannerz suggests "a reasonably large and permanent concentration of people within a limited territory as a common characteristic of all cities and other urban places."[1] This definition depends on what is considered "reasonably large and permanent" or how a territory is defined and thereby "limited." Following descriptions of small cities and their territories, such as those of the Greek *poleis*,[2] Andean cities,[3] and others in the Americas and elsewhere,[4] population estimates of the smallest towns or minimal urban places range in the low thousands, whereas medium-sized ones range into the tens of thousands. Their sizes generally range between about 50–150 ha and, if we include smaller examples, towns rather than major cities, they often range much smaller. The territories they inhabit typically range from 100–500 km², which are often distributed in peer-polities with weakly developed regional hierarchies, each occupying areas usually in the tens of thousands of square kilometers.

Hannerz goes on to say: "The beginnings of urbanism are now generally identified with a broad type of ritual-political centre . . . [from which] divine monarchs and priesthoods . . . controlled countryside peasants . . . [and] from whom they exacted a surplus . . . [and] small 'tribal' shrines were elaborated as complexes of monumental architecture."[5] The focus on ritual-political aspects of early complex societies shares critical aspects of what are glossed as "theater states," where the surplus was symbolic and sociopolitical, rather than strictly economic, within mixed, undulating landscapes of greater and lesser land use and size, rather than a simple town/country distinction,[6] a pattern also described as the "ritual phase of political economy."[7] The "galactic polity,"[8] with its mandala orientation of networks of social value and power, is one example, notably the self-scaling quality based on the interaction of broadly shared religious values and ritual performance with dynamic social, political, and ecological conditions. In the Americas, major ceremonies of social and symbolic reproduction (successions), embedded in the built environment and associated with monumental plaza-temple complexes, major causeways within settlements and networks of roads linking them, were critical to religious-cum-political authority or theocracy and power derived from within rather than over other people.[9]

Following these parameters, Amazonian examples seem to fall within the minimal range of urban places, but do any of them amount to actual cities? That Amazonian urbanism does not fit classical models should perhaps come as no surprise; as with many other settings in the non-Western world, the fit is awkward. Settlements of significant size with highly constructed and managed core areas, towns, or super-villages were common in this late prehistoric landscape. In most cases, it seems that a more diffuse settlement pattern is typical, with potentially large regional populations but only modest centers, perhaps due in part to the constraints of tropical forest ecology. Most regional specialists today agree that in the past Amazonian cultural variation included diverse small- to medium-sized polities, which were (1) densely settled with highly productive forest farming and wetland management economies; (2) regional in scope, including large peer-polity territories up to 50,000 km², and linked into supraregional geopolitical systems and interaction beyond simple reciprocal exchange systems, such as the Amazon River floodplains, with the celebrated ceramic arts and polychrome elite wares, and southern transitional forest macro-regions, with their remarkable constructed politico-ritual centers (plazas or diverse forms); and (3) hierarchical, including clear settlement and spatial hierarchies, as well as partially endogamous elite groups, rituals, and other esoteric knowledge, dispositions, and symbols, such as names and body adornments. It also included diverse, nonhierarchical, and even mobile, egalitarian, and politically autonomous communities (although the ratio of smaller to larger may have been inverted over the past five centuries due to Native American depopulation).

In Amazonia, as with many small- to medium-sized polities, major feasts were central to social and symbolic reproduction and intra- and intergroup interaction, notably including political rivalry between local and regional chiefs, which in this case would be between leaders of hierarchical clusters.[10] In Amazonia, Julian Steward and Louis Faron long ago noted that "in eastern Bolivia, a men's ceremonial house, based on the Amazonian pattern, was magnified to state significance."[11] The plaza-temple-idol complexes or "theocratic chiefdoms," as they referred to them, were highly variable and discontinuous across broad regional political economies. They inspired the broad category of chiefdoms, first introduced to describe southern Amazon groups like the Xingu,[12] but later used as a gloss for a wide range of societies across the globe, particularly in the Americas and Global South, which clearly de-emphasized remarkable variation among these nonegalitarian, nonstate, regionally integrated sociopolitical formations.[13] Indeed, although plazas have been discussed and analyzed as elements of egalitarian self-organization (everyone has a front-row seat), they often represent hierarchically ordered sociospatial cartographies which, like their Andean counterparts,[14] were containers of symbolic or cosmic power, wielded by chiefs or priests as part of canonistic religious and ritual practices tied to this laterally explicit and expansive ceremonial architecture.

In the Upper Xingu, plazas, temples, and idols are central to local culture today. They were also critical to the garden cities of the past, as the glue and currency of political integration of the regional peer-polity. In contemporary communities, plaza rituals are the primary sites for public construction and display of political authority. It is hypothesized here that it was equally or more so in the past, being perhaps the most critical feature of both local and regional sociopolitical integration. In the present case, social and political integration is tightly tied to public ritual, architecture, and place, rather than control over economic commodities, bureaucratic apparatus, modes of production, or instruments of direct coercion. The question remains: Where does the village end and the town or city begin? Are Xinguano plazas just big tribal "shrines" made of thatch and wood, ceremonial "huts," or do they represent monumental architecture, one which is laterally complex but vertically flat? As Henri Lefebvre notes about architecture in general, such variation isn't a surprise: "How can we classify architectural works, determine types? How can we periodize architectural history based on those classifications? It's not obvious that accurate periodization would mean the exclusion of all other forms of classification. The multiplicity of classifications, here or elsewhere, is the primordial truth, which relativizes scientific authority."[15]

The Xingu, like western African examples of nonnucleated or clustered towns with no overarching or centralized, state-focused power structure, beg the question: Is there urbanization or polity without cities?[16] If so, what is the range of complex polities without cities[17] or, conversely, cities without states?[18] Specifically, do networks of walled towns and satellite villages count? These do not conform to classic urban-rural models (typically framed as differences in economic and administrative functions between social, cultural, religious, and political centers and their agricultural hinterlands), even admitting the far greater (and often smaller) variation than once assumed[19]—but if not urbanized, what do we call these complex networks? Regardless of what we call the largest settlements, or even how large they are in terms of population relative to one another, the present case provides an unparalleled instance in Amazonia to accurately measure settlement morphology and variation within and between settlements in clusters, as well as relations between them and broader constructed or "domesticated" landscapes (an urban ecology) of the terminal Pre-Columbian period.

The Human Footprint of Amazonian Urbanism

Suffice it to say, definitions of what constitutes early urbanism across the globe vary substantially. Many recent discussions highlight features of urbanized landscapes comparable to Amazonian examples, particularly in other tropical forest regions across the globe. The question we might ask is not what urbanism is, but instead what urbanism does: What is the urban ecology of these societies? Erik Andersson suggests that "urbanization results in an environment that is compositionally more heterogeneous, geometrically more complex, and ecologically more fragmented, and may represent the most complex mosaic of vegetative land cover and multiple uses of any landscape."[20] What then is the signature, or footprint, of complex human settlements patterns, whether we call them urban or not?

In the forested areas of the southern Amazon headwater basins, located along the Brazil–Bolivia border and in central Brazil, there is substantial evidence of large, densely settled populations and large-scale anthropogenic impacts on the natural environment, including complex systems of earthworks, causeways, fish weirs and ponds, raised fields, forest islands (ancient settlements), and other diverse archaeological features in extensive domesticated landscapes.[21] Early ethnohistoric reports (1600–1850) also describe regional enclaves of large, densely settled populations, typically speakers of Arawak languages and culturally affiliated groups, across the southern transitional moist tropical forests, clearly the remnants of sociopolitically integrated Pre-Columbian regional systems.[22]

In southeastern Amazonia, transitional moist forests are intermediate between the closed broad-leaved evergreen humid forests of Amazonia and the more open woodlands of the central Brazilian Cerrado; they supported at least two primary regional systems in the headwater basins of the Tapajós and Xingu Rivers. Recent studies using remote-sensed data suggest that the pattern of settled plaza communities is part of a broader pattern spread across the southern Amazonian transitional forests.[23] Antônio Pires de Campos describes one such polity, the "Pareci nation" in the Upper Tapajós River in 1720: "These people exist in such vast quantity that it is not possible to count their settlements or villages, [and] many times in one day's march one passes ten or twelve villages, and in each one there are from ten to thirty houses . . . even their roads they make are very straight and wide, and they keep them so clean that one will find not even a fallen leaf."[24]

The Upper Xingu is the easternmost regional culture in the southern transitional forests. No historical records are available before 1884, but archaeological research provides clear evidence of the scale and organization of discrete late Pre-Columbian and early historical regional occupations, the ancestors of the contemporary Kuikuro (Xinguano). Archaeology in this area has documented late Pre-Columbian, recent historical, and contemporary contexts, in landscapes that show a continuous record of habitation by related (Xinguano) peoples over the past millennium. It is the best-known case of large-scale, densely settled prehistoric populations and semi-intensive techno-economic systems in the Brazilian Amazon at the time of European contact. This enables us to address change in coupled socio-ecological systems, including the nature and scale of sustainable and intensive systems of indigenous land use at their height (ca. 1250–1650), as revealed by visible archaeological features and associated forest floral communities in contemporary landscapes, as well as by changes in population and land use over the past three centuries related to punctuated demographic decline (to near collapse by the mid-1900s) and "forest fallowing." This highlights active cultural responses to environmental changes from ca. 1650 to 1950, including climate change, depopulation, globalization, and the place of contemporary indigenous groups in scientific research, both as research subjects and as fully engaged partners in the coproduction of knowledge aimed at sustainability in the Amazon.

Xingu Garden Cities: An Urban Ecology

The Upper Xingu is among the clearest examples of a complex indigenous socio-ecological system, preserving the most obvious anthropogenic footprint of terminal Pre-Columbian complex societies across the region.[25] It is also unique in the southern transitional forests of the Amazon, as the largest contiguous tract of tropical forest still under indigenous resource management, which today is an island of forest within the

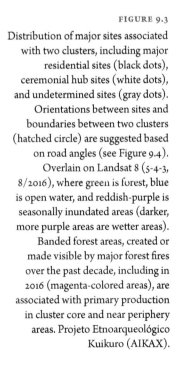

FIGURE 9.3

Distribution of major sites associated with two clusters, including major residential sites (black dots), ceremonial hub sites (white dots), and undetermined sites (gray dots). Orientations between sites and boundaries between two clusters (hatched circle) are suggested based on road angles (see Figure 9.4). Overlain on Landsat 8 (5-4-3, 8/2016), where green is forest, blue is open water, and reddish-purple is seasonally inundated areas (darker, more purple areas are wetter areas). Banded forest areas, created or made visible by major forest fires over the past decade, including in 2016 (magenta-colored areas), are associated with primary production in cluster core and near periphery areas. Projeto Etnoarqueológico Kuikuro (AIKAX).

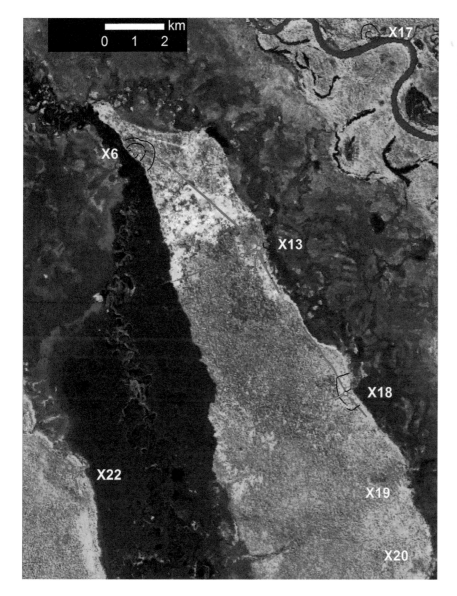

FIGURE 9.4

Distribution of sites associated with the northern cluster, including ceremonial hub site (X13), two first-order residential sites (X6 and X18), two second-order residential sites (X17 and X22), and two tertiary permanent plaza villages (X19 and X20). GPS-mapped roads are shown as red lines and major ditch earthworks at X6, X17, and X18 in black lines (Landsat 7, 5-4-3, 8/2008). Current Kuikuro village and formal road (*tangiña*) are to the right of X6. Projeto Etnoarqueológico Kuikuro (AIKAX).

Território Indígena do Xingu (TIX), with predominantly deforested areas outside of it. The TIX, the first demarcated indigenous area in the Amazon (1961), preserves the most intact system of traditional knowledge among descendants of these ancient complex polities. The forested environments themselves preserve an unparalleled record of the postcontact (post-1500) "fallowing" of much of the landscape, associated with the demographic collapse of Amerindian populations from the sixteenth to the twentieth century, but also this rich and detailed history.

Early agriculturalists living in plaza villages arrived in the Upper Xingu region between ca. 800 and 1200 BP, if not before, and established a significantly different regime of human-environmental interaction than previous groups in the region. Several significant periods of transformational change in the evolving regional system can be

Major earthworks associated with northern cluster core settlements X6 and X13 with GPS-mapped road/plaza berms in yellow line and major ditches in blue line. Smaller peripheral plazas are inferred to be staging areas for primary plaza rituals, like campsites positioned just outside plaza villages today. Projeto Etnoarqueológico Kuikuro (AIKAX).

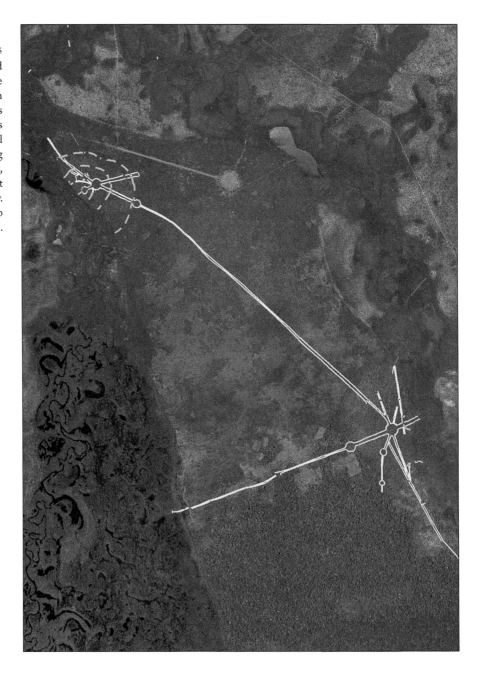

reconstructed from research to date (supported by thirty carbon-14 dates):[26] (1) initial colonization by settled agriculturists, approximately 800 BP or before, ancestral to later Xinguano periods (pre-Galactic Period); (2) enlargement and structural elaboration of major settlements, ca. 1250–1300, marked by large-scale constructions (roads, canals, weirs, ponds, defensive walls, and other engineered features) and integration in hierarchical clusters (Galactic Period); (3) population decline and fallowing of landscapes, ca. 1550–1700 (Transitional Period); (4) geographic compression, depopulation, and

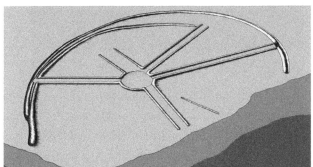

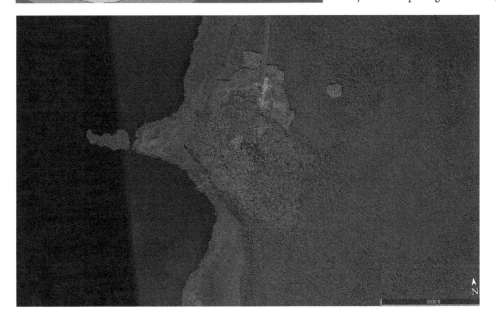

FIGURE 9.7

Reconstruction of the Pre-Columbian town of X11. Reproduced from Michael Heckenberger, "Lost Garden Cities: Pre-Columbian Life in the Amazon," *Scientific American*, October 2009.

ethnogenesis of the multilingual contemporary society, including population stabilization in the scale-adjusted settlement pattern of one or a few small villages related to discrete local groups in the regional cultural system, 1700–1850; and (5) acute depopulation after the mid-1800s from 1850 to 1960 followed by post-1980 demographic and socioeconomic rebound and current growth of all descendant groups (late Xinguano Period).

During the late Pre-Columbian or Galactic Period, three levels of sociopolitical organization can be identified: (1) the decentralized peer-polity extending across the basin (over an area of roughly 50,000 km²); (2) the hierarchical galactic cluster, composed of eight to twelve permanent plaza settlements, in territories of some 250–400 km², with clearly defined core areas (approximately 50 km²) composed of four walled residential centers (20–50 ha) and a central ceremonial site or hub (Figures 9.3–9.5); and (3) the individual settlement (Figures 9.6 and 9.7). The focus here is the intermediate form, described as garden cities, which emerge around 1250 and disintegrate after roughly 1650, but with elements that continue in the knowledge and practices of descendant indigenous peoples.

Regional Planning

Participatory survey and mapping with trained indigenous assistants has identified twenty-eight major Pre-Columbian archaeological sites, identified based on the presence of *egepe* forest areas (associated with Amazonian dark earths or ADE) and co-occurring archaeological ceramics (*egeho*) as well as historical villages (*etepe*).[27] Once

FIGURE 9.8
a) Survey and mapping
training workshop in
Kuikuro village of Ipatse;
and b) Laquai Kuikuro
mapping Pre-Columbian
road berm that bisects
modern-day fence around
manioc garden, July 2003.
Projeto Etnoarqueológico
Kuikuro (AIKAX).

located, all sites were positioned with real-time GPS or on satellite images in the few
cases where GPS was unavailable (Figure 9.8). All sites were positioned at regular intervals along forest/wetland margins and linked by a region-wide system of broad, straight
roads. All sites were integrated in internally hierarchical clusters of settlements, in
approximately 1250–1650. Positioning, stratigraphic evidence, and radiocarbon dating
from two major residential sites (X6 and X11) and one ceremonial hub site (X13), as well
as ceramics and detailed mapping at additional sites, suggest that most if not all of the
identified residential sites were occupied ca. 1250–1650 within one of the two hierarchical
clusters. This suggests that settled agricultural populations underwent radical reorienta-
tions around 1250, as documented in settlement expansion and major road and plaza constructions, clearly indicated by well-dated earthworks within and between settlements.

Mapping of major earthworks at these sites reveals an elaborate regional plan, including major excavated ditches surrounding the largest settlements, which are up to 15 m wide and 5 m deep (Figure 9.9); linear mounds positioned along roads and public plaza areas; and a variety of wetland constructions, such as raised causeways, bridges, river obstructions (weirs), canals, and artificially modified ponds. Mapping of all major occupation sites and road networks in the northern cluster, combined with archaeological testing at several larger sites, enables an accurate reconstruction of a multicentric or "galactic" settlement organization. Each galactic cluster or "garden city" was composed of four major towns with peripheral ditched walls (20–50 ha), unwalled ceremonial hub sites, smaller peripheral villages (less than 10 ha), and hamlets in peripheral areas. Plaza towns were distinguished by major ditches (500–2,000 m long), defining settlement boundaries, associated with a palisade wall, and, in some cases, located within settlements. These are inferred to be small, independent polities with territories of roughly 250 km^2, which were integrated in a regional peer-polity of twenty-five or more such clusters (over an area greater than 50,000 km^2).

Overall, landscape transformation associated with the galactic clusters may have rivaled other social formations called "urban," although these settlements lacked many of the material trappings seen as critical elsewhere: for example, full-time craft specialization, stone or even vertical earthen monuments and structures, and certainly the bureaucratic or coercive apparatus of the state. Still, today there are systems of tribute, surplus, and infrastructural elaboration. The residents keep "livestock" in managed fish ponds, in domesticated landscapes. And, they have sophisticated astronomical, architectural, geometric, and calendrical systems, as shown in the settlements' precise orientations and alignments. These premodern social formations represent an integrated regional system which cultivates connectivity, not only through complicated systems of social interaction, but also through "traffic" with the natural world, including diverse nonhuman beings. Although diffuse and "flat," these self-organized systems, which seem to link everything with everything else, organized large, dense regional populations and semi-intensive forest and wetland production systems in Pre-Columbian clusters.

Research on settlement and road networks documents a highly patchy and textured landscape due to mosaic conditions in this transitional area, sensitivity to climate change, and long-term human manipulation. At the broadest level, the entire ecological province of the southern transitional forests was composed of areas of intense anthropogenic influence in forested headwater basins of the southern Amazonian tributaries. However, evidence suggests that rather than denuding forests, the residents were managing them and converting them into patchier forests. (The timber needed to support a single settlement would, in and of itself, constitute semi-intensive extraction.) In a long-term system of resource recycling, they connected diverse ecological areas through developed systems of cyclical extraction within fixed zones. In terms of settlement size and density, populations were clearly much larger in the Pre-Columbian past than in historical times: one hundred times the twentieth-century low of approximately five hundred. What was also distinctive about the preindustrial systems were

a

b

c

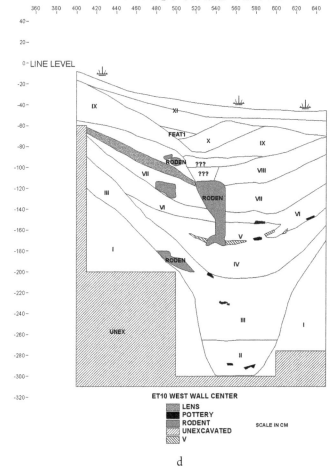

d

FIGURE 9.9

a) Inner ditch at X6; b) excavation trench bisecting outer peripheral ditch at X6, which is dated to ca. 1400 and represents substanial fourteenth-century expansion of the site; and c–d) photograph and profile of excavation trench bisecting inner ditch at X6, showing funnel shape with basal portions inferred to have been footing for palisade wall and multiple stages of infilling after construction, ca. 1250. Projeto Etnoarqueológico Kuikuro (AIKAX).

the highly partitioned and patchy landscapes created by semi-intensive agricultural and wetland land use.

The Galactic Period, defined by the emergence and then dissolution of the integrated supralocal clusters, was characterized by semi-intensive land use, more rigidly defined regional hierarchies, and partitioned or "zoned" land use. During the Galactic Period, a radical reorientation and integration of settlement patterns occurred in ca. 1250–1350. Throughout this time, settlements were expanded and integrated through major road-building projects, indicated by well-dated earthworks within and between settlements, including over a dozen carbon-14 determinations. This includes enlargement and structural elaboration of major settlements, ca. 750–350 BP, marked by large-scale constructions (roads, canals, weirs, ponds, defensive walls, and other engineered features) and integration in hierarchical clusters. Environmental impacts also intensified, ultimately leading to highly anthropogenic and even engineered landscapes from at least approximately 750–350 BP. The system collapsed soon after European contact, roughly 1550–1650, and was reconstituted at a much smaller scale, with much land returning to forest, demographic and socioeconomic rebound post-1970, and restabilization by descendant groups.

In the better-known northern (Ipatse) cluster, settlements were positioned at forest/wetland interfaces at regular intervals and linked by a region-wide system of broad, straight roads. Clusters were composed of large (45 ha or more) and medium (less than 30 ha) plaza towns, smaller (less than 10 ha) plaza villages, and small (nonplaza) hamlets. Basic mapping of major earthworks was conducted in and around fourteen sites and detailed mapping of earthworks was conducted at eight (X6, X11, X13, X17–20, X22). Earthworks include peripheral ditches and low linear berms (0.5–1.5 m high) situated at the margins of public plaza areas and major roads (greater than 10 m wide) and forming more than 40 km of a contiguous network of curbed roads between settlements, as well as gates, bridges, and weirs.

Settlement Morphology

Extensive residential occupations are documented across interior portions of walled settlements, including structural remains (house and trash midden areas) and ceramic cooking utensils, covering more than 20 ha in first-order settlements. Small nonwalled plaza villages are similar in size and form to contemporary villages. In addition to their larger size and structural elaboration, including gates, roads, and secondary plazas (possible ritual staging areas), walled towns are distinguished by their position relative to the cluster center. The largest residential centers are located roughly equidistant (3–5 km) from the exemplary center (X13) to the northwest and southeast; medium-sized centers are located to the northeast and southwest, roughly 8–10 km from the center. To determine the distribution of residential quarters within areas enclosed by ditches, extensive surface collection (2 m² units) was conducted at X6 (2,059 units), X11 (1,996 units), and X13 (330 units). Surface collection units were collected in 1 m² subunits and placed along linear transects (at an interval of 10 m) positioned at 50 m intervals across X6 and

X11, and in 100 m² collection/testing areas (10 m grid) at X6 (nine areas with 770 units) and X13 (three areas with 330 units).

More detailed investigations were conducted at X6 and X13 due to the proximity of the Kuikuro village, including three hundred soil augers (8 cm), sixty test pits (0.5 m²), fifteen excavation trenches (10 m² or more), eighty excavation units (1 m²), and fourteen excavation strips (0.5 × 5 m) to locate structures and a large block (340 m²) exposing a house (carbon-14 dated to approximately 1450). Detailed analysis of highly varied ADE and non-ADE soils in the Upper Xingu documents great variation in organic material and chemical alteration of soils, including quite subtle and even negative results from clearly anthropogenic areas.[28] These findings generally confirm the large size of late prehistoric communities and indicate accretional deposits across the majority of the sites, including areas of high and low frequency and identifiable function (house, ADE midden, public space, work space, traffic, and non-ADE gardening areas).[29]

Fifteen trench excavations were positioned to bisect ditch/gate/parapet earthworks and road and plaza curbs, which preserve well-stratified cultural contexts for understanding site chronology and layout (see Figure 9.9). Securely dated contexts place initial Xinguano tradition occupations of X6, X11, and X13 at 600–900 CE (based on one early date, 640–690 CE, and five dates of approximately 900–1000 CE), although there are indications of earlier occupations (one carbon-14 date from mixed basal ditch deposits is 190–60 BCE). Dates related to the late prehistoric clusters were obtained from samples hand-collected from the obvious interface of stratified pre-earthwork deposits and overburden from earthwork construction. At X6, the greater number of excavated contexts enabled careful selection of samples from intact deposits at the overburden interface, including 590±60 BP, 670±60 BP, 690±60 BP, 700±70 BP, and 710±50 BP (Beta-176139, 177724, 88362, 78979, and 176136). These deposits capped by overburden are easily identified and are close approximations of initial earthwork construction (approximately 1250–1300), resulting in remarkably consistent dates at about 1300. At X11, the interface is bracketed by two dates of 440±70 BP (Beta-72262) and 900±60 BP (Beta-72263), and X13 by 690±60 BP (Beta-88632) and 910±80 (Beta-88363).

Previous research included detailed studies of ADE, household production, and archaeological ceramics.[30] It is clear that there was significant variation in deposits across large sites as reflected in ceramic distribution and functional variation,[31] as well as soils, including a wide range of ADE, public areas, and other open spaces interpreted as community gardens. Soils from archaeological, historical, and current villages show significant variation, including ADE and non-ADE areas, but exhibit characteristic features of anthropogenic soils in terms of organics, texture, and soil chemistry (notably calcium, magnesium, zinc, and phosphorus, among others).[32]

It is inferred that the area delimited by the four primary residential satellites formed the residential and production core of each galactic cluster. This was distinct from non-walled satellites, similar in size to modern villages. In core areas, it is suggested that semi-intensive land use in mosaic secondary forest-parkland settings was distinct from mixed land-use regimes and high forest (called *itsuni* by the Kuikuro) in areas of smaller unwalled settlements, situated in a hinterland periphery. Even larger-scale terraformed features of the built environment are suggested by anthropogenic influences on the overall forest and wetland structure, including lakes and large ponds along rivers and streams.

Xinguano settlement patterns and landscapes (and social philosophies) show a scalar or self-organizing quality, which is reflected in sociospatial patterns (household, settlement, galactic cluster). They provide a point of departure to consider change at different sociohistorical or temporal scales: household levels, community levels, and ultimately regional levels. Whether splitting the initial state from chiefly forms of power or lumping them into one general category of theocratic polities, the partitioning of the built environment is quite clear and easily measured in this case. It is always tied to clear and obvious symbols of rank and genealogy (east–west, right–left, and center–edge orientations noted above), as well as special woods, designs, and ornaments used in chiefs' houses and on chiefs' bodies, including the plaza flute/mask house, flanking the communal burial ground to the west and adjacent to the ritual field for chiefly rites of passage. This local "cartography" is a great boon to the archaeologist due to the high visibility of low, linear mounds, which were placed along roads and at the margins of circular plazas and ritual staging areas, creating an almost unbroken settlement feature that extends across the entire landscape (Figure 9.10).

Without belaboring the point, plazas are everywhere in the Xingu, particularly in late prehistoric galactic clusters (they are the nodes in the galactic structure). It is not certain, however, that all circular curbed structures are plazas, or whether all central plazas are cemeteries, let alone the possible differences between cemeteries within clusters. "Xinguano society" and its constituent peer communities, single or a few closely related villages, well described ethnographically since the 1880s,[33] share this plaza-ritual complex. These also suggest basic features of sociopolitical organization and ideology, showing tremendous resiliency over the past five centuries despite acute depopulation. All communities are linked by roads and coparticipation in chiefly rites of passage and other rituals; a regional system of economic specialization and equivalencies underpins local exchange throughout historical memory and continues today. Shared features, which have endured from the earliest pre-Galactic Period occupations, beginning over a millennium ago, include ring plaza villages and associated plaza rituals, co-participation in ritual events or feasts, well-planned and maintained primary causeways and roads, manioc-based agriculture and arboriculture, wetland fisheries management, and, notably, the self-scaling properties of these systems that are carefully partitioned according to a calculus of center and periphery—from house, to village, to countryside, to wilderness. There were substantial differences, however, not only in terms of the degree of such built environments but in their fixity. It is inferred that villages will split up to a certain point, then optimal site areas and internal politics will demand a structural change, witnessed in this case by the major constructions in towns occupied in 1250–1350 and only abandoned after 1550.

In contemporary society, established by the early Xinguano period, there are two levels of sociopolitical integration: *otomo* and regional (*kuge*, or real "people"). The intermediate

FIGURE 9.10

Aerial photograph (1967) of the Pre-Columbian site of Jacaré (X9), located to the left of what was then a military training base in the Xingu indigenous area. Note the plaza and radial road berms, oriented to cardinal directions, and the oval of anthropogenic forest within peripheral ditch (palisade wall) earthworks. Projeto Etnoarqueológico Kuikuro (AIKAX).

level of sociopolitical organization—small territorial clusters or polities—are known strictly from the archaeology of the late prehistoric period. The form and orientations of settlement spatial organization, notably circular plazas and radial roads, document a regional pattern of political and ritual integration based on the internal ranking of closely related linguistic/residential groups, *otomo*.[34] Within *otomo*, relations of sociopolitical subordinacy are marked in formal chiefly ceremony and works projects, notably the mortuary feast (Kwryp), where chiefly ancestors are ranked according to social hierarchies of the living. The local chiefly individuals and families, called *anetü* (or *anetão* in plural), are identified by diverse markers of rank, including sun-diadem headdresses, jaguar claws and skins, body paint, and the *uengïfi* (kwyrp) tree, a singular species, chief of the forest, and the tree from which the mother of primordial ancestors (the Sun and Moon) was carved, which today is used in burial structures, ceremonial houses, and the house of the *anetão*.

Ecology of Xingu Garden Cities

The Upper Xingu case is an example of multicentric preindustrial urbanism, composed of small-scale hierarchical settlement clusters. These were integrated in territorial units defined by core areas, specifically, the four major residential settlements precisely positioned in relation to the ceremonial hub site, rather than clear boundaries and peripheral satellites. These existed across the Upper Xingu basin as discrete micropolities in a basin-wide peer-polity nation extending over some 50,000 km². This multicentric pattern of dense settlement and intensive land use differs dramatically from both ethnographic indigenous patterns (twentieth-century) and contemporary (post-1950) nonindigenous urbanization and frontier development in the Amazon.[35] Whether defined as urbanized or not, these areas of complex socioecological systems (for example, associated with small- to medium-sized premodern complex societies) show very different dimensions of ecological resiliency than areas of little direct human impact, as portrayed by ethnographic and ecological studies in the twentieth century.

The cultural pattern of root crop agriculture and fishing, plaza settlement organization, regional integration, and hierarchical sociopolitical organization is characteristic of Xinguano people through the known cultural sequence (from before 1200 BP to the present). It is a long-standing ethnographic case study of indigenous land use in recent times, including staple manioc agriculture supplemented by arboriculture of tropical fruit trees as well as "house gardening" and fairly intensive fishing and wetland management.[36] The contemporary agricultural countryside is a mosaic of managed fields of mono-crop manioc (*Manihot esculenta*) converted to orchards of *pequi* trees (*Caryocar*), and large areas of *sapé* grass (*Imperata*) which is mixed with secondary forest in various stages of regrowth (Figure 9.11). It is also the most intact system of traditional knowledge among descendants of ancient complex polities in the broad Amazon, and thus one of the few places where contemporary observations about indigenous agriculture, land use, and settlement patterns can be systematically linked with archaeological and oral historical evidence, within an unbroken cultural continuum extending from before 1000 BP to the present.

There is clear continuity in settlement locations, as well as in domestic activities and ceramic technology.[37] Settlement patterns and land use, both in the past and today, conform to several factors: (1) location along ecotones of upland forest and wetlands, of diverse kinds, including large channelized rivers, with oxbow and side-channel lakes, marshy rivers and streams, and associated ponds and lakes; (2) land use, associated with a techno-economy of fixed-area manioc cultivation and fishing, which shows a concentric pattern of garden areas around settlements; and (3) culturally specific ideas of social organization and cosmology, notably tied to sundial-like partitions of settlement space, according to basic east–west/north–south orientations and 45-degree divisions.

These cultural landscapes preserve an unparalleled record of the "fallowing" of the forests and wetlands associated with the demographic collapse of Amerindian populations from the sixteenth through the twentieth centuries. In recent times (1950 to today), small semipermanent villages (one to five Kuikuro villages, 2–6 ha in size, with 100–350 persons each) still substantially restructure tropical forest landscapes. In prehistory, the settlement pattern consisted of much larger and more densely settled villages. These early agricultural populations did not denude the landscape of trees, as commonly practiced in modern developmental practices, but instead created patchy (spatially and seasonally) mosaic patterns of land use. Like today, these incorporated diverse forest and wetland management strategies, for example patchy land use relating to long-term rotational cycles of multicrop agriculture and arboriculture, large-scale wetland management, and forest "connectivity" through habitat corridors.

a

b

c

d

FIGURE 9.11

a) Manioc processing pots, including a griddle
and pot for cooking broth (tapioca), which
are identical to Pre-Columbian examples;
b) manioc flour storage silos, which are used
to store flour for major community rituals
in chiefs' houses and contain up to 2,000 kg;
c) hammock being woven of buriti palm and
cotton, the two primary industrial crops; and
d) spinning cotton in-house, alongside fishing
trap, manioc-carrying baskets (hanging), and
bottle gourd (*Lagenaria siceraria*) scoops.
Projeto Etnoarqueológico Kuikuro (AIKAX).

In 1960, when the TIX was established and the regional population was at its historical nadir, there were roughly 500 persons living in seven villages—following epidemics between the late 1880s and 1960s, resulting in a substantial population reduction estimated at over 3,000 persons in thirty or more villages. Today, regional population is distributed in twenty-four villages, with the largest villages between 350 and 400 persons and larger villages commonly between 150 and 200 persons, again with a regional population in the low thousands over the TIX's roughly 20,000 km². These villages are all less than 10 ha in size, with a concentric ring of gardening areas and working forests, but far removed from one another.

Although basic features of socioeconomic organization, settlement pattern, and land use were typical from the earliest-known plaza occupations (1200 BP or before) to the present, the highly engineered and precise pattern of landscape partitioning and semi-intensive land use in selected areas was restricted to late Pre-Columbian times. The fixed placement of settlements and roads radiating out from them also rigidly partitioned production landscapes, particularly in core areas of clusters, where it is inferred that semi-intensive land-use practices (slash-and-char) were typical. Core areas were surrounded by a peripheral "green belt" of mixed land use in mosaic forest and, in turn, large tracts of unfelled forest between clusters, although the vast extent of modified soils and associated vegetation (called *egepe* by Kuikuro) extend over much of the area between sites in clusters, as well as substantial extractive forest management in intervening areas between clusters. Hybrid production technologies included intensified systems of land use in forested areas, including management of secondary succession to expand production of industrial tree crops, rather than simple expansion of slash-and-burn farming. In other words, forests were converted to other forests, rather than open farming areas, including banded forest features recognized in satellite images.

The Upper Xingu is a prime example of highly anthropogenic forest landscapes characterized by "intermediate disturbance." This refers to regions more heavily impacted than areas of extensive secondary succession described for twentieth-century indigenous groups (slash-and-burn), but less than the primary succession related to mechanized agropastoral development and industrial urbanism.[38] Clear evidence of substantial human alteration of the landscape in prehistoric times is found in vegetation (patchiness resulting from differential succession) and anthrosols (ADE), as well as in the widespread distribution of archaeological remains in deposits currently forested over.[39] Past systems of semi-intensive land use, based on patchy land use and long-term rotational cycling, converting forest to forest overtime rather than permanently open agricultural areas, present viable alternatives to primary conversion or extensive slash-and-burn, both of which can substantially degrade forest cover when intensified.[40] Indeed, contemporary forest and wetland processes suggest that anthropogenic forests are more differentially impacted than nonfelled areas of forest, notably more susceptible to burning in their current long-abandoned state. But during the Pre-Columbian period of maximal land use and management, they were likely more resilient than never-felled forest areas due to human constructions that controlled water, fire, and other natural forces.

It is inferred that production landscapes were divided into three spatially and technologically distinctive subsystems, including (1) highly managed core areas, formed by hub site and largest walled satellites (roughly 50 km²), which included ADE farming, concentrated specialty species, fruit tree orchards, seasonally burned fields of grass, and scrub forest in mosaic parkland settings; (2) a "green belt" peripheral area of mosaic high forest and agricultural production, which may cover an additional 100 km²; and (3) large tracts of unfelled forest in areas at the edge of and between clusters, which served as working forest and forest preserves (more than 100 km²). This overall system of resource management promoted and maintained these forests, which were different in composition from natural forests, notably in terms of increased patchiness and species concentration.

This responds to arguments about past production systems that narrowly focus on certain food crops, notably maize and manioc, and agricultural limitations under typical slash-and-burn technology. In most agricultural systems, population growth results in more intensive regimes of shorter and shorter fallow periods, or technological innovations, but extensive slash-and-burn agriculture is only sustainable with very long fallow periods. In the Amazon, soil fertility management favors charcoal introduced for soil amelioration through slash-and-char of aboveground biomass, rather than conversion to carbon dioxide through burning (slash-and-burn).[41] Robert Carneiro describes Kuikuro practices that include elements of both semi-intensive slash-and-char and extensive slash-and-burn (more common in recent times in mature forest with metal and motorized tools).[42] He suggested that expanding basic technology, applied uniformly across more extensive production landscapes, could yield manioc to support settlements of up to 2,000 persons. This predicts simple falloff in use as one moves away from individual settlements, identical to patterns typical of recent villages, which he suggested would be apparent in charcoal in soils.[43] However, this does not factor in known site densities and hierarchical multicentric organization, nor in the management of resources other than food crops.

The alternative is that Pre-Columbian production landscapes were composed of hybrid systems, including semi-intensive resource management within distinctive concentric zones. This predicts more standardized land-management strategies, roughly defined by enduring settlement and road networks which intensified both food and industrial crop production in specific zones. While soil fertility management for food crops was critically important in past production systems, other aspects of forest resource and land management may have been equally important, notably arboriculture of high-demand species, notably those associated with *egepe* soils. These include timber for house posts and low walls; agricultural fences and constructions in Pre-Columbian towns; saplings of small-leaved *pindaíba* (*Xylopia brasiliensis* spp.), used almost exclusively today for house beams (40–50 per house); and several bast trees (Figures 9.12 and 9.13). Buriti palm (*Mauritia flexuosa*), an important industrial crop with fruits that provide abundant fish food in managed ponds, was also potentially managed in wetland areas to a greater degree than today, although still highly abundant, particularly in areas of Pre-Columbian sites.

FIGURE 9.12

a) House structure prior to thatching, with central posts, side posts, and vertical and horizontal beams, typically made using from *pindaíba* (*Xylopia brasiliensis*) sapling and young trees; b) nearly completed house during final thatching stage, using *sapé* grass (*Imperata*) that is harvested in abandoned garden areas; c) wooden sacred idols made for Kwryp represent recently deceased chiefs in front of ceremonial flute house, *kuakutu*; and d) burning of garden areas in village peripheral areas sometimes poses danger to houses. Projecto Projeto Etnoarqueológico Kuikuro (AIKAX).

Pre-Columbian land use was not primarily aimed at long-term conversion of forests to open farmland, except in very restricted core areas. Instead it typically converted forested areas into diverse types of anthropogenic forest within an integrated production system, including managed forest and wetlands, which promoted forest integrity. Specific areas of forest production were expanded, such as wetland extraction of buriti palms, secondary forest management, and strip forest management, in part to meet the structural requirements of perishable architecture, but these practices maintained or even

FIGURE 9.13

a) Block excavation of Pre-Columbian house at X6, showing darkened area associated with central hearth areas in lower center, estimated to be about 250 m², also the average of contemporary Kuikuro houses; b) excavation of hearth area by Kuikuro participants; c) exposed ceramic griddle support (*undagi*) and fragments of manioc cooking pot (*ahukugu*) in central hearth area; and d) house structure in Kuikuro village that burned in 2005. Projeto Etnoarqueológico Kuikuro (AIKAX).

expanded forest cover. The long-term effect was increased patchiness, including artificially high proportions of certain species, but without adversely affecting forest cover and biodiversity. This hypothesis is supported by preliminary palynology of a Xingu radiocarbon-dated lake-bottom piston core, which indicates that tree species dominated after approximately 4000–3500 BP, replacing dominant grasses in the mid-Holocene in the context of warmer and drier conditions.[44] These suggest that production systems included mechanisms that increased forest resilience, such as patch maintenance and connectivity in fire-adapted landscapes (Figure 9.14), which were in part an adaptation

a

b

c

d

FIGURE 9.14

Manioc gardens are planted across broad areas—which have internal divisions, including fences to deter animals and control burns—that define separate gardens of individual families. Fire is widely used by the Kuikuro to open grass area, new gardens, and other areas, but it can also pose serious threats to houses (note manioc from silos rescued in grain bags) as well as forest areas during dry periods, such as in the current warm and dry climate of the past decade, when large-scale forest burns have impacted thousands of hectares. Projeto Etnoarqueológico Kuikuro (AIKAX).

or preadaptation to the Medieval Warm Period, approximately 900–1300. Likewise, the complex systems of fisheries management or "fish farming" are also impacted by and even act as responses to drier climate and fire, as true today under current conditions of desiccation and fire vulnerability during the Medieval Warm Period (Figures 9.15 and 9.16).

This suggests that techno-economic systems, which supported large Pre-Columbian populations, not only altered forest conditions but also maintained or may have even expanded forest in the southern Amazon. Specifically, it is suggested that significant population growth and organizational change in approximately 1250–1650, as

a

b

c

FIGURE 9.15

a) Major fish weir across the Angahuku
River, named after the buriti palms
(*Mauritia flexuosa*) that line this and
other watercourses; b) conserved fishing
traps used in a similar fish weir along an
Ipatse stream during the wet season; and
c) woman fishing with a dunk-trap in
an artificially modified pond associated
with Pre-Columbian site X13 along an
Ipatse stream. Projeto Etnoarqueológico
Kuikuro (AIKAX).

a

b

FIGURE 9.16

a) Possible Pre-Columbian fish-farming complex at large Tafukuno Lake exposed by major forest fires in 2017; and b) close-up of larger pond area. Projeto Etnoarqueológico Kuikuro (AIKAX).

reflected in the size and integration of settlements, was not correlated with a simple conversion of forest to open farming land, but instead that forest was converted to increasingly managed forest. The Upper Xingu and other areas of the forested Amazon may thus represent slow conversion cycles of natural to working forests which, rather than outright denuding the landscape, effectively concentrated forest and wetland resources in some areas under regimes of intensive management while leaving other areas sparsely utilized, including buffer areas or ecological set-asides.

In the Upper Xingu, large and densely settled regional populations (estimated at 50,000 or more) and semi-intensive land use converted broad areas of the tropical forest ecosystem into managed forests, parklands, and mosaic agricultural countryside.[45] These areas reverted to forest following catastrophic depopulation from approximately 1600 to 1950, but a dramatic demographic rebound following vaccination programs[46] is rapidly converting forested landscapes in the Upper Xingu once again. This conclusion has obvious implications for how we conceive of biodiversity, including not only genetic and phenotypic variation but also functional variation within dynamic ecosystems and domesticated landscapes heavily influenced by human forces, commonly overlooked in conservation and sustainability studies in the region. It also represents a subtle bio-power in its early Amazonian form, which not only organizes human subjects but also nature, providing clues to maintaining the ecological resilience of these systems.

Discussion

In *Garden Cities of To-morrow* (1902), Ebenezer Howard laid out his utopian plan for a new and improved form of urbanism. It aimed to curb the pollution, social degradation, and alienation of humans from nature caused by crowding in cities through the careful design of traffic patterns and partitioning: the original "smart city."[47] Although formulaic—half blueprint, half ledger—the core design proposed an organic mix of centers of social and cultural activities, parks, plazas, and arcades, and concentric rings of residential, agricultural, and minor industry, bisected by radial segments, a forerunner of the urban ecology of the Chicago school. The innovation he envisioned was traffic, socioecological connectivity networks between people working and living together in systems that intermingled nature, production, and residence. At a certain moment, the imagined garden city would bud off to create new neighborhoods, new garden cities, to the north, south, east, and west, extending the bundle of social relations. But through careful planning and monitoring, his design was meant to distribute resources equitably and embrace social diversity.

Had he known of them, the ancestors of the contemporary Xingu nation might have merited a chapter: the prototypical garden cities of yesterday. The model was rooted in an ancient design, with elements of the tribalism still characteristic of medieval towns in temperate European forests, nodes in networks of lived space and forest that created patchiness across broad regions, as opposed to the classic model of urbanism based on a singular core or city, an agricultural periphery, and wilderness. As Jacques Le Goff noted of temperate Europe in medieval times: the Western forest civilizations were the "photographic negative" of the oasis civilizations in the Mediterranean and south-west Asia.[48] Preindustrial forest settings across the globe, in fact, only weakly fit the expectations of classical models. Notably, full-blown cities are the rarity, absent really in the Amazon, but might have also inspired alternative urbanisms, neither tribal nor civic, rural nor urban, but networked urbanism—more about planning and saturation than numbers, traffic patterns, and landscape, although numbers across the Americas were respectable for the medieval world. However, as true of other "revolutions," such as the transition to settled life or agriculture, which also does not conform to models of a "Neolithic Revolution,"[49] urbanism, urbanization, and the impulse toward aggregation, integration, and planning in the Amazon remained a kind of absolute "other" to Western historical experience: urbanism without cities.

A growing number of cases from tropical regions document alternative forms of highly complex and heterogeneous human landscapes. Multicentric networks of towns, villages, and garden cities seems as likely a label as any, particularly in the Amazon. More than a label, it also provokes dialogue or even a conceptual "bombshell," the alter ego of city-based urbanism, or urban society, as known in the classical world. The garden city, or galactic urbanism, doesn't imply everything that cities and urban society are not. It is not an initial form on its way to full-scale urbanism, nor are city-based and galactic urbanism mutually exclusive, as Howard recognized clearly. There is also the ability of indigenous forms of knowledge to inform Western science. Theirs is a science of the concrete, ours of models and theorems. Codiscovery helps to define the hybrids, their knowledge and ours, not to set it down as the Amazonian variant of what elsewhere might be called urbanization, or at least urban planning.

The garden city model may be more appropriate to describe more diffuse but no less multifaceted or multilayered urbanism. In terms of regional planning and integration, or socioecological connectivity, the Amazonian examples rival many small- to medium-sized preindustrial urban societies. Why not, as Howard suggested, have ten towns of 3,000, rather than a city of 30,000 people (or 300,000), partitioning them into habitation nodes and districts that fold within them nature and agricultural production, diffuse population and industry, nested hierarchies of living space, country-side, and wilderness, connecting things up, within towns, districts, urban clusters, and regions. This confounds the definition of "urban" based on monumental architecture and socioeconomic distinction, everything from city to village society, mechanical and organic solidarity, and in its place a connected network of communication or public areas.

The regional planning and socioecological connectivity of Pre-Columbian Xinguano polities represent remarkable achievements, as impressive as other world areas in 1492. Xingu towns were fairly small in terms of settlement size, 50 ha in the largest cases. However, these were not independent communities, but part of a network of places, oriented in a precise grid, and should be considered as units. It is this that defines the garden city; it is hierarchical, diarchic, and heterarchical all at once. There were over 100 ha of residential areas within walled towns (some over 150 ha), with the core area between them about 50 km², about half the size of Howard's model garden city, within an overall sustaining area of about 400 km², with numerous satellite villages, often in between clusters. In short, this settlement pattern can be fruitfully considered as a unique Amazonian form of incipient or early urbanism, specifically in terms of the overall manipulation of the landscape or urban ecology. The galactic settlement pattern, unique to the period 1250–1650, creates a lattice- or gridlike distribution across broader landscapes, which over the past millennia has become a basic conditioning aspect of ecology in this area, affecting all levels of biodiversity.

The Xingu case documents regional population sizes and intervention in the natural environment rivaling examples of preindustrial urbanism worldwide, particularly examples from major forested regions. These remarkably flat and convoluted urban settings created an ever-expanding latticework of dwelling places, with concentric zones around them radiating deep into forestland, including working forests, channelized and ponded wetlands, and straight, wide roads, which seem to connect everything with everything else. Whatever we call them, the recognition of complex coupled human-environmental systems, rivaling other world areas in terms of regional population densities and impacts on the natural environment, informs contemporary debate on climate change, conservation, and development; the pride of place of descendant Native American peoples; and their place in contemporary dialogues.

The archaeological consensus that much of the Amazon's tropical forests are anthropogenic refutes the centuries-old trope of tropical primitivity, or "tropicality,"[50] although this image is still widely accepted by natural scientists, policy makers, and the popular media. The idea of Xingu "garden cities," therefore, responds to recent debate over anthropogenic influences in Amazonia. It counters the still widespread assumption among many scientists, and in the popular media, that sparse populations dominated the broad region, with a few enclaves of settled peoples, notably—as argued by most scholars over the past five decades—the floodplain region.[51] In other words, most of the region was considered "terra nullius" and is, therefore, open to development or conservation today as outsiders see fit. The Xingu case adds to a growing body of evidence that Pre-Columbian complex societies inhabited diverse areas of Amazonia and had dramatic impacts on local and regional biodiversity. The same was true for western portions of the southern transitional forests, in eastern Bolivia and adjacent Brazil, and likely the whole southern forest fringe.

This informs questions of maintenance and restoration of tropical forests, particularly in transitional areas sensitive to climate change.[52] It informs us about how large, settled populations dealt with changing climates in the past, notably the warmer and drier climates during the late Medieval Warm Period in South America.[53] Notably, the patchy anthropogenic forests created by late Pre-Columbian societies may have been adaptive responses to a warmer climate from approximately 900 to 1300,[54] and could reveal important alternative strategies of sustainable land use that inform practices and even policy in the face of climate change in the region today. The fires that have ravaged many forest areas in recent years, for instance, may well have been a major cause of the constructions in the past. Fire was and is today the principal technology of land use and resource management, and the well-maintained roads, ditches, and partitioning of production, forest, and wetland areas served for fire control. These communities developed means to support fairly large regional populations through forest and wetland technologies that worked with the natural environment, not against it. Indigenous resource management strategies hold important clues not only to understanding the past, but also to creating alternative approaches to sustainable regional development.

Suddenly, some of the best solutions for "saving" the Amazon are provided by its indigenous peoples, particularly semi-intensive resource management and adaptive responses developed by Pre-Columbian groups. The "old ways" may hold answers, alternative homegrown solutions, to future problems as local populations grow and efforts increase to maintain or restore forests, bringing us again to the garden cities of tomorrow, rather than yesterday. This is a potentially vital resource for future land use and resource management in the Upper Xingu and other indigenous areas (20 percent of the Brazilian Amazon), particularly in similar areas of semi-intensive management in the southern Amazon as the region is increasingly vulnerable to new drivers of change (for example, climate change and infrastructure development) and to external pressure for natural resources.

The present case emphasizes interdisciplinary and intercultural interactions as a central part of research design and aims to develop mutually intelligible and dialogic participatory methods to promote coproduction of knowledge and novel research directions and synergies. This requires expanding or even exploding many common themes derived from Western historical experience and knowledge production. In the world of contemporary research, knowledge production with indigenous peoples involves understanding non-Western views regarding diverse others, among them scientists, and creating hybrid problem-and-solution-based learning strategies, itself a process of familiarization and productive consumption.[55] These are not only "types," sociohistorical varieties, but "bombs," incendiary devices that use radical difference as a counter-political move mobilizing culture, national identity, and "others" to combat the normative views that not only dominate reconstructions of past human achievements but also, as often as not, aim to extinguish or dampen the cultural life force of subaltern peoples who fall outside the mainstream of Western historical experience.[56]

Through training and coparticipation in research, the tools and technologies for understanding change in human-natural systems in the Amazon will be placed in the hands of indigenous peoples themselves. At the very least, it is something that they—indigenous peoples—can understand and build upon, in what Paulo Freire aptly calls a "pedagogy of hope,"[57] creating knowledge hybrids uniquely suited to the changes they currently face. Indeed, it is in this area—strategic alliances among scientists, conservationists, and local populations—that studies of the Amazonian past have pride of place, drawing our attention to the value of the past as a model for the future. In short, rather than environmental hot spots of biodiversity, scientists, as well as policy makers and the broader public, should focus on socioecological "hope spots,"[58] not only recognizing that Amazonian landscapes are as cultural as elsewhere in other forested areas of the preindustrial world, but that indigenous technological achievements, still practiced in attenuated form by descendant populations in the postindustrial world, inform us as much about the future as they do about the past.

Acknowledgments

Research on the archaeology and indigenous history of the Upper Xingu, initiated by the author in 1992, has been sponsored in Brazil by the Museu Nacional, Universidade Federal do Rio de Janeiro (UFRJ), Museu Antropológico, Universidade Federal de Goiás, and Museu Paraense Emílio Goeldi. All have been critical in the formulation of the ideas presented here and are warmly acknowledged. The research has been supported by National Science Foundation Archaeology regular grants (BCS 0004487, BCS 0353129, BCS 1660459), and synergistic activities and community-based projects have been supported through multiple grants since 1992 by the William Talbott Hillman Foundation. Drs. Bruna Franchetto (UFRJ), Carlos Fausto (UFRJ), and Eduardo Góes Neves (Universidade de São Paulo), in particular, have contributed substantially to the interdisciplinary Projeto Etnoarqueológico Kuikuro over the past two decades, conducted in collaboration with the Associação Indígena Kuikuro do Alto Xingu (AIKAX). The Kuikuro community, particularly Chief Afukaka Kuikuro and his family, are especially thanked.

Notes

1   Ulf Hannerz, "City," in *Encyclopedia of Social Sciences*, ed. Adam Kuper and Jessica Kuper (Cambridge, Cambridge University Press, 1996), 86.

2   Mogens Herman Hansen, *Polis: An Introduction to the Ancient Greek City-State* (Oxford: Oxford University Press, 2006).

3   Adriana Von Hagen and Chris Morris, *The Cities of the Ancient Andes* (London: Thames and Hudson, 1998).

4   Gary Feinman and Joyce Marcus, eds., *Archaic States* (Santa Fe: School of American Research Press, 1998); and Kent Flannery, "Childe the Evolutionist: A Perspective from Nuclear America," in *The Archaeology of V. Gordon Childe*, ed. David Harris (Chicago: University of Chicago Press, 1994), 101–20.

5   Hannerz, "City," 86.

6   Clifford Geertz, *Negara: The Theatre State in Nineteenth-Century Bali* (Princeton: Princeton University Press, 1980).

7   Aiden Southall, "The Segmentary State and the Ritual Phase of Political Economy," in *Beyond Chiefdoms: Pathways to Complexity in Africa*, ed. Susan Keech McIntosh (Cambridge: Cambridge University Press, 1999), 31–38.

8   Stanley Tambiah, *Culture, Thought, and Social Action: An Anthropological Perspective* (Cambridge, Mass.: Harvard University Press, 1985).

9   Arthur Demarest and Gregory Conrad, eds., *Ideology and Pre-Columbian Civilization* (Santa Fe: School of American Research Press, 1992); George Lau, *Ancient Alterity in the Andes: A Recognition of Others* (New York: Routledge, 2012); Jerry Moore, *Cultural Landscapes in the Ancient Andes: Archaeologies of Place* (Gainesville: University Press of Florida, 2005); and Prudence Rice, *Maya Political Science: Time, Astronomy, and the Cosmos* (Austin: University of Texas Press, 2004).

10 Michael Dietler and Brian Hayden, *Feasts: Archaeological and Ethnographic Perspectives on Food, Politics, and Power* (Washington, D.C.: Smithsonian, 2001).

11 Julian Steward and Louis Faron, *Native Peoples of South America* (New York: McGraw Hill 1959), 2.

12 Kalervo Oberg, "Types of Social Structure among the Lowland Tribes of South and Central América," *American Anthropologist* 57 (1955):472–87.

13 Timothy Pauketat, *Chiefdoms and Other Archaeological Delusions* (Lanham, Md.: Altamira Press, 2007).

14 Moore, *Cultural Landscapes in the Ancient Andes*.

15 Henri Lefebvre, *Toward an Architecture of Enjoyment* (Minneapolis: University of Minnesota Press, 2014), 143.

16 Roderick McIntosh, *Ancient Middle Niger: Urbanism and the Self-Organizing Landscape* (Cambridge: Cambridge University Press, 2005).

17 Carole L. Crumley, "Historical Ecology: A Multidimensional Ecological Orientation," in *Historical Ecology: Cultural Knowledge and Changing Landscapes*, ed. Carole L. Crumley (Santa Fe: School of American Research Press, 1994), 1–16.

18 Gregory Possehl, "Sociocultural Complexity without the State: The Indus Civilization," in Feinman and Marcus, *Archaic States*, 261–92.

19 George L. Cowgill, "Origins and Development of Urbanism: Archaeological Perspectives," *Annual Review of Anthropology* 33 (2004):525–49; and Norman Yoffee, *Myths of the Archaic State: Evolution of the Earliest Cities, States, and Civilizations* (Cambridge: Cambridge University Press, 2005).

20 Erik Andersson, "Urban Landscapes and Sustainable Cities," *Ecology and Society* 11 (2006):34.

21 For example, Charles R. Clement, William Denevan, Michael Heckenberger, André Braga Junqueira, Eduardo G. Neves, Wenceslau G. Teixeira, and William Woods, "The Domestication of Amazonia before European Conquest," *Proceedings of the Royal Society B* 282, no. 1812 (2015), https://doi.org/10.1098/rspb.2015.0813; William Denevan, *Cultivated Landscapes of Native Amazonia and the Andes* (Oxford: Oxford University Press, 2001); Clark Erickson, "The Domesticated Landscapes of the Bolivian Amazon," in *Time and Complexity in Historical Ecology: Studies in the Neotropical Lowlands*, ed. William Balée and Clark L. Erickson (New York: Columbia University Press, 2006), 235–78; Michael Heckenberger and Eduardo Neves, "Amazonian Archaeology," *Annual Review of*

Anthropology 38 (2009):251–66; Heiko Prümers, ed., *Loma Mendoza: Las excavaciones de los años 1999–2002* (La Paz: Plural Editores, 2015); Martti Pärssinen, Denise Schaan, and Alceu Ranzi, "Pre-Columbian Geometric Earthworks in the Upper Purús: A Complex Society in Western Amazonia," *Antiquity* 83 (2009):1084–95; Anna Roosevelt, "The Development of Prehistoric Complex Societies: Amazonia, a Tropical Forest," in "Complex Polities in the Ancient Tropical World," ed. Elisabeth A. Bacus and Lisa J. Lucero, special issue, *Archaeological Papers of the American Anthropological Association* 9, no. 1 (January 1999):13–33; Stephen Rostain, *Islands in the Rainforest: Landscape Management in Pre-Columbian Amazonia* (Walnut Creek, Calif.: Left Coast Press, 2012); Denise Schaan, *Sacred Landscapes of Ancient Amazonia: Historical Ecology of Social Complexity* (Walnut Creek, Calif.: Left Coast Press, 2011); John Walker, *Agricultural Change in the Bolivian Amazon* (Pittsburgh: University of Pittsburgh, 2004); and John Walker, "Regional Associations and Ceramic Assemblages in the 14th Century AD Mamoré Basin," *Andean Past* 10 (2012):241–61.

22 William Denevan, *The Aboriginal Cultural Geography of the Llanos de Mojos of Bolivia*, Ibero-Americana 80 (Berkeley: University of California Press, 1996).

23 Jonas de Souza Gregorio, Denise Pahl Schaan, Mark Robinson, Antonia Demasceno Barbosa, Luiz E. O. C. Aragão, Ben Hur Marimon Jr., Beatriz Schwantes Marimon, Izaias Brasil da Silva, Salman Saeed Khan, Francisco Ruji Nakahara, and José Iriarte, "Pre-Columbian Earth-Builders Settled along the Entire Southern Rim of the Amazon," *Nature Communications* 9, no. 1125 (2018), https://www.nature.com/articles/s41467-018-03510-7; Michael Heckenberger, *The Ecology of Power: Culture, Place, and Personhood in the Southern Amazon, A.D. 1000–2000* (New York: Routledge, 2005); and Heckenberger and Neves, "Amazonian Archaeology."

24 Author's translation of Antônio Pires de Campos, "Breve Notícia que Dá o Capitão Antonio Pires de Campos do Gentio que Há na Derrota da Viagem das Minas de Cuyaba e Seu Recôncavo," *Revista trimestral do Instituto Histórico, Geográfico e Ethnográfico do Brasil* 5 ([1720]1862):443–44.

25 Michael Heckenberger, J. Christian Russell, Carlos Fausto, Joshua R. Toney, Morgan J. Schmidt, Edithe Pereira, Bruna Franchetto, and Afukaka Kuikuro, "Pre-Columbian Urbanism, Anthropogenic Landscapes, and the Future of the Amazon," *Science* 321 (2008):1214–17.

26 Heckenberger, *Ecology of Power*.

27 Michael Heckenberger, "Mapping Indigenous Histories: Cultural Heritage, Collaboration, and Conservation in the Amazon," *Collaborative Anthropology* 2 (2009):17–23.

28 Morgan Schmidt, "Reconstructing Tropical Nature: Prehistoric and Modern Anthrosols (Terra Preta) in the Amazon Rainforest, Upper Xingu River, Brazil" (PhD diss., University of Florida, 2010).

29 Schmidt, "Reconstructing Tropical Nature"; and Joshua Toney, "The Product of Labor: Pottery Technology in the Upper Xingu, Southern Amazon, Brazil, A.D. 800–1800" (PhD diss., University of Florida, 2012).

30 Schmidt, "Reconstructing Tropical Nature"; and Toney, "Product of Labor."

31 Toney, "Product of Labor."

32 Schmidt, "Reconstructing Tropical Nature."

33 Bruna Franchetto and Michael Heckenberger, eds., *Os Povos do Alto Xingu: História e Cultura* (Rio de Janeiro: Editora UFRJ, 2001); Bruna Franchetto, ed., *O Alto Xingu: Uma Sociedade Multi-lingue* (Rio de Janeiro: Museu Nacional, 2011); and Heckenberger, *Ecology of Power*.

34 Bruna Franchetto, "Falar Kuikuro: Um Estudo Ethnoliguistica" (PhD diss., Museu Nacional, Universidade Federal do Rio de Janeiro, 1987); and Heckenberger, *Ecology of Power*.

35 John Browder and Brian Godfrey, *Rainforest Cities: Urbanization, Development, and Globalization of the Brazilian Amazon* (New York: Columbia University Press, 1997).

36 Robert Carneiro, "The Knowledge and Use of Rain Forest Trees by the Kuikuru Indians of Central Brazil," in *The Nature and Status of Ethnobotany*, ed. Richard I. Ford (Ann Arbor: Museum of Anthropology, University of Michigan, 1978), 201–6; and Robert Carneiro, "The Cultivation of Manioc among the Kuikuru Indians of the Upper Xingu," in *Adaptive Responses in Native Amazonians*, ed. Raymond B. Hames and William T. Vickers (New York: Academic Press, 1983), 65–111.

37 Heckenberger, *Ecology of Power*; Schmidt, "Reconstructing Tropical Nature"; and Toney, "Product of Labor."

38 William Balée, "The Research Program of Historical Ecology," *Annual Review of Anthropology* 35 (2006):75–98; Denevan, *Cultivated Landscapes of Native Amazonia and the Andes*; and William Balée, *Cultural Forests of the Amazon: The Historical Ecology of People and Their Landscapes* (Tuscaloosa: University of Alabama Press, 2013).

39 For example, William Woods, Wenceslau G. Teixeira, J. Lehmann, C. Steiner, A. M. G. A. WinklerPrins, and L. Rebellato, eds., *Amazonian Dark Earths: Wim Sombroek's Vision* (New York: Springer, 2009).

40 William F. Laurance, Mark A. Cochrane, Scott Berger, Phillip M. Fearnside, Patricia Delamônica, Christopher Barber, Sammya D'Angelo, and Tito Fernandes, "The Future of the Brazilian Amazon," *Science* 291, no. 5503 (2001):438–39.

41 Christoph Steiner, "Slash and Char as Alternative to Slash and Burn: Soil Charcoal Amendments Maintain Soil Fertility and Establish a Carbon Sink" (PhD diss., Universität Bayreuth, 2006); and Woods et al., *Amazonian Dark Earths*.

42 Carneiro, "Cultivation of Manioc among the Kuikuru Indians of the Upper Xingu."

43 Also see Crystal McMichael, Dolores Piperno, Mark Bush, Miles R. Silman, Andrew R. Zimmerman, Marco F. Raczka, and Luiz C. Lobato, "Sparse Pre-Columbian Human Habitation in the Western Amazon," *Science* 336 (2012):1429–31.

44 Paulo Oliveira, personal communication, 2007.

45 Heckenberger et al., "Pre-Columbian Urbanism."

46 Introduced after 1954, a measles epidemic reduced the indigenous population by 25 percent to approximately 500 persons.

47 Ebenezer Howard, *Garden Cities of To-morrow* (1902; reprint, Boston: MIT Press, 1965).

48 Jacques Le Goff, *Medieval Civilization, 400–1500* (Oxford: Blackwell, 1988).

49 Eduardo Neves, "Não Existe Neolítico ao Sul do Equador: As Primeiras Cerâmicas e Sua Falta de Relação com Agricultura," in *Novos Olhares sobre as Cerâmicas Arqueológicas da Amazônia*, ed. Cristiana Barreto, Helena Pinto Lima, and Carla Jaimes Betancourt (Belém: IPHAN, Ministério da Cultura, 2016), 32–39; and Eduardo G. Neves and Michael J. Heckenberger, "The Call of the Wild: Rethinking Food Production in Ancient Amazonia," *Annual Review of Anthropology* 48 (2019):371–88, http://doi.org/10.1146/annurev-anthro-102218-011057.

50 For example, Susanna Hecht, *The Scramble for the Amazon and the "Lost Paradise" of Euclides da Cunha* (Chicago: University of Chicago Press, 2013); and Hugh Raffles, *In Amazonia: A Natural History* (Princeton: Princeton University Press, 2002).

51 For example, Mark B. Bush, Crystal H. McMichael, Dolores R. Piperno, Miles R. Silman, Jos Barlow, Carlos A. Peres, Mitchell Power, and Michael W. Palace, "Anthropogenic Influence on Amazonian Forests in Pre-History: An Ecological Perspective," *Journal of Biogeography* 42, no. 12 (2015), http://dx.doi.org/10.1111/jbi.12638; McMichael et al., "Sparse Pre-Columbian Human Habitation in the Western Amazon"; and Dolores Piperno, Crystal McMichael, and Mark Bush, "Amazonia and the Anthropocene: What Was the Spatial Extent and Intensity of Human Landscape Modification in the Amazon Basin at the End of Prehistory?," *Holocene* 25 (2015):1588–97.

52 David Lamb, Peter Erksine, and John Parrotta, "Restoration of Degraded Tropical Forest Landscapes," *Science* 310 (2005):1628–32; Marcia N. Macedo, Michael T. Coe, Ruth DeFries, Maria Uriarte, Paulo M. Brando, Christopher Neill, and Wayne S. Walker, "Land Use-Driven Stream Warming in Southeastern Amazonia," *Philosophical Transactions of the Royal Society B: Biological Sciences* 368 (2013), https://doi.org/10.1098/rstb.2012.0153; Daniel Nepstad, Stephen Schwartzman, B. Bamberger, M. Santilli, D. Ray, P. Schlesinger, P. Lefevbre, A. Alencar, E. Prinz, Greg Fiske, and Alicia Rolla, "Inhibition of Amazon Deforestation and Fire by Parks and Indigenous Lands," *Conservation Biology* 20 (2006):65–73; and A. Carla Staver, Sally Archibald, and Simon Levin, "The Global Extent and Determinants of Savanna and Forest as Alternative Biome States," *Science* 334 (2009):230–32.

53 Yair Rosenthal, Braddock Linsley, and Delia Oppo, "Pacific Ocean Heat Content during the Past 10,000 Years," *Science* 342 (2013):617–21; M. Vuille, S. J. Burns, B. L. Taylor, F. W. Cruz, B. W. Bird, M. B. Abbott, L. C. Kanner, H. Cheng, and V. F. Novello, "A Review of the South American Monsoon History as Recorded in Stable Isotopic Proxies over the Past Two Millennia," *Climate of the Past* 8 (2012):1309–21; and Luiz Carlos Ruiz Pessenda, Paulo Eduardo De Oliveira, Milene Mofatto, Vanda

Brito de Medeiros, Ricardo José Francischetti Garcia, Ramon Aravena, José Albertino Bendassoli, Acácio Zuniga Leite, Antonio Roberto Saad, and Mario Lincoln Etchebehere, "The Evolution of a Tropical Rainforest/Grassland Mosaic in Southeastern Brazil since 28,000 ^{14}C yr BP Based on Carbon Isotopes and Pollen Records," *Quaternary Research* 71, no. 3 (May 2009):437–52.

54 John Carson, Bronwen Whitney, Francis Mayle, José Iriarte, Heiko Prümers, J. Daniel Soto, and Jennifer Watling, "Environmental Impact of Geometric Earthwork Construction in Pre-Columbian Amazonia," *Proceedings of the National Academy of Sciences of the United States of America* 111 (2014):10497–502; John Carson, Jennifer Watling, Francis Mayle, Bronwen Whitney, José Iriarte, Heiko Prümers, and J. Daniel Soto, "Pre-Columbian Land Use in the Ring-Ditch Region of the Bolivian Amazon," *Holocene* 25 (2015):1285–1300; and Robert Dull, Richard Nevle, William Woods, Dennis Bird, Shiri Avnery, and William Denevan, "The Columbian Encounter and the Little Ice Age: Abrupt Land Use Change, Fire, and Greenhouse Forcing," *Annals of the Association of American Geographers* 100, no. 4 (2010):755–71.

55 Carlos Fausto, *Warfare and Shamanism in Amazonia* (Cambridge: Cambridge University Press, 2012); and Bruno Latour, "From the World of Science to the World of Research," *Science* 280 (1998):208.

56 Philippe Descola, *Beyond Nature and Culture* (Chicago: University of Chicago Press, 2013); Bruno Latour, "Perspectivism: 'Type' or 'Bomb'?," *Anthropology Today* 25, no. 2 (April 2009):1–2; and Eduardo Viveiros de Castro, *The Relative Native: Essays on Indigenous Conceptual Worlds* (Chicago: University of Chicago Press, 2015).

57 Paulo Freire, *The Pedagogy of Hope: Reliving Pedagogy of the Oppressed* (New York: Continuum Publishing, 1994).

58 Brett Garling, "Hope Spots: An Actionable Plan to Save the Oceans," *National Geographic*, June 8, 2016, https://blog.nationalgeographic.org/2016/06/08/hope-spots-an-actionable-plan-to-save-the-ocean/.

"when the King breaks a town he builds another"

Politics, Slavery, and Constructed
Urban Landscapes in Tropical West Africa

J. CAMERON MONROE

OR MUCH OF THE TWENTIETH CENTURY, HISTORIANS AND ARCHAE-
ologists viewed sub-Saharan Africa as a region lacking a deeply rooted urban
history, and the impressive scale of many precolonial African towns was interpreted
as the product of intrusive Islamic or European influences.[1] Following Africa's independence era, a generation of archaeologists, working in diverse regions across the
continent, sought to reveal the local origins and deep histories of many of Africa's urban
communities.[2] Painstaking archaeological research revealed ancient urban traditions
across the continent, ushering in a veritable golden age in the study of African cities
(Figure 10.1).[3] In West Africa, much of this research targeted medieval trading centers
and regional capitals in the Sahelian zone, sites that were articulated into trans-Saharan
trading networks in the late first and early second millennia CE. In tropical West Africa
to the south, historical and archaeological research in Ghana and Nigeria revealed
expansive cities that emerged at the same time as these Sahelian trading centers to
the north. Archaeological evidence from communities such as Ile-Ife, Benin City, and
others attested to the deep local roots of urbanism in the forest zone, suggesting that
long-distance forces also may have stimulated their growth and evolution over time.

Although this research went far in putting West African cities on the map, later critiques highlighted the overemphasis on cities and city walls, and the lack of attention
paid toward the broader constellation of settlements into which they were situated.[4]
Additionally, others have noted the difficulty in applying this model in the forest zone,
where site visibility inhibits the adoption of a regional approach.[5] In this essay, I explore
how survey methodologies designed to infer settlement in such contexts may help to
illuminate the nature of urban landscape structure and origins, casting valuable new

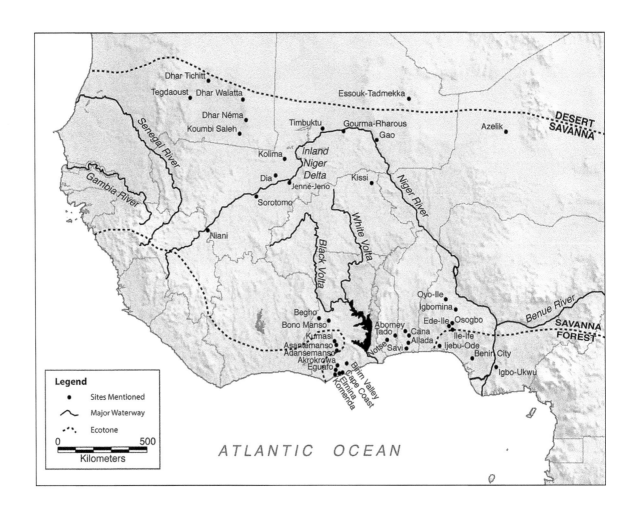

FIGURE 10.1

Map of West Africa
identifying key
archaeological sites,
geographical features,
and environmental
zones. Drawing by
J. Cameron Monroe.

light on the forces encouraging the rise of urbanism across the region. In the first half of the essay, I explore how archaeologists have conceptualized urban landscapes in West Africa, highlighting the complex interplay between local and long-distance forces in shaping urban trajectories, and emphasizing certain issues that have constrained the archaeological visibility of cities in more forested zones. In the second half of the essay, I outline recent regionally oriented archaeological research in Southern Bénin, which focuses on tracing broader settlement landscapes in the era of the transatlantic slave trade. Drawing on research I have conducted at Cana, an urban center of the precolonial Kingdom of Dahomey, I trace how long-distance forces created a unique political climate which impacted the overall character of urban landscapes dramatically. I highlight how urban-rural dynamics, in this context, was driven by elite political agendas, fueled in large part by the transatlantic slave trade.

Seeing the City in West Africa

For much of the twentieth century, external Middle Eastern and European forces provided ready explanations for the emergence of cities across sub-Saharan Africa.[6]

264   J. CAMERON MONROE

Justification for this idea lay in the fact that many African settlements did not fit early models of the city, defined in terms of a series of specific traits: large and nucleated populations, monumental architecture, and a literate class that fostered religion, the arts, and government.[7] Urbanism, so defined, became a hallmark of civilization, intrinsically associated with the emergence of the state. African communities that did not evince all of these requisites of urbanism were viewed as merely extensions of an undifferentiated rural countryside rooted in a peasant mode of production.[8] However, evidence for urban civilization in Africa, classically defined, was forthcoming in many areas. When encountered, it was attributed to a bewildering variety of migrations and influences from the outside world,[9] an argument that supported the imperialist logic of European colonial enterprises in Africa.[10]

In West Africa, specifically, evidence for the emergence of cities in the context of expanding Islamic and European world systems was readily available, and arguments for exogenous stimulus were embraced wholeheartedly.[11] Muslim chroniclers left clear historical evidence for networks of expansive cities and states that flourished across the savanna regions during the early second millenium CE.[12] Early excavations in these cities produced Middle Eastern trade goods and evidence for Islamic religious practices. Many concluded that such cities were the product of enterprising colonists from elsewhere.[13] Similar arguments were posed for West African cities encountered during the Atlantic Era.[14] Presumed the product of outside influences, West African cities stood divorced from indigenous cultural traditions.

Despite the tenacious grip this model has held on our understanding of the sub-Saharan African past, archaeological research has done much to dispel myths of cityless Africa in the precolonial era.[15] The decades following independence, in particular, witnessed a sea change in the way scholars approached urbanism. On the one hand, a proliferation of archaeological surveys and excavations at precolonial sites provided new, and early, chronologies for major cities and towns, demonstrating their undeniably indigenous roots.[16] Archaeologists thus rejected diffusionist arguments that precolonial urban communities arose as the lonely outposts of foreign settlers. Additionally, scholars began to appreciate the significant diversity of examples on the African continent as a whole, and in West Africa in particular.[17]

Importantly, scholars began to call for a more systematic approach to understanding African cities.[18] African archaeology has long been dominated by an overtly historical approach to the study of early cities that sought to verify or reject chronologies and descriptions of towns derived from the documentary record.[19] Since the 1980s, however, archaeologists working across the continent have explored a wider range of case studies, more closely engaging broader archaeological debates on the nature of urbanism and social complexity, and experimenting with systematic research methods focused on the regional nature of urban traditions.[20]

Research conducted in a tradition of intensive regional survey, specifically, has encouraged Africanists to see beyond trait list approaches in favor of a *functional* definition of the city, providing a new theoretical tool kit with which to examine the origins and nature of cities across the continent.[21] According to this model, urban communities were differentiated from, but closely integrated with, their rural hinterlands, emerging through intertwined processes involving settlement population growth, economic specialization, and regional integration.[22] *Urbanism* is thus intimately tied to *ruralism*,[23] twin processes wherein emerging population centers provide specialized services to a broader hinterland.[24] The study of urbanism thereby turned its attention from the analysis of cities themselves to the study of the regional settlement systems. The functional model has rapidly transformed our understanding of the emergence of urban centers across sub-Saharan Africa.[25] Indeed, research on precolonial urbanism in the last few decades has revealed the complex ties between African towns and their rural hinterlands across the continent, demonstrating that African communities began to pass the "urban threshold" long before Islamic or European influence became a factor.[26]

In the Western Sudan, regionally oriented archaeology has proven particularly powerful in exploring the rise of cities and protocities in the absence of the state. Archaeological survey in the Dhar Tichitt region of Mauritania reveals the presence of complex settlement hierarchy as early as the second millennium BCE, yet one bearing precious little evidence for social status differentiation or inequality of any kind.[27] Systematic survey around the sites of Jenné-Jeno, Dia, and Timbuktu, furthermore, has revealed clustered settlement mounds that suggest an urban tradition engaged in interregional trade as early as the mid-first millennium CE (Figure 10.2).[28] This tradition bears all the hallmarks of a network of regional capitals emerging through intensifying urban-rural dynamics largely in the absence of significant long-distance trade. Research in the Inland Niger Delta and adjacent regions, however, has fundamentally shifted our paradigmatic assumptions about the origins and nature of such communities, revealing *heterarchical* forms of social organization that resisted centralized authority for centuries.[29] Here, decentralized economies underwrote a social structure that resisted centralization for a millennium, possibly as an adaptation to severe environmental unpredictability.[30] The origins of West African urban communities have been pushed back significantly by regionally oriented research, providing alternative perspectives on the origins and nature of urbanism in the centuries prior to the advent of Islam into the Sudan. Notably, however, this regional system was ultimately upset substantially by the influx of trans-Saharan commerce, resulting in the abandonment of many sites, and the expansion of trading entrepôts and imperial capitals that would serve as important nodes in long-distance trade.

Whereas the origins of cities in the Western Sudan have a much deeper history than once appreciated, research at medieval town sites has identified clear evidence for the impact of long-distance factors on regional urban systems. Research in the Sahara and on its fringes, for example, has revealed multiple trading entrepôts in which urban settlement organization and social life was dominated by the shifting tides of long-distance economic forces.[31] Excavation at sites such as Tegdaoust, Essouk-Tadmakka, and Koumbi Saleh suggests that such sites originated as the ephemeral settlements of nomadic Berbers in the first millennium CE. By the early second millennium CE, they had transformed into major towns serving almost entirely as nodes in long-distance exchange networks, linking the savanna with the broader medieval North African and Near Eastern worlds. Yet these were fragile experiments in urbanism. Indeed, as trade

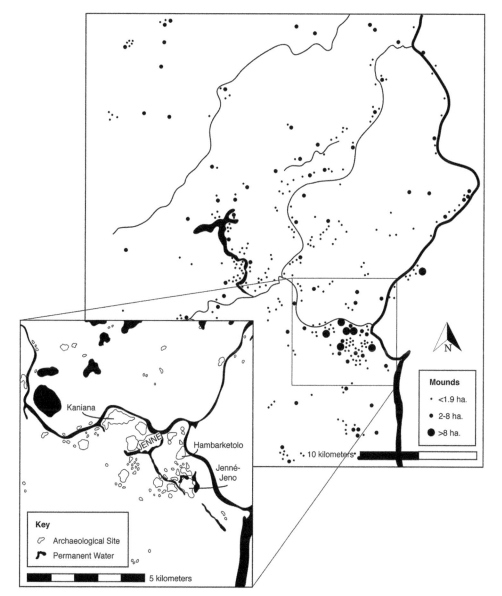

FIGURE 10.2

Map of the urban core and hinterland survey results at Jenné-Jeno, Mali. Note the clustered settlement pattern in the urban core, which has been interpreted as representing a *heterarchical* urban social configuration. Reproduced from Susan Keech McIntosh, "Modeling Political Organization in Large-Scale Settlement Clusters: A Case Study from the Inland Niger Delta," in *Beyond Chiefdoms: Pathways to Complexity in Africa*, ed. Susan Keech McIntosh (New York: Cambridge University Press, 1999), fig. 5.3.

routes shifted and empires fell, these trading entrêpots of the Western Sudan declined and were abandoned.

Additionally, however, historical and archaeological evidence from the Western Sudan reveals how regional capitals may take on many of the qualities of such entrêpots as a result of foreign colonizing efforts or rapidly intensifying long-distance trade. We have clear archaeological evidence for a "twin city" at Gao, and suggestive historical evidence for such a community at Koumbi Saleh, which contained distinct local and foreign communities at the peak of its prosperity (Figure 10.3).[32] Such intermediate forms were functionally differentiated from their rural hinterlands, serving as redistributive centers for rural surplus production and industrial activities, yet they also played

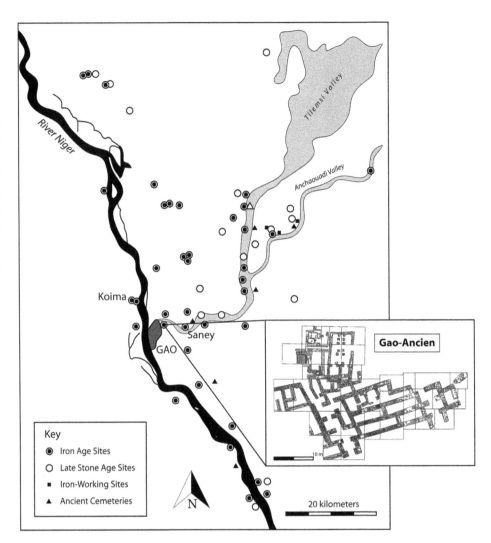

FIGURE 10.3

Map of the dual settlement at Gao as well as sites in its rural hinterlands. Note the presence of a possible palace building at Gao-Ancien, which was the indigenous settlement component. Reproduced from Timothy Insoll, *Islam, Archaeology and History: Gao Region (Mali) ca. AD 900–1250* (Oxford: British Archaeological Reports, 1996).

a major role in fostering long-distance trade, linking interregional and global systems of production, exchange, and consumption. In such contexts, however, the material rewards of trade were consumed by an emerging elite class culturally united by Islamic faith. Exotic trade goods from North Africa, and beyond, provided symbolic sources of social distinction for political elites struggling to assert their authority. High quantities of Islamic pottery and glass objects, as well as forest products, such as ivory, found at sites across the region attest to the importance of material wealth acquired through long-distance trade to elite power strategies. Long-distance trade thus encouraged new forms of social differentiation. Across the Western Sudan, the stimulus toward urbanism was thus a combination of opportunities seized upon by local political entrepreneurs as well as mercantile interests introduced from abroad.

Farther to the south, opportunistic research across the forest zone and its fringes has identified a host of major historical sites dating broadly to the late first through mid-second millennium CE. Beginning in this period, towns formed along the northern

forest fringe of modern Ghana, and by the fifteenth century, Akan towns coalesced around opportunities yielded by trans-Saharan demand for forest products, notably gold, ivory, and kola.[33] Deep within the forest zone to the south, Akan communities produced impressive earthworks around substantial communities between the ninth and fourteenth centuries.[34] Although often interpreted essentially as fortifications, such landscape features also served an important symbolic role in materializing social space.[35] In Nigeria's forest zone, furthermore, urbanism emerged in relation to a combination of local and long-distance forces. Rulers of the city of Ile-Ife emerged along the northern fringe of the forest zone and likewise tapped into opportunities for trade provided by the expansion of Sudanic polities; other Yoruba city-states proliferated across the Nigerian forest by the fifteenth and sixteenth centuries.[36] To the south, similar factors encouraged the rise of the capital of the Edo Kingdom of Benin, an expansive regional polity that was probably the source of several forest resources for the northern trade (Figure 10.4).[37] The extensive earthwork systems surrounding the urban cores of Benin City, Ile-Ife, and Oyo-Ile represent centralized control over vast quantities of labor. The widespread distribution of such wall systems has also been identified in the hinterlands around Benin City, adding new insights into the limits and structure of urban-rural relations in this polity (Figure 10.5).[38]

The advent of the transatlantic trade had significant consequences for the urban dynamics in coastal West Africa and its hinterlands. In coastal Ghana, the construction of European forts set off a chain reaction whereby communities situated on the distant periphery of the savanna mercantile network found themselves at the center of new economic activity. New towns emerged and settlements in their rural hinterlands diminished significantly as a result. In Southern Bénin, European fort building was

FIGURE 10.4

A seventeenth-century representation of a royal procession at Benin City, Nigeria. Note the spired structures in the foreground (representing the king's palace) as well as city walls in both the foreground and distance. The original caption reads: "A. The queens' palace. B. The enclosure of the royal court. C. Its entry. D. Other palaces of this court. E. The King's Solemn Exit. F. Nobility on horseback. G. Musicians in attendance. H. Jesters and dwarves I. Musicians leading tigers." Olfert Dapper, *Description de l'Afrique* (Amsterdam, 1686), courtesy of the Bibliothèque nationale de France, Paris.

FIGURE 10.5

Map of the earthwork
enclosures surrounding
Benin City. The lobate
sections may have served
as territorial markers
for dispersed lineage
groups within this urban
landscape. Reproduced
from Graham Connah,
*African Civilizations: An
Archaeological Perspective*,
2nd ed. (Cambridge:
Cambridge University
Press, 2016), fig. 7.9.

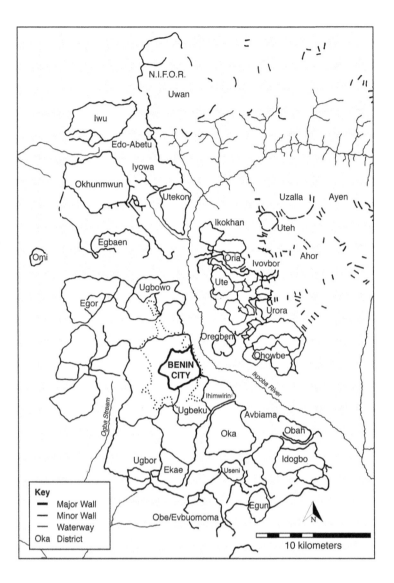

much more limited, reflecting an elevated degree of regional control enforced by local
lords. However, the long-term impacts of the slave trade on urbanism in this region are
clear. Here, expansive regional capitals that predated the slave trade became implicated
in the exchange of human captives for material resources that served to underwrite their
political authority.[39] Competition for these resources led to interpolity wars as well as
internal factionalism. Cities such as Savi, the capital of the Kingdom of Hueda, failed
to maintain control over their territories and fragmented.[40] Others, such as Abomey
and Cana in Dahomey (described below), managed to extend direct control into their
rural hinterlands, and refashioned the cultural fabric of urban centers in the process.[41]
Here, then, we see how the influx of long-distance economic forces had important consequences for the expression of power across local settlement systems.

The rapid growth of scholarly interest in the nature of West African cities has, therefore, taken our understanding of the origins of urban-rural dynamics in exciting new

directions, revealing the autochthonous roots of cities across the region. However, archaeologists continue to recognize that long-distance trade and intercultural contact was a substantial force for shaping the contours of urbanism across West Africa. Indeed, it is clear that in many West African contexts, long-distance forces sometimes overshadowed local regional dynamics in shaping urban trajectories.[42] Because the functional model is implicitly geared toward explaining locally evolving urban-rural settlement systems, interpreting the impact of interregional and global forces on urban settlement has proven difficult. Scholars have thus rightly called for an approach to urbanism which can successfully account for how local urban-rural dynamics were entangled within interregional and global economic and political forces unleashed by contact with expanding world systems, what Adria LaViolette and Jeffrey Fleisher have called a *multiscalar* perspective.[43]

Recent archaeologies of urban spaces focusing on diversity, agency, and power highlight a potential path toward understanding how multiscalar forces impacted the nature of urban communities in the past. On the one hand, comparative archaeological analyses of cities have revealed significant variation in urban form across a broad range of cultural contexts, demonstrating culturally specific patterns in how cities were designed and experienced in the past.[44] Indeed, comparative archaeological research on urbanism has distinguished between cities that served as *regional capitals* (cities which evolve through the processes of settlement differentiation and integration with their rural hinterlands), *disembedded capitals* (cities that are implanted in political neutral zones and are largely divorced from their rural hinterlands), and *trading entrepôts* (cities which are implanted or strongly influenced by foreign economic interests and are also largely divorced from their rural hinterlands).[45] Such variability in urban trajectories suggests the importance of historical contingency rather than universal processes in shaping urban trajectories.

Additionally, however, recent archaeological analyses have problematized the idea of the city itself as a material statement of corporate unity, exposing the often contentious nature of urban social dynamics.[46] Rather than a clearly definable settlement "type," or even a range of "types," with equally definable social, economic, and political functions, cities emerge as a palimpsest of social and cultural practices, produced through the negotiation of a variety of often competing interests of individuals and factions.[47] Indeed, rather than a homogeneous analytical category, archaeologists are rethinking the urban setting as an arena for the contestation of power. Forces operating at multiple geographic scales (*local/regional/global*) can impact the choices made by political agents living in cities and their hinterlands, resulting in heterogeneous material traces that we seek to unravel as archaeologists.

These conceptual shifts in our understanding of the nature of urban communities call for an approach that integrates a wider range of data sets generated at multiple geographic scales, often referred to as a landscape approach to archaeology. In forested zones of West Africa, however, where cultural practices limit settlement density and site visibility is incredibly poor, the adoption of such an approach has been bedeviled by the basic methodological problem of seeing archaeological remains across the region.[48] For one, even the largest settlements are defined by relatively low-density, graduated settlements in which houses are interspersed with gardens and small fields. Additionally, buildings across the region are constructed with perishable materials such as earth and thatch. These quickly melt into low mounds in the intense tropical rains once abandoned, and remain largely hidden in the dense vegetation that characterizes the region. Additionally, slash-and-burn agriculture and the practice of distributing kitchen waste across fields to increase the fertility of the fragile tropical soils encourages horizontal settlement shifting and the widespread distribution of artifacts. Combined, these factors have produced a regional pattern characterized by shallow archaeological deposits, dispersed over wide areas, and interspersed with areas covered in a low-density blanket of artifacts. How can we begin to study the nature of urban regional systems in forested West Africa if seeing cities, let alone rural villages, presents serious methodological challenges? For the rest of this essay, I will illustrate how the use of nonsite archaeological methods and geographic information systems can bridge this gap, revealing hitherto unseen urban patterns, and revealing that urbanism in the Kingdom of Dahomey was driven by elite political agendas, fueled in large part by the transatlantic slave trade.

Urban Landscapes on the Abomey Plateau, Bénin

The Atlantic Era, which spanned the sixteenth through nineteenth centuries, was a period of intense commercial integration linking key economic players in Western Europe, the Americas, the Indian Ocean littorals, and much of West and Central Africa. The period was marked by dramatic increases in the volume of commerce at regional and global levels,[49] and both the nature and structure of political organization in West Africa was transformed radically. Beginning in the second half of the seventeenth century, as long-distance commerce became dominated by the export of human captives in the transatlantic slave trade, West African political economies transformed dramatically, resulting in a complex network of polities linking coast and interior in new ways.[50]

If trans-Saharan economic forces impacted the nature of urban trajectories to the north, then Atlantic commercial processes during the era of the slave trade had even greater impacts on communities across the coastal reaches of the forest zone and its hinterlands.[51] Royal capitals of the kingdoms actively engaged in the Atlantic slave trade expanded rapidly, providing safe haven both for those fleeing slave-raiding neighbors as well as for those profiting from the new economic opportunities introduced by Atlantic commerce. New towns emerged in the interior to control important nodes in regional exchange systems. Populations flocked to the European-controlled coastal communities, resulting in towns with populations in the tens of thousands.[52] Others were depopulated, reflecting a pattern of de-urbanization.[53] Still others fled conflict to mountainous regions, building complex defensive systems to avoid capture, yet remaining articulated into broader economic currents.[54] Overall, the period was one of major demographic upheaval that resulted in new political and economic landscapes structured as much to resist the onslaught of expansionist polities as to maintain order and foster trade.[55]

Archaeological research on the relationship between urban communities and transatlantic commercial forces across the coast and its littorals has expanded dramatically

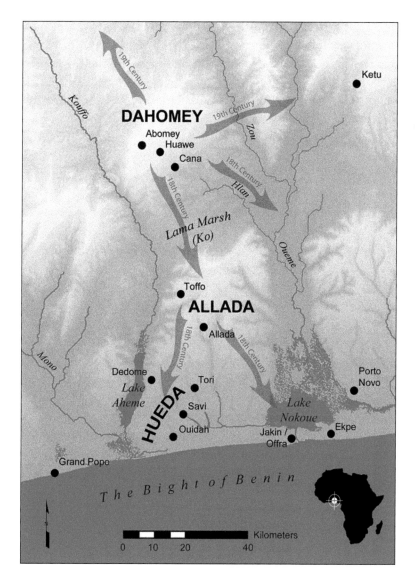

FIGURE 10.6

Regional map of
seventeenth-century
polities in Southern Bénin,
West Africa. Drawing by
J. Cameron Monroe.

in recent years. Substantial archaeological research on European coastal forts and their associated African settlements has been conducted in coastal Ghana, Senegal, and the Gambia.[56] Similarly, research in the Republic of Bénin has examined royal capitals and their rural hinterlands, exploring the relationship between long-distance trade and urban transformation in the Atlantic Era.[57] These efforts have successfully combined site-based and systematic regional approaches to examine how West African urban-rural dynamics were shaped and transformed by the opportunities and constraints provided by the advent of transatlantic commerce in the sixteenth century.

At the dawn of the Atlantic Era, dozens of large urban polities with complex political economies were well established on the Slave Coast of West Africa, which spanned the coastal regions of Togo, Bénin, and southwest Nigeria. The Kingdom of Dahomey arose on the Abomey Plateau of the Republic of Bénin during the seventeenth century as a minor polity providing captives for trade with its powerful coastal neighbors Allada and Hueda (Figure 10.6). In the early eighteenth century, Dahomey waged an extensive military campaign, conquering its southern rivals, and wresting control over the primary trade route to the coast, launching two centuries of political expansion. Throughout this period, Dahomean power depended on control over long-distance trade routes servicing the slave trade, as well as a sustained flow of resources from the countryside. Available historical and archaeological evidence allows us to paint a general picture of the nature of precolonial settlement on the Abomey Plateau, suggesting the emergence of a mature multitiered settlement hierarchy by the nineteenth century.

More than a decade of research by the Projet Bénino-Danois d'Archéologie (BDArch), an international team of researchers from the University of Copenhagen and the Direction du patrimoine culturel du Bénin, has identified a regional cultural sequence extending into the Stone Age.[58] BDArch's work along the Sodohomé channel, a water displacement system, has revealed iron-producing villages characterized by a shifting settlement pattern that extended back to the first millennium BCE. This work has produced tantalizing hints of the deep history and dynamic nature of settlement on the Abomey Plateau in the pre–Atlantic Era. However, because the research has been so geographically localized, it can say precious little about the overall nature of regional settlement during this period.

By the seventeenth century, oral historical evidence begins to add to the story. Oral sources indicate that the region was occupied by a decentralized confederacy of Guedevi chiefdoms living in minor towns distributed across the Abomey Plateau. According to these same traditions, this regional order was upset by the arrival of the Fon, or Dahomean, royal dynasty and their subsequent expansion across the plateau. Thus Abomey, originally a Guedevi settlement, emerged in the seventeenth century as the political capital of the nascent state of Dahomey. Oral sources claim that over the course of the seventeenth century, the Fon dynasty subjugated a series of Guedevi chiefdoms distributed across the plateau, setting the groundwork for political expansion to the south.

Documentary sources indicate that during the eighteenth and nineteenth centuries, the Abomey Plateau was characterized by a multicentric urban pattern centered on two neighboring cities: Abomey and Cana (Figure 10.7). For Abomey, we have rich historical and architectural detail from which to draw interpretations. Abomey in this period was an expansive community surrounded by a rectilinear wall-and-ditch system, an anomaly in the urban ditches of West Africa (Figure 10.8). This urban complex was defined by elite and commoner residences, marketplaces, quarters for craft guilds, and temples—indeed, all the characteristics of urban life (Figure 10.9). Royal palace compounds, the political nexuses of this urban community, were centers for public display and decorated with royal heraldry and images of conquest, representing the power and authority of the king (Figures 10.10 and 10.11). Abomey was also quite large by contemporary standards. By the late eighteenth century, its population may have reached 24,000 inhabitants;[59] during the subsequent century, reported population figures range from 30,000[60] to 40,000,[61] and as high as 60,000 inhabitants.[62] Abomey shares, therefore, significant features with urban communities in the forest zone.

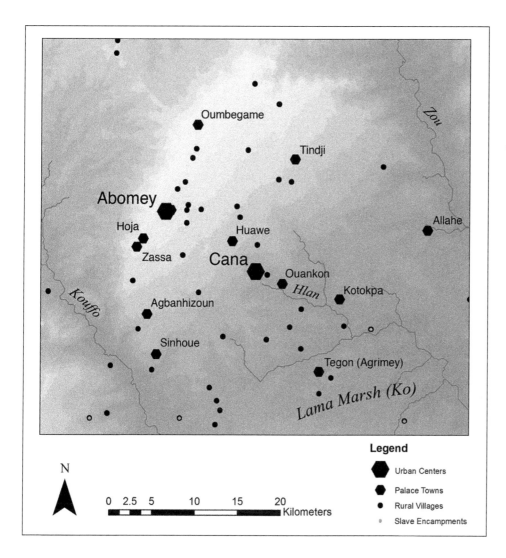

FIGURE 10.7

Urban centers, towns, and villages on the Abomey Plateau in the precolonial era, derived from ethnohistorical sources. Drawing by J. Cameron Monroe.

Nearby Cana, located 11 km to the southeast, also emerged as a major economic center on the plateau during this same period.[63] Cana also originated as a Guedevi settlement prior to the arrival of the Fon on the plateau. Cana boasted major regional markets, serving as an important node in regional administration and interregional trade routes,[64] and its population in the eighteenth century may have reached as many as 15,000 inhabitants.[65] Despite evidence for population decline by the late nineteenth century, Cana continued to support a substantial population numbering anywhere from 5,000[66] to 25,000 inhabitants.[67]

Although a good deal can be said about these cities themselves, the same is not yet true of the broader settlement system into which they were articulated. European travelers were rarely permitted to wander freely throughout the kingdom, biasing the record toward a limited number of larger settlements visited with regularity. As J. A. Skertchly wrote: "Many of the larger towns are built in the midst of large forests at a distance from the main road, so that it is quite possible to be within half a mile of a place of considerable

FIGURE 10.8
Views of the Abomey city wall
and moat (*agbodo*): a) view of
the moat following clearing; b)
excavation profile of Abomey
moat; and c) historical drawing
of wall segments flanking
city gates. Photograph by
J. Cameron Monroe, 2001;
drawings reproduced from
Klavs Randsborg and Inga
Merkyte, *Bénin Archaeology—
The Ancient Kingdoms*, 2 vols.
(Oxford: Wiley-Blackwell,
2009); and Frederick E.
Forbes, *Dahomey and the
Dahomans; Being the Journals
of Two Missions to the King of
Dahomey and Residence at His
Capital in the Years 1849 and 1850*
(London: Frank Cass
and Company, 1851),
1:facing page 69.

a

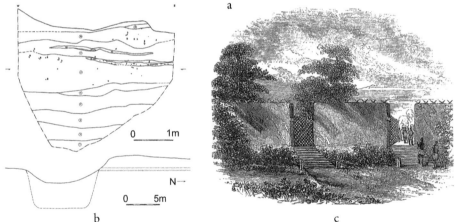

b   c

importance, while nothing but a few miserable huts and the Denun or custom house is visible."[68] Despite this historical invisibility, data from the early colonial period may be of some use for estimating population figures for the Abomey Plateau during the period immediately prior to the onset of the colonial era. Auguste Le Hérissé, who had colonial census records from 1908 at his disposal, placed the population of the Abomey Plateau at 120,000 individuals. Based on the aforementioned population estimates for Abomey and Cana, anywhere from 24 to 71 percent of the entire population of the plateau lived in these two urban centers.[69]

The remaining precolonial population lived in towns and villages scattered across the region. A number of additional minor towns may have functioned as secondary centers in the overall regional settlement system. Oral sources suggest that on the eve of the fall of Dahomey to France (1894), King Béhanzin divided traditional authority

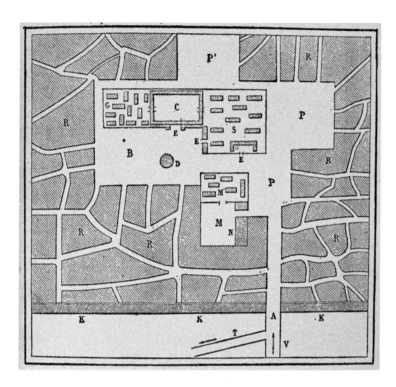

FIGURE 10.9

Plan of Abomey in 1856. "A. Bridge and town gate from Kana. B. The main square. C. The King's palace; courtyard with rooms for official receptions. D. The sacrificial hut of the main square. E. Gates to King's palace. G. Irregularly placed huts for housing the Amazons. K. Ditch and wall around the town. M. Meu's house. N. Hut in Meu's compound. P. Squares planted with trees for markets. R. Maze of small streets and lanes between compound walls. S. Huts of the 'wives'. T. Road to Prince Badahun's house. V. Road from Kana to Abomey." Reproduced from Richard Francis Burton, *A Mission to Gelele, King of Dahome* (London: Tinsley Brothers, 1866).

FIGURE 10.10

Depiction of ceremonies conducted before the Abomey palace during Annual Customs of 1850. Reproduced from Frederick E. Forbes, *Dahomey and the Dahomans; Being the Journals of Two Missions to the King of Dahomey and Residence at His Capital in the Years 1849 and 1850* (London: Frank Cass and Company, 1851), 2:facing page 75.

FIGURE 10.11

Bas reliefs from
the royal palace of
King Guezo (Musée
historique d'Abomey)
depicting military
conquest. Photographs
by J. Cameron Monroe.

beyond Abomey among seven noble families, resulting in an equal number of colonial-era kingships. These were located at Allahé, Cana, Djidja, Ounbegame, Sinhoué, Tindji, and Zogbodomey, respectively.[70] These settlements, along with Abomey, are also listed among eleven important regional markets of the nineteenth century, suggesting that they played an important economic role in the rural economy of the Abomey Plateau much earlier.[71] They were nowhere near as large as Cana and Abomey, however. Population figures for Zogbodomey in this period suggest it never surpassed 900 inhabitants.[72] The remainder of the region's population was distributed in smaller villages and hamlets of a few hundred people or less.[73] The village of Wodonun, for example, was "completely hidden from the road, and contains perhaps twenty families."[74]

The limited historical evidence available suggests the presence of a three-tiered settlement hierarchy during the period of Dahomean political expansion: major urban centers, regional market centers, and rural villages. This pattern was marked by a dramatic level of nucleation around twin urban centers Abomey and Cana, which served as the major political and economic hubs for its broader hinterlands during the Atlantic Era—functional urbanism classically defined. Were Abomey and Cana part of a mature urban system that evolved gradually and organically out of intensifying functional relationships between urban centers and hinterland communities? And can we see traces of this process prior to the expansion of Dahomean political authority in the Atlantic Era? Given the great success at identifying the deeply rooted nature of urban traditions in other parts of West Africa, I initially expected that this would be the case. However, archaeological and ethnohistorical data suggest that urbanism here was a relatively recent and politically structured phenomenon.

The regional distribution of royal palace complexes across the Abomey Plateau, for example, provides a valuable perspective on the changing relationship between these Dahomean cities and their broader hinterlands over the course of the eighteenth and nineteenth centuries. From 2000 to 2002, the Abomey Plateau Archaeological Project documented twenty-seven palace sites built by Dahomean monarchs across the region (Figures 10.12 and 10.13). These were massive complexes, ranging in size from 1 ha to 34 ha. Surface collections and targeted test excavations, interpreted in coordination with relevant oral and documentary data, date each of these structures to within a century at minimum, and often to within the reign of a particular Dahomean king. Patterns in the regional distribution of royal palace sites provide a valuable perspective on the changing relationship between Dahomean cities and their broader hinterlands over the course of the seventeenth through nineteenth centuries.[75]

Seventeenth-century palace construction was limited to the capital, Abomey, which served in this period as the central node in Dahomey's sphere of influence. Provincial elites were thus left largely to their own devices and were tenuously integrated into Abomey's political orbit. Following the conquest of its southern neighbors, Dahomey waged a relentless campaign to project its authority outward from the capital, a strategy aimed at integrating the provinces and the capital in response to the particular demands of Atlantic commerce.[76] During the eighteenth century, the monarchy built palaces in towns and cities on the major highways along which Dahomey delivered human captives to the Atlantic coast and received imported goods in return. In contrast, nineteenth-century palaces were located in rural zones at a distance from urban centers. These patterns reflect changes in the European demands for African exports, from human captives to agricultural commodities by the second quarter of the nineteenth century.[77] Dahomean rural expansion thus resulted in economically integrated countryside, in which the political elite increasingly circumscribed rural production and exchange.

Was the nascent state constructing such sites to solidify its control in existing towns? Or were these projects a critical contributing factor in the growth of urban communities themselves? Ethnohistorical evidence suggests the latter. Concomitant with

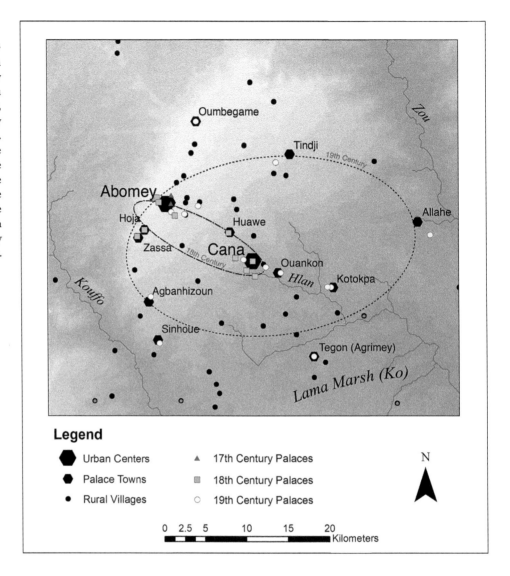

Dahomean military expansion into neighboring frontiers in the Atlantic Era was the uprooting and influx of various ethnic groups throughout the kingdom. Dahomean kings adopted a complex resettlement strategy to integrate these new groups. One nineteenth-century source claims, for example, that following King Agaja's conquest of the village Akpweh, he resettled the majority of its inhabitants in a series of local villages near Abomey. Yoruba captives were resettled in a village called Lefu-Lefu near Abomey under King Gezo, and his successor, King Glele, resettled captives from Takon and Ishagga in similar villages. Indeed, as Richard Francis Burton noted, "when the King breaks a town he builds another, and is supposed to place there the poor remnants of his captives."[78]

The aforementioned palace construction campaigns were a centrally important component of settlement strategies designed to integrate newly conquered peoples across Dahomey. For example, Edna Bay has noted that Akan smiths and jewelers, who fled Asante in the late eighteenth century, were forcibly settled at the palace town of

FIGURE 10.13

Ruins of the country palace of King Glele, Cana-Mignonhi. Photograph by J. Cameron Monroe.

Hoja under the patronage of King Kpengla.[79] Oral sources from Abomey and Cana, for example, contain complex narratives of resettlement, war, and slave trading in which the state had a heavy hand in structuring the social landscape of these cities. Lineage histories from Abomey demonstrate the close synergy between the spatial distribution of noble and common lineages and royal palace construction campaigns.[80] For each palace constructed at Abomey, both noble and common lineages were installed in neighboring quarters, and many of these lineages were of nonlocal origin. In the Adandokpodji quarter of Abomey, for example, members of the royal lineage were installed alongside descendants of captives of war brought to Dahomey during the reign of King Kpengla. Similarly, King Tegbesu settled ritual specialists brought from the Aja region of modern Togo at Agblome, south of Adandokpodji. This pattern continued into the nineteenth century as kings incorporated foreigners into Abomey in communities adjacent to the walls of their palaces. Palace sites at Abomey thus served as anchors for the diverse communities that arose around their walls. Each community established, furthermore, served as a microcosm of the kingdom as a whole, with palace residents, noble elites, and commoners living in relative proximity to one another.

Oral traditions collected at Cana tell a similar story.[81] These largely confirm commonly cited histories, which suggest that the Guedevi were established in Cana by the seventeenth century. The area inhabited by these autochthonous residents is now located on the eastern edge of the modern town at Cana-Kbota. Oral data suggest that Cana grew substantially over time, as Dahomean kings built royal palaces and installed subjects across a relatively open landscape.[82] This practice resulted in rapid urban growth over time, and just like the pattern observed at Abomey, palaces facilitated the integration of new peoples into Dahomean urban society. Thus, palace construction campaigns were not just geared toward integrating city and countryside in the Atlantic Era. They were also an important strategy for integrating conquered people into Dahomey, serving as a major factor in driving the urbanization process itself.

Regional Archaeology at Cana, Bénin

Since 2007, the Abomey Plateau Archaeological Project has targeted the microregion around Cana to understand the historical roots and local dynamics of urbanism in this one particular town. Between 2007 and 2013, a systematic pedestrian survey was completed within a 10 km diameter octagonal zone around Cana. This survey was designed to assess the timing and nature of urban nucleation at Cana to help deduce whether or not urban/rural differentiation was a pre-Dahomean phenomenon on the Abomey Plateau.

The nature of farming practices across the region shaped our research strategy substantially. Tropical West African soils rapidly decline in productivity once farmed and require long fallow periods before fully recovering, encouraging the use of "slash-and-burn" agricultural regimes.[83] Such regimes, in turn, encourage the lateral movement of farmsteads, resulting in a settlement pattern marked by significant horizontal shifting and population dispersal. Slash-and-burn agricultural practices also influence the spatial structure of individual communities with important archaeological implications. Villages are typically surrounded by a concentric land-use pattern marked by declining agricultural intensity with distance,[84] a pattern often referred to as "land zoning"[85] or the "ring system of cultivation."[86] The area around the homestead is under intensive, permanent production. Beyond the homestead, however, fields may be maintained in concentric circles, which have longer fallow periods at greater distance from the homestead.

Across this region, agricultural and trash disposal practices coordinate to render the material traces of settlement ambiguous (Figure 10.14). Today, trash disposal targets borrow pits and old structures in and around households within core settlement areas. Such contexts, therefore, contain the highest density of artifacts. Beyond the core settlement, however, the distribution of kitchen waste across fields introduces material culture into cultivated areas, particularly those zones adjacent to settlements. Burton noted this practice on the plateau in the nineteenth century, writing that "the women ridge the ground neatly with their little hoes, and some, more industrious, dispose over their crofts the huge heaps of kitchen-midden that have grown about their houses."[87] Additionally, a wide range of material culture is brought to fields during its use life. Such items include implements, food and beverage containers, cooking utensils, and other items used to repair tools or prepare cultivated products for transport to market. These practices result in a blanket of artifacts around settlements and across agricultural fields.

In light of these issues, I expected a regional settlement pattern characterized by a broad palimpsest of artifacts, dating to multiple periods, and largely invisible in heavily

FIGURE 10.14

Trash disposal and field use patterns observed in the Cana region: a–b) trash disposal within settlements; c–d) trash dispersal across active fields; and e–f) material culture use in active fields. The widespread distribution of trash around settlements and in field systems in the past renders rural village sites difficult to distinguish archaeologically. Photographs by J. Cameron Monroe.

FIGURE 10.15

FIGURE 10.15
View of archaeological village site identified in the Cana region. Note the presence of a shallow depression (possibly a trash pit) and associated baobab. Photograph by J. Cameron Monroe.

vegetated areas. Within this low-density blanket of features and artifacts, however, I assumed that we might be able to distinguish between 1) core areas of settlement characterized by high densities of artifacts and features, and 2) areas devoted to farming containing lower densities of artifacts and no features. This assumption proved correct.

The aforementioned ethnographic observations fundamentally structured the Cana Archaeological Survey, and we adopted a nonsite approach to identify feature and artifact densities across the region. In four seasons of survey, we ran paired survey lines radiating north and south of the main road through modern Cana. We excavated 50 × 50 cm hoe test pits placed along each survey line at 50 m intervals to recover subsurface artifacts. We intensively surveyed all agricultural fields encountered with good surface visibility in order to identify visible settlement features. In all, we covered 1.5 km² of ground (2 percent of the region), excavated 1,322 test units, surveyed 242 fields, and mapped over 300 features using mapping-grade GPS units. Eighty-seven percent of hoe test pits excavated were positive for artifacts, confirming expectations that clearly bounded settlements would be difficult to identify.

Pedestrian survey was successful in identifying a diverse assemblage of features, including small-scale linear ditches, architectural mounds, and depressions that were presumably borrow pits for extracting clay for building purposes (Figures 10.15 and 10.16). We frequently encountered baobab trees alongside such features. Baobabs often serve as the ritual and spatial focal point of village communities across the region (Figure 10.17), and thus provided a useful index of archaeological settlements. Additionally, we identified numerous subterranean structures or souterrains, which may have been used

a

b

FIGURE 10.16

Sample of sites identified on the Abomey Plateau: a–b) iron slag mounds and an example of slag recovered at Ouhli; c) subterranean (souterrain) site; d) earthen mounds at Alladaho; and e–f) refuse and refuse pits in Saclo. Photographs by J. Cameron Monroe.

c

d

e

f

THE RECEPTION AT KANA.

FIGURE 10.17

J. A. Skertchly received by King
Glele and his court at Cana in
1871. Note the presence of the
large baobab tree providing
shade for the open courtyard
in which the ceremonies
took place. Such trees are
visible across the landscape
and are a useful index for
identifying archaeological
sites. Reproduced from J. A.
Skertchly, *Dahomey as It Is:
Being a Narrative of Eight
Months' Residence in That
Country* (London: Chapman
and Hall, 1874), 128.

as defensive structures during slave raids. The majority of archaeological sites identified
included clusters of mounds, depressions, and baobabs, and occasionally souterrains,
reflecting a typical village layout in which borrow pits surround domestic compounds
and open courtyards, and shade trees are distributed throughout (Figure 10.18). The
distribution of archaeological features suggests, on the surface, nucleation around Cana
and relatively low-density settlement across the rural landscape (Figure 10.19). Features
are densely clustered in the area closest to Cana's six royal palace complexes, in a second
zone on the northeast of the survey universe around Sodohomé, and in a limited number of much smaller pockets throughout the countryside. However, surface visibility
along survey lines was exceedingly low, and we rarely encountered such features outside
of open fields. Additionally, the density of such fields tended to be highest near Cana.
To control for this bias, I used data from subsurface test units to identify settlement in
zones covered in vegetation.

Interpolating artifact counts from these units produced a coarse perspective on settlement density across this region. This analysis reveals two high-density occupation

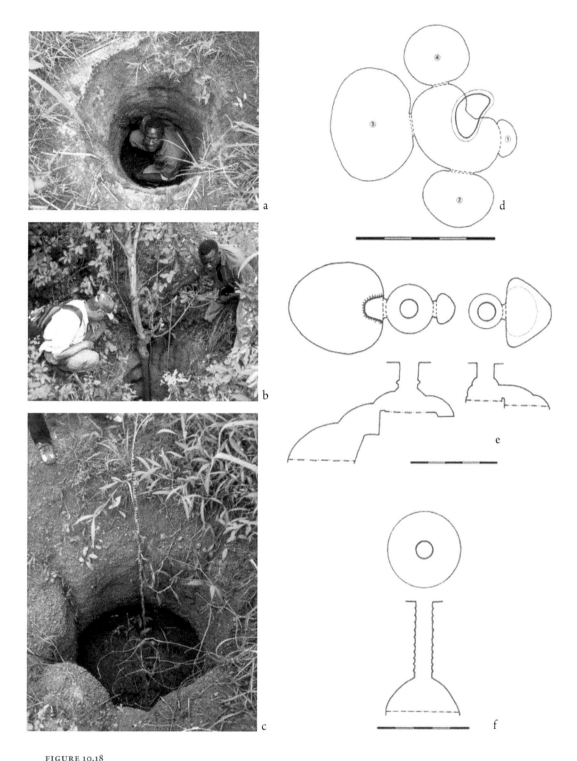

FIGURE 10.18

Subterranean chambered structures (souterrains) identified in regional survey: a–c) views of souterrain entrances in the Cana region; d) plan of chambered souterrain; and e–f) plan (above) and section (below) of souterrains in the Bohicon region. Reproduced from Klavs Randsborg and Inga Merkyte, *Bénin Archaeology—The Ancient Kingdoms*, 2 vols. (Oxford: Wiley-Blackwell, 2009).

FIGURE 10.19

Regional distribution of
archaeological features around
Cana and its royal palaces.
Archaeological features
cluster most strongly near
historic period palaces, yet
are represented in the rural
hinterlands as well. Drawing by
J. Cameron Monroe.

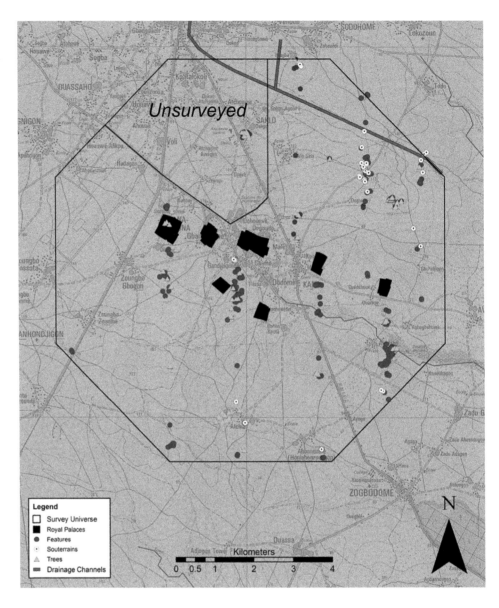

zones (Figure 10.20). The first is located on the northeastern reaches of the survey universe, enveloping the sites of Sodohomé and a series of slag mounds. The second is located around Cana, near its six royal palaces. This latter area covers approximately 11 km², closely approximating Frederick E. Forbes's nineteenth-century estimate of 10 km² as a whole. At a broad regional level, therefore, the results of the feature survey were supported. However, this higher-density zone was undoubtedly the product of patchy urban settlement. In the nineteenth century, Burton described Cana in much the same way: "A neerer glance at the habitations showed us that they are ... heaps of haycock huts or penthouse thatches enclosed in 'compounds' of mud wall or palm-leaf, and jealously detached. There is palpably more field than habitation, and far more fallow than field."[88] Burton's quote provides a more realistic perspective on urban

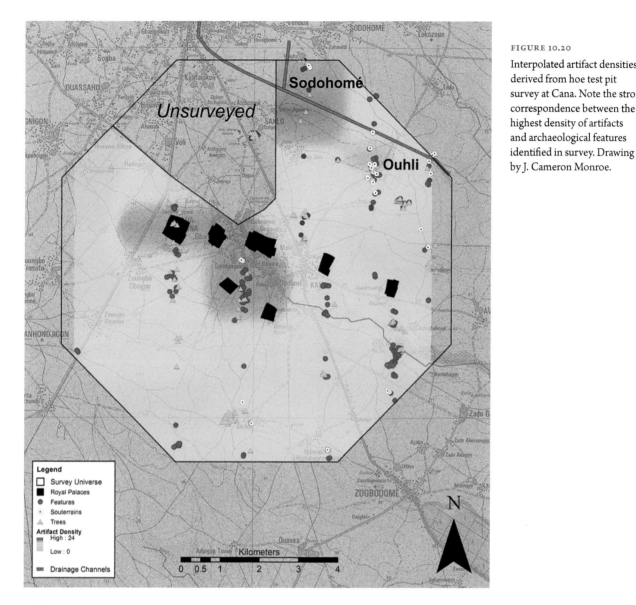

FIGURE 10.20

Interpolated artifact densities derived from hoe test pit survey at Cana. Note the strong correspondence between the highest density of artifacts and archaeological features identified in survey. Drawing by J. Cameron Monroe.

Cana in the nineteenth century, demanding a method for accounting for such settlement patchiness.

A number of geospatial statistics are commonly mobilized to tease out density patterns within such data sets. The Hot Spot Analysis tool in ArcGIS, for example, uses spatial regression statistics (specifically Getis-Ord Gi*) to identify statistically significant high and low values in a neighborhood of adjacent points. Hot Spot Analysis proved useful for differentiating higher- and lower-density artifact patterns in the survey universe. Across the survey universe, statistically significant artifact concentrations along survey lines corresponded strongly with the distribution of features in areas with good visibility. Thus, high-density artifact concentrations were probably the locations' core settlements situated within a blanket of low-density artifact noise across the region.

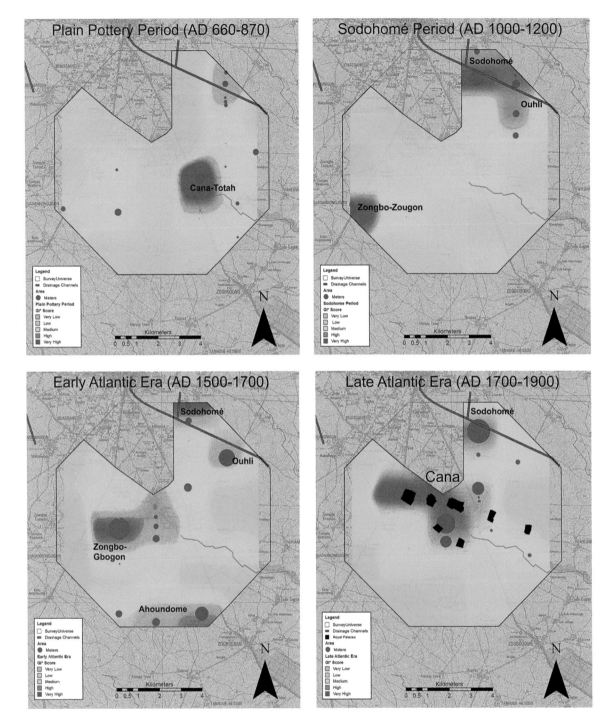

FIGURE 10.21

Comparison of high-density settlement zones identified using the Getis-Ord Gi* statistic in ArcGIS, with broader artifact dispersal patterns over time. Note that the greatest period of settlement nucleation coincides with the construction of historic palace sites at Cana. Drawing by J. Cameron Monroe.

Existing ceramic chronologies for the region, furthermore, allowed me to date these clusters and to outline settlement patterns over four cultural periods spanning the first and second millennia (Figure 10.21). This analysis suggests small-scale settlement in the southeast and northeast in the Plain Pottery Period (660–870), settlement expansion in the northeast during the Sodohomé Period (1000–1200), larger-scale settlement around Zounbo-Gbogon during the early Atlantic Era (1500–1700), and rapid nucleation around Cana's historic palaces during the later Atlantic Era (1700–1900), the period of Dahomean political expansion. Notably, the period of greatest urban nucleation, chronologically associated with the rise of Dahomey, was also marked by near-complete rural abandonment. These data confirm that during the later Atlantic Era, settlement does appear more nucleated around Cana than in previous periods, supporting the ethnohistoric evidence that urban settlement at Cana was a phenomenon closely associated with the rapid rise of the Dahomean state.

Conclusions

The rapid expansion of archaeological research across West Africa in the past few decades has contributed valuable new insights into the local origins and regional nature of cities across the region. Whereas much research remains focused on dating urban origins and tracing long-distance contacts, archaeologists increasingly deploy a *functional model* of the city to understand urban communities within their regional contexts. This intellectual turn has rapidly advanced our understanding of the great diversity, as well as the early onset, of urbanism across West Africa, pushing the origins of cities deep into prehistory and rejecting external stimulus as the only explanation for their rise. Yet, despite the undeniable antiquity of urban traditions in West Africa, long-distance trade clearly had a major impact on urban developmental trajectories over the last two millennia. Scholars have yet to adequately explain how long-distance forces articulated into local community dynamics to shape urban trajectories across the region. The research presented here was driven by the essential question of whether the emergence of urban landscapes in Dahomey was 1) a deeply rooted precontact phenomenon resulting from the close articulation of towns and their respective countrysides, or rather 2) a state-driven process spurred by long-distance forces of the Atlantic Era. A multiscalar landscape approach incorporating palace distributions, regional settlement data, oral historical sources, and artifactual evidence supports the argument that urbanism was largely a state-driven process.

Settlement patterns prior to the eighteenth century appear relatively dispersed across the microregion around Cana, shifting from low-density artifact scatters to full-fledged village sites over the course of the Iron Age. In the eighteenth century, however, Cana emerged on the world stage as a major city involved in the transshipment of human captives to coastal slave traders. The archaeological evidence described above reveals that regional settlement coalesced around Cana proper only during this period. What forces encouraged this shift? Were settlers attracted by economic opportunities provided by an expanding urban community? Ethnohistorical evidence, collected in oral interviews across Cana, suggests that families came to the town starting in the eighteenth century to serve the interests of a revenue-hungry elite class. Most came from hundreds of kilometers away, and many through predatory slave raids by Dahomey itself. The timing of settlement nucleation at Cana suggests that such resettlement schemes did not necessarily articulate into an existing precontact urban center, but, rather, drove the process of urbanism itself. Collectively, our data suggest that urbanism at Cana was largely a state-driven process, supporting an explicitly *political* rather than a *functional* model of the city.

Now, is this political model one that could be marshaled to explain the dramatic urban patterns witnessed elsewhere in the forest zone? Probably not. Dahomey was a truly exceptional example of the imposition of state power on the everyday lives of West African subjects, one born of the particularly complex power dynamics of the era of the slave trade. However, the research presented here hopefully provides an example of how exploring urban transformation at multiple spatial scales and drawing on multiple lines of archaeological and ethnohistorical evidence can provide us with a more nuanced perspective on the factors that drove the formation of urban landscapes across tropical West Africa in the precolonial era.

Notes

1. Roderick J. McIntosh, "Western Representations of Urbanism and Invisible African Towns," in *Beyond Chiefdoms: Pathways to Complexity in Africa*, ed. Susan Keech McIntosh (Cambridge: Cambridge University Press, 1999), 56–65; and Roderick J. McIntosh, *Ancient Middle Niger: Urbanism and the Self-Organizing Landscape* (Cambridge: Cambridge University Press, 2005).

2. Thurstan Shaw, "'Filling Gaps in Afric Maps': Fifty Years of Archaeology in Africa" (Fifteenth Annual Hans Wolff Memorial Lecture, African Studies Program, Indiana University, 1984).

3. Augustin Holl, "Background to the Ghana Empire: Archaeological Investigations on the Transition to Statehood in the Dhar Tichitt Region (Mauritania)," *Journal of Anthropological Archaeology* 4 (1985):73–115; Adria LaViolette and Jeffrey Fleisher, "The Archaeology of Sub-Saharan Urbanism: Cities and Their Countrysides," in *African Archaeology: A Critical Introduction*, ed. Ann Brower Stahl (Malden, Mass.: Blackwell, 2005), 327–53; McIntosh, *Ancient Middle Niger*; Roderick J. McIntosh and Susan Keech McIntosh, "Cities Without Citadels: Understanding Urban Origins along the Middle Niger," in *The Archaeology of Africa: Foods, Metals, and Towns*, ed. Thurstan Shaw, Paul Sinclair, Bassey Andah, and Alex Okpoko (London: Routledge, 1993), 622–41; and Paul Sinclair, Innocent Pikirayi, Gilbert Pwiti, and Robert Soper, "Urban Trajectories on the Zimbabwean Plateau," in Shaw et al., *Archaeology of Africa*, 705–31.

4. Susan Keech McIntosh and Roderick J. McIntosh, "The Early City in West Africa: Towards an Understanding," *African Archaeological Review* 11 (1984):73–98.

5. Graham Connah, "Urbanism and the Archaeological Visibility of African Complex Societies," *Journal of African Archaeology* 6 (2008):233–41.

6. Roland Anthony Oliver and J. D. Fage, *A Short History of Africa* (Baltimore: Penguin Books, 1962).

7. V. Gordon Childe, "The Urban Revolution," *Town Planning Review* 21 (1950):3–17; and Gideon Sjoberg, *The Preindustrial City* (Glencoe, Ill.: Free Press, 1960).

8. Catherine Coquery-Vidrovich, "The Process of Urbanization in Africa (From the Origins to the Beginnings of Independence)," *African Studies Review* 34, no. 1 (1991):1–98.

9. C. G. Seligman, *Races of Africa* (London: T. Butterworth, 1930); John Hanning Speke and James Augustus Grant, *Journal of the Discovery of the Source of the Nile*, 2nd ed. (Edinburgh; London: W. Blackwood and Sons, 1864), 247; R. N. Hall, *Prehistoric Rhodesia* (Philadelphia: George W. Jacobs, 1909); Leo Frobenius, *The Voice of Africa; Being an Account of the Travels of the German Inner African Exploration Expedition in the Years 1910–1912* (London: Hutchinson, 1913); W. M. Flinders Petrie, *The Making of Egypt* (London: Sheldon Press, 1939); and Walter B. Emery, *Archaic Egypt* (London: Penguin Books, 1961).

10. Brian Fagan, "Two Hundred and Four Years of African Archaeology," in *Antiquity and Man: Essays in Honour of Glyn Daniel*, ed. J. D. Evans, Barry Cunliffe, and Colin Renfrew (London: Thames and Hudson, 1981), 42–51; Ann B. Stahl, "Perceiving Variability in Time and Space: The Evolutionary Mapping of African Societies," in McIntosh, *Beyond Chiefdoms*, 39–55; and Peter Robertshaw, *A History of African Archaeology* (London: J. Currey, 1990).

11. Nehemia Levtzion, *Ancient Ghana and Mali* (London: Methuen, 1973).

12. Levtzion, *Ancient Ghana and Mali*; and E. W. Bovill, *The Golden Trade of the Moors* (New York: Oxford University Press, 1958).

13. Levtzion, *Ancient Ghana and Mali*.

14. Frobenius, *Voice of Africa*; Oliver and Fage, *Short History of Africa*; and Ivor Wilks, *Forests of Gold: Essays on the Akan and the Kingdom of Asante* (Athens: Ohio University Press, 1993).

15. LaViolette and Fleisher, "Archaeology of Sub-Saharan Urbanism."

16. Shaw et al., *Archaeology of Africa*; Graham Connah, *African Civilizations: An Archaeological Perspective*, 2nd ed. (Cambridge: Cambridge University Press, 2001); Peter Mitchell, *African Connections: An Archaeological Perspective on Africa and the Wider World* (Walnut Creek, Calif.: AltaMira Press, 2005); and Shaw, "'Filling Gaps in Afric Maps.'"

17. LaViolette and Fleisher, "Archaeology of Sub-Saharan Urbanism," 343.

18. Bassey Andah, "An Archaeological View of the Urbanization Process in the Earliest West African States," *Journal of the Historical Society of Nigeria* 8, no. 3 (1976):1–20; and McIntosh and McIntosh, "Early City in West Africa."

19 McIntosh and McIntosh, "Early City in West Africa."

20 Jeffrey Fleisher and Stephanie Wynne-Jones, "Authorisation and the Process of Power: The View from African Archaeology," *Journal of World Prehistory* 32, no. 4 (2010):177–93; Roland Fletcher, *The Limits of Settlement Growth: A Theoretical Outline* (New York: Cambridge University Press, 1995); Roland Fletcher, "African Urbanism: Scale, Mobility and Transformations," in *Transformations in Africa: Essays on Africa's Later Past*, ed. Graham Connah (London: Leicester University Press, 1998), 104–38; Susan Keech McIntosh, "Pathways to Complexity: An African Perspective," in McIntosh, *Beyond Chiefdoms*, 1–30; J. Cameron Monroe and Akin Ogundiran, "The Power of Landscape in Atlantic West Africa," in *Power and Landscape in Atlantic West Africa: Archaeological Perspectives*, ed. J. Cameron Monroe and Akin Ogundiran (New York: Cambridge University Press, 2012), 1–48; Ann B. Stahl, "Ancient Political Economies of West Africa," in *Archaeological Perspectives on Political Economies*, ed. Gary M. Feinman and Linda M. Nicholas (Salt Lake City: University of Utah Press, 2004), 253–70; Paul Sinclair, "The Archaeology of African Urbanism," in *The Oxford Handbook of African Archaeology*, ed. Peter Mitchell and Paul Lane (New York: Oxford University Press, 2013), 689–703; and Andah, "Archaeological View of the Urbanization Process in the Earliest West African States."

21 LaViolette and Fleisher, "Archaeology of Sub-Saharan Urbanism"; and McIntosh and McIntosh, "Cities Without Citadels."

22 Robert McCormick Adams, *Heartland of Cities: Surveys of Ancient Settlement and Land Use on the Central Floodplain of the Euphrates* (Chicago: University of Chicago Press, 1981); Charles Redman, *The Rise of Civilization: From Early Farmers to Urban Society in the Ancient Near East* (San Francisco: W. H. Freeman, 1978); and Richard E. Blanton, "Anthropological Studies of Cities," *Annual Review of Anthropology* 5 (1976):249–64.

23 Norman Yoffee, "The Process of Ruralization in Social Evolutionary Theory" (paper presented at the 51st Annual Meeting of the Society for American Archaeology, New Orleans, 1986).

24 Blanton, "Anthropological Studies of Cities."

25 McIntosh and McIntosh, "Early City in West Africa."

26 LaViolette and Fleisher, "Archaeology of Sub-Saharan Urbanism"; McIntosh, *Ancient Middle Niger*; McIntosh and McIntosh, "Cities Without Citadels"; Sinclair et al., "Urban Trajectories on the Zimbabwean Plateau"; and Holl, "Background to the Ghana Empire."

27 Holl, "Background to the Ghana Empire"; Patrick J. Munson, "Recent Archaeological Research in Dhar Tichitt Region of South Central Mauritania," *West African Archaeological Newsletter* 10 (1968):6–13; and Kevin C. MacDonald, Robert Vernet, Marcos Martinón-Torres, and Dorian Q. Fuller, "Dhar Néma: From Early Agriculture to Metallurgy in Southeastern Mauritania," *Azania: Archaeological Research in Africa* 44, no. 1 (2009):3–48.

28 Roderick J. McIntosh and Susan Keech McIntosh, "The Inland Niger Delta before the Empire of Mali: Evidence from Jenne-Jeno," *Journal of African History* 22 (1981):1–22; Susan Keech McIntosh, *Excavations at Jenné-Jeno, Hambarketolo, and Kaniana (Inland Niger Delta, Mali), the 1981 Season*, University of California Publications in Anthropology 20 (Berkeley: University of California Press, 1995); Susan Keech McIntosh and Roderick J. McIntosh, *Prehistoric Investigations in the Region of Jenne, Mali: A Study in the Development of Urbanism in the Sahel* (Oxford: British Archaeological Reports, 1980); Susan Keech McIntosh and Roderick J. McIntosh, "Archaeological Reconnaissance in the Region of Timbuktu, Mali," *National Geographic Research* 2, no. 3 (1986):302–19; Douglas P. Park, "Prehistoric Timbuktu and Its Hinterland," *Antiquity* 84 (2010):1–13; Rogier Bedaux, *Recherches archéologiques à Dia dans le Delta intérieur du Niger (Mali): Bilan des saisons de fouilles, 1998–2003*, CNWS Publications (Leiden: Research School of Asian, African, and Amerindian Studies, Leiden University, 2005); Rogier Bedaux, Kevin C. MacDonald, Alain Person, Jean Poleta, Kléna Sanogo, Annette Schmidt, and Samuel Sidibé, "The Dia Archaeological Project: Rescuing Cultural Heritage in the Inland Niger Delta (Mali)," *Antiquity* 75, no. 290 (2001):837–48; and Téréba Togola, *Archaeological Investigations of Iron Age Sites in the Mema Region, Mali (West Africa)* (Oxford: Archaeopress, 2008).

29 Susan Keech McIntosh, "Modeling Political Organization in Large-Scale Settlement Clusters: A Case Study from the Inland Niger Delta," in McIntosh, *Beyond Chiefdoms*, 66–79.

30 Roderick J. McIntosh, "The Pulse Model: Genesis and Accommodation of Specialization in the Middle Niger," *Journal of African History* 34 (1993):181–220.

31 Sam Nixon, "The Archaeology of Early Islamic Trans-Saharan Trading Towns in West Africa: A Comparative View and Progressive Methodology from the Entrepot of Essouk-Tadmekka" (PhD diss., Institute of Archaeology, University College London, 2008); Sam Nixon, "Excavating Essouk-Tadmakka (Mali): New Archaeological Investigations of Early Islamic Trans-Saharan Trade," *Azania* 44 (2009):217–55; Sophie Berthier, *Recherches archéologiques sur la capitale de l'empire de Ghana: Étude d'un secteur d'habitat à Koumbi Saleh, Mauritanie: Campagnes II-III-IV-V (1975–1976)–(1980–1981)* (Oxford: Archaeopress, 1997); Denise R. Robert, "Les Fouilles de Tegdaoust," *Journal of African History* 11, no. 4 (1970):471–93; D. Robert, S. Robert, and Jean Devisse, *Tegdaoust I: Recherches sur Awdaghost* (Paris: Arts et Metiers Graphiques, 1970); C. Vanacker, *Tegdaoust II: Fouille d'un Quartier Artisanal* (Paris: Memoires de l'Institut Mauritanien de la Recherche Scientific, 1979); Jean Devisse, *Tegdaoust III: Recherches sur Awdaghost, Campagnes 1960–1965 Enquetes Generales* (Paris: Editions Recherche sur les Civilizations, 1983); and Jean Polet, *Tegdaoust IV: Fouille d'un Quartier de Tegdaoust (Mauritanie Orientale: Urbanisation, Architecture, Utilisation de l'espace construit)* (Paris: Editions Recherche sur les Civilisations, 1985).

32 Mamadou Cissé, "Archaeological Investigations of Early Trade and Urbanism at Gao Saney (Mali)" (PhD diss., Rice University, 2011); Shoichiro Takezawa and Mamadou Cissé, "Discovery of the Earliest Royal Palace in Gao and Its Implications for the History of West Africa," *Cahiers d'études africaines* 4, no. 208 (2012):813–44; Mamadou Cissé, Susan Keech McIntosh, Laure Dussubieux, Thomas Fenn, Daphne Gallagher, and Abigail Chipps Smith, "Excavations at Gao Saney: New Evidence for Settlement Growth, Trade, and Interaction on the Niger Bend in the First Millennium CE," *Journal of African Archaeology* 11, no. 1 (2013):9–37; Timothy Insoll, "Iron Age Gao: An Archaeological Contribution," *Journal of African History* 38, no. 1 (1997):1–30; Timothy Insoll, *Islam, Archaeology and History: Gao Region (Mali) ca. AD 900–1250* (Oxford: British Archaeological Reports, 1996); Timothy Insoll, *Urbanism, Archaeology and Trade: Further Observations on the Gao Region (Mali), the 1996 Fieldseason Results*, British Archaeological Reports (Oxford: Archaeopress, 2000); and Berthier, *Recherches archéologiques*.

33 Merrick Posnansky, "Archaeology and the Origins of the Akan Society in Ghana," in *Problems in Economic and Social Archaeology*, ed. Gale de G. Sieveking, Ian H. Longworth, Kenneth E. Wilson, and Grahame Clark (London: Duckworth, 1976), 49–58.

34 Gerard Chouin and Christopher DeCorse, "Prelude to the Atlantic Trade: New Perspectives on Southern Ghana's Pre-Atlantic History (800–1500)," *Journal of African History* 51 (2010):123–45.

35 Nii Otokunor Quarcoopome, "Notse's Ancient Kingship: Some Archaeological and Art-Historical Considerations," *African Archaeological Review* 11, no. 1 (1993):109–28; Merrick Posnansky, "Notsé Town Wall Survey," *Nyame Akuma* 18 (1981):56–57; and Dola Aguigah, "La Site de Notsé: Contribution à l'Archéologie du Togo" (PhD diss., Université du Paris I, 1986).

36 Akinwumi Ogundiran, "Four Millennia of Cultural History in Nigeria (ca. 2000 B.C.–A.D. 1900): Archaeological Perspectives," *Journal of World Prehistory* 19, no. 2 (2005):133–68; and Robert Sydney Smith, *Kingdoms of the Yoruba* (London: Methuen, 1969).

37 Graham Connah, *The Archaeology of Benin: Excavations and Other Researches In and Around Benin City, Nigeria* (Oxford: Clarendon Press, 1975).

38 Patrick Darling, *Archaeology and History in Southern Nigeria: The Ancient Linear Earthworks of Benin and Ishan* (Oxford: British Archaeological Reports, 1984).

39 Michael Houseman, Christiane Massy, Blandine Legonou, and Xavier Crepin, "Note sur la structure évolutive d'une ville historique. L'example d'Abomey (République populaire du Bénin)," *Cahiers d'Études africaines* 26, no. 104 (1986):527–46; J. Cameron Monroe, *The Precolonial State in West Africa: Building Power in Dahomey* (New York: Cambridge University Press, 2014), 167–73; J. Cameron Monroe, "In the Belly of Dan: Space, History and Power in Precolonial Dahomey," *Current Anthropology* 52, no. 6 (2011):769–98; and Suzanne Preston Blier, "Razing the Roof: The Imperative of Building Destruction in Danhomè (Dahomey)," in *Structure and Meaning in Human Settlements*, ed. Tony Atkin and Joseph Rykwert (Philadelphia: University of Pennsylvania, 2005), 165–84.

40 Kenneth Kelly, "The Archaeology of African-European Interaction: Investigating the Social Roles of Trade, Traders, and the Use of Space in the Seventeenth- and Eighteenth-Century Hueda Kingdom, Republic of Bénin," *World Archaeology* 28, no. 3 (1997):351–69; Kenneth Kelly, "Using Historically Informed Archaeology: Seventeenth and Eighteenth Century Hueda-Europe Interaction on the Coast

of Bénin," *Journal of Archaeological Method and Theory* 4, nos. 3–4 (1997):353–66; Neil L. Norman, "Hueda (Whydah) Country and Town: Archaeological Perspectives on the Rise and Collapse of an Atlantic Countryside and Entrepôt," *International Journal of African Historical Studies* 42, no. 3 (2009):387–410; and Neil L. Norman, "From the Shadow of an Atlantic Citadel: An Archaeology of the Huedan Countryside," in Monroe and Ogundiran, *Power and Landscape in Atlantic West Africa*.

41 Monroe, *Precolonial State in West Africa*.

42 LaViolette and Fleisher, "Archaeology of Sub-Saharan Urbanism."

43 LaViolette and Fleisher, "Archaeology of Sub-Saharan Urbanism."

44 Bruce G. Trigger, *Understanding Early Civilizations: A Comparative Study* (Cambridge: Cambridge University Press, 2003); Deborah L. Nichols and Thomas H. Charlton, *The Archaeology of City-States: Cross-Cultural Approaches*, Smithsonian Series in Archaeological Inquiry (Washington, D.C.: Smithsonian Institution Press, 1997); James L. Boone, J. Emlen Myers, and Charles Redman, "Archeological and Historical Approaches to Complex Societies: The Islamic States of Medieval Morocco," *American Anthropologist* 92, no. 3 (1990):630–46; Richard G. Fox, *Urban Anthropology: Cities in Their Cultural Setting* (Englewood Cliffs, N.J.: Prentice-Hall, 1977); Blanton, "Anthropological Studies of Cities"; George L. Cowgill, "Origins and Development of Urbanism: Archaeological Perspectives," *Annual Review of Anthropology* 33 (2004):525–49; William T. Sanders and David Webster, "The Mesoamerican Urban Tradition," *American Anthropologist* 90, no. 3 (1988):521–46; McIntosh and McIntosh, "Cities Without Citadels"; and McIntosh, *Ancient Middle Niger*.

45 Blanton, "Anthropological Studies of Cities"; Boone, Myers, and Redman, "Archeological and Historical Approaches to Complex Societies"; Richard G. Fox, "Regal-Ritual Cities," in Fox, *Urban Anthropology*; Sjoberg, *Preindustrial City*; Paul Wheatley, *The Pivot of the Four Quarters: A Preliminary Enquiry into the Origins and Character of the Ancient Chinese City* (Edinburgh: Edinburgh University Press, 1971); Sanders and Webster, "Mesoamerican Urban Tradition"; Gordon Willey, "The Harvey Lecture Series: The Concept of the 'Disembedded Capital' in Comparative Perspective," *Journal of Anthropological Research* 35, no. 2 (1979):123–37; and Richard E. Blanton, *Monte Albán: Settlement Patterns at the Ancient Zapotec Capital*, Studies in Archeology (New York: Academic Press, 1978).

46 David Anderson and Richard Rathbone, *Africa's Urban Past* (Oxford: James Currey, 2000); Norman Yoffee, *Myths of the Archaic State: Evolution of the Earliest Cities, States, and Civilizations* (Cambridge: Cambridge University Press, 2005); Monica L. Smith, *The Social Construction of Ancient Cities* (Washington, D.C.: Smithsonian Institution Press, 2003); Adam T. Smith, *The Political Landscape: Constellations of Authority in Early Complex Polities* (Los Angeles: University of California Press, 2003); McIntosh, *Ancient Middle Niger*; McIntosh and McIntosh, "Cities Without Citadels"; and Arthur A. Joyce, "Theorizing Urbanism in Ancient Mesoamerica," *Ancient Mesoamerica* 20, no. 2 (2009):189–96.

47 Cowgill, "Origins and Development of Urbanism."

48 Connah, "Urbanism and the Archaeological Visibility of African Complex Societies."

49 Philip D. Curtin, *The Rise and Fall of the Plantation Complex: Essays in Atlantic History*, 2nd ed. (Cambridge: Cambridge University Press, 1998).

50 David Eltis, Stephen D. Behrendt, David Richardson, and Herbert S. Klein, *The Trans-Atlantic Slave Trade: A Database on CD-ROM* (Cambridge: Cambridge University Press, 1999).

51 Ray A. Kea, *Settlements, Trade, and Polities in the Seventeenth-Century Gold Coast* (Baltimore: Johns Hopkins University Press, 1982); and Martin A. Klein, "The Slave Trade and Decentralized Societies," *Journal of African History* 42 (2001):49–65.

52 Christopher DeCorse, *An Archaeology of Elmina: Africans and Europeans on the Gold Coast, 1400–1900* (Washington, D.C.: Smithsonian Institution Press, 2001).

53 Kea, *Settlements, Trade, and Polities in the Seventeenth-Century Gold Coast*.

54 Klein, "Slave Trade and Decentralized Societies"; Scott MacEachern, "Selling the Iron for Their Shackles: Wandala–Montagnard Interactions in Northern Cameroon," *Journal of African History* 34, no. 2 (1993):247–70; Philip Lynton de Barros, "The Rise of the Bassar Chiefdom in the Context of Africa's Internal Frontier," in Monroe and Ogundiran, *Power and Landscape in Atlantic West Africa*, 255–77; and Christopher DeCorse, "Fortified Towns of the Koinadugu Plateau: Northern Sierra Leone in the Pre-Atlantic and Atlantic Worlds," in Monroe and Ogundiran, *Power and Landscape in Atlantic West Africa*, 278–308.

55 Monroe and Ogundiran, "Power of Landscape in Atlantic West Africa."

56 Christopher DeCorse, "Culture Contact, Continuity and Change on the Gold Coast, AD 1400–1900," *African Archaeological Review* 10 (1992):163–96; Christopher DeCorse, "Culture Contact and Change in West Africa," in *Studies in Culture Contact: Interaction, Culture Change, and Archaeology*, ed. James G. Cusick (Carbondale: Center for Archaeological Investigations Southern Illinois University, 1998), 358–77; Christopher DeCorse, "The Europeans in West Africa: Culture Contact, Continuity and Change," in Connah, *Transformations in Africa*; DeCorse, *Archaeology of Elmina*; Christopher DeCorse, "Archaeological Fieldwork at Bunce Island: A Slave Trading Entrepôt in Sierra Leone," *Nyame Akuma* 82 (2014):12–22; Liza A. Gijanto, "Exchange, Interaction, and Change in Local Ceramic Production in the Niumi Commercial Center on the Gambia River," *Journal of Social Archaeology* 11, no. 1 (2011):21–48; Ibrahima Thiaw, "Slaves without Shackles: An Archaeology of Everyday Life on Gorée Island, Senegal," in *Slavery in Africa: Archaeology and Memory*, ed. Paul Lane and Kevin C. MacDonald (New York: Published for the British Academy by Oxford University Press, 2011), 147–65; Merrick Posnansky and Albert Van Dantzig, "Fort Ruychaver Rediscovered," *Sankofa* 2 (1976):7–18; and Albert Van Dantzig, *Forts and Castles of Ghana* (Accra: Sedco, 1980).

57 Kelly, "Archaeology of African-European Interaction"; Kelly, "Using Historically Informed Archaeology"; Kenneth Kelly, "Change and Continuity in Coastal Bénin," in *West Africa during the Atlantic Slave Trade: Archaeological Perspectives*, ed. Christopher DeCorse (New York: Continuum International Publishing Group, 2001), 81–100; Kenneth Kelly and Neil Norman, "Historical Archaeologies of Landscape in Atlantic Africa," in *Envisioning Landscape: Situations and Standpoints in Archaeology and Heritage*, ed. Dan Hicks, Laura McAtackney, and G. J. Fairclough (Walnut Creek, Calif.: Left Coast Press, 2007), 172–93; Norman, "Hueda (Whydah) Country and Town"; Neil L. Norman, "Feasts in Motion: Archaeological Views of Parades, Ancestral Pageants, and Socio-Political Process in the Hueda Kingdom, 1650–1727 AD," *Journal of World Prehistory* 23, no. 4 (2010):239–54; Norman, "From the Shadow of an Atlantic Citadel"; Neil L. Norman and Kenneth Kelly, "Landscape Politics: The Serpent Ditch and the Rainbow in West Africa Landscape Politics," *American Anthropologist* 104, no. 1 (2006):98–110; J. Cameron Monroe, "Continuity, Revolution, or Evolution on the Slave Coast of West Africa: Royal Architecture and Political Order in Precolonial Dahomey," *Journal of African History* 48 (2007):349–73; J. Cameron Monroe, "Dahomey and the Atlantic Slave Trade: Archaeology and Political Order on the Bight of Benin," in *The Archaeology of Atlantic Africa and the African Diaspora*, ed. Toyin Falola and Akin Ogundiran (Indianapolis: Indiana University Press, 2007), 100–121; J. Cameron Monroe, "Power by Design: Architecture and Politics in Precolonial Dahomey," *Journal of Social Archaeology* 10, no. 3 (2010):477–507; Monroe, "In the Belly of Dan"; J. Cameron Monroe, "Urbanism on West Africa's Slave Coast: Archaeology Sheds New Light on Cities in the Era of the Atlantic Slave Trade," *American Scientist* 99, no. 5 (2011):400–409; J. Cameron Monroe, "Building the State in Dahomey: The Political Economy of Landscape on the Bight of Benin," in Monroe and Ogundiran, *Power and Landscape in Atlantic West Africa*, 191–222; and Monroe, *Precolonial State in West Africa*.

58 Klavs Randsborg and Inga Merkyte, *Bénin Archaeology—The Ancient Kingdoms*, 2 vols., Centre of World Archaeology Publications 7 (Oxford: Wiley-Blackwell, 2009).

59 Robert Norris, *Memoirs of the Reign of Bossa Ahádee, King of Dahomy* (London: Printed for W. Lowndes, 1789), 92.

60 Frederick E. Forbes, *Dahomey and the Dahomans; Being the Journals of Two Missions to the King of Dahomey and Residence at His Capital in the Years 1849 and 1850* (London: Frank Cass and Company, 1851), 1:14.

61 Louis Brunet and Louis Giethlen, *Dahomey et dépendances: Historique général, organisation, administration, ethnographie, productions, agriculture, commerce* (Paris: A. Challamel, 1900), 48.

62 Alexandre L. d'Albéca, *La France au Dahomey* (Paris: Hachette, 1895), 63.

63 Edna Bay, "On the Trail of the Bush King: A Dahomean Lesson in the Use of Evidence," *History in Africa* 6 (1979):1–15; and Karl Polanyi, *Dahomey and the Slave Trade: An Analysis of an Archaic Economy* (Seattle: University of Washington Press, 1966).

64 Justin Fakambi, *Routes des esclaves au Bénin (ex-Dahomey) dans une approche régionale* (Ouidah: Musée d'histoire de Ouidah, 1993).

65 Norris, *Memoirs of the Reign of Bossa Ahádee*, 82.

66 J. A. Skertchly, *Dahomey as It Is: Being a Narrative of Eight Months' Residence in That Country* (London: Chapman and Hall, 1874), 111.

67 Albéca, *La France au Dahome*, 63.

68 Skertchly, *Dahomey as It Is*, 43.

69 Auguste Le Hérissé, *L'ancien royaume du Dahomey: Moeurs, religion, histoire* (Paris: Emile Larose, 1911), 44; and J. Cameron Monroe, "The Dynamics of State Formation: The Archaeology and Ethnohistory of Pre-Colonial Dahomey" (PhD diss., University of California, Los Angeles, 2003), 222.

70 Da Langanfin Aïhotogbe Glele, interview by the author, 2001, Cana, Bénin.

71 Da Langanfin Aïhotogbe Glele, interview by the author, 2001, Cana, Bénin.

72 John Duncan, *Travels in Western Africa, in 1845 & 1846, Comprising a Journey from Whydah, Through the Kingdom of Dahomey, to Adofoodia, in the Interior* (London: R. Bentley, 1847), 1:213.

73 Monroe, "Dynamics of State Formation," 219–20.

74 Skertchly, *Dahomey as It Is*, 107.

75 Monroe, "Continuity, Revolution, or Evolution"; Monroe, "Dahomey and the Atlantic Slave Trade"; Monroe, "Urbanism on West Africa's Slave Coast"; Monroe, "Building the State in Dahomey; and J. Cameron Monroe, "Cities, Slavery, and Rural Ambivalence in Precolonial Dahomey," in *The Archaeology of Slavery: A Comparative Approach to Captivity and Coercion*, ed. Lydia Wilson Marshall, Center for Archaeological Investigation Occasional Paper 41 (Carbondale: Southern Illinois University Press, 2015), 192–214.

76 Monroe, "Continuity, Revolution, or Evolution."

77 Monroe, "Continuity, Revolution, or Evolution."

78 Richard Francis Burton, *A Mission to Gelele, King of Dahome* (London: Tinsley Brothers, 1864), 1:285.

79 Edna Bay, *Asen, Ancestors, and Vodun: Tracing Change in African Art* (Urbana: University of Illinois Press, 2008).

80 Houseman et al., "Note sur la structure évolutive d'une ville historique."

81 Monroe, "In the Belly of Dan."

82 Monroe, "In the Belly of Dan."

83 B. N. Okigbo, "Shifting Cultivation in Tropical Africa-Definition and Description," in *The Future of Shifting Cultivation in Africa and the Task of Universities: Proceedings of the International Workshop on Shifting Cultivation*, ed. Arthur H. Bunting and Edward Bunting (Rome: FAO, 1982), 18–36; H. Ruthenberg, "From Shifting Cultivation to Semi-Permanent and Permanent Farming in the African Savannas," in *International Workshop on Farming Systems* (Ithaca, N.Y.: International Crops Research Institute for the Semi-Arid Tropics, Cornell University, 1974), 325–49; and Peter Hague Nye and D. J. Greenland, *The Soil under Shifting Cultivation*, Commonwealth Bureau of Soil Science Technical Communication (Farnham Royal: Commonwealth Agricultural Bureaux, 1960).

84 Glenn Davis Stone, *Settlement Ecology: The Social and Spatial Organization of Kofyar Agriculture*, Arizona Studies in Human Ecology (Tucson: University of Arizona Press, 1996), 46.

85 A. T. Grove and Frances M. G. Klein, *Rural Africa*, Cambridge Topics in Geography Series (Cambridge: Cambridge University Press, 1979).

86 D. W. Norman, Emmy Bartz Simmons, and Henry Merlin Hays, *Farming Systems in the Nigerian Savanna: Research and Strategies for Development* (Boulder, Colo.: Westview Press, 1982); and Hans Ruthenberg and J. D. MacArthur, *Farming Systems in the Tropics*, 3rd ed. (Oxford: Clarendon Press, 1980).

87 Burton, *A Mission to Gelele*, 2:248.

88 Burton, *A Mission to Gelele*, 1:190.

EPILOGUE

This remarkable collection of essays clearly opens far more avenues of inquiry than it answers. The questions offered in the introductory essay, of when the phenomenon of urban landscapes emerged and how the relationship between cities and landscapes defined urban processes, are now grounded in a series of nine projects that engage traditional historic and archaeological methodologies alongside cutting-edge technological approaches to revealing land use. The paradigm of what we understood as a limited diversity of urban forms has shifted to a broader combination of processes as well as to a more nuanced discussion of their difference and specificity. This shift is underpinned by the ongoing deconstruction of the dualities of the urban landscape and its hinterland, revealing a broad spectrum of spatial organizations that defy what we believed we knew about urbanism and its forms in the land. This work grew out of a more specific focus on urban landscapes, alongside an access to and use of new remote-sensing technologies as well as digital image analysis and modeling. Applied to preindustrial urban landscapes, these new approaches have generated new knowledge and contribute to enriching urban history.

Expanding our understanding of possible forms and organizational relationships of urban landscapes offers alternative visions to historians, humanists, and social scientists. As recalled by Georges Farhat, the monothetic, unilinear definitions of urbanization have proved far too rigid and essentializing, revealing a Western viewpoint that lends little to understanding urban landscapes in non-Western environments. The scholarship shared in this volume focuses on explorations of what urbanism might be even in its "smallest, most diffuse, and non-Western" forms; it considers how urban traditions might be understood more through regional relationships and landscapes than through any centrally oriented urbanism, or how early Mesopotamian urban landscapes might have "invented themselves" within a localized framework. Many of the essays depict what might be described as urbanism without cities; for example, urbanism on the Indian subcontinent might be more usefully understood as the network of residents "engaged with the surrounding countryside in order to address basic needs in increasingly sophisticated ways."

No longer limited by the rigid parameters of most modern definitions of urbanism, the essays in this volume suggest that the urban process is specific to the place defined by its technical and environmental frameworks as shaped by local historical worldviews, and thus should be understood through such particularities. In this view, Western urbanism, even when considering a city as canonic as Rome, is re-read through a ceremonial praxis informed by water, flooding, and the detritus of abandoned buildings. Cahokian and Bhubaneswarian urbanism are equally informed by ceremony and ritual, but in different environments; through their specific cultural lenses, they contribute to a new understanding of the histories of urban landscapes and their development.

Equally significant, this volume outlines the potential of applying new technologies and digital tools to aid in revealing unseen settlement patterns that suggest newly defined large-scale and low-density preindustrial urbanism. This is a significant contribution to the scholarship of urbanism in the humanities and social sciences as well as in the design and planning disciplines. It is also in this work that it becomes evident how much research there is left to pursue. Rather than closing the box with a handful of new urban landscape types, it suggests a multitude of types and relationships along the urban-rural continuum. With the built-unbuilt duality excised from the analysis, complicated networks and webs of human-environmental interactions are uncovered, grounding new and alternative explorations of urban landscapes. In total, this volume presents urban landscapes as a medium for worldviews, as Farhat notes. The work comprises a carefully curated collection of insights into the exchange of perspectives that are central to comprehending preindustrial urban landscapes and the associated process of urbanization.

But where do we go from here? We have yet to fully grapple with the question of when, why, and how the phenomenon of urban landscapes emerged and coalesced into settlements. While we can now consider early Mesopotamian urban settlements as self-organized megasites demonstrating low-density models that vary in scale, we must now consider them in the context of alternative urban forms and governance in the Amazon, Asia, and West Africa. With a much more nuanced global inquiry, the role of environmental and cultural specificities rises as paramount to any investigation of universal urban processes and/or forms. Such research grounds further the opportunity to build on the urban environmental humanities to expose and leverage critical intersections of history and landscape with scholarship in geography and archaeology, and perhaps most potently with that in the field of political ecology, from scholars such as Eric Swyngedouw, Marie Kaike, and Matthew Gandy. This might catalyze robust questions of social organization, labor, and the spatial traces of power and hierarchy, especially as it might be evident in land-tenure practices in the preindustrial era. It will be fruitful as well to align with scholars in genetics, neural science, and machine intelligence as new tools of inquiry and analysis produce alternative data and novel frameworks of study. For too long we have used tools to merely replace each other without challenging our intentions, a digital version of existing scholarship. And yet the tools discussed in this volume suggest that we may be gathering data we have not yet imagined, leading to questions that have yet to be anticipated, as we approach the project with an immense curiosity, openness, and creativity grounded in the rigor of historical scholarship.

Dumbarton Oaks has stewarded the discipline of landscape history for almost seventy-five years. With the expansion made possible by the Mellon Foundation's initiative in Architecture, Urbanism, and the Humanities, we have been able to extend the scholarship to include urbanism as a process and cities as built environments that were once thought outside the purview of landscape but that significantly contributed to deconstructing the very boundaries between the built and unbuilt, the constructed and the natural, the city and the land. By traversing this edge, as with the forest edge, we identify a remarkable diversity of approaches, methods, forms of analysis, and readings of what we mean by the urban landscape and its process of becoming. Future research will be able to draw on the potential of even more powerful technologies as existing tools are refined and new tools are created. This should lead to scholarship that further builds upon and challenges the ideas and questions currently under investigation.

Thaïsa Way
Director, Garden and Landscape Studies

CONTRIBUTORS

JEAN-BAPTISTE CHEVANCE graduated from the Ecole du Louvre, Paris, in 1997, then obtained a master's degree and a PhD on Khmer archaeology in 2011. He simultaneously worked for various institutions in Cambodia, including at the Ecole Française d'Extrême-Orient (EFEO), the Institut National de Recherches Archeologiques Preventives (INRAP), and the Cambodian APSARA National Authority. In 2007, he founded and has continued to direct the Archaeology and Development Foundation (ADF). This charity focuses on the Phnom Kulen archaeological sites with a humanitarian aspect: it ensures that the Cambodian people living around the sites are directly involved in their protection and that their livelihoods are improved in the process. He has conducted with the ADF team many archaeological studies on the Phnom Kulen, which have had a significant impact on the knowledge of the Angkor region and, more generally, of the Khmer empire.

HENDRIK W. DEY is professor in the Department of Art and Art History at Hunter College, CUNY. He received his BA in Classics from Middlebury College and his PhD in Classical Art and Archaeology from the University of Michigan. His research centers on urbanism and urban history in Europe and the Mediterranean from Late Antiquity through the Middle Ages. He is the author of *The Aurelian Wall and the Refashioning of Imperial Rome, AD 271–855* and *The Afterlife of the Roman City: Architecture and Ceremony in Late Antiquity and the Early Middle Ages*, as well as the coauthor (with Paolo Squatriti and Deborah Deliyannis) of *Fifty Early Medieval Things: Materials of Culture in Late Antiquity and the Early Middle Ages*. He codirects the Caesarea Coastal Archaeology Project, an underwater excavation at the city of Caesarea Maritima in Israel.

GEORGES FARHAT is a licensed architect (DPLG, Paris-Belleville) and landscape historian (PhD, Paris-Sorbonne). An associate professor at the University of Toronto, he previously taught at the school of architecture of Versailles, where he is a founding member of the Léav, its laboratory. His research unfolds at the intersections between territorial organization and design techniques, looking into historical appropriations of optics, the historiography of perspective, and epistemologies of landscape and urbanism. Farhat cocurated the exhibition and coedited the companion book

André Le Nôtre in Perspective at the château de Versailles (2013–2014). He is the editor of *Fragments d'un paysage culturel: Institutions, arts, sciences et techniques* (2006) and *Les années 1960 hic et nunc: Architecture, urbanisme, paysage* (2010). He has received numerous awards (Académie d'architecture, Society of Architectural Historians, Foundation for Landscape Studies, Council on Botanical and Horticultural Libraries, and CIVA-Bruxelles) and grants (Centre des Monuments Nationaux, Centre de recherche du château de Versailles, Agence française de développement, and Descartes Centre-Utrecht University). He serves on many advisory boards and has chaired the senior fellows committee at Dumbarton Oaks.

MICHAEL HECKENBERGER, professor at the University of Florida, has worked with indigenous peoples for over twenty years, focusing on the Upper Xingu region of Brazil. Work by him and his team reveals unique patterns of late Pre-Columbian settlement and land use, based on long-term participatory research in collaboration with the Kuikuro indigenous peoples. The context-sensitive and place-based approaches also inform work on urban landscapes in São Paulo. In addition to numerous articles, his books include *The Ecology of Power* (2005), *Archaeology of the Amazon* (forthcoming, with Eduardo Neves), *Os Povos do Alto Xingu* (2001, with Bruna Franchetto), and *Time and Memory in Indigenous Amazonia* (2007, with Carlos Fausto). He is currently working on *Tropical Garden Cities* and *Heart of the City: Centro, São Paulo*.

J. CAMERON MONROE is associate professor of anthropology and the founding director of the Archaeological Research Center at the University of California, Santa Cruz. Specializing in the archaeology of urban landscapes and state formation in West Africa and the African diaspora, he has led a major research project on the archaeology of Dahomean urbanism in West Africa since 2000, and he launched a new research project on the early nineteenth-century kingdom of Haiti in 2015. He serves on the editorial board of *Azania: Archaeological Research in Africa* and has published in various journals, including *African Archaeological Review, Historical Archaeology, Journal of African History, Journal of Social Archaeology,* and *Current Anthropology*. His book, *The Precolonial State in West Africa: Building Power in Dahomey* (2014), was selected as a Choice Outstanding Academic Title for 2015.

TIMOTHY R. PAUKETAT is director of the Illinois State Archaeological Survey and professor of anthropology and medieval studies at the University of Illinois. He earned his doctorate at the University of Michigan (1991) and taught at the University of Oklahoma (1992–1996) and SUNY-Buffalo (1996–1998). He has researched Pre-Columbian eastern North America for thirty years, with a special interest in the city of Cahokia, its immigrant farmers, and its historical connections across the Mississippi Valley and into Mesoamerica. More generally, his research examines the relationships of religion, material culture, and nonhuman phenomena to human history by focusing on the objects, substances, and phenomena through which people realize their humanity. He is the author and editor of sixteen books, including *An Archaeology of the Cosmos* (2013), *Medieval Mississippians* (2014, with Susan M. Alt), and *The Archaeology of Ancient North America* (2020, with Kenneth E. Sassaman).

JORDAN PICKETT is an archaeologist and assistant professor in the Department of Classics at the University of Georgia. He earned his PhD from the University of Pennsylvania in 2015, and he has held postdoctoral fellowships at the University of Michigan and Florida State University. He researches the historical landscapes and environments of the eastern Mediterranean, with particular emphasis on the transformation of Roman cities during Late Antiquity and the early medieval period, with resultant publications in the *Dumbarton Oaks Papers, Journal of Archaeological Science, Quaternary Science Reviews*, and *Human Ecology*. He has worked with survey and excavation projects across the Mediterranean, in Italy, Ukraine, Jordan, Greece, and Turkey, and is currently a principal investigator for a survey of Byzantine fortifications at Sardis. At the time of writing, he is preparing a monograph concerned with the vulnerability, adaptation, and transformation of Roman water infrastructure during Late Antiquity.

PRIYALEEN SINGH is professor in the Department of Architectural Conservation at the School of Planning and Architecture, New Delhi. She has master's degrees in both landscape architecture and architectural and urban conservation. She was awarded the Charles Wallace India Trust scholarship to complete a master's degree in conservation from the Institute of Advanced Architectural Studies, University of York, and subsequently received the Commonwealth Scholarship to pursue her D.Phil. from the same institution on "Changing Attitudes to Design with Nature in the Urban Indian Context." As a practicing conservation architect and landscape architect, she has worked on several urban conservation and historic landscape conservation projects. She is presently researching lesser-known Indian landscape design traditions from the sixteenth to eighteenth centuries. She is also compiling a National Register of Historic Gardens of India and continues to be involved in contemporary landscape design and urban conservation issues in India.

MONICA L. SMITH is professor of anthropology at the Institute of the Environment and Sustainability at the University of California, Los Angeles. She holds the Navin and Pratima Doshi Chair in Indian Studies and serves as the director of the South Asian Archaeology Laboratory at the Cotsen Institute of Archaeology. Her research focuses on urbanism and the development of social complexity, and her primary fieldwork region is in India and Bangladesh, with additional field experience in Egypt, England, Italy, Tunisia, Turkey, and Madagascar. Her books include *A Prehistory of Ordinary People* (2010) and *Cities: The First 6,000 Years* (2019), as well as the edited volumes *The Social Construction of Ancient Cities* (2003) and *Abundance: The Archaeology of Plenitude* (2017).

JASON A. UR is professor of anthropology and the director of the Center for Geographic Analysis at Harvard University. He specializes in early urbanism, landscape archaeology, and remote sensing, particularly the use of declassified U.S. intelligence imagery. He has directed field surveys in Syria, Iraq, Turkey, and Iran. He is the author of *Urbanism and Cultural Landscapes in Northeastern Syria: The Tell Hamoukar Survey, 1999–2001* (2010). Since 2012, he has directed the Erbil Plain Archaeological Survey in the Kurdistan Region of northern Iraq. He is also preparing a history of Mesopotamian cities.

INDEX

Page numbers in *italics* indicate illustrations.

C

Caesarea Maritima (Israel), 131
Cahokia (United States), 20–21,
    89–106; affective properties of,
    91–93, 102; Cahokia precinct,
    95–96, *96, 97,* 101, 102, *103,*
    104; deliberate demise of, 103;
    Charles Dickens's account of
    climate and frogs of, 93–95, *94;*
    "Downtown Cahokia," 95; East
    Saint Louis precinct, *96,* 96–97,
    101, 103; Emerald Acropolis, 91, *98,*
    98–100, *99,* 101; geoarchaeology
    and historical ecology of, 12;
    geographic, climatological, and
    biological factors, 91–93; maize
    agriculture in, 89, 91, 92, 94–95, 104;
    maps, *90, 93;* Medieval Climatic
    Anomaly (ca. 800–1300) and, 89,
    92, 105; Monks Mound, *96, 97;*
    New Materialist approach to, 91,
    104; nodal sites, 100, 102; non-
    anthropocentric agency in, 89–91,
    104–6; ontology and worldview,
    100, 102–4, *103, 104;* pol-and-thatch
    constructions, 97, *98;* precincts
    of, 95–98, *96;* Rattlesnake Mound, 95,
    97, 98; Saint Louis precinct, *96, 98,*
    99; shrine complexes, 95, 98–100;
    steam baths, 101, 102; Woodhenge,
    91, *104*
camay, 15
Cana (Kingdom of Dahomey): African
    urbanism and, 23, 264, 270; in
    Atlantic Era, 274–75, *275, 276, 278,*
    279, 280, 281; regional archaeology
    at, 282–91, *283–90;* rise of, 291–92
Caracol (Belize), 11–12
Carneiro, Robert, 247
Carson (United States), 102
central place theory, 6
Charlemagne, 141n133
Chersonesus (Crimea), *116,* 130, 139n106
Chevance, Jean-Baptiste, 21–22, 148,
    165, 173, 303
Childe, V. Gordon, 6, 8, 14, 20, 27n25,
    27n29, 37–38, 39, 41, 50, 51, 167n3
chinampas, 15, 16, 31n79
Choricius, 136n54
Christaller, Walter, 6
city/hinterland binary, 3–6, *7*
city-states (self-organized, high-
    density urban areas), 20, 38, 51–56,
    52–55
classical world. *See* Roman and
    Byzantine aqueducts and water
    management; Rome, classical
Codex Iustinianus, 137n59

coined money and urban development,
    162, 171n59
Collins site (United States), 100
Columella, 118
Conneller, Chantal, 3
conservation of historic urban
    landscapes, 219
Constantine I (emperor), *70*
Constantine V (Roman emperor),
    141n128
Constantinople, 119, *120, 129,* 132,
    137n59, 139n99, 141n128, 141n130
convergence or nucleation of
    settlements, 132
Corinth (Greece), 132
Cowgill, George L., 7–8, 41
Crouch, Dora, 118

D

Dagens, Bruno, 176
Dahomey, Kingdom of (Africa), 23,
    264, 270, 272–80, *273, 280,* 291–92.
    See also Cana; tropical West Africa
dark earths, 13, 227, 236, 241, 246, 247.
    See Amazonian dark earths
deforestation, 12, 186, 188, *189,* 190, 233
DeLanda, Manuel, 104
Delaporte, Louis, 176
Deleuze, Gilles, 104
Delhi (India), 195, 220nn7–8
Dey, Hendrick W., 20, 61, 303
Dhar Tichitt region (Mauritania), 266
Dhauli (India), 154
Dhauligiri (India), 196
Dia (Africa), 266
Dickens, Charles, 93–95
Diocletian (Roman emperor), price
    edict of, 147n62
disaggregated settlements, 132
Dumbarton Oaks, urban landscape
    studies at, ix–x, 301
Dupont, Pierre, 176

E

earthworks, 19–21. *See also* Cahokia;
    medieval Rome; Mesopotamia
ecological anthropology, 13, 30n69
"ecology of materials," 3
"economic rent," scheme of land, 6, *7*
Einsiedeln Itineraries, 68, 69, 82, 84n11
Ekamra Chandrika, 196, 202
Ekamrakshetra (temple town of
    Bhubaneswar, India), 22, 193–219;
    ashtaāyatanās (eight sacred areas),
    201–2, 220–21n23; Brahmeswara
    temple complex and tank, *194;*

conservation of historic urban
    landscapes and, 219; Kapileswara
    temple tank, *216;* Kedar Gouri
    temple and Gouri tank, 201,
    210; Kedareswara temple and
    Kedarkunda tank, 201; Lingaraj
    (deity) and life of, 196, 202, 221n24;
    Lingaraj temple and Bindusagar
    tank, 199–200, *200,* 202, 204, 207,
    208; maps, *197, 199;* modern urban
    life in, 211–13, *212–13;* monastic
    establishments, 204, 221n26;
    Mukteswara temple and tank,
    201, *203;* nature and culture,
    links between, 194–95; New
    Bhubaneswar, 214–19, *215, 217, 218,*
    222n37; open space systems of, 204–
    7, *205–7, 210,* 217–19; origins, 195–96;
    pradakshinā or circumambulation
    route, 201; *prasādam* and other
    activities providing agricultural and
    trade employment, 203–4, *204–7,*
    211, 212; Rameswara temple and
    tank, *198, 213;* sacred geography,
    importance of water to, 199–204,
    200–203, 220n12; Sisupalgarh and, 21,
    196; topography, 196–99; trees and
    tree cults, 204, 207–12, *209, 210, 211,*
    213, 216–17, *217,* 221n30
Emerson, Ralph Waldo, 225
Ephesus (Turkey), 21, 122–27, *123–27,*
    130, 132
Erdosy, George, 150, 151, 154
erosion, at Mahendraparvata
    (Cambodia), 186–88, *187, 189*
Esan-Edo agglomerations (Nigeria), 10
Essouk-Tadmakka (Africa), 266
Evans, Damian, 11
Eye Temple, Tell Brak (Mesopotamia),
    49, *50*

F

Farhat, Georges, x, 1, 303–4
farming. *See* agriculture
Faron, Louis, 230
fiefdom, *seigneurie,* or manor, 16–17
Fisher Mounds complex (United
    States), *100,* 102
Fleisher, Jeffrey, 271
Fletcher, Roland, 10, 21
Food and the City (2015), ix
Forbes, Frederick E., 288
forestry: concept of forest-urban
    settlements, 12; medieval Western
    forest civilizations, 254. *See also*
    tropical West Africa; Xingu garden
    cities

in, 148; natural environment, interaction with, 178, *179*, 183–86, *185*; natural resources, impact on, 186–88, *187*, *189*; Pleu Cere (laterite stairway), 188; urban network of, 178–83, *179–82*; Western discovery and study of, 176–77

Maidanetske (Ukraine), 10

maize agriculture in Cahokia, 89, 91, 92, 94–95, 104

manor, fiefdom, or *seigneurie,* 16–17

Mansārā, 194

Marx, Karl, 121

Maya, 145

Māyāmātā, 194

McEwan, Colin, 30n72

Medieval Climatic Anomaly/Warm Period (ca. 800–1300), 89, 92, 105, 250, 255

medieval Rome, 20, 61–82; Campus Martius, 62, 63, *64*, 65, 68, 69, 72, *74*, *75*, 76, 79, 82, 83n5, 85n26; centralization of population near Tiber, 76, 82; Crypta Balbi, 62, 79, 80, 87n52; demographic and economic boom of eleventh through thirteenth centuries, 75–78, 82; flooding problems in, 72–74, *74*, 78, 80; Forum Holitorium, 63, *64*, 65, 68, 71, 73, *74*, *75*, 76; gristmills, water-powered, 76, 86n33; ground-level rise as deliberate elevation of Via Papalis, 78–82, *79*, *81*, 87n46, 88n59; Jewish community in, 77; Lateran Cathedral/Palace, *68*, 69, *70–71*, 79, 80; population collapse, from late antiquity, 61, 71–72, 76, 85n19; *porticus maximae,* 67, *67–68*, 69, 78; ruins of ancient Rome, effects of, 61, 72–74, *73*, 76, 88n60; sources and methodology, 62–63; Temple of Apollo, collapse of, *73*; Theater of Marcellus, 65, *66*, 68, *73*, 77, 81; Theater of Pompey, 63, *65*, 68, *74*, *75*; Vatican basilica of St. Peter, 67, 69, *70–71*, 74, 79, 80; Via Lata, 69, 80, *81*, 87n46, 87n51, 88n39; Via Papalis replacing Via Triumphalis as processional route, 61–62, *68*, 68–75, *70–71*, 78–79; Via Triumphalis, in classical and late antique periods, 61–62, 63–68, *64–67*, 83–84n6, 83n3, 84n9; Via Triumphalis, no artificial elevation of, 80–81; Via Triumphalis (*via mercatoria*), medieval use of, 69, 74–78, *75*, *78*, 81–82

medieval Scandinavian port cities, 172n76

megasites, 8–10, 20, 38, 43–46, *44*, *45*, 300

Megasthenes, 168n11

Melosi, Martin V., 8

Mesopotamia, 20, 37–56; bottom-up and self-organized nature of urbanism in, 20, 38, 53–56, *55*; Childe's "Urban Revolution" model and, 37–38, 39, 41, 50, 51; city-states (self-organized, high-density urban areas), 20, 38, 51–56, *52–55*; as Fragile Crescent versus Fertile Crescent, 145; geography and chronology of, 38–43, *39–42*; growth pattern, obscurity of, at Uruk, 39–41, 50–51, *51*; Indus cultural area compared, 146; low-density urbanism in, 20, 38, 46–50, *47–50*, 300; megasite of Khirbat al-Fakhar, 20, 38, 43–46, *44*, *45*, 48; patrimonial household in, 14; remote sensing technologies, use of, *43*, 44; temple redistribution economy of, 169n23; trackways and formation of cities in, 53–56, *54*, *55*, 59n32

metabolism, urban, 8, 28n42

Miksic, John N., 6–7

mills/gristmills/water mills: classical Roman and Byzantine, 121–22, 137n62; in late antique/medieval Roman world, 76, 86n33, 127

Minoans, 118

Mokissos (Cappadocia), *116*, 129

Monks Mound, Cahokia (United States), 96, *97*

Monroe, J. Cameron, 23, 263, 304

monsoon landscapes of Indian subcontinent, 21, 143–66; development of urbanism in South Asia and, 146–47, *147*; drought management, 165; Dry Zone, 157; excess water management in, 163–65, *164*, 172n71; flexibility, sustainability, and resilience of, 161–63, 165; gendered division of labor and, 162–63, 171nn60–61; modern dams and, 169n24; "normal floods," 143, 148, 152, 157, 163; religious institutions and, 146–47, 149, 154–57, *159*, 162, 168–69n22, 169n25; rice cultivation in, *144*, 148–49, 157–58, *164*; rural-urban migration and interdependence, 145, 149, 157; seasonally variable climate and agriculture of, 143–45, *144*, 148, 163–65, *164*, 168n12, 168n16; social and environmental power of monsoon, 147–49; transportation, 161–62, 171n56; urban centers in, 149–61 (*see also specific cities*); walls and ramparts, 150, 169nn26–27

Moore, Christopher R., 148

Mughal India, 195

Mycenaeans, 118

Myra (Lycia), 130

N

natural/built environment binary, 3–6, *7*

Nebelivka (Ukraine), 10

Nebuchadnezzar (Babylonian ruler), 42

Neoplatonism, 33n92

New Delhi (India), 220n5

New Materialism, 91, 104

Nicholas V (pope), 78

Nicopolis ad Istrum (Bulgaria), *116*, 129

Nile Valley, flood patterns in, 148

Nineveh, 42

nixtamalization, 92

nucleation or convergence of settlements, 132

Nymphaeum Traiani, Ephesus, 124–25, *126*

O

oasis civilizations of Mediterranean and southwest Asia, 254

Obion complex (United States), 100

Oc-Eo (Cambodia), 190

Olynthus (Greece), *116*, 118

Ooty (India), 220n5

Ostia (Italy), *116*, 136n53

Oyo-Ile (Africa), 269

P

panchavati, 204

Paris: François de Belleforest's description of (1575), 32n85; modern urban landscape studies of, 32nn86–87; *seigneuries* and parishes in, 16–17, *18*; techno-environmental framework of, 17–19, *18*; Truschet and Hoyau, *Ici est le vray pourtraict naturel de la ville, cité, université, & faubourgz de Paris* (ca. 1550), 2, *4–5*, *17*, *18*

parishes, 17

Paschal II (pope), 79, *81*

Pataliputra (now Patna, India), 150, 168n11

Pauketat, Timothy R., 20–21, 89, 304–5

Paul, B. K., 148
Pella (Greece), *116*, 132
Pergamum (Turkey), *116*, 118
Perge (Anatolia), 131
Petra (Jordan), 122
Phanom Rung (Thailand), 183
Philostratus, 135n27
Phnom Kulen (Cambodia). *See* Mahendraparvata
Phrygian Hierapolis, 132
Pickett, Jordan, 21, 115, 305
pilgrimage: in Cahokia, 100; in India, 146, 149, 151, 157, 162, 164, 195, 196, 200–201, 207, 213; in medieval Rome, 67, 76; in Roman/Byzantine world, 130, 133
Pires de Campos, Antônio, 231
Plato, 117–18
Pliny the Elder, 118, 135n24
Pliska (Bulgaria), 133, 141n134
Pompeii, 119, 136n53
Pottier, Christophe, 11, 165
preindustrial urban landscapes, ix–x, 1–24, 299–301; challenging preconceptions about, ix–x, 2, 23–24; defining/redefining, 6–8, 168n11, 299–300; in geoarchaeology and historical ecology, 12–13, *13*; natural/built and city/hinterland binaries, 3–6, *7*; remote sensing technologies transforming understanding of, 8–12, *9–11*; rural-urban continuum, 145, 149, 157, 167n3, 266, 271, 300; techno-environmental frameworks of, 2–3, *3–4*, 17–19, *18*, 24, 115–16; terminology of, 2, 25n1; worldviews and, 13–19, *14–18*. *See also* earthworks; forestry; waterscapes
Pre Rup (Cambodia), 177
Preslav (Bulgaria), *116*, 133, 141n134
Priene (Western Anatolia), *116*, 118
processual archaeology, 6, 27nn31–32
Procopius, 139n99
Pseudo-Jahiz, 141n133
Puranas, 22, 196, 201–2, 208, 210, 220n9, 220n12, 221n33
Pylos (Greece), 118

R

Rattlesnake Mound, Cahokia (United States), 95, *97, 98*
remote sensing technologies, 8–12, *9–11, 43, 44*, 189, 231
Renfrew, Colin, 8

rice cultivation in Indian subcontinent, *144*, 148–49, 157
Rig Veda, 146, 200
River Cities, City Rivers (2018), ix
Roman and Byzantine aqueducts and water management, 21, 115–33; access to water, 119–21, 136nn55–56; afterlives of, 76, 86nn32–33, 127–32, *128–31*; Bronze and Iron Age aqueducts, open-flow systems of, 118; cisterns, 118, 119, 124, 127–29, *129*, 130, 131, 133, 135n24, 135n27, 136n41, 138n91, 139n102, 139nn97–100; *civitates* and *poleis* administrative structure, based on, 116–17, *117*, 119, 134n10, 142n137; consumption, commodification, and display issues, 119–21, 135n20, 137n59; development and use of, 118–22, *120, 121*; Ephesus as case study of, 21, 122–27, *123–27*, 130, 132; inverted siphons, 118, *120*, 121, *131*; irrigation, 122; Islamic conquests and, 132–33, 140n113, 141n122, 141n133; mills, 121–22, 127, 137n62; political map of Roman empire (ca. 114 CE), 115, *116*; population densities and, 119; spring water, preference for, 117–18, 119, 135n24; techno-environmental frameworks of, 115–16; thematic capitals, 129–30, *130*; wells, 118–19, *123*–24, 127, 130–33, 135n27, 136n53, 140n119, 141n129, 142n136. *See also specific cities*
Romanian-Ukrainian Cucuteni-Trypillia civilization, 10
Rome, classical: aqueducts of, 118, 119; flour mills, water-powered, 122; Via Triumphalis, 61–62, *63–68, 64–67*, 83–84n6, 83n3, 84n9
Rome, medieval. *See* medieval Rome
Rong Chen (Cambodia), 177
rural-urban continuum, 145, 149, 157, 167n3, 266, 271, 300

S

Sakada, Sakhoeun, *181*
Sambor Prei Kuk (Cambodia), 176, 183
Samos (Greece), *116*, 118
Sanchi (central India), 149, 171n61
SAR (synthetic-aperture radar), 8, *9*
Savi (Kingdom of Hueda), 270
Scandinavian port cities in the Middle Ages, 172n76
scheme of land "economic rent," 6, *7*
Schmidt, Christopher W., 148
Sdok Kak Thom stela (Angkor, Cambodia), 176

seigneurie, fiefdom, or manor, 16–17
Sennacherib (Neo-Assyrian ruler), 42
Shahjahan (Mughal emperor), 220n7
Shahjahanabad (India), 220n7
Sharma, G. R., 169n27
Shaw, Julia, 149
Shimla (India), 220n5
Side aqueduct (southern Anatolia), *117*, 119, 131, 140n114
Silvester (pope), *70*
Singh, Priyaleen, 21, 22, 193, 304
Sirmium (Balkans), *116*, 131, 140n112
Sisupalgarh (India), 21, 149, 150, *153*–56, *153–57*, 163–64, 166, 169n24, 170nn36–37, 196–97
Sixtus IV (pope), 78
Skertchly, J. A., 275–76, *286*
slash-and-burn (swidden) agriculture, 161, 186, 188, 190, 246–47, 272, 282
slave trade and urban tropical West Africa, 23, 264, 269–70, 272–74, 279, 281, 291–92
Smith, Michael E., 8, 28n40
Smith, Monica L., 21, 143, 305
souterrains in Cana (Bénin), 23, 284–86, *287*
Steward, Julian H., 6, 22, 27n30, 230
Stobi (Balkans), *116*, 131, 140n111
St. Silvester Chapel, SS. Quattro Coronati (Rome), fresco, 69, *70*
Sutcliffe, John, 149
Svanadri Mahodaya, 196, 202
swidden (slash-and-burn) agriculture, 161, 186, 188, 190, 246–47, 272, 282
Swyngedouw, Eric, 300
synthetic-aperture radar (SAR), 8, *9*

T

Talapada (India), 157, 164
techno-environmental frameworks, 2–3, *3–4*, 13, 19, *18*, 24, 115–16
Tegbesu (king of Dahomey), 281
Tegdaoust (Africa), 266
Tell Abada (Mesopotamia), *41*
Tell Asmar (ancient Eshnunna, Mesopotamia), 52
Tell Brak (Mesopotamia), 41, 42, *46–50, 47–50*, 54, 57n1
Tell Chuera (Mesopotamia), 52–53
Tenochtitlan (Mexico), 16, *17*
Teotihuacan (Mexico), *15*, 15–16, *16*
thauma, 121
thematic capitals in Byzantine empire, water resources in, 129–30, *130*
Theodore the Studite, 139n105

DUMBARTON OAKS COLLOQUIUM ON THE HISTORY OF LANDSCAPE ARCHITECTURE

Published by Dumbarton Oaks Research Library and Collection, Washington, D.C.

The Dumbarton Oaks Colloquium on the History of Landscape Architecture series volumes are based on papers presented at scholarly meetings sponsored by the Garden and Landscape Studies program at Dumbarton Oaks. These meetings provide a forum for the presentation of advanced research on garden history, landscape architecture, and urban landscapes; they support a deepened understanding of landscape as a field of knowledge and as a practice carried out by landscape architects, landscape artists, and gardeners.

Further information on Garden and Landscape Studies publications can be found at www.doaks.org/publications.